EZRA AND THE LAW
in History and Tradition

STUDIES ON PERSONALITIES OF THE OLD TESTAMENT

James L. Crenshaw, Series Editor

EZRA AND THE LAW

in History and Tradition

LISBETH S. FRIED

The University of South Carolina Press

Published by the University of South Carolina Press
Columbia, South Carolina 29208

www.sc.edu/uscpress

Manufactured in the United States of America

23 22 21 20 19 18 17 16 15 14   10 9 8 7 6 5 4 3 2 1

Library of Congress Cataloging-in-Publication Data

Fried, Lisbeth S.
Ezra and the law in history and tradition / Lisbeth S. Fried.
pages cm. — (Studies on personalities of the Old Testament)
Includes bibliographical references and index.
ISBN 978-1-61117-313-0 (hardbound : alk. paper) 1. Ezra (Biblical figure) I. Title.
BS580.E9F75 2014
222'.7092—dc23

2013024196

This book was printed on a recycled paper with 30 percent postconsumer waste content.

To my students in the Emeritus Program at
Washtenaw Community College

CONTENTS

ILLUSTRATIONS

SERIES EDITOR'S PREFACE

Critical study of the Bible in its ancient Near Eastern setting has stimulated interest in the individuals who shaped the course of history and whom events singled out as tragic or heroic figures. Rolf Rendtorff's *Men of the Old Testament* (1968) focuses on the lives of important biblical figures as a means of illuminating history, particularly the sacred dimension that permeates Israel's convictions about its God. Fleming James's *Personalities of the Old Testament* (1939) addresses another issue, that of individuals who function as inspiration for their religious successors in the twentieth century. Studies restricting themselves to a single individual—for example, Moses, Abraham, Samson, Elijah, David, Saul, Ruth, Jonah, Job, Jeremiah—enable scholars to deal with a host of questions: psychological, literary, theological, sociological, and historical. Some, like Gerhard von Rad's *Moses* (1960), introduce a specific approach to interpreting the Bible, hence provide valuable pedagogic tools.

As a rule these treatments of isolated figures have not reached the general public. Some were written by outsiders who lacked a knowledge of biblical criticism (Freud on Moses, Jung on Job) and whose conclusions, however provocative, remain problematic. Others were targeted for the guild of professional biblical critics (David Gunn on David and Saul, Phyllis Trible on Ruth, Terence Fretheim and Jonathan Magonet on Jonah). None has succeeded in capturing the imagination of the reading public in the way fictional works like Archibald MacLeish's *J. B.* and Joseph Heller's *God Knows* have done.

It could be argued that the general public would derive little benefit from learning more about the personalities of the Bible. Their conduct, often less then exemplary, reveals a flawed character, and their everyday concerns have nothing to do with our preoccupations from dawn to dusk. To be sure, some individuals transcend their own age, entering the gallery of classical literary figures from time immemorial. But only these rare achievers can justify specific treatments of them. Then why publish additional studies on biblical personalities?

The answer cannot be that we read about biblical figures to learn ancient history, even of the sacred kind, or to discover models for ethical action. But what remains? Perhaps the primary significance of biblical personages is the light they throw on the imaging of deity in biblical times. At the very least, the Bible constitutes human perceptions of deity's relationship with the world and its creatures. Close readings of biblical personalities therefore clarify ancient understandings of God. That is the important datum which we seek—not because we endorse that specific view of deity but because all such efforts to make sense of reality contribute something worthwhile to the endless quest for knowledge.

James L. Crenshaw
Duke Divinity School

PREFACE

Although the figure of Ezra appears in only six chapters in the Hebrew Bible, he has sparked the imagination of writers, scholars, and tradents for almost two and a half millennia. Ezra's activities are described in chapters 7–10 of the Book of Ezra and in chapter 8 of the book of Nehemiah. He also makes a cameo appearance in Nehemiah 12. These two biblical books deal with the period of the return of Judeans to Judah under Cyrus the Great and tell how the returnees rebuilt Jerusalem and their temple. Ezra is described in these books as bringing the Torah (the Pentateuch, the Five Books of Moses) to Judah and reading it to the populace there.

The biblical story of Ezra inspired later writers and scholars. Fourth Ezra, written after the fall of the second temple, portrays Ezra as having dictated the entire Bible from memory since the original had been destroyed in the fire that destroyed the temple. Rabbinic traditions hail Ezra as a hero, the equal of Moses himself, and as the last prophet, the prophet Malachi. In contrast, several Church Fathers, as well as many medieval Samaritan and Muslim scholars, argue that Ezra falsified the text when he rewrote it and that the Bible we have now is not the same text that Moses had written but another. Modern biblical scholars attribute to Ezra the creation of Judaism and assert that without him Judaism would not exist.

Who was the real Ezra? What did he actually do? And how and why did all these conflicting and some rather unflattering views of him develop over the ensuing 2,400 years?

After a brief introduction, I present in chapter 2 the man whom I believe to be the real historical Ezra. This man would not be recognized in any of his other portrayals, not even in the Ezra depicted in the Hebrew Bible! In subsequent chapters I describe each of the other views of him and discuss how each originated and why. Each chapter discusses one ancient understanding of God, of his laws, and of the path toward salvation. It describes a journey of more than two thousand years that wends its way from ancient Judea and Arabia to modern Europe and the United States.

I want to express my appreciation to Peter Machinist for suggesting this book topic to me and to James Crenshaw for accepting my proposal for a volume on

Ezra in history and tradition for his series Personalities of the Old Testament. It is truly an honor. I also thank him for the many profound suggestions for improvement he made on an earlier version. I would like to thank Debra Dash Moore and the Frankel Center of Judaic Studies as well as the Department of Near Eastern Studies at the University of Michigan for their continued support and encouragement. Without it, this book (and all my books and articles) would be impossible. Along with them I thank Jonathan Rodgers, head of the Near Eastern Collection at the University of Michigan Library; Karl Longstreth of the Clark Map Library at the University of Michigan; and Kim Schroeder of the Visual Resources Collection and Media Services, Department of History of Art, at the University of Michigan for all their efforts on behalf of this project. I want also to thank Natalie Niell for the wonderful work she did on all the indices.

My wonderful husband, Michael Fried, prepared the bibliography, and he and my friend Moshe Sharon read every word of the manuscript and critiqued it. Thank you, thank you. All remaining errors and problems are of course my own. My students of the Emeritus Program at Washtenaw Community College spent eight weeks reading, discussing, and commenting on the entire text and the ideas behind it. It is to them that I dedicate this book.

I

Introduction to the Continuing Story of Ezra, Scribe, and Priest

The biblical character of Ezra appears in only six chapters in the entire Bible, yet he has sparked the interest and concern of writers for more than two thousand years. He has been labeled a "second Moses" by the authors of the Talmud and a falsifier of the biblical text by Samaritan, Christian, and Muslim medieval scholars. Modern commentators have claimed he created Judaism, and without him Judaism would not exist. This book attempts to describe and to understand these conflicting images as well as to find the historical Ezra buried in the biblical text.

Ezra's activities are described in chapters 7–10 of the book of Ezra and in chapter 8 and 12 of the book of Nehemiah. These two books, Ezra and Nehemiah, are the only narrative books of the Bible that deal with the period of the return of Judeans to Judah after the Babylonian exile. In 586 B.C.E. Judah was conquered by Nebuchadnezzar, king of Babylon. In the process, the temple was destroyed and the bulk of the population deported to Babylon or killed—either in the ensuing battles or by starvation and illness during the sieges of the cities.[1] In October 539 B.C.E., however, Cyrus the Great of Persia conquered Babylon, and that spring, in 538 B.C.E., he issued an edict permitting the Judeans to return home to Judah and to rebuild their cities and their temple (Ezra 1:1–4).[2] The books of Ezra and Nehemiah tell the story of the Judean return to Judah and of their rebuilding their temple and their city. If it were not for these two books we would know nothing about this important period of history.

The Story of the Return—Ezra Chapters 1–6

The book of Ezra is not all of a piece, however. In fact it is pretty much a hodgepodge. The first six chapters tell the story of the return to Judah and Jerusalem and of the rebuilding of the temple there, but they also tell of a squabble between the returnees and a second group of people, perhaps Samaritans (Ezra 4). Having been excluded from participating in the building of the temple, this second group writes a complaint to the Persian king Artaxerxes about the returnees. That king then puts a stop to the building process, which lasts until the reign of Darius.

Ezra Scribe and Priest. From *Promptuarii Iconum Insigniorum a Seculo Hominum*, published by Guillaume Rouillé, 1553.

These first six chapters of the book of Ezra have led to much confusion. There are five Persian kings named Artaxerxes and three kings named Darius. (For the list of Persian kings, see Appendix 1). Most people think that the Darius under whom the temple was completed and dedicated was Darius I (522–486 B.C.E.), but no king named Artaxerxes ruled before him. Only Cyrus and his son, Cambyses, ruled before Darius. This has caused some researchers to contend that the temple was not completed until Darius II (424–405), who ruled after Artaxerxes I,[3] but this seems too late a date for the second temple's dedication, and it leads to other difficulties.[4] Those who contend that the temple was dedicated in the time of Darius I, however, have to explain the apparent intrusion into the temple-building story of a letter to a later king.[5] Ezra himself does not appear until chapter 7 of the book named for him; the story of the return ends before the story of Ezra begins.

The Story of Ezra in Ezra Chapters 7–10, Nehemiah Chapter 8

Ezra arrives in Judah in the seventh year of a king Artaxerxes, and at this point the temple has already been built and dedicated. Scholars are divided over which Persian King Artaxerxes is meant of the five who bore that name (again, see Appendix 1). The debate is primarily between Artaxerxes I (465–424 B.C.E.) and Artaxerxes II (405–359 B.C.E.). If Ezra arrived in the seventh year of Artaxerxes I, then he preceded Nehemiah (who arrived in 445 B.C.E., the twentieth year of that king). If he arrived in the seventh year of Artaxerxes II, then he followed him. The date of Ezra's arrival is explored in the following chapter on the historical Ezra. It is concluded there that the reign of Artaxerxes II is most plausible. This means that, contrary to the order of the presentation in the biblical text, Ezra followed Nehemiah by almost half a century.

Ezra is presented to the reader of Ezra chapter 7 as both a scribe and a priest. According to the biblical text, he arrives in Judah and Jerusalem thinking only of teaching Torah (the laws of Moses) there. Apparently he comes with a mandate from Artaxerxes to do so, as well as a command from him to inspect Jerusalem according to the law of God, which he has in his hand, and to appoint judges and magistrates to enforce these laws. This relationship with the Torah is Ezra's most important and most enduring characteristic and the reason why Ezra appears in postbiblical Jewish, Christian, Samaritan, and Islamic texts. It also is the reason why biblical scholars have attributed to Ezra the origin of Judaism.

Soon after Ezra's arrival, officials approach him, complaining about the treachery of the many intermarriages between the people Israel and the "peoples of the lands" (Ezra 9:1–2). Although it is not explicitly stated, it is apparently on the basis of the laws of Moses that Ezra has brought with him that the officials complain to him about the intermarriages. Ezra reacts to the news with shock—he tears his hair and beard, rends his clothes, and fasts until evening. He is afraid to pray to God, stating that he is too ashamed and embarrassed to lift his face to him. "Our iniquities have risen higher than our head," he says. Ezra argues that we had been driven off our land because of our sins and have only now returned, and we are again provoking God with this treachery. After Ezra warns the people that these intermarriages might cause them to be driven off their land again, the people agree to a mass divorce. This story is told in Ezra 9–10.

Scholars wonder how the officials who complained to Ezra about the intermarriages would know that this was a "treachery" against God since Ezra had not yet taught them the law. In fact, we do not read of him preaching the law to the assembled populace until the book of Nehemiah (Nehemiah 8). According to the biblical timeline, Ezra arrives in the seventh year of Artaxerxes; only thirteen years later, when Nehemiah arrives, is Ezra shown reading the law. Some scholars want to rearrange the chapters, therefore, so that the story of Ezra's law reading is told in the book of Ezra immediately after the story of his arrival. They argue that originally it had actually been placed between Ezra chapter 8 (Ezra's arrival) and chapter 9 (when the officials complain),[6] but there is no external evidence for this.

These stories provide a basis of what can be known about Ezra. Combining their content with what is known of Persian administrative practices, scholars try to disentangle the historical Ezra from the person presented in the biblical text. My efforts in this regard are in chapter 2, while chapter 3 discusses Ezra as he was seen by the biblical writers.

First Esdras—The Law Triumphant

The story of Ezra is told again in the Apocrypha, a set of books written in Greek by Jews, probably in Alexandria, Egypt, and probably in the early Ptolemaic period (323–200 B.C.E.). Because this rewritten Ezra[7] was placed before our canonical

Ezra-Nehemiah in the new Greek translation (called the Septuagint), it came to be known as 1 Esdras, or Esdras α. First Esdras overlaps in the gist (but not necessarily in every detail) with the last two chapters of 2 Chronicles, with the book of Ezra, and with the story in Nehemiah of Ezra reading the law. It also adds a story about three bodyguards of King Darius, one of whom is Zerubbabel, the Davidic heir and a Persian governor of Yehud (as this Persian province was known).[8] Josephus (writing between 70 and 95 C.E.) uses the text of 1 Esdras for this portion of his history of the Jews, rather than the canonical Ezra-Nehemiah, no doubt because the order of the chapters in 1 Esdras makes better sense.

First Esdras stresses that it is because of the sins of the people and their wickedness that the kingdom fell to Babylon. As in the canonical book, Ezra returns to Judah immediately after the temple's rebuilding and dedication. He quickly learns of the perfidy of the people in their intermarriages and, as in canonical Ezra, he prays and mourns. As in canonical Ezra, the people undergo a mass divorce, but, in contrast to the canonical books, in 1 Esdras the narrative moves immediately to Ezra's reading the law. The entire story of Nehemiah is omitted. There is nothing in it about Nehemiah's building the wall or about any of his reforms. The only section included from the book of Nehemiah in 1 Esdras is the story of Ezra reading the law, and with this triumphant story the book ends. First Esdras as well as Josephus's use of it is discussed in chapter 4.

Fourth Ezra, the Ezra Apocalypse

First Esdras leaves us with the world apparently perfected through Torah, but all goes horribly wrong again when the second temple is destroyed—this time by Rome. Although it purports to be about the fall of the first temple to Babylon, 4 Ezra is actually a Jewish response to this new horror. Fourth Ezra begins with Ezra in Babylon lamenting the destruction of the temple and the exile of his people. He asks how God could have allowed this to happen to his own people, the people whom he loves of all the earth. How could he have turned his beloved over to the people of Babylon who do not know him and do not know his covenant? The Babylonians are not better than the Judeans; they are not freer from sin. Ezra asks about God's sense of justice: "Are the deeds of those who inhabit Babylon any better? Is that why it has gained dominion over Zion? For when I came here [to Babylon] I saw ungodly deeds without number, and my soul has seen many sinners during these thirty years. And my heart failed me, because I have seen how you endure those who sin, and have spared those who act wickedly, and how you have destroyed your people, and protected your enemies, and have not shown to anyone how your way may be comprehended" (4 Ezra 3:28–31).

This has been the Jewish lament over the ensuing two thousand years of Jewish history. I say two thousand years and not twenty-five hundred, because it can be discerned from the text of 4 Ezra itself that it was written not after the destruction of the first temple by Babylon in 586 B.C.E. but after the destruction of the second temple by Rome in 70 C.E. Where Babylon is read in this story, Rome must be substituted. So Ezra, like Job, asks where God's justice is, and like the book of Job it provides various answers, none of which are particularly helpful. During the course of his questioning, Ezra sees visions of the end time and the ultimate triumph of good over evil, but even these visions fail to satisfy. After being shown how the world will end and the disasters that will be meted out to those who fail to follow God's commands, Ezra asks to be imbued with the spirit of holiness that he might write down the law, God's Torah. The Book of the Law was burned in the conflagration that destroyed the temple, and without it people will not know what God is asking of them. Ezra wants "people to be able to find the path, so that those who want to live in the last days may do so" (4 Ezra 14:22).

Ezra is granted his desire and is given a magic potion to drink; after he drinks it, his heart pours forth understanding, and wisdom increases in his breast, and his spirit retains its memory (4 Ezra 14:40). During the ensuing forty days and forty nights Ezra dictates not only the twenty-four books [of the Bible] that are to be made public but also the seventy books that are to be given only to the "wise among your people, for in them is the spring of understanding, the fountain of wisdom, and the river of knowledge" (4 Ezra 14:47). Ezra is thus granted this one ability to save his people, for if survival depends upon following God's law, then the only recourse is to read that law, to learn what it is, and to follow it. I discuss this apocalyptic story of Ezra in chapter 5.

Translations of 4 Ezra

Fourth Ezra struck the imagination of later Christian writers, and translations were continually being made of it, up through the Middle Ages and later. It was translated by Christians first from Hebrew into Greek, then into Latin, and from there into Syriac, Ethiopic, Armenian, and three separate independent Arabic translations. These various translations are discussed in Appendix 2.

Christian Additions to 4 Ezra

Not only were many translations made of 4 Ezra, but early Christian writers appropriated this Jewish text by adding two chapters to the beginning (called 5 Ezra) and two chapters at the end (called 6 Ezra). These three sections (5 Ezra, 4 Ezra, and 6 Ezra) are referred to together as II Esdras. According to 5 Ezra especially, the people whom God loves are no longer the Jewish people but the Christian. Faith in the Risen Christ is the solution to Roman persecution, not Torah. These Christian additions are discussed in chapter 6.

Ezra's Tours of Hell

The apocalyptic nature of 4 Ezra and the visions in it of the end time initiated great elaborations of the story among medieval Christian writers. In these stories, Ezra tours hell, sees the horrific tortures that the sinners undergo there, and begs God to forgive them. In most of these stories, God refuses to relent since these sinners had ample time to repent of their sins while they were yet alive. After death, the die has been cast. These apocalypses, assuredly the forerunners of Dante's Inferno, are discussed in chapter 7.

Ezra in Medieval Islamic, Samaritan, Christian, and Jewish Scholarship

In 4 Ezra, the point is clearly made that the original Torah of Moses, which had lain protected in the Jerusalem temple, had been destroyed in the conflagration that destroyed the city. Because of Ezra's faith and his merit before God, God provides a potion that enables Ezra to dictate to "ready scribes" the twenty-four books of the Bible that he is to make public, as well as the seventy secret texts that are to be revealed only to the wise. The twenty-four biblical books include, of course, the five books of Moses, the Torah. Samaritan and Islamic medieval scholars, as well as several of the Church Fathers, have argued that Ezra falsified the Torah when he rewrote it and that the Torah we have now could not be the text that Moses wrote. These Church Fathers claimed that if we had the original Torah of Moses, Jesus's coming and resurrection would have been more clearly revealed than it is now; Muslim scholars claim that had we the original Torah of Moses, Mohammed would surely have been revealed in it. Also absent from Ezra's Torah is any mention of the resurrection of the dead or of the rewards of heaven to the righteous and the punishments of the damned in hell, crucial features of the Quran. Since none of these things are mentioned in it, Ezra's Torah could not be the original one. Besides the Church Fathers and Islamic scholars, Samaritan writers also claim that Ezra falsified the Torah. They argue that their Samaritan Torah is the original Torah of Moses, whereas Ezra's Torah, the one that Jews use today, is false. It is false since it does not mention Mount Gerizim as the place where God caused his name to be placed, a place that Samaritans venerate as the holiest site on earth.

In sharp contrast to Christian, Samaritan, and Islamic scholarly traditions, the rabbis hail Ezra as a second Moses. To the rabbis, Ezra is a hero, the last prophet—namely the prophet Malachi. They consider him to be one of the founders of the Great Assembly, the assembly that they say ruled Judah under the Romans. These competing claims of Samaritan, Christian, Islamic, and Jewish early medieval writers are addressed in chapter 8.

Ezra in Modern Scholarship

Modern biblical scholars have attributed the creation of Judaism to Ezra and have asserted that without Ezra's bringing the Torah to Jerusalem, Judaism would not exist. The seventeenth-century scholars Spinoza and Hobbes began this line of thought when they argued that Ezra did not simply recite the Torah from memory (as described in 4 Ezra) and did not simply bring it back from Babylon, where it had been preserved by the exiles (as described in 1 Esdras and canonical Ezra-Nehemiah) but that Ezra actually wrote it. Maybe he had some documents that he drew on, but basically he wrote it de novo. Eighteenth-century scholars drew on the work of Spinoza and Hobbes but decided that the Torah could not have been written by one person and was really a haphazard combination of four separate documents. The haphazardness of the combination accounts for the contradictions and repetitions in the Pentateuch. Nineteenth-century scholars went further and concluded that the laws of the Torah were not Israelite at all, that they did not go back to the period of the Exodus or even to the period of the Judean Monarchy. Rather, all these laws were only a manifestation of the great guilt that the Jews felt after their temple was destroyed in 586. These laws were created by Ezra and by the priests who took charge of the community after their return from Babylon. They were mandated as the Judean constitution by the Persians, thereby creating Judaism. This theory continues in various forms today and is discussed in chapter 9.

2

The Historical Ezra

As stated in chapter 1, the material about the person of Ezra is to be found only in chapters 7–10 of the book that bears his name, as well as in Nehemiah 8. He also makes a cameo appearance in Nehemiah 12:36 at the dedication of Jerusalem's city wall, but this is all there is. There are no contemporary nonbiblical references to him. So, we must ask, did he really exist? Was he an historical character? Or was he simply a creation of the imagination of the biblical writer(s)?

It should not surprise that the question is raised. Appearance in the biblical text is no guarantee of historicity. The stories of Jonah, Esther, Ruth, and Daniel, to take some examples, are fictional stories, novellas really.[1] They were written by Jews in antiquity to express an idealized past or perhaps to set an example for Jewish behavior in the diaspora, extolling the exemplary virtues of the protagonists. Of course, biblical books may also be about real people. The kings of Judah and Israel, for example, definitely existed. But to which category does the story of Ezra belong?

Torrey, writing in 1910, gives a resounding "Fiction!" to this question.[2] He argues that the whole "Ezra Memoir," in Ezra 7:27–10:44, plus the extended story of Ezra in Nehemiah, was written by the same biblical writer, the language being the same throughout. That is, he contends that both the sections written in the first person (Ezra 7:27–9:15, customarily attributed to Ezra himself), as well as the sections written in the third person (Ezra 10, Neh. 8), were all written by the same biblical writer. He concludes that this writer could not have been Ezra and that there was no real Ezra at all. The biblical writer used the first person solely to imitate Nehemiah's first-person memoir and to lend authenticity to his report. In a detailed linguistic study, Kapelrud too finds no differences between the first-person and third-person texts and agrees they were all written by the same person. This was obviously not Ezra, since Ezra would not refer to himself in the third person.[3] He too concludes that there was no person Ezra. Mowinckel claims that the use of the first person as a literary technique has "seduced" (*verleitet*) the reader into accepting the first-person narrative as Ezra's authentic memoir.[4]

Mowinckel finds reason to accept an actual Ezra behind the text, however. He does not think that a biblical writer, writing in Jerusalem, would know about a River Ahava (Ezra 8:15) or about a cult-place called Casiphia nearby where Levites

Persian Nobles and Officials. East facade of the Apadana, Wing A. Photo 1973. Courtesy of Margaret Cool Root.

might be found (Ezra 8:17).[5] Unfortunately, these places have never been located, and these names too may have been fabricated by the biblical writer to provide authenticity. Mowinckel sees in the first-person account an underlying text that has been added to by a second biblical writer and concludes, therefore, that there must have been an underlying source to which the biblical writer had added. He attributes this original source to Ezra. Evidence for a basic first-person account that has been added to, however, does not prove that this underlying text was written by the historical Ezra or even that there was an Ezra.

Yonina Dor has recently argued for several authors of Ezra 9 and 10 on the basis of the different uses of person and of the different vocabularies in the texts.[6] Yet, even she notes a strong similarity of vocabulary between the introduction to the prayer in Ezra 9 (9:1–5) and parts of Ezra 10, in spite of the difference in person used (first person in Ezra 9, third in Ezra 10).[7] Between the prayer itself and Ezra 10 she finds only a weak connection.

The alternation between the first and the third persons in literary texts has been studied recently with respect to the narrative in Acts.[8] There, "we" passages occur in the last half of the book and alternate with "he" passages, that is, with a third-person narrative. The presence of the "we" passages has indicated to traditional readers an eye-witness account. A survey of ancient literature makes clear, however, that the use of the first or third person in antiquity differs from our own. Thucydides, who wrote the *History of the Peloponnesian War* in the mid-fifth century B.C.E., customarily refers to himself, an actor in the events, in the third person (*Hist.* 1.1.1; 2.70.4; 5.26.1). The use of the third person to describe events in which the author himself took part was intended to lend an air of detachment and objectivity to the narrative. Thucydides also uses the first person to refer to himself when he claims that he has interrogated his sources carefully, has lived through it all, and understands it all (1.1.3; 1.20.1; 1.21.1). Thus, the same author makes use of both the first and the third person to refer to himself depending upon his literary goals. Polybius, writing in the second century B.C.E. on the rise of Rome to power, makes use of both the first and the third person in the same way that Thucydides does, referring to himself now in the first-person singular, now in the third person. He also uses the first-person plural occasionally, most notably in his prayer to the gods for his safe return from Rome (39.8.3–8). Polybius explains the variety of his choices for grammatical person: "so that we do not offend by . . . continuously mentioning our name, or that we should fall into a boorish rhetorical style without being aware of it by constantly interjecting 'of me' or 'on account of me'" (36.12.3). Thus, alternation in person was also used to avoid undue repetition.

Given the fact that most scholars find no real linguistic differences between the "I" and the "he" passages in the narrative of Ezra 7:27–10:44, we may conclude that the choice of person in Ezra (as well as the choice of vocabulary) has to do only with the rhetorical goals of the writer and cannot help us to determine whether it is in fact an historical person who is being described. The third person was used in contemporary literature to indicate objectivity, while the first person was used to indicate personal integrity and trustworthiness.[9] These characteristics are seen in the Ezra narrative. The first-person singular account in 7:27–9:5 not only indicates Ezra's personal integrity, trustworthiness, and personal involvement in the affairs he describes but also lends historicity and an aura of reliability to the narrative. The author then, like Polybius, switches from the first-person singular to the first-person plural in his prayer (Ezra 9:6–15) in order to convey solidarity and identification with his people. The account in Ezra 10 of the mass divorce of mixed marriages is described in the third person in an attempt to distance the main character, Ezra, from the events described and to convey objectivity and detachment. Ezra's detachment is emphasized further in that the impulse for the mass divorce is put into the mouth of Shecaniah ben Jehiel, not of Ezra himself. The unity of style across the "I" and the "he" passages makes it possible, therefore, that one person wrote both, referring to Ezra now in the first person and now in the third. The fact that the "we" passages in Acts do not cohere with Paul's actual letters reminds us, however, that the use of the first person is a rhetorical strategy and does not necessarily indicate the historicity of the protagonist or an authentic memoir. Nor does it indicate the opposite, as Thucydides's histories reveal.

Ezra's Letter from Artaxerxes

Because there is no external source for Ezra and because the use of person in the text does not indicate author, reasonable people will disagree as to Ezra's existence and activities. As a way out of the impasse, I propose to look at the text from a distinctly historical, rather than literary, point of view. The text of Ezra-Nehemiah as a whole was clearly written in the Hellenistic period. It refers to Darius, the Persian, the last king of Persia (Neh. 12:22): "In the days of Eliashib, Joiada, Johanan, and Jaddua, the heads of ancestral houses were recorded, as well as the priests, until the reign of Darius the Persian." Eliashib, Joiada, Johanan, and Jaddua were the last four priests of Judah until the Macedonian conquest under Alexander the Great, and Darius the Persian, that is, Darius III, was the last Persian king.[10] Thus, we can assume a Hellenistic, and most probably a Ptolemaic, date for the composition of the book as a whole. If so, it is not likely that the author(s) would be greatly informed about the realia of life under the Persians, so if we do find something that is definitely of a Persian context, we can tend toward accepting it as historically authentic. If it smacks of Greek influences, we can assume it was written by the biblical author and assume it is not authentic. This is not a foolproof approach, since there were Greek influences on the Levant even under the Persians,[11] and Alexander continued many Persian administrative practices.[12] Still, no method is foolproof—Juha Pakkala and Jacob Wright have used the same type of literary-critical methods with the goal of arriving at the basic, most original layer of the text of Ezra-Nehemiah, and yet they reached different, sometimes opposite conclusions.[13] The avowedly historical-critical method used here provides another approach out of the dilemma but will not satisfy everyone.

The quest for the historical Ezra begins properly with Artaxerxes's letter (Ezra 7:12–16).[14] The goal here is to determine whether there is anything in the letter that smacks of the historically plausible under the Achaemenids. The introduction to the letter (Ezra 7:11) is in Hebrew, while the letter itself is in Aramaic, the diplomatic language of the Persian Empire. The Aramaic has both Persian period linguistic forms and late Hellenistic forms in it, suggesting a letter written in the Persian period that had been updated in Hellenistic times.[15]

According to the Hebrew introduction, the letter is a copy of an order that King Artaxerxes gave to Ezra, as well, presumably, a letter of introduction to carry with him as he journeyed from Babylon to Judah. This may be compared to Nehemiah's request for a letter that would guarantee him safe passage from the governors of all the provinces that he would traverse on the way from Susa to Jerusalem (Neh. 2:2). This type of letter, dated to the end of the fifth century B.C.E., was found in Egypt. Written by Arsames, the Persian satrap of Egypt, it guaranteed one of his officials safe passage from Susa to Egypt as well as provisions from the governors of the various provinces through which the official would cross on his way.[16] The letter authorizes the various governors to dispense rations of flour and beer for the travelers and fodder for the horses at each stop, to be reimbursed later by Arsames. Without such a letter, travel was impossible.

Admittedly, Artaxerxes's letter as presented here does not do that. It does not state that the various governors should provide rations for Ezra and his fellow travelers at each of the rest stops they would encounter on the way. It does state, however, that the travelers have the permission of the king to travel to Judah from Babylon (v. 13) and that the silver, the gold, and the vessels that they are carrying are sent from the king and his counselors (vss. 15–20). Being declared an envoy of the king should guarantee Ezra and his entourage safe passage as well as provisions throughout the king's territories. Still, it is not exactly the sort of letter one would expect, and so scholars have debated its authenticity at least since the time of Wellhausen (1878).[17]

Ezra as the King's "Ear," or Episkopos

We read in the letter (Ezra 7:14) exactly what task the king was assigning to Ezra: "Accordingly you are being sent from before the king . . . to act as the 'King's Ear' over Judah and Jerusalem by means of the *dātā* of your god which is in your hand." The ellipsis hides the phrase "and his seven counselors." The Persian king's "seven counselors" has been a literary topos, a popular ascription to the Persian monarch by non-Persian writers since antiquity (see, for example, Esther 1:14). There is no mention of them in any document attributed to the Persians themselves, however. The Persian king was sovereign and did not share power.[18] We may conclude that the reference to the seven advisers was added by the biblical writer to lend putative Persian coloring to the missive.

The phrase translated here as "to act as King's Ear" is the Aramaic infinitive לְבַקָּרָא, *lebaqqārā',* which means "to act as a *mebaqqer.*"[19] The two Greek versions of Ezra—the straight Greek translation of Ezra-Nehemiah, as well as 1 Esdras (to be discussed in chapter 4)—translate this phrase with the verb ἐπισκέπτομαι, which means "to hold the office of *Episkopos*" (ἐπίσκοπος), that is, to hold the office of one who "watches over, who acts as overseer, or guardian," specifically, to act as the "King's Eye" (or King's "Ear").[20] We may assume that the Jews in Alexandria who translated the text into Greek understood the term and its role. Moreover, the *mebaqqer* of the community of the Dead Sea Scroll sect at Qumran also functioned as an *Episkopos.*[21]

The *Episkopoi* were common in the contemporary Athenian Empire.[22] They were sent out by Athens to inspect subject peoples on an ad hoc basis.[23] They toured states conquered by Athens to ensure that these territories continued to function in the interests of the empire.[24] These officials had no enforcement capabilities but exercised their influence through persuasion or, if necessary, through the local Athenian garrison commanders and the garrisons posted throughout the territories. According to one decree promulgated in 453–452 B.C.E. in Erythrai, a city on the coast of present-day Turkey, *Episkopoi* were sent from Athens to oversee (with the assistance of the Athenian soldiers garrisoned there) the selection of 120 Erythraean city council members and to supervise the investigation into their qualifications. That is to say, the *Episkopoi* were actually to select the council members who would run this putatively independent *polis.* According to another decree, ca. 447 B.C.E., *Episkopoi* in the allied states throughout the empire were directed to supervise (and compel) the collection of the annual tribute to Athens.

Most important for the present purpose, the Athenian office of *Episkopos* had a Persian origin. It was based on that of the Achaemenid "King's Eye" or "King's Ear."[25] These Persian officials were ubiquitous in the empire and are even mentioned as the *gauškaya* ("Ears") in a petition from the Persian garrison on the Nile island of far-off Elephantine, the southern tip of the Persian Empire.[26] Quoted here are the last two lines of a judicial request from 410 B.C.E.: "If inquiry be made of the judges, police, and King's Ears who are appointed in the province of Tshetres, it would be [known] to our lord in accordance to that which we say."[27] Although the text is written in Aramaic, all the words peculiar to the judicial system are Persian. The word used here for inquiry is *azad* and is Persian; the word for "police," *typatya*ʾ, is the Old Persian **tipati-* with an Aramaic suffix; the word for "King's Ears" is *goškia*ʾ, from the Old Persian **gaušaka*ʾ ("hearers"), again with an Aramaic suffix. These latter are the intelligence officers (Greek *episkopoi*) known from classical sources.[28] The "King's Ears" were thus a fixed part of the investigative apparatus of an Achaemenid province; they were sent from Susa or Babylon to all parts of the empire.[29]

Xenophon (*Cyropaedia* VIII 6:13–16) describes the role: "[He] makes the circuit of the provinces . . . to help any satrap that may need help, to humble any one that may be growing rebellious, and to adjust matters if any one is careless about seeing the taxes paid or protecting the inhabitants, or to see that the land is kept under cultivation . . . and if he cannot set it right, . . . it is his business to report it to the king." Artaxerxes's letter appoints Ezra to an avowedly investigative role in the satrapy, and, since this is how the Greek translators understood his role and since we know that Artaxerxes did in fact send out *gauškaya,* "King's Ears," to Judah and to the satrapy of Beyond-the-River, as well as to Egypt and all the provinces, one may reasonably conclude that one such person sent was named Ezra and that this was what our Ezra was appointed to do—to be the "King's Ear," his *Episkopos.*

As Xenophon informs us, the "King's Eye" or the "King's Ear" worked outside the official apparatus of the governmental bureaucracy, reporting directly to the king (*Oecon.* iv 6, 8; *Cyrop.* VIII 16). He traveled throughout the empire only rarely with soldiers or imperial guards.[30] If we accept that a man named Ezra was sent to Judah by a King Artaxerxes to *lebaqqer,* that is, to act as the Eye or Ear of the king in Judah and Jerusalem and perhaps in the whole satrapy Beyond-the-River (7:25–26), then his duties would have included those enumerated by Xenophon: to humble any governor who grew rebellious, to see to it that taxes were paid and that the land was cultivated (and taxes paid on it), and to help or humble the Persian satrap. Primarily he was to make sure that nothing was amiss, and if it was, to report it directly to the king.

Some express surprise that a non-Persian from Babylon, one of Judean descent at that, would have been given this important role. However, the many Babylonian documents written in Persepolis reveal the large number of Babylonian scribes and officials who operated in the top echelons of power within the central bureaucracy of the Achaemenid Empire.[31] These Babylonians were instrumental in giving and transmitting orders. It should not surprise any reader that among these Babylonian officials would also be Babylonians of Judean descent. We know of one such Babylonian of Judean ancestry who served as the viceroy of Egypt under Arsames, 'Anani,[32] and another, Gedalyahu (BM 74554), who served in the same role for the satrap of Babylon and Beyond-the-River in the thirty-sixth year of Darius I.[33] The fact of Ezra's Judean descent would not have prevented him from serving in the role of *Episkopos,* the intelligence officer, in the satrapy Beyond-the-River.

By Means of the Dātā of Your God That Is in Your Hand

According to Artaxerxes's letter, Ezra was to conduct his office of "King's Ear" (or "King's Eye") by means of "the *dātā* of your [Ezra's] god that is in your hand" (Ezra 7:14). The Persian word *dātā* in this verse (and elsewhere) is usually translated "law" and is conventionally interpreted to mean that Ezra was to investigate Judah and Jerusalem in order to determine whether the populace there was following the Torah, the law that Ezra is reputed to have carried with him from Babylon (Neh. 8). (For the conventional interpretation, see chapter 3 and any of the commentaries on Ezra.) As discussed earlier, the office of "King's Ear" was a common office throughout the empire, and it is unlikely that someone in this official capacity would have needed a knowledge of the Torah or of the law of YHWH to carry it out.

What then was meant by the phrase "by means of the *dātā* of your god"? There are two ways to consider this—one is according to how the biblical writer would have interpreted it, which is discussed in chapter 3. A second way is the way in which a Persian king might have intended it in an authentic letter, and this is the way it is considered here.

Dātā, "Right Decisions," in Persian Imperial Inscriptions

In order to understand Artaxerxes's letter in a Persian context, one must understand the Persian implications of *dātā.* The word *dātā* in the phrase "by means of the dātā of your god that is in your hand" (Ezra 7:14) is not Hebrew or even

Aramaic but Persian. To understand the verse, therefore, we must understand its meaning in its native Persian context. The first Achaemenid occurrence of the word is in the Behistun Inscription of Darius I (520 B.C.E.): "Says Darius the king: 'Within these countries, the man who was loyal, him I rewarded well; he who was evil, him I punished well; by the favor of Ahura Mazda these countries showed respect for my *dātā*—as was said to them by me, thus was it done'" (lines 20–24).[34]

As Kent punctuates his translation, the term *dātā* refers to the word of the king, and "what was said by me" explains "my *dātā*." The text could also be punctuated to indicate two separate entities, one being "my *dātā*," the other being "what was said by me," but that is less likely. If Kent's understanding and punctuation are correct, then "my *dātā*" should be translated as "my word." Other texts are similar. The following is from Darius' Inscription A at Naqš-i-Rustam reads, "Says Darius the king: 'By the favor of Ahura Mazda these are the countries which I seized outside Persia: I ruled over them; they bore tribute to me; what was said to them by me, that they did; my *dātā*—that held them firm'" (lines 15–30).[35] Again, *dātā* is parallel to "what was said by me"; this includes the words, decisions, decrees, and edicts of the king.

The phrase also appears in Darius's Inscription E at Susa: "Says Darius the king: 'Much which was ill-done, that I made good. Provinces were in commotion; one man was smiting the other. The following I brought about by the favor of Ahura Mazda, that the one does not smite the other at all, each one is in his place. My *dātā*—of that they feel fear, so that the stronger does not smite nor destroy the weak'" (lines 30–41).[36] This last phrase, "so that the stronger does not smite nor destroy the weak," appears in the prologue and epilogue of Hammurabi's Code and provides part of the rationale for the "just decisions" (*dīnāt mīšarîm*) that constitute this collection. The Akkadian translation of the Persian word *dātā* in the Behistun Inscription by *dinātu,* "decisions" or "judgments," confirms the relationship between the "just decisions" or "words" of Hammurabi's Laws and Darius's intention in the inscription. *Dinātu,* in both, refers to the king's words, his just decisions, righteous verdicts, and statements.[37] This is how it should be translated here.

More relevant perhaps is Xerxes's reference to the *dātā* of the Persian high god, Ahura Mazda, in the so-called Daiva Inscription (Inscription H of Xerxes at Persepolis): "You who [shall be] hereafter, if you shall think, 'Happy may I be when living and when dead may I be blessed,' have respect for that *dātā* which Ahura Mazda has established; worship Ahura Mazda and Arta reverently. The man who has respect for that *dātā* which Ahura Mazda has established, and who worships Ahura Mazda and Arta reverently, he both becomes happy while living and becomes blessed when dead" (lines 46–56).[38] The Persians had no law codes, so the *dātā* that Ahura Mazda has established can only be right order, justice, fairness, with each person in his proper place as described elsewhere in the inscriptions.[39] The *dātā* of the god is his word, but also the word, the order, the righteous decisions of the king. The words pronounced by the king are established by the god as part of the right order that exists in the world. There is no difference between the word (*dātā*) of the king and the right order (*dātā*) established by Ahura Mazda, the god.[40]

Dātā in Babylonian Texts from the Time of Darius

Besides royal inscriptions, the word *dātā* also appears in five Babylonian texts from the time of Darius.[41] Among them is "*akî da-a-ta ša šarri ušallam*" ("He will replace [the slave] according to the *dātā* of the king").[42] Another is "*akî da-a-ti šarri miksu ana* É.LUGAL *inandin*" ("He will deliver the toll to the royal exchequer according to the *dātā* of the king").[43]

The *Assyrian Dictionary of the Oriental Institute of the University of Chicago* translates *dātā* in both these cases as "the decree," that is, according to "the decree of the king." Thus, the term is interpreted as referring not to a written law, permanent or temporary, but to an ad hoc royal statement. A third text from the fourteenth year of Darius is similar:[44] "*a-ki-i da-a-tu*$_4$ *ša da-ri-a-muš* LUGAL *ina* UKKIN ^{lú}*a-kad*^{ki}*-ú-a gab-bi it-ta-na*$^{??}$*-šu [a-na]? di-i-ni mu-a-tu*$_4$ *a-ki-i da[a- tu*$_4$*] ša* LUGAL *di-i-ni* [erasure]" ("According to the *dāta* of Darius the king, given in the assembly of all Akkad, for this capital lawsuit according to the *dāta* of the king, the court case").

This case concerns a dispute about the performance of an *ilku*-task that was satisfied in silver. The case was presented before the highest official of the main temple in Akkad and before the assembly of its citizens, but the damage to the obverse of the tablet prevents determining its exact circumstances. Here, again, however, the "*dāta* of the king" is not a "law," which would affect the legal behavior of society at large, but simply an order instructing the temple personnel how to handle the assets of the crown.[45] The king issues a decision here regarding a situation that involved his own monetary interests.

One final text is a court case that involved the kidnapping of a slave from the house of her owner: "$^{lú.d}$30*-ma-gi-ir ù* [^{lú}di.kud^{meš}] ^{lú}*ki-na-at*^{meš}*-šu da-a-ti ip-tu-ú-ʾ-i*" ("The *simagir* and the judges, his colleagues, opened the *dāta* [of the king?]").[46] This is the only reference to the *dāta* as a physical object. It is evidently a sealed document or envelope that had to be opened.[47] Here the term refers to a written rescript from the king in answer to a specific query by the judges regarding this case.[48]

Dātā on the Trilingual Inscription of Xanthus

A final occurrence of the word *dātā* occurs in line 19 of the Aramaic version of the Trilingual Inscription from Xanthus, dated to the close of the Achaemenid Empire (338/337 B.C.E.).[49] The inscription, written in Aramaic, Lycian, and Greek, commemorates the creation of a cult or sanctuary (כרפא in Aramaic, βωμός in Greek) for the Carian god Kandawatz (or King), at Xanthus (Arna), the capital of the Persian satrapy of Lycia. The inscription sets forth the fiscal regulations that would govern the estate of the newly installed Carian god and his priest and outlines the economic prerogatives of the priest and the complementary responsibilities of the city of Xanthus and its neighboring villages. According to the inscription, the villagers have exempted the new priest from public tax burdens and have taken these burdens upon themselves. The word *dātā* appears in line 19 of the Aramaic version. דתה דך כתב זי מה(ח)סן אף ("This decree [*dātā*] he [Pixodarus] has written which he retains also."). Thus, Pixodarus, the Carian satrap of Lycia, has decreed in favor of setting up the statue of a Carian god within the temple of the Lycian gods in Xanthus, the capital of Lycia. This would have been only for the benefit of the Carian soldiers of the garrison installed there. The Persian word *dātā* on line 19 of the Aramaic text should be translated "word," or "decree" as it is translated everywhere else. Pixodarus decrees and confirms the Lycian agreement to install the Carian god King in their local sanctuary. The term does not refer to a written law or law code.

It must be concluded, on the basis of the wide variety of Persian period texts reviewed here, that the *dātā* of the king refers to the king's word, his orders and decrees, not to a law code, written or unwritten, neither of which ever existed in the Persian Empire.[50] The *dātā* of the god refers to that god's decrees, of course, but in a Persian context it actually refers to the word of the king, to his pronouncements, his ad hoc decisions, and his edicts. It also refers generally to the justice, the right order, and the right action that the god establishes on the king's behalf. Xerxes's Daiva Inscription refers to the *dātā* of the god Ahura Mazda, but it could refer to any god. The *dātā* that Ahura Mazda has established is the *dātā* that any god would establish; it is the word or decree of the king, including right order, justice, fairness, with each person in his proper place as described in the Persian inscriptions.

Construing the letter as a genuine missive from Artaxerxes, the Achaemenid king, then this can only be what the *dātā* of Ezra's god denotes—it is, first of all, the word of King Artaxerxes himself and includes right order, justice, and fairness, with each person in his proper place. This is the means by which Ezra is to serve in his office of *Episkopos,* as the "King's Ear"; he is to ensure that the word of the king is upheld and that right order, justice, and fairness exist in the Persian province of Yehud (Judah) and in the city of Jerusalem. There would have been no implication on the part of Artaxerxes that Ezra's god would have had a different conception of "right order," of justice or of fairness, than would Artaxerxes himself or Ahura Mazda, the high god of the Persian Empire.

The Dātā ("Word") of Your God That Is in Your Hand

What about the phrase "in your hand"? According to Ezra 7:14, Ezra was "to act as the 'King's Ear'" over Judah and Jerusalem by means of the "word" (*dātā*) of your (Ezra's) god *which is in Ezra's hand.* Even though the term *dātā* never refers to a physical object in Persian texts, Grätz argues that the phrase "in your hand" in 7:14 does imply a physical object, the written Pentateuch.[51] He cites in support the various verses in the Hebrew Bible that employ the phase "in your hand" to refer to a physical object. He does not mention the numerous verses that use it figuratively, however. The biblical text refers to the "power and might which are in your hand" (1 Chron. 29:12; 2 Chron. 20:6), "the people who are in your hand" (Joshua 9:25), the "kingdom of Israel which is in your hand" (1 Samuel 24:20), the "iniquity which is in your hand" (Job 11:14), and the "times which are in your hand" (Psalms 31:15). The expression is common in the ancient world to convey the notion of being "under your control" or "at your disposal." It occurs in Darius's Behistun Inscription (IV:36): "The lie made [these nine kings] rebellious, . . . afterwards Ahura Mazda put them into my hand; as was my desire, so I did unto them" and in a court case from the Persian period: "*dinam ša ina qatikunu ibaššu šuḫiza*" ("Try the case according to common legal practices" [lit., the practices "that are in your hand"]).[52] In this last example, judges are commanded in reality to "try the case according to existing norms," and again, the phrase "in your hand" does not imply a physical object.

Who Was Ezra's God?

What about the reference to "your [Ezra's] god"? Is this YHWH? This is certainly the understanding of the biblical writer (Ezra 7:6, 10) to be discussed in chapter 3, but what would it have meant to Artaxerxes, the Persian king? Who would Artaxerxes have assumed Ezra's god to be? Would Artaxerxes have known YHWH? Artaxerxes's letter in fact identifies Ezra's god. He is not YHWH. Rather, he is "the God of Heaven" (אֱלָהּ שְׁמַיָּא) (7:12). Although much of this verse has been supplemented by the biblical writer, the phrase "God of Heaven" is likely authentic. It is used not only here but also in a letter sent in 407 B.C.E. from Judeans manning a Persian garrison on the Nile island of Elephantine in southern Egypt.[53] The letter was written by the Judean priest on the island and his colleagues at the temple of YHW there to Bagavahya, the Persian governor of Judah.[54] In the letter, the writers explain that since the time that their temple was destroyed (three years before) they have been fasting and praying to "YHW Lord of Heaven." They state further that if the temple is rebuilt, Bagavahya will have great merit before "YHW, God of Heaven." The Persian governor, Bagavahya, responds that the Judean priests may say to the satrap of Egypt that the temple of the "God of Heaven that is in Elephantine should be rebuilt as it was formerly."[55] He thus uses the phrase "God of Heaven" to refer to the Judean god. The letters between the Judeans at Elephantine and the Persian officials in Judah demonstrate that the terms "God of Heaven" and "Lord of Heaven" were titles that Judeans applied to their god when communicating with non-Judeans and that were also used by non-Judeans in return to refer to the Judean god. To complicate matters further, a separate god, Ba'al Shamem, literally "Lord of Heaven," appears at the head of the Phoenician pantheon in both tenth- and seventh-century-B.C.E. Phoenician inscriptions.[56] In the Hellenistic period, this god, Ba'al Shamem, was also assumed to be that god who was called Zeus among the Greeks (Eusebius, *Praeparatio Evangelica* I 10,7); that is, it became the title applied to the head of every local pantheon.[57] As can be seen from the Elephantine material, this usage of the term for the generic high god was also common in the Persian period. It would also have been understood as the title of the god who was called Ahura Mazda among the Persians. Indeed, Schmid suggests that the Priestly source in the Pentateuch, written in the Persian period, uses the word Elohim (usually translated simply as "God") to indicate the generic high god and that it served as "an inclusive cipher for Ahura-mazda, Zeus, or YHWH."[58] The use of the phrase "God of Heaven" in a letter from Artaxerxes suggests therefore that Artaxerxes was referring to the generic great high god, not to any actual particular god.

Indeed, there is evidence that the Persians did make room for unknown gods in their dealings with the many peoples of their empire. The phrase "great god" appears on two texts from the Persepolis Fortification Tablets.[59] These texts, from Persepolis, one of the three capitals of the Persian Empire, deal with the administrative transfer of food commodities in the years between 509 and 494, the thirteenth to the twenty-eighth year of Darius I. One text refers to a delivery of two *marriš* of beer for the Aramean god Adad plus two more *marriš* for "their great god," making a total of four. A second text refers to a delivery of 3 BAR of grain for the offering of "the great god." The great god is not named in these texts, and the phrase seems to be a circumlocution for a god unknown to them. Thus, there is no need to assume that Artaxerxes refers to the actual god YHWH and his Torah, although this is certainly how the biblical writer interprets it (see chapter 3); rather, Artaxerxes would have been referring to the "high god" of Ezra's pantheon, whoever that happened to be.

Ezra's Second Task: To Appoint Judges

According to Artaxerxes's letter, besides acting as the "King's Ear" (Ezra 7:14), Ezra was to appoint judges for the satrapy Beyond-the-River (the official title of the satrapy that extended from the River Euphrates to the Mediterranean Sea and beyond, including Cyprus). We read: "Now, you, Ezra, according to the wisdom of God[60] which is in your hand[61], appoint . . . judges[62] who may serve as judges for all the peoples who are in [the satrapy of] Beyond-the-River" (Ezra 7:25–26).

This is Ezra's second task: he was to appoint judges. This does not imply that no judges were present in the satrapy in the 140 years prior to his arrival. Rather, Ezra would simply have filled vacancies and certified those already in office as worthy of continuing. The judges he was responsible for would have been the so-called royal judges common throughout the empire (since he was appointing them as an agent of the king). Royal judges served as judges for all the people in a satrapy and would have done so in the satrapy Beyond-the-River. As evident in the many Persian period documents from Egypt, these royally appointed judges would have been ethnic Persians.[63] In addition to the documentary evidence of the many ethnic Persian judges in Egypt, the Greek authors report that the Persian kings sent Persians into all the conquered areas to serve as judges.[64] According to Herodotus (*History* III:31): "Royal judges are men selected out from among the Persians to be so until they die or are detected in some injustice. It is they who decide suits in Persia and who interpret the established customs [θεσμός] of the land; all matters are referred to them."

These royal judges served throughout the empire, not just in Persia proper. This is seen not only in the Egyptian Aramaic papyri but also in Babylonian tablets and in the Elamite texts from Persepolis. All these testify to the presence of royal and provincial judges (*databara* in Old Persian) throughout the empire. As noted, these royal judges were all ethnically Persian.[65] The highest judicial authority in a satrapy was the satrap, but, perhaps to prevent him from gaining too much power, royal judges were appointed by the king or his agent. Immediately upon the Achaemenid occupation of Babylon, for example, local judges were replaced by Persians. A tablet from Nippur in Babylon refers to the Persian Ishtabuzanu, "judge of the canal of Sîn," a position later inherited from him by his son Humardātu.[66] The receipt of a loan by the Babylonian Marduk-naṣir-apli of the house of Egibi was registered in the Babylonian city of Nippur in the presence of the Persian judge Ummadātu, son of Udunātu.

It appears that Ezra, as *Episkopos,* was charged by the king with the task of appointing these royal judges for the satrapy Beyond-the-River. This was not unusual and is similar to the task of the Athenian *Episkopos* who was sent to Erythrai to "help" appoint the members of the *boulē,* that Greek city's governing body.

Appointing these royal judges throughout the satrapy would not have given Ezra "unlimited power" in the satrapy, as has been suggested. He would not have had the power to dismiss them, for example, since, once appointed, these royal judges could be removed only by the king himself. Of course, he certainly would have reported their behavior to him.

According to the text of Ezra 7:25 cited earlier, the king directs Ezra to appoint royal judges who are to "serve as judges for all the peoples in the satrapy Beyond-the-River—for all knowing the *dātê* of your god, and for whoever does not know, you [pl., the judges][67] will instruct [him]." What are the *dātê* of your [Ezra's] god? As discussed earlier, they are the "words" not of YHWH in particular, but of the "God of Heaven," the universal great high god, and, of course, they are the words of Artaxerxes the king. These "words" of the god are simply "right actions," "correct behavior," with no cultural or ethnic connotations to them. There would have been no implication, in a genuine letter from Artaxerxes, that those who knew how to behave correctly would have been only those Judeans scattered throughout the satrapy who refrained from eating pork. Such ethnic customs could not have been known, much less enforced, by the Persian judges whom Ezra appointed. Rather, "all who know the just decisions of your god" are all people, Judeans and non-Judeans throughout the satrapy, who know how to comport themselves properly in an ordered society.

We may conclude that this was the role of the historical Ezra: to serve as *Episkopos,* the "King's Ear," in Judah and Jerusalem. Beyond that, he was to act as the king's agent in appointing the royal judges for the satrapy of Beyond-the-River. If this is accepted, then we may use Artaxerxes's letter to inform us further about the historical Ezra. The presence of archaic Persian period linguistic forms (in Ezra 7:16, 17, 18, 24) and of Persian loan words (Ezra 7:17, 21, 23, 26) suggests that an original Persian period letter formed the basis of Ezra 7, which was then updated by the biblical writer in the Hellenistic period.[68] The hypothesis that the biblical writer used an existing royal authorization to a real historical Ezra is supported by the fact that he never shows Ezra actually inspecting the people or appointing judges.[69] It is unlikely that the author of the biblical narrative would have created an imaginary letter just to authorize Ezra's doing something that he never shows him actually doing! While the bulk of the letter may been added to by the biblical writer in the Hellenistic period (and this is discussed in chapter 3), it is likely that within the verses discussed (14, 16–26) lies an authentic core.

The Date of Ezra's Arrival

Assuming an historical Ezra, we may discuss the date of his arrival, specifically the chronological order of Ezra and Nehemiah. Such discussions have been ongoing since Van Hoonacker first broached the issue in 1890.[70] Van Hoonacker proposed that Ezra followed Nehemiah and arrived in the seventh year of Artaxerxes II, not the first. One may read the arguments for and against in any commentary. I add an additional reason in favor of the later date for the historical Ezra, but readers should also consult chapter 3.

The events told in the book of Ezra last one year—from the first day of the first month (Ezra 7:9) until the first day of the first month of the following year (Ezra 10:17). This is an appropriate length of time for the service of the "King's Ear," or *Episkopos.* According to the portion of Artaxerxes's letter that can be considered authentic, Ezra brought exemptions from taxes and tribute for the cultic personnel of the temple of YHWH in Jerusalem (Ezra 7:24). If this is historic, then these exemptions would have included release from corvée labor. This type of release from taxes and corvée labor was frequent in the Persian Empire. Cyrus remitted taxes and corvée labor for the citizens of Babylon when the city opened its gates to him (Cyrus Cylinder, lines 25–26). Gadatas, probably the governor of Lydia, had exacted tribute and corvée labor from the priests of Apollo contrary to Darius's wishes (Gadatas Letter, lines 19–29). Evidently, Darius (or Cyrus) had granted them exemption from both, and Darius kept that promise.[71] The priest of the Carian god, King, at Xanthus in Lycia was granted exemption from public burdens, that is, taxes and corvée labor, by Pixodarus, the last satrap of Caria and Lycia (Xanthus Stele, line 11, Greek text).[72]

I suggest that such is the case here as well. The first exemption that Ezra brings is from מִנְדָּה, *mindâ.* The term is from the Akkadian *maddattu* (*mandattu*), meaning "tribute" but also "work assignment."[73] The second term, בלו, *bĕlô,* is from the Akkadian *biltu* and means "taxes." The third term is הֲלָךְ, *halāk,* from the Akkadian *ilku.* It refers to conscripted work performed for a higher authority, that is, corvée labor.[74] While *maddattu* and *halāk* were also known in the Hellenistic period, the term *bĕlô* is not attested in Aramaic texts later than the Persian period and so provides evidence for the authenticity of this part of the letter.[75] If the meanings of their cognate Akkadian terms apply, then these exemptions released the temple personnel from both taxes and corvée labor. Since work on city walls was corvée labor, it is not likely that the temple personnel would have participated in building Jerusalem's city wall as they apparently had during the governorship of Nehemiah (Neh. 3) if they had previously been granted an exemption from such duties. If Ezra 7:24 is historical, then Ezra must have followed Nehemiah, and the cultic personnel would have been granted release from such duties only in the reign of Artaxerxes II. Some have objected, however, that Nehemiah states that he secured the willing cooperation of the people and that the wall building was therefore not corvée labor but volunteerism.[76] This is admittedly how Nehemiah portrays the situation, but the reader is not obligated to trust Nehemiah's version as an unbiased portrayal of reality, especially when he mentions the *śabāl* (Neh. 4:4 [English translation: 4:10]), a "gang of workmen at forced labor").[77] We may conclude that Ezra arrived after Nehemiah, very likely in the reign of Artaxerxes II (405–359 B.C.E.), during the high priesthood of Joḥanan (Ezra 10:6), the grandson of that Eliashib who was high priest during the time of Nehemiah.[78]

Ezra and the Mixed Marriages

When Ezra arrives in Jerusalem we are told that "officials," *śārîm,* approach him to complain that the people Israel was not separating itself from the "peoples of the lands." Can this event be historic? It is impossible to say. Who would these officials, these *śārîm,* have been? The basic meaning of the term is that of a military leader or commander.[79] In Genesis 21:22, 32, for example, he is the *śar ṣābā',* the general of the army. In Exodus 1:11 the phrase שָׂרֵי מִסִּים (*śārê misîm*) refers to the "commanders of a work force," so called because of the soldiers through whom they ensure the workers' compliance. In Exodus 18:21 Jethro tells Moses to appoint commanders (*śarîm*) of thousands, of hundreds, of fifties, and of tens to judge the people (cf. 2 Chron. 1:2; 8:9, 10). This military organization reflects that of the Persian army (Herod VII 81). It is also exemplified in the records from the Persian garrison at the Nile island of Elephantine (fifth to fourth century B.C.E.). The archive of papyri found there illustrates that the garrison was similarly organized, with a Persian commander over "the thousands" and primarily Persian (but also Babylonian) captains over "the hundreds" and the "tens."[80] That these *śarîm* were military commanders is also demonstrated by the reference to them in the story of the wall building in Nehemiah 3:9–19:

> Next to them Rephaiah son of Hur, commander [*śar*] of half the district of Jerusalem, made repairs. . . . Next to him Shallum son of Hallohesh, commander [*śar*] of half the district of Jerusalem, made repairs, he and his daughters. . . . Malchijah son of Rechab, commander [*śar*] of the district of Beth-haccherem, repaired the Dung Gate. . . . And Shallum son of Col-hozeh, commander [*śar*] of [half] the district of Mizpah, repaired the Fountain Gate. **16**After him Nehemiah son of Azbuk, commander [*śar*] of half the district of Beth-zur, repaired. . . . Next to him Hashabiah, commander [*śar*] of half the district of Keilah, made repairs for his district. After him . . . Binnui, son of Henadad, commander [*śar*] of half the district of Keilah; next to him Ezer son of Jeshua, commander [*śar*] of [half the district of] Mizpah, repaired.

These commanders over the various districts within Judah were necessarily military officers since they would have required troops to enforce their decisions.[81] Indeed, these commanders would have used their troops to build Jerusalem's city wall. Evidence from an archive of Aramaic letters from the fourth-century-B.C.E. Persian province of Bactria (present-day Afghanistan) shows that Persian troops were regularly used in this manner.[82] The Bactrian archive includes chancellery copies of official letters from Akhvamazda, satrap of Bactria, to Bagavant, governor (*peḥah*) of a province in northern Bactria. In one letter Akhvamazda responds affirmatively to a previous request made by Bagavant that he (Bagavant) be allowed to release the troops at his disposal from their current activity of building the city wall around Nikhšapaya, a city in the extreme northern end of his province, and use them instead to gather in the harvest before the locusts consume it. Thus, as governor, Bagavant had troops at his disposal, and, moreover, he had been commanded to use his troops to build a city wall. This is also what Nehemiah did. As provincial governor he was able to use the troops garrisoned throughout his province to build a city wall around Jerusalem. As was true elsewhere in the Achaemenid Empire, each of the district commanders within the province would have had charge of a garrison, and, as governor, Nehemiah could commandeer their troops to build the city wall.

We may conclude that if this half-verse, Ezra 9:1a, were indeed from the memoir of an historical Ezra during the reign of Artaxerxes, and it is indeed a big if, then these would have been military commanders who approached Ezra, and they would have been officials of the Persian Empire, as was the case everywhere. The issue then would be whether these military officers would have concerned themselves with such matters as intermarriage in the provinces and, if so, why.

Life in Contemporaneous Athens

Why would a Persian official have complained to Ezra, the new *Episkopos,* about intermarriages between peoples of different ethnicities?[83] Why would he have cared? It is interesting to note, however, that a similar ban on intermarriages was enacted in contemporaneous Athens. In 451–450, Pericles, a prominent and influential statesman and general of Athens, persuaded the Athenian Assembly to pass a law that required that for anyone to be considered an Athenian citizen he had to have two Athenian parents. According to Plutarch (*Pericles* 37.2), however, this was a law "about bastards," not about citizenship per se. Aristotle also reports on the law: "And in the year of [the archonship of] Antidotus, owing to the large number of the citizens, an enactment was passed on the proposal of Pericles prohibiting a person from having a share in the city who was not born of two citizens" (Aristotle, *Athenaion Politeia* 26:3).

For the first time Athenian citizens now had to prove descent from an Athenian mother, that is, a woman whose father was a citizen. Those unable to prove this were reckoned bastards. Though not often stated, this law recognized for the first time the status of the Athenian woman and may have even elevated it.[84] The decree of 451/450 was followed by a public scrutiny (διαψηφισμός) in 445, when the Egyptian king sent grain to be distributed to Athenian citizens. "And so [in 445] when the king of Egypt sent a present to the people [of Athens] of forty thousand measures of grain, and this had to be divided up among the citizens, there was a great crop of prosecutions against citizens of illegal birth by the law of Pericles, who had up to that time escaped notice and been overlooked, and many of them also suffered at the hands of informers. As a result, a little less than five thousand were convicted and sold into slavery, and those who retained their citizenship and were adjudged to be Athenians were found, as a result of this selection, to be fourteen thousand and forty in number" (Plutarch, *Pericles* 37.3–4).

Indeed, exactly 4,760 Athenians were struck from the citizenship rolls then as being of "impure birth" and not entitled to the grain.[85] Deprived of their rights as citizens, they had no recourse to the protection of the courts; if murdered, their family had no right of vengeance. Many fled or were exiled. Confiscation of property and often loss of life followed even those allowed to remain in Athens. Those who sued for their citizenship rights and lost their suit were executed. These laws were allowed to lapse during the Peloponnesian Wars, but in 403 they were reinforced and strengthened. Another census and mass exile ensued. Manville characterizes these periodic "scrutinies" as "reigns of terror."[86] Davies notes the constant status anxieties that are reflected in contemporary tragedies.[87]

Laws elaborating on the prohibition of intermarriage between Athenians and foreigners followed upon Pericles's citizenship law. Two laws in particular are noteworthy, both quoted in Demosthenes, *Against Neaira* LIX:16, 52.[88]

> If a foreign man lives as husband with an Athenian woman in any way or manner whatsoever, he may be prosecuted before the *thesmothetai* by any Athenian wishing and entitled to do so. If he is found guilty, both he and his property shall be sold and one-third of the money shall be given to the prosecutor. The same rule applies to a foreign woman who lives with an Athenian as his wife, and the Athenian convicted of living as husband with a foreign woman shall be fined a thousand drachmas. (Demosthenes, *Against Neaira* LIX:16)
>
> If any Athenian gives a foreign woman in marriage to an Athenian citizen, as being his relative, he shall lose his civic rights and his property shall be confiscated and one-third shall belong to the successful prosecutor. Those entitled may prosecute before the *thesmothetai,* as in the case of usurpation of citizenship. (Demosthenes, *Against Neaira* LIX:52)

These laws imply that a mandatory divorce took place in all marriages between an Athenian and a non-Athenian, whether male or female. According to the law, the foreigner living as a spouse with an Athenian shall be sold into slavery and his or her property confiscated (with one-third given to the man who brings the suit). Since women did not give themselves in marriage, anyone giving a foreign woman to an Athenian in marriage was also subject to sanctions. This was then the situation in fifth- and fourth-century Athens.

Why was this law enacted? One problem with foreign marriages was inheritance. Sons of foreign women or, rather, grandsons of foreign men could wind up inheriting land in Athens. Technically speaking, women did not inherit, but wealthy women received a premortem inheritance through their dowries, and these could include lands and estates, as well as sums of money easily turned into land. Women without brothers also received a postmortem inheritance. In this way, a woman served as a conduit, conducting her father's estate to her sons. Sons of brotherless women were often adopted into the household of their maternal grandfather, and, if the women were foreign, these non-Athenian grandsons could wind up owning land in Athens and achieving civil power there.

The law in Athens succeeded in sharply reducing foreign marriages. While common before, they are unknown after Pericles's law of 450.[89] Moreover, charges of "foreign birth" and "treachery" were the most common allegations scrawled on potsherds used to ostracize politicians from the city.[90] The main effect of the law, however, was on the large number of men serving as imperial officials in cities throughout the Athenian empire.[91] In prohibiting their fraternization with locals, the law prevented families in other cities from accessing property in Athens through the marriage of their daughters to Athenians. If Athenian men married abroad, their children would not inherit Athenian land. Claims of kinship could never lead non-Athenians to power or influence at Athens.

A second purpose may have been to prevent the Athenian aristocracy from forming dynastic alliances with wealthy families from other states—not only those with which Athens had hostilities, like Sparta, but also with those dependent states that paid tribute to the coffers of the Athenian League.[92] Any of these alliances could easily have upset the balance of power. Such alliances would provide a power base outside the *polis,* a power base that could threaten Athenian autonomy.

Persian Concerns

Would the Persians have had an equivalent concern about foreign marriages? We know very little about Achaemenid marriage practices, but foreign marriages seem to have been generally avoided.[93] Whereas intermarriages were common between the ruling Mermnad dynasty (680–547) and the Sardian aristocracy of Asia Minor before the Persian conquest, for example, they are completely absent from the documentation of the Achaemenid period. Cambyses II, Cyrus's son, entered into marriages with the daughters of both Persian nobles and non-Persian royalty, but he was the last to do so.[94] Darius I, the usurper, married the wives of his predecessors, Cambyses II and Bardiya (Smerdis), and also their sisters, but only to emphasize his right to the throne.[95] His successors all married within the royal family (half sisters or close cousins). Other members of the royal household married offspring of Persian satraps and military commanders in order to strengthen the bonds between them and the king[96] and also to prevent Persian officials in the satrapies from marrying local women. Marriages between Persian officials and local dynasts were frowned upon since they could create alliances that would exert a centrifugal force away from the central power base in Susa and threaten the status quo. All provincial governors had garrisons and militias at their disposal to control the populace and to collect taxes and tribute from them to send on to Susa. These resources tended to increase the desire of local governors for independence and autonomy.[97] Marriages across provinces between ruling governors and local dynasts would have pooled these resources and threatened resistance against Persia. Nehemiah and Josephus report marriages between the families of Sanballat, the governor of Samaria, and Eliashib, the Judean high priest (Neh. 13:28; *Ant.* XI:2); between the families of Tobiah, the governor of Ammon, and that of the high priest of Judah (Neh. 13:4; *Ant.* XII iv:160); and between the family of Tobiah and the nobility of Judah (Neh. 6:18). These marriage alliances across the provinces of Beyond-the-River may have been seen by the Persian officials as threatening to create a power base and source of wealth independent of the king.[98] In fact, bans on intermarriages were carried out in other bureaucratic empires with the same objective. Akbar, one of the descendants of Gengis Kahn, established a military occupation in China and forbad intermarriage among the various ethnic groups there.[99] Lucius Aemilius Paulus, Roman general in 168 C.E., divided Macedonia into four separate provinces; he then forbade intermarriage and land ownership across the boundaries (Livy XLV.29).[100] The deified Augustus established a code of rules for the administration of the Privy Purse, a code maintained for 200 years. This code consisted of over 100 laws that greatly restricted interaction among ethnic groups. The goal was *divide et impera.*[101] It seems reasonable then to suppose that Persian officials would have approached Ezra upon his arrival to complain about the numerous intermarriages that were taking place in Judah, especially since "[Persian] military officers and prefects [הַשָּׂרִים וְהַסְּגָנִים] were the first in this treachery" (Ezra 9:2). As the new *Episkopos,* the agent of the king, it would have been natural for Persian officials in Judah to complain to him about this upon his arrival.

The Mass Divorce

Although we may assign Ezra's overwrought reaction to the news to the biblical writer, since it seems unbecoming to a Persian *Espiskopos,* it is possible that in Jerusalem as in Athens a mass divorce may have been ordered. It is equally possible that the entire episode is a creation of a biblical writer, writing in the Greek period and aping the Athenians. It is peculiar that the major instigator appears to be Shecaniah ben Jehiel from Elam (Ezra 10:2), as his own father seems to be listed among the transgressors (10:26). Had Jehiel the Elamite taken a local woman in marriage as a secondary wife, whose children now posed a threat to Shecaniah's inheritance?

Conclusion

In sum, we may conclude that Ezra was a Persian official, one of the hundreds of *gaushkaiya* ("King's Ears") sent throughout the empire to inspect it to determine if the satrap and the governors in it were conducting their affairs properly in the service of the king. Ezra's task was to serve in this role in Judah and Jerusalem. He was also charged with appointing, for the entire satrapy of Beyond-the-River, those royal Persian judges that were found throughout the empire. He arrived in the seventh year of Artaxerxes II and likely returned to Babylon or Susa after his one-year term of office expired. Whether or not he instituted a mass divorce, we cannot know.

Everything else asserted about Ezra we may assign to the biblical writers as well as to ancient, medieval, and modern scholars and tradents who followed upon them. It is to the first of these that we now turn.

3

Ezra in the Hebrew Bible

The story of Ezra was created by biblical writers writing not from the perspective of the Persian period (to which we date the historical Ezra) but from that of the Hellenistic period. Indeed, references in Nehemiah 12:22 to the high priest Jaddua (who according to Josephus [*Jewish Antquities* 11:326–33] was visited by Alexander the Great) and to the last Persian king, Darius III, demand a Hellenistic date for Ezra-Nehemiah as a whole. It is possible to narrow this date further. It has been convincingly shown by scholars that the apocryphal 1 Esdras (see chapter 4) is based on the canonical books of Ezra-Nehemiah, so the canonical books must have been written first.[1] Since the story of the three youths in 1 Esdras was likely written during the early Ptolemaic period, that is in the third century B.C.E.,[2] our canonical Ezra would either have been written then or earlier, in the time of Alexander the Great, at the end of the fourth century.

Ezra's Priestly Genealogy

The story of Ezra begins in Ezra 7 with a presentation of his priestly genealogy. It is nearly identical to the high-priestly genealogy in 1 Chronicles 5:29ff (English translation: 6:3ff), except that six names are omitted from the center of this list (Amariah–Johanan):

1 Chronicles 5:29–41	Ezra 7:1–5
Aaron	Aaron
Eleazar	Eleazar
Phineas	Phineas
Abishua	Abishua
Bukki	Bukki
Uzzi	Uzzi
Zerahiah	Zerahiah
Meraioth	Meraioth
Amariah	
Ahitub	
Zadok	

1 Chronicles 5:29–41	**Ezra 7:1–5**
Ahimaaz	
Azariah	
Johanan	
Azariah	Azariah
Amariah	Amariah
Ahitub	Ahitub
Zadok	Zadok
Shallum	Shallum
Hilkiah	Hilkiah
Azariah	Azariah
Seraiah	Seraiah
Jehozadak	Ezra

The Chronicler states that the Jehozadak who ends the list in Chronicles is the very same one who was exiled to Babylon (1 Chron. 5:49 [English translation: 6:15]). Seraiah, his father, was therefore the one who was killed by the hand of the Babylonian king at Riblah (2 Kings 25:18–21). By providing Ezra with this same

Ezra Preaches to the People. Woodcut, *Die Bibel in Bildern*, 1860, by Julius Schnorr von Carolsfeld.

genealogy, the author assumes him to be the son of the last high priest of Judah, brother of the Jehozadak who was exiled, and uncle of the Jeshua son of Jehozadak, the high priest of the restoration period under Darius I.

The absence of six names in the middle of Ezra's genealogy cannot imply that Ezra is closer by six generations to Aaron, Moses's brother, than Jehozadak is. Since three of the names omitted—Zadok, along with his father, Ahitub, and his son Ahimaaz—are the three priests whom we know about from the stories of David and Solomon (cf. 2 Sam. 8:17; 15:2), it is possible that the Chronicler added these famous names plus three others to the shorter list that appears in Ezra.[3] A second possibility is that these names were omitted from the list in Ezra due to haplography (that is, the scribe's eye jumped to the same set of three names, Amariah, Ahitub, and Zadok, that is repeated further down on the list), so that the list in Chronicles is the original one. Middle names on a list are more likely to be omitted when reciting a list than the names at either the beginning or the end, consistent with the notion that the longer list in Chronicles is the original one and that the names in the middle of the list were lost in transmission.

In any case, the author of our passage used this priestly genealogy to provide Ezra with a high-priestly pedigree. The genealogy was intended to demonstrate that Ezra was a legitimate descendant of Aaron, a member of the high-priestly family, son of the last high priest, brother of Jehozadak, and uncle of Jeshua ben Jehozadak, the high priest of the restoration period (Ezra 1–6). It does not seem likely that this genealogy was taken from Ezra's actual memoir.[4] It is more likely that since genealogies have specific purposes, a genealogy going back to Aaron, the first high priest, was supplied by the biblical writer in order to legitimate Ezra's activities surrounding the law and that this genealogy has nothing to do with the historical Ezra.[5] He may not even have been a priest at all. The phrase "the priest" is included after Ezra's name in Ezra 10:10 but is not present in the corresponding text in 1 Esdras 9:7. This is so even though 1 Esdras expands Ezra's priestly role everywhere else, even making him a high priest, ὁ ἀρχιερεὺς (1 Esdras 9:39, 40), when he is never called this in the Hebrew version.[6] It seems likely therefore that had the phrase "the priest" been present in 1 Esdras's source at Ezra 10:10, 1 Esdras would have included it. This suggests that references to Ezra as a priest were added late in the transmission process. Ezra's father may have been named Seraiah, and the biblical writer may have assumed him to be the Seraiah who was the last high priest under the Judean monarchy and so supplied the appropriate genealogy. If so, then Ezra's true genealogy was unknown, and Ezra was not of the high priestly line and probably not a priest at all, since priests kept careful track of their lineage (cf. Ezra 2:62).

Indeed, if Ezra did in fact arrive in Judah during the reign of any king Artaxerxes, however, then historically speaking, it is impossible for him to be the uncle of Jeshua son of Jehozadak. Even if he arrived in 458 B.C.E., in the seventh year of Artaxerxes I, he could not have been the son of someone who died when Jerusalem fell to Babylon, in 586 B.C.E., 128 years before. This genealogy would be reasonable, however, if the biblical author assumed that the Darius who was king when Jeshua son of Jehozadak was high priest (Ezra 5:2) and the Artaxerxes who was the king when Ezra arrived in Jerusalem (Ezra 7:1), were one and the same, that is, that Artaxerxes was simply the throne name of Darius. This is the rabbinic understanding (see chapter 8).

The Date of Ezra's Arrival According to the Biblical Writer

The story of Ezra begins with the phrase "after these things." A form of this phrase occurs twelve times in the Hebrew Bible. Whenever it occurs, its use suggests that the exact chronological relationship between two related events is not clear to the writer. In every case, however, the second, subsequent event is viewed as occurring within the lifetime of the protagonist of the first event. (See, for example, Genesis 15:1; 22:1, 20; 39:7; 40:1; 48:1.) It is instructive to consider 1 Kings 21:1 and the corresponding text in the Greek Septuagint version (3 Reigns 20:1). The phrase "after these things" is present in the Hebrew 21:1 but absent in the Septuagint. This is because Kings 21 in the Hebrew relates an event in the life of Ahab, the protagonist of the previous chapter. Indeed, the purpose of the phrase is to tell the reader so. Chapters 20 and 21 are reversed in the Greek, however, so that chapter 21 of the Hebrew text now follows chapter 19. The protagonist of 1 Kings 19 is Elijah, not Ahab. Not being about the same protagonist, the phrase "after these things" is omitted.

This consistent use of the phrase implies that the events of Ezra 7 were construed by the biblical writer as occurring within the lifetime of King Darius, the protagonist of Ezra 6. Ezra's arrival is dated to the first month of the seventh year of a King Artaxerxes (Ezra 7:7). This date is not likely to be authentic. The biblical writers, writing in the Hellenistic period, knew from Artaxerxes's letter that Ezra arrived during the reign of a King Artaxerxes, but, as is discussed further later, they considered Artaxerxes to be the throne name of every Persian king. In this view, the Darius under whom the temple was dedicated had the throne name Artaxerxes! The writer who inserted the phrase "after these things" assumed that Ezra's arrival in Jerusalem would have occurred immediately following the events of Adar, the twelfth month, of Darius's sixth year, when the temple was finally completed and dedicated, and so it is put to the first month of the seventh year. Thus, the phrase "after these things" should be read as "immediately after these things" from the point of view of the literary construction of the story. This writer may also have been the one who added those first six chapters of the return to the story of Ezra-Nehemiah.[7] The phrase indicates that in the mind of its author, no chronological separation existed between the temple's rebuilding and dedication and Ezra's bringing the law to Jerusalem.[8]

In fact, the chronology that forms the background to the book Ezra-Nehemiah is not the conventional chronology. According to the conventional chronology, the list of Persian kings from Cyrus to Darius III spans more than two hundred years (from 550 to 333) and includes ten kings. (The list of Persian kings with their dates is in Appendix 1.) The conventional chronology is based on the writings of the Greek historians (for example, Herodotus, Xenophon), on dated administrative texts from Babylon and Egypt, and on the inscriptions of the Persian kings themselves. The conventional chronology is also matched to eclipses of the sun and moon and is correct.[9]

The chronology that forms the backbone of the book of Ezra-Nehemiah differs from the conventional one, however. The chronology assumed in Ezra-Nehemiah is revealed in the book of Daniel 11:1–2, written in the mid-second century B.C.E. According to the book of Daniel, there were only three kings of Persia who succeeded Darius the Mede, and the last one (the fourth in the series) was the one who fought Alexander the Great: "As for me, in the first year of Darius the Mede, I stood up to support and strengthen him [Darius]. 'Now I will announce the truth to you. Three more kings shall arise in Persia. The fourth shall be far richer than all of them, and when he has become strong through his riches, he shall stir up all against the kingdom of Greece'"(Dan. 11:1–2).

This is a prediction after the fact (*vaticinium ex eventu*), that is, the writer is writing from the vantage point of the days of Antiochus IV, almost two hundred years after the fall of Persia to Alexander. If, as is likely, his primary information about the chronology of the Persian period came from the book Ezra-Nehemiah, then we can use these verses in Daniel to understand how the chronology of the Persian period was perceived in later Judean thought. Darius the Mede does not appear in Ezra, so the three kings mentioned in Daniel that appear after this Darius must be named in Ezra-Nehemiah. If the first mention of each king reveals the order of their reigns, the order of the Persian kings is Cyrus (Ezra 1:1), Xerxes (= Ahasuerus; Ezra 4:6), Artaxerxes (Ezra 4:7), and Darius (Ezra 4:24). There is another Artaxerxes whose seventh year is mentioned in Ezra 7:1 and another whose twentieth year is mentioned in Nehemiah 2:1. Since at most three kings were assumed to cover the entire Persian period after Darius the Mede, the Talmud (*Rosh Hashanah* 3b) and Rashi (Comment on Ezra 7:1) both concluded that Artaxerxes was the throne name taken by every Persian king. It applied equally to Cyrus, Xerxes, and Darius. This was likely the underlying assumption of the final author of Ezra-Nehemiah as well. The seventh year of Artaxerxes, when Ezra is reported to have come to Jerusalem, is, in this view, the seventh year of Darius. The temple is consecrated in the twelfth month of Darius's sixth year (Ezra 6:15), and Ezra starts out on his journey a few days later on the first day of the first month of Darius-Artaxerxes's seventh year (Ezra 7:7). That is, the Artaxerxes who is king in Ezra

7-Nehemiah 13 is actually (according to this way of thinking) Darius the Persian, the same Darius in whose reign the temple was dedicated and (in this view) the same Darius who fought Alexander.

This yields three Persian kings after Darius the Mede (who appears only in Daniel)—Cyrus, Ahashuerus (Xerxes), and Darius the Persian. The Persian period is compressed in this way into a very short time. According to this view, Cyrus reigned for three years (Dan. 10:1), Ahashuerus-Artaxerxes reigned for twelve years (Esther 3:7), and then Darius-Artaxerxes reigned for at least thirty-two years (Neh. 13:6), for a total of forty-seven years. Nehemiah reports, moreover, that in the thirty-second year of (Darius -) Artaxerxes he was recalled to Persia, and after some time he returned to Judah and finished his term, presumably under that same king. This likely was seen as rounding out the Persian period to a nice fifty years. This seems to have been the chronology in the mind of the historian who edited Ezra-Nehemiah. It explains Ezra's genealogy and the order of the kings in Ezra, as well as all the names in the heading of the list in Ezra 2. With a Persian period of only fifty years from the first return to the advent of Alexander the Great, all the preeminent men of the period could have been contemporaries. Naturally, they all would have returned at the first moment possible under Cyrus. Some—like Ezra (ʿAzariah), Nehemiah, and Mordechai (who all appear in the list of returnees in Ezra 2 = Nehemiah 7)—must have gone back to Susa at some point since they are reported active there after Cyrus's reign. There was apparently no doubt, in the narrator's mind at least, that if they were alive they would have gone up to Israel immediately under Cyrus even if they went back to Babylon later. According to this understanding, since the second temple was reputedly dedicated seventy years after the destruction of the first one (Jer. 29:10; Zech. 1:12), Ezra could have been as young as seventy when he led a group back to Judah.

Ezra as Scribe

According to the biblical text, Ezra was a scribe (Ezra 7:6). Scribes fulfilled many functions in the Achaemenid Empire, most often simply writing letters and contracts for the illiterate majority of the population (as is witnessed by Jeremiah 36:32 and by the Aramaic papyri from Elephantine).[10] Kings, satraps, governors, priests, and judges also employed scribes to read to them and to write what they dictated. Scribes also served in a notary function, certifying contracts and notarizing receipts and disbursements from the royal storehouses located in each of the provinces.[11] We read that Nehemiah appointed Zadok, the scribe, as one of the treasurers over the temple storehouse (Neh. 13:13). He served under Shelemiah, the priest, probably as chief accountant and record keeper of the temple funds.

Scribes also served in highly placed official positions in provincial, satrapal, and royal administrations.[12] The title *si-pir-ri* (scribe) appears on a Babylonian tablet dated to the twenty-fourth day of the sixth month of the thirty-sixth year of Darius I, that is, October 4, 486 B.C.E.[13] On the tablet, a record of a transfer of barley, two men, Libluṭ and Gedalyahu, are each given the combined title of scribe and *bēl ṭè-e-mu* (viceroy), and, according to the tablet, they each served directly under the satrap of Babylon and Beyond-the-River. (This large satrapy was divided into two separate satrapies later, during the reign of Xerxes.) It may be that one of the men served as secretary and viceroy for the half-satrapy of Babylon while the other served in this double role for the half-satrapy of Beyond-the-River. One of the officials on the tablet has the Judean name Gedalyahu (Yahu, or YHWH exalts). He was likely a Babylonian of Judean descent, and he may have been the one assigned to the subsatrapy Beyond-the-River.

Scribes were included in almost every area of temple and court administration throughout the ancient Near East and Egypt. They filled diplomatic, political, notarial, and fiscal tasks at all levels of imperial administration. Beyond their bureaucratic and administrative functions, however, scribes were also considered to be steeped in the wisdom traditions of their cultures. Following a literary vein that goes as far back as Egypt's Middle Kingdom, Ben Sira (ca. 196 B.C.E.), describes the wisdom of the scribe, the γραμματεὺς, the same title that Ezra receives in Greek Ezra.[14]

> The wisdom of the scribe depends on the opportunity of leisure; only the one who has little business can become wise.
>
> 25 How can one become wise who handles the plow, and who glories in the shaft of a goad, who drives oxen and is occupied with their work, and whose talk is about bulls? He sets his heart on plowing furrows, and he is careful about fodder for the heifers.
>
> 27 So too is every artisan and master artisan who labors by night as well as by day; those who cut the signets of seals, each is diligent in making a great variety; they set their heart on painting a lifelike image, and they are careful to finish their work.
>
> 28 So too is the smith, sitting by the anvil, intent on his iron-work; the breath of the fire melts his flesh, and he struggles with the heat of the furnace; the sound of the hammer deafens his ears, and his eyes are on the pattern of the object. He sets his heart on finishing his handiwork, and he is careful to complete its decoration.
>
> 29 So too is the potter sitting at his work and turning the wheel with his feet; he is always deeply concerned over his products, and he produces them in quantity.
>
> 30 He molds the clay with his arm and makes it pliable with his feet; he sets his heart to finish the glazing, and he takes care in firing the kiln.
>
> 31 All these rely on their hands, and all are skillful in their own work.
>
> 32 Without them no city can be inhabited, and wherever they live, they will not go hungry.

Yet they are not sought out for the council of the people, nor do they attain eminence in the public assembly. They do not sit in the judge's seat, nor do they understand the decisions of the courts; they cannot expound discipline or judgment, and they are not found among the rulers.
34 But they maintain the fabric of the world, and their concern is for the exercise of their trade.

How different the one who devotes himself to the study of the law of the Most High! He [the scribe] seeks out the wisdom of all the ancients, and is concerned with prophecies; he preserves the sayings of the famous and penetrates the subtleties of parables; he seeks out the hidden meanings of proverbs and is at home with the obscurities of parables. He serves among the great and appears before rulers; he travels in foreign lands and learns what is good and evil in the human lot. He sets his heart to rise early to seek the Lord who made him, and to petition the Most High; he opens his mouth in prayer and asks pardon for his sins.
6 If the great Lord is willing, he will be filled with the spirit of understanding; he will pour forth words of wisdom of his own and give thanks to the Lord in prayer.
7 The Lord will direct his counsel and knowledge, as he meditates on his mysteries. He will show the wisdom of what he has learned, and will glory in the law of the Lord's covenant.
9 Many will praise his understanding; it will never be blotted out. His memory will not disappear, and his name will live through all generations.
10 Nations will speak of his wisdom, and the congregation will proclaim his praise. (Sir 38:24–39:10)

These two images of the scribe, the court official and the wisdom scholar, play out in the biblical traditions of Ezra. The first appears in the letter from Artaxerxes, in which he is presented as a high court official, and the second in the descriptions of Ezra reading and discussing the law of Moses in Nehemiah 8. It is according to this second role of the scribe, however, that Ezra is introduced as a "scribe skilled in the law of Moses" (Ezra 7:6). The phrase "skilled [or ready] scribe" (סֹפֵר מָהִיר, *sōfēr māhîr*) appears also in Psalm 45:2 (English translation: 45:1), and a similar usage of the adjective "skilled" or "ready" occurs in Proverbs 22:29. The complete phrase "skilled [or ready] scribe" also occurs in the Aramaic *Parables of Aḥiqar.*[15] This fictional text, of Mesopotamian origin, was found in a fragmentary copy on the Nile island of Elephantine, dating to the late fifth century B.C.E. Ezra's two scribal identities, as both court official and wisdom teacher, are also assigned to Aḥiqar in the *Parables of Aḥiqar.* According to the narrative, Aḥiqar was a "wise and skilled scribe" (סֹפֵר מָהִיר, *sōfēr māhîr*), a court adviser to Sennacherib the king of Assyria (705–681 B.C.E.), and bearer of Sennacherib's royal seal. After the narrative introduction, Aḥiqar is shown reciting parables to his nephew by which he imparts to him the wisdom of the ages. The text of Aḥiqar thus reveals the two images of the scribe that we see in Ezra: court administrator and wisdom teacher. The language of the parables indicates they were composed around 700 B.C.E, whereas the language of the narrative that frames the sayings is later, stemming from the sixth century B.C.E.[16] In view of how widespread the story was (traveling all the way from Mesopotamia to the Nile island of Elephantine) and how late it was being read there (end of the fifth century), it would very likely have been known to the author of Ezra and to his readers. Ezra's description as "skilled scribe" may have been intended to convey to readers a similarity between Aḥiqar and Ezra, implying that Ezra's relationship to Artaxerxes was the same as that of Aḥiqar's to Sennacherib and implying also that Ezra was a knower of parables and knowledgeable in the wisdom of the god of heaven.

It is obvious, of course, that Ezra did not have the sort of relationship with Artaxerxes that Aḥiqar had with Sennacherib, or Ezra would have remained at court in Susa as adviser to the king. He would not have been sent to the satrapy of Beyond-the-River. Indeed, as *Episcopos* he would most likely have had a scribe himself, rather than have been one. The biblical writer introduces Ezra as both priest and scribe of the law of Moses in order to prepare the reader for the scene in which Ezra reads the law to the assembled congregation (Neh. 8). That scene is the climax of both these books.

Ezra's Task in Biblical Tradition—to Teach Torah

According to the biblical writer, the purpose of Ezra's trip to Judah was to teach law and ordinance in Israel (Ezra 7:10), and, according to that writer, his mission was self-initiated, not imposed from above.[17] In this view, Ezra came to Jerusalem for the express purpose of studying and teaching Torah, the Mosaic law code, in Israel. He did not come in order to act as the spy, or as "King's Ear," nor did he come to appoint judges in the satrapy Beyond-the-River. In fact, he is never portrayed as doing any of these things in the biblical text. According to the biblical writer who introduces him, he came only to teach YHWH's laws, and this was not *to* Israel but *in* Israel. If it were *to* Israel, he could have remained in Babylon and taught the commandments to the Judeans who remained there. Instead, he came to Judah. It seems that to the biblical writer, then, the holiness of the land demanded a greater obedience to the Torah than was required of the Judeans in Babylon. Only now that the temple had been built and dedicated did the land become so holy that the law, the Torah of YHWH, had to be installed and obeyed in it.

Ezra Inquires of the Torah

According to the biblical writer, moreover, Ezra did not come only to teach the law; "Ezra had set his heart to inquire [לדרוש *lidêrôš*] of the Torah of YHWH"

(Ezra 7:10). The expression "inquire of YHWH" or "inquire of God," usually refers to inquiry through a seer, prophet or medium (for example, 1 Sam. 9:9; 28.7; 1 Kings 22:8). This form of the verb occurs thirty-six times in the Hebrew Bible and in all but three it is used to denote the act of seeking an oracle from a god, either directly or by means of a medium or prophet. One of these three instances is in this passage, where an oracle is sought from a text. A second occurs in Ezra 10:16, in which inquiry is made by the judges to determine who has married foreign women. A third occurs in Deuteronomy 22:2 when someone comes to inquire after a lost object, but the use of the term *lidêrôš* in these latter two passages may imply that inquiry was made by divination. The term is used most often to refer to seeking an oracle from other gods (for example, Exod. 18:15; Deut. 12:30), from the dead (Deut. 18:11; Isaiah 8:19), from a seer (1 Sam. 9:9), from a medium (1 Sam. 28:7; Isaiah 8:19), or from a prophet of YHWH (1 Kings 22:8; Ezek. 20:3). Employing this phrase in the context of the Torah indicates that the scroll itself has become an oracular device,[18] a medium through which God may be accessed. A precise description of this activity is found in 1 Maccabees 3:48: "And they opened the Book of the Law to inquire into those matters about which the Gentiles consulted the images of their gods."

If this analysis is correct, then by the time this verse in Ezra was written, the scroll itself had taken on a hypostatic character and had become the icon of the god,[19] a portal into his presence.[20] Because it was an icon of the god, only priests could touch it to avoid the sacred contagion that surrounded it. This is why Ezra was made a priest and given a high priestly genealogy by the biblical writer. We see this concept of sacred contagion, for example, in the story describing the ark's being brought up to Jerusalem (2 Sam. 6:2–7), for the ark too was a medium by which YHWH could be accessed:

> [2] David and all the people with him set out and went from Baale-judah, to bring up from there the ark of God, which is called by the name: "YHWH of hosts who is enthroned on the cherubim."
>
> [3] They carried the ark of God on a new cart, and brought it out of the house of Abinadab, which was on the hill. Uzzah and Ahio, the sons of Abinadab, were driving the new cart [4] with the ark of God; and Ahio went in front of the ark. . . .
>
> [6] When they came to the threshing floor of Nacon, Uzzah reached out his hand to the ark of God and grasped it, for the oxen shook it.
>
> [7] YHWH's anger was kindled against Uzzah; and God struck him there because he reached out his hand and touched the ark; and he died there beside the ark of God.

Uzzah died because he touched the ark without being of the priestly or Levitical castes. The same contagion is seen in the rabbinic attitude toward the Torah scroll.[21] The rabbis knew that Ezra's Torah would defile the hands if taken out of the temple. According to the Talmud (*Kelim* 15:6): "Ezra's book [the Torah scroll that he brought to Jerusalem] when taken out [of the temple] defiles the hands, and not only Ezra's book, but also the Prophets and the Five Books [of the Writings]."[22]

This notion of "defiling the hands" implies a tradition of a sacred contagion inherent in the Torah scroll. This contagion is conveyed not by the meaning of the laws and commandments but is a contagion inherent in the scroll itself, a physical contagion dangerous to all but the high priests to whom, according to Josephus, Ezra's Torah was entrusted (Josephus, *Contra Apionem* 1:29).[23]

The Torah scroll as the icon of the god is revealed again in the description of the Torah reading in Nehemiah (Neh. 8:5–6): "And Ezra opened the book in the sight of all the people, for he was standing above all the people; and when he opened it, all the people stood up. Then Ezra blessed YHWH, the great god, and all the people answered, 'Amen, Amen,' lifting up their hands. Then they bowed their heads and bowed down [יִּשְׁתַּחֲוּ] to YHWH with their noses to the ground."

The verb יִּשְׁתַּחֲוּ, *yištaḥawū,* to bow down, is used numerous times in the Hebrew Bible, often to denote respect; David, for example, bows down before King Saul (1 Sam. 24:9). However, it is also the very action that Moses takes when YHWH stands before him on Mount Sinai (Exod. 34:8) and that Bilam makes before the angel of YHWH (Num. 22:31). It is thus a reaction to the presence of the divine. This is the only time in the Hebrew Bible that people are shown bowing down before a text, however, and here too it conveys more than simple respect. The ceremony described in Nehemiah 8 in which the people bow down before the Torah scroll when Ezra lifts it up suggests that at this point the Torah scroll has become more than a simple piece of writing, more than a simple wisdom text. It has been exalted into the physical sign of YHWH's presence, his location on earth.[24] Here, too, as in Ezra 7:10, in Nehemiah 8:1–6, the Torah scroll is seen as a manifestation or an epiphany of the god YHWH and as a medium through which God may be accessed.

Ezra as Teacher of Torah

Ezra set his task not only to inquire of the Torah of YHWH but to do so "in order to do and to teach in Israel statute and ordinance" (Ezra 7:10). Since Nehemiah 8 is the only passage that actually shows Ezra teaching statutes and ordinances in Israel, this verse in Ezra 7 foreshadows the story of Ezra's reading the law told in Nehemiah 8. The verse in Ezra looks forward to Nehemiah 8:1, in which Ezra is told to bring the Torah scroll. In Nehemiah 8:1, Ezra the *sofer* (scribe) is told to bring the *sefer* (the book of the law of Moses) and to read it to the people assembled before him in Jerusalem. The similarity between the two verses is striking:

Ezra 7:6	**Neh. 8:1**
This Ezra went up from Babylon	They told
He was a ready scribe	Ezra the Scribe
	To bring the book
of the Torah of Moses	of the Torah of Moses
which YHWH God of Israel gave	which YHWH commanded Israel

The biblical writer, writing in the Hellenistic period, thus had an entirely different understanding of Ezra's task from what Artaxerxes intended. As suggested in the previous chapter, Artaxerxes instructed Ezra "to serve as *Episkopos,* that is, as the 'King's Ear,' over Judah and Jerusalem by means of the decrees [*dātā*] of . . . [the] god [of heaven]," which Ezra had at his disposal (Ezra 7:14; see chapter 2). According to the biblical writer, however, the meaning of the phrase was completely different—the *dātā* of Ezra's god that he held in his hand could be nothing else than the written Torah of Moses. In this biblical understanding, the Achaemenid ruler, Artaxerxes, had sent Ezra to Judah and Jerusalem only to determine the extent to which the Torah of Moses was being obeyed there.[25]

Indeed, this has been the traditional interpretation of the verse. The question has always been only whether the Torah Ezra brought was a new law that Ezra composed himself or was one with which the people of Judah and Jerusalem were already familiar.[26] The Apocalyptic 4 Ezra (see Introduction and chapter 5 on 4 Ezra) shows Ezra dictating from angelic revelation the twenty-four books of the Hebrew Bible plus seventy secret texts, all of which had previously been destroyed. In this tradition Ezra rewrote the Torah from memory and earned the title of the "second Moses."

The biblical writer who introduces Ezra in Ezra 7:1–10 assumed that Ezra had brought a copy of the original Mosaic Torah to Judah and Jerusalem. He likely based this assumption on the Persian word *dātā,* which appears in Artaxerxes's letter. By the time of his writing (in the Hellenistic period), this word had been incorporated into the Hebrew and Aramaic languages with an entirely different meaning than it had in Persian. Instead of the term referring to ad hoc royal decrees that had only temporary validity and restricted applicability, a permanent written law code was now in mind. The change in meaning is visible in the Aramaic portions of Daniel, likely written over the course of the third century B.C.E.[27] The original Persian understanding of the term is employed in Daniel 2:9, where it refers to a decree of the king applicable only once and only to Daniel. The later Hellenistic meaning is employed in Daniel 6, however. There, the several references to the *dātā* of the Persians and the Medes suggest a permanent collection of codified laws. This is not historical, since no such law code ever existed. It represents a completely Greek (even an Athenian) understanding of law.

Ezra Reads the Torah

Nehemiah 8, in which Ezra reads the Torah to the assembled population, is the climax of the book of Ezra-Nehemiah.[28] Nehemiah 8, moreover, presents the only passages in Ezra-Nehemiah where Ezra is actually shown reading and teaching Torah. In contrast to the passage that introduces the person of Ezra (Ezra 7:1–10) and that anticipates the law reading of Nehemiah 8, the primary story of Ezra as presented in Ezra 7:27–10:44 knows nothing of any law code or of any law of Moses. The only occurrence of the word "*tôrâ*" in these chapters is in the mouth of Shecaniah, not Ezra, when the former argues before the assembled populace that we should "put away our foreign wives and the children born to them" and that it should be "done according to torah" (וְכַתּוֹרָה יֵעָשֶׂה) (Ezra 10:3). Since there is no other reference to a law of Moses or to a book of the law in any verse that may reasonably be assigned to an Ezra source (that is, in Ezra 7:27–10:44), it is probable that Shecaniah's plea should be translated "let it be done rightly" or "let it be done as God would want us to do it." The meaning of *tôrâ* here would then be as it is in the oldest portions of the biblical canon—"teaching," "instruction," "right behavior" (for example, Prov. 6:20, "do not abandon the torah [the teaching] of your mother" [אַל־תִּטֹּשׁ תּוֹרַת אִמֶּךָ]). No book of laws need be implied. Thus, if it were not for the law reading as presented in Nehemiah 8, the person of Ezra would never have been associated with a written Torah scroll.

Scholars who have examined the question have concluded, moreover, that the story of Ezra's law reading is an addition to Nehemiah's memoir and was not originally part of it.[29] If we look for the word *tôrâ* in what is considered the authentic portions of Nehemiah's memoir (the first-person accounts: Neh. 1:1–3, 11c; 2:1–7:4; 11:1–2; 12:27–43; 13:4–31) dated to the mid-fifth century and the reign of Artaxerxes I, we see that the word *tôrâ* never appears.[30] In fact, the historical Nehemiah, governor of Judah under Artaxerxes I, knows nothing about either a Torah or a law code. He does not refer to any law code when he reprimands the Judean nobles for demanding interest from their own kin or for selling them abroad (Neh. 5). He does not refer to a law code when he refuses to enter the temple (Neh. 6:11), when he expels Tobiah from his rooms at the temple compound (13:8), when he remonstrates with temple officials for not ensuring that the Levites received their tithes (13:11), when he chastises the merchants for selling their wares on the Sabbath (13:17), and not even when he contends with Judean nobles for marrying non-Judeans (13:25). He knows about Solomon (13:26) but not about Moses. Scholars have been able to find numerous parallels between Nehemiah's activities and the written Torah,[31] but Nehemiah himself refers to no written law code and no Moses. While exhibiting familiarity with many Judean customs and traditions, he was not familiar with the concept of a written code of law, a Torah. The historic Nehemiah thus did not know Ezra's law reading. This lends support to those who date Ezra to the seventh year of Artaxerxes II, 398 B.C.E. If Ezra had indeed read the Torah then, Nehemiah would not have known about it.

Some scholars solve the problem of Nehemiah 8's apparent dislocation by assuming that the story of the law reading was originally set between Ezra 8 and 9.[32] According to the present formulation of these chapters, Ezra comes to Judea to teach the law in the seventh year of Artaxerxes I (458; Ezra 7:10, 14, 25)[33] but does not read it to the people until thirteen years later, in the time of Nehemiah, in the twentieth year of that king (Neh. 2:1; 8:2). Nor is there anything in Nehemiah 8 as it now stands that can account for the sackcloth and ashes in Nehemiah 9:1. In Nehemiah 8 the people are told not to be sad, for joy in YHWH is strength (Neh. 8:10). Now, three days later, they are fasting in sackcloth and ashes! Nehemiah 8 does not logically precede Nehemiah 9 but could motivate Ezra 9. In Nehemiah 8, Ezra reads the law, and as a result, in Ezra 9, officials approach Ezra to complain that the people of Israel have not separated themselves from the peoples of the lands. Without Nehemiah 8 and the story of Ezra's reading the law, the concern of the officials in Ezra 9 appears unmotivated. From a source critical point of view, Nehemiah 8 with the story of the law reading seems to belong to a separate Ezra story, and most scholars assume it originally was placed between Ezra 8 and 9.

There is evidence, however, to indicate that Nehemiah 8 was not written by the author of the material that we have in Ezra 7:27–10:44 and that it should not be moved from its present position. This can be readily shown by the choice of the Hebrew word to express the verb "to assemble."[34] The word used for "assembled" in Nehemiah 8:1 is based on the root *asaf* (אסף), and it is used twice more in the same pericope (Neh. 8:13; 9:1). It appears only once in all of Ezra 7–10 (Ezra 9:4), however.[35] The word used most commonly in Ezra 7–10 for "to assemble" is based on the root קבץ, *qbṣ,* and it is used five times (Ezra 7:28; 8:15; 10:1, 7, 9). It is unlikely that the author of Ezra 7–10, who uses קבץ consistently in 7–8 (twice) and in 9–10 (three times), would now use only אסף in an intervening chapter (the law reading in Neh. 8). It seems time therefore to sever the law reading and references to the "book of the law of Moses" from the story of Ezra. The author of the Ezra story (Ezra 7:25–10:44) is not the author of Nehemiah 8.[36]

A Covenant Renewal Ceremony (Nehemiah 8–10)

If whoever wrote the story of the law reading did not write the rest of the story of Ezra, why did he write this part? And, having written it, why did he insert it into the middle of Nehemiah's memoir and not in the book of Ezra? As suggested earlier, he was likely the one who also wrote the introduction to Artaxerxes's letter and the introduction to the story of Ezra. It is only there that it is said that Ezra came to Israel to teach the law of YHWH, and only in Nehemiah 8 is Ezra shown actually teaching it. If he wrote the introduction to the story of Ezra only to foreshadow the law reading, which he does not relate until Nehemiah 8, he must have been the one who combined these two previously independent books. If he also wrote the introductory words "after these things," which seems likely, then he would also have been the one who prefaced his combined Ezra-Nehemiah story with the story of the temple's rebuilding and dedication (Ezra 1–6). But why would he have done all this? If he had both Ezra's story (Ezra 7:27–10:44) and Nehemiah's memoir at his disposal, why did he not insert his story of the law reading into the story of Ezra? Why did he insert it into the middle of Nehemiah's memoir?

Nehemiah 8–10 forms the climax of the books Ezra-Nehemiah.[37] In Nehemiah 8, Ezra reads the Torah of Moses to all the people, who weep when they hear it (Neh. 8:9b). He admonishes them to be glad, for joy in YHWH is strength (8:10). The people celebrate, eat, drink, and send gifts (8:12). In their long prayer that follows (Neh. 9), the Levites recount the wonders God has done for them from the time he brought them out of Egypt to the present (Neh. 9:4–25);[38] they confess that in spite of everything that God has done, they and their ancestors have been disobedient (Neh. 9:26–30). Now, because YHWH is a just god, he has handed them over to the peoples of the lands, making them slaves in their own country to the kings that he has set over them (9:36–37). According to Nehemiah 10:1 [English translation: 9:38], it is because of all this that "we," the undersigned, make a firm agreement, an *'Amānāh,* to keep the Torah of YHWH and not to forsake his temple. Because this section climaxes in Nehemiah 10 with the signing of this *'Amānāh,* this whole section (Neh. 8–10) has been dubbed a "covenant renewal ceremony."[39]

Although this section climaxes the books, it is not a literary unity and therefore cannot be a historical one. As noted earlier, there is nothing in Nehemiah 8 as it now stands that can account for the sackcloth and ashes in 9:1. Thus, from a source critical point of view, Nehemiah 8 and the story of the law reading should be peeled away from Nehemiah 9 and 10.

But Nehemiah 9 and 10 do not form a literary unit either. The extensive penitential psalm in Nehemiah 9 is too general to have arisen either from the reforms of Ezra or Nehemiah or even from the biblical writer's own concerns with the problems of intermarriage.[40] The sins confessed in the prayer reflect only a general disobedience; intermarriage is not cited. The prayer was evidently not composed for the present context but more likely stems from another occasion and was included in its present position by the biblical writer.[41] These source critical results leave the agreement (*'Amānāh*) in Nehemiah 10 without a motivation either in the prayer (Neh. 9) or in Ezra's law reading (Neh. 8). The agreement in Nehemiah 10 either was thus composed de novo by the biblical writer for its present position or is based on a temple archival document.[42]

The story of the law reading is not historical but rather was created for a specific literary purpose. Evidence discussed earlier suggests that the biblical writer who introduced the person of Ezra in Ezra 7:1–10 (and who did not write the rest of Ezra's story) was the one who wrote the story of Ezra's reading the law (Neh. 8:1–6, 9b, 10, 12). Though not historical, the effect of the story of the law reading is profound, for it evokes in the mind of the reader awe and veneration for the Torah scroll, indeed not for its contents (which the reader does not know) but for the scroll itself.[43] In contrast to the assembled populace, the reader does not hear a word of the book; he apprehends its nature only from observation of the assembled Israelites' reaction to it.[44]

Is the 'Amānāh a Covenant Oath?

Nehemiah 8–10 is consistently referred to as a covenant renewal ceremony, that is, a treaty between God and the people,[45] but the treaty form as it existed in the ancient Near East has been extensively studied. Vassal treaties, parity treaties, loyalty oaths, and unconditional grants have been dissected and found to reveal a remarkable similarity of structure.[46] A preamble identifies the parties, narrates their relationship, and gives their titulary. In vassal treaties, an historical prologue presents the saving acts of the sovereign to his vassal. This introduction is followed by a list of stipulations that states the obligations of each; the gods of each are called upon to witness the covenant and enforce the sanctions; and finally the sanctions—the blessings and curses that would follow from either obedience or betrayal—are listed. In the case of all but the parity treaty, the stipulations are commands imposed by the stronger party onto the weaker. In a parity agreement, the stipulations are imposed on each by each.

Baltzer argues that Nehemiah 9–10 exhibits the basic structure of a vassal treaty.[47] Nehemiah 9 contains the historical prologue and relates God's saving acts toward his people; Nehemiah 10:1 states that the following is a firm "covenant" (which is how he translates *'Amānāh*); a curse is mentioned in 10:30; and the stipulations are stated in vss. 29–40. Baltzer does note important differences, however.[48] Rather than promising not to forsake YHWH, the participants promise in Nehemiah 10 "not to abandon the house of our god" (Neh. 10:39). Moreover, the stipulations are not stated as imperatives or jussives as would be expected but are expressed as voluntatives in the first-person plural. To Baltzer, these differences from the typical covenant ceremony reflect the passage of time. By the Persian period, he suggests, there was no longer anyone able to pronounce commandments in God's name. God's voice belonged to the past.

McCarthy agrees that these differences from the usual covenant renewal ceremony reveal the passage of time and show only what the postexilic author thought that covenant renewal ceremonies should look like."[49] To McCarthy, the relationship of Nehemiah 9–10 to traditional covenant forms is so tenuous that a shift in the concept of covenant renewal must have occurred in the Persian period. Yet, if no prophet speaks God's word to the populace, the second party to the agreement is absent, and God isn't really here at all, can the *'Amānāh* reasonably be called a covenant? If the redactor wrote a covenant renewal ceremony de novo, he would surely have included the covenant partner. It seems more likely therefore that he used an authentic document from the temple archives to create his covenant renewal ceremony. If so, what type of document might it have been?

Does the 'Amānāh Reflect a Religious Association in Yehud?

Not often considered in this connection is the idea that the *'Amānāh* of Nehemiah 10 may have been the foundation document for a temple cult guild or association.[50] Solon's Law on Associations, probably written in Athens in 594, provides a contemporary understanding of the institution: "If a demos [δῆμος] or members of a phratry or of a cultic society [ὀργεῶνες] or of a ship-command or messmates or members of a burial society or revelers or people going abroad for plunder or for commerce make an arrangement concerning these matters [matters appropriate to their association] among themselves, it is to be valid unless the written statues of the People forbid it."[51]

According to Solon's Law, an association is a group of people that is able to issue edicts binding on its members. Such a group may be permanent and lasting over many generations, like the *phratry* or the *demos;* or it may be transient, a group of men who agree on a common commercial or military venture. The group may have been organized for a public purpose (for example, the *phratry* or the *demos*) or for a purely private purpose (revelers). Membership may be voluntary (as with the revelers) or involuntary (as with the *demos*). The crucial distinction is that the group of people must be capable of regulating itself by enforceable rules.

One type of association cited by Solon is the cult guild (ὀργεῶνες). Temple cultic associations were well known throughout the Greco-Persian world. Weisberg has recognized a Craftsmen's Guild at the temple of Eanna in Uruk from the fourth year of Cyrus;[52] De Cenival has documented associations of Egyptian priests as early as the twenty-ninth year of Amasis (541 B.C.E.);[53] and Jones has studied the cultic associations of classical Athens (594–321).[54] The ubiquity of the institution makes it reasonable to propose that a cultic association also existed at the temple of YHWH in Jerusalem and to suggest that its foundation document lies behind the text of Nehemiah 10. To test this hypothesis, I compared the structure and content of the *'Amānāh* in Nehemiah 10 against that of the foundation document for a Ptolemaic Egyptian cultic association and against that of the Babylonian craftsmen's guild.[55] The three documents were found to be very similar. Their structure and the great majority of their terms and conditions are analogous; this is especially true of the association of the Egyptian temple priests and the *'Amānāh* described in Nehemiah 10. In both these documents, the members agree to provide for all their temples' operating needs, and these needs are spelled out in great detail. There are, moreover, strong similarities in structure, content, and purpose, suggesting that, like the agreement among the Egyptian temple priests, the *'Amānāh* too was the foundation document for a temple association. It can be concluded that the document used to form the basis of Nehemiah 10 was simply the foundation document for a temple association in Jerusalem, the type of association that was common throughout the Greco-Roman world. This was used by the author of our chapter to create a covenant renewal ceremony in which the document was signed only as a result of the law reading. Thus, both the prayer and the document antedated the story of the law reading and were used by the biblical author to formulate what has been termed by scholars a covenant renewal ceremony.

Ezra—a Second Moses—Brings the Torah into the Temple

Now we can understand the author's arrangement of Ezra 7-Nehemiah 13.[56] He has sandwiched his story of Ezra reading the Torah and his entire covenant renewal ceremony (Neh. 8–10) between two lists of the legitimate population of Judah and Jerusalem. He prefaces the ceremony with the list in Nehemiah 7 of those who returned from the captivity and who were settled in their towns (Neh. 7:6, 7). He follows it with Nehemiah's statement that the city is now repopulated (Neh. 11:1–2) and with a second list of those settled in Jerusalem and the surrounding villages (Neh. 11, 12). Next, he prefaces the first population list (Neh. 7) with Nehemiah's account of his trip to Judah to rebuild the city wall, an account of the wall building itself, and the portion of Nehemiah's memoir that ends with the comment that the wall is completed and the doors hung (Neh. 7:5). He follows the second population list in Nehemiah 11 and 12 with Nehemiah's description of the wall's dedication (Neh. 12:27ff), the ascent onto the wall, and the ceremonial celebration and the sacrificial feasting in the temple. The author has thus surrounded the covenant renewal ceremony first and most nearly with the legitimate population of Judah and second and outermost with the creation, completion, and dedication of the city wall. The wall has become a fence, not only around the people, but around the Torah itself. Inside the dedicated wall is the rightful population of Judah, and in the center of that population is the Torah.

In bringing the law to Judah and Jerusalem, the author portrays Ezra as a second Moses. The sequence of events told mythically in the story of the Exodus—the move from bondage to God's holy habitation, the people's purification for three days before hearing the law, the thunder and lightning, and the people's trembling—is all repeated—albeit prosaically—in the story of Ezra. To begin with, in the Book of Exodus, Moses brings the people from bondage to God's holy mountain on the first day of the first month (Exod. 12:2; 13:4). Ezra too brings the people from captivity to the site of God's habitation, the temple, setting out on the first day of the first month (Ezra 7:9). Ezra states that although we are slaves, God has not abandoned us but brought us to the site of his residence (Ezra 9:9).

Second, Moses brings the people to the foot of the mountain of God in order to read them the law (Exod. 19–20). To the biblical writer that is also why Ezra comes to the site of the temple of God—to read the people the law (Ezra 7:10). In his prayer, Ezra confirms that the people Israel have been living in bondage (Ezra 9:8, 9), but even in their present servitude God has given them a stake in his holy place (מְקוֹם קָדְשׁוֹ,) and a new life in God's dwelling. Moses arrives at the mountain to form a covenant between God and Israel (Exod. 19). When Ezra arrives at the house of YHWH, he is told that there is hope for Israel against the divine anger if they form a new covenant with God (Ezra 10:2, 3).

Third, Moses informs the people that God is about to make an agreement with them and that if they obey his words, they will be his treasured possession (Exod. 19:5). Even before they hear his conditions, the people answer Moses: "All that YHWH has spoken, we will do" (Exod. 19:8). So too with Ezra: before they hear what he has to say, they answer Ezra in one voice: "Yes, according to your instructions upon us we will do" (Ezra 10:12).

The people give their assent to both Moses and Ezra prior to hearing the conditions to be placed upon them. Frank Polak has shown that this type of preliminary agreement is the initial step in treaty arrangements in Mari, Mesopotamia, and Ugarit.[57] It is not a final ratification of the agreement but rather affirms that the proceedings may go forward. The preliminary acceptance of the Sinai covenant takes place in a ceremony at the bottom of the mountain of God before all the people and their elders (Exod. 19:7, 8). In the Ezra story, it takes place in the square facing the temple before a great assembly of the people as well as before the officials of the priests and the Levites (Neh. 8). If God can be assumed to dwell on the mountain in the Exodus story and in the temple in the book of Ezra-Nehemiah, then the location of these events vis-à-vis the deity is the same. It is close to but outside God's residence; the site approaches the border between the holy and the profane.[58]

After the people's initial acceptance of the covenant, Moses ascends to the mountain top in order to receive the divine instructions regarding its terms. When he comes down, he does not read the law to the people but instructs them first to purify themselves, to wash their clothes, and to avoid women for three days (Exod. 19:14–16). They obey his wishes and meet, trembling, at the bottom of the mountain:

> And Moses came down from the mountain to the people and he consecrated the people and they washed their clothes, and he told the people to get ready for the third day, and not to go near a woman.
>
> And it was on the morning of the third day and there was thunder and lightning, with a heavy cloud on the mountain, and the sound of a very loud blast on the trumpet, and all the people in the camp trembled (Exod. 19:14–16).

This scenario is repeated in the book of Ezra. Ezra instructs the people to appear before him in three days (10:8). On the third day the people assemble in Jerusalem, trembling because of the heavy rain (10:9). Ezra tells them that they must put away their [foreign] wives. In the Exodus story, they put their wives away for three days only as part of their purification rites prior to hearing the law. In the Ezra story, they put them away permanently. The ideological purpose of the narrator may be the same, however, to indicate that the people have purified themselves prior to hearing the law.[59]

In the canonical Ezra, the purification and the mass divorce of chapter 10 are followed not by the Torah reading, which is delayed until Nehemiah 8, but by the story of Nehemiah's coming to Jerusalem to build a wall.[60] The story of the wall is interposed between the people's purification and the Torah reading, but this placement is purposeful. It follows the story of Moses. Before Moses descends from the mountain, before he relates God's commands, God tells him to place a border around the people, lest they touch the Mountain of God and perish: "You shall place a border around the people, saying: Be careful not to go up upon the mountain or touch the edge of it. Anyone who touches the mountain shall be put to death" (Exod. 19:12). In the book of Exodus, the people arrive at the foot of the mountain trembling in fear and awe. God again tells Moses to warn the people not to approach the mountain or to get too close, not to break through the boundary, or they will die (Exod. 19:21).

YHWH's command to Moses to place a boundary around the law inserts itself between the people's purification and the law reading. The account of Nehemiah's wall building (Neh. 3) is also inserted after the people have divorced their wives (Ezra 10) but before Ezra reads the Torah (Neh. 8). In this way, the author creates Ezra as a second Moses not only in the fact that Ezra brings the law to the people but in the entire sequence of covenantal events. Most striking in this regard is that the episodes that contain the journey to God's holy habitation, the subsequent purification of the people by separating from their wives, the wall building, and the Torah reading are preceded in the accounts of both Moses and Ezra by the command to appoint judges. Prior to approaching the wilderness of Sinai, Jethro tells Moses to teach the people the statutes and the laws, to inform them in the way that they should go (Exod. 18:20), and to appoint judges over them (18:22). Similarly, prior to his trip to Judah, Ezra is told by King Artaxerxes to appoint judges and to teach the people the laws (Ezra 7:14, 25). In this way, too, the author consciously presents Ezra as a second Moses.

Moses's reading the law (Exod. 20–23) is followed in Exodus 24 by the story of Moses purifying the people by anointing them with blood, the blood of the covenant (Exod. 24:8). The leaders of the people (Moses, Aaron, Nadab, Abihu, and the seventy elders) then climb the mountain until they see the God of Israel (24:10). They see God, and they eat and drink (Exod. 24:11). They have crossed the border that hitherto separated the divine and the profane spheres and entered the abode of the divine.[61]

The story of Ezra parallels that of Moses's covenantal ceremony but again more prosaically. Ezra reads the law (Neh. 8), and it is ratified by the leaders of the people when they sign the ratification document (Neh. 10). The ratification is followed by a list of the people (Neh. 11) and by the dedication of the city wall (Neh. 12:27ff). We then read: "Then the priests purified themselves; and they purified the people and the gates and the wall" (Neh. 12:30).

According to this biblical writer, after the Torah reading, while the people are all there in front of the water gate of the city wall, the priests begin to purify themselves and the people, as well as the gates and the wall (Neh. 12:30).[62] This is the culmination of the covenant renewal ceremony, and parallels Moses's purifying the people by anointing them with the blood of the covenant. It should be noted that the purpose of purification rituals was always to enable a person to enter sacred space. In Leviticus 12:4 a woman is purified after her period so that she may enter the sanctuary. In Genesis 35 Jacob purifies himself and his household in order to go to Bethel and build an altar (Gen. 35:2, 3). According to Numbers 8, the Levites must be purified before they can enter the Tabernacle and serve YHWH, and, according to the Chronicler (2 Chron. 29:12–19), the temple had to be purified after Ahab's desecrations in order for it to be usable again, presumably in order for YHWH to inhabit it. Thus, here, too, in Nehemiah 12, the people are being purified in order to enter a sacred space.

The dedication itself consists of two thanksgiving processions in which the purified people go around the top of the purified city wall in two directions and meet within the temple, the house of God: "So both companies of those who gave thanks stood in the house of God" (Neh. 12:40). There they offer sacrifices and rejoice, with music and singing, women and children also experiencing the joy of the celebration (Neh. 12:43). God had caused them to rejoice. These sacrifices and celebrations form the climax of Ezra-Nehemiah. Their feasting and celebrating in the temple parallel those of Moses, Aaron, Nadab, Abihu, and the seventy elders who saw God and ate and drank (24:10–11).

But what exactly is being celebrated in Nehemiah 12? Is it just the completion of the wall? If so, why does the procession not just conclude with the two groups simply meeting on the other side of the wall from where they began, showing that the wall was now complete? Why does it end inside the house of God?

The wall forms the boundary between the sacred city that houses the temple and the profane world outside it, but why is the wall itself purified? Purification of a city wall is unique in the biblical text,[63] but there are parallels in the ancient Near East. During Nabonidus's dedication of Shamash's temple, Ebabbar, Nabonidus drenches the door posts, locks, bolts, and door leaves with oil in preparation for the entry of the god (*Nabonidus* #6, col. II:13–15).

The door posts, locks, bolts and door-leaves
I drenched with oil
and for the entry of their exalted divinity
I made the contents of the temple full of sweet fragrance.
The Temple, for the entry of Shamash my lord,
its gates were wide open, and it was full of joy.[64]

The anointment of the door posts, locks, bolts, and door leaves enabled the god, Shamash in this case, to pass from the area of the profane into an area now made sacred by his presence.

We do not know how Jerusalem's city walls were purified or with what, whether it was by oil or blood, by sacrifices, or by water in which the ashes of the red heifer were mixed (all of these are mentioned in biblical purification rites). When the purification rites are completed, however, the leaders of the people ascend the wall. They walk around on it in both directions until they come to the house of God (Neh. 12:40). With Ezra the priest-scribe leading the way (Neh. 12:36), they stand inside the house of God and give thanks, offering sacrifices and rejoicing (Neh. 12:43). By entering the temple, they have entered the sphere of the divine.

Purification of the wall suggests that a god was to enter the city. I suggest that according to our author, Ezra, the *sofer* of the book of the words of the commandments of YHWH, was still carrying the Torah from when he had read it to the populace and that he carried it while he walked upon the wall, that he carried it into the temple, and that he installed it in its place.[65] This is why the city wall itself had to be purified—because Ezra, bearing the Torah, the physical manifestation of YHWH's presence, was to walk upon it.

The festive meal (which presumably accompanied the sacrifices) seals the covenant in both the Exodus story and that of Ezra-Nehemiah. In both stories, it occurs only upon passing from the profane into the divine realms of the mountain and the temple. This alternation in venue is common to treaty texts from Mari. The agreement is ratified first in the locale of one king and then in the locale of the other.[66]

The comparison of these treaties with the Sinai covenant yields a profound insight. In the Sinaitic pericope, the first reading of the law occurs at the bottom of the mountain in the profane realm, the locale of all the people. A second covenant ratification ceremony occurs on top of the mountain in the divine realm where the leaders who have been anointed seal it with a communal meal with the deity. The two realms, the profane and the divine, are the locations of the two parties to the covenant at Sinai. This is echoed in the story of Ezra-Nehemiah. The law is read in the square before all the people, in front of the water gate, that is, east of the city and outside it, in the realm of the profane. After this, the anointed leaders mount the consecrated city wall and walk around it until they are standing in the House of God (Neh. 12:40). They have entered the realm of the divine. There they rejoice, offer sacrifices, and presumably partake of the sacrifice, sharing a meal with the deity whose icon, the Torah, had been ushered into the temple (Neh. 12:43).

The Existential Threat of the Mixed Marriages

Rejoicing with the Torah in the Temple occurs only after the mass divorce, and it is to this subject that we now turn. When Ezra first arrives in Jerusalem he is greeted by a group of officials who complain about marriages with "the peoples of the lands." A mass divorce follows. Whereas, historically speaking, the mass divorce may have been instigated by Persian officials (*śarîm*) as a way of ensuring Persian hegemony (see chapter 2), the biblical writer construed something far different from it. He saw in the mixed marriages a threat to the Judeans' very presence on their land.[67] He shows Ezra exhibiting shock and dismay upon hearing the news and characterizes his response as one of extreme mourning—Ezra fasts, pulls out his hair, and tears his garments (Ezra 9:3, 5). This stereotypical mourning rite is also seen in the description of the desolation of Moab after its destruction by the Babylonians: "For every head is shaved and every beard cut off; on all the hands there are gashes, and on the loins sackcloth. On all the housetops of Moab and in the squares there is nothing but lamentation" (Jeremiah 48:37–38).

This stereotyped response is shown as well in the portrayal of Ezra. The goal of the self-immolation is the same—to show repentance and contrition and so to avert the evil decree. The underlying assumption everywhere is the also same—all the horrific events that happen to a person are a consequence of his own actions.[68] The Babylonian conquest of the land and the destruction of the Jerusalem temple, for example, were acts of God, brought about by his anger against the people's sins: "Because our ancestors had angered the god of heaven, he gave them into the hand of King Nebuchadnezzar of Babylon, the Chaldean, who destroyed this house and carried away the people to Babylonia" (Ezra 5:12).

The temple's destruction and the exile of the people prove God's anger. The Babylonians are an unwitting tool of the god of heaven; like the Assyrians before them, they are the rod of YHWH's anger (Isaiah 10:6). Rather than seeing the exile as caused by repeated rebellions and failures to pay Babylon the tribute owed her (2 Kings 24:1, 20), the biblical writers (both of Ezra and of the book of Kings) internalized the guilt and concluded that the people had sinned against God. To the writer of Kings, the exile was a just punishment, because Zedekiah, the king, "did what was evil" and "Jerusalem and Judah so angered YHWH that he expelled them from his presence" (2 Kings 24:20). The author of Kings leaves the precise reason for God's anger unspecified; it is some nameless "evil" of their king that brought the destruction and the exile. The author of Ezra states that the exile was caused by the sins of the whole people, not just their king, and by their failure to keep the commandments (Ezra 9:13, 14). God is always in control; whatever happens happens only because God wills it. More important, God is just. Evil is deserved.[69] The only conclusion that can be derived from misfortune, injury, or death is that the victim had sinned.[70] Bad things do not happen to good people;[71] indeed, the fact of the injury or death proves that the person had sinned. If "bad things" happened to "good people," then it would mean that either God was not just or that God was not in charge and had no power. Either conclusion was untenable and, for that matter, unbiblical.[72] (This view is questioned in the biblical book of Job and in 4 Ezra; see chapter 5.)

Ezra brings the Torah back to Judah, but, whether or not the people knew the commandments, they were still responsible for them. Ezra states: "shall we break the commandments again?" (9:14). In other words, it is because we have broken the commandments in the past that we were cast out of the land; shall we risk breaking them again when in doing so might cause God to destroy us entirely? "After all that has come upon us for our evil deeds and for our great guilt, seeing that you, our God, have punished us less than our iniquities deserved and have given us such a remnant as this, shall we break your commandments again and intermarry with the peoples who practice these abominations? Would you not be angry with us until you destroy us without remnant or survivor?" (Ezra 9:13, 14).

The commandment that Ezra is concerned about most is the command against intermarriage, but commentators have been hard pressed to find such a generic command in our present written Pentateuch.[73] The classic prohibition against intermarriage in the Torah is Deuteronomy 7:1–6, which forbids marriage with the seven Canaanite peoples:

> When YHWH your god brings you into the land that you are about to enter and occupy, and he clears away many nations before you—the Hittites, the Girgashites, the Amorites, the Canaanites, the Perizzites, the Hivites, and the Jebusites,[74] seven nations mightier and more numerous than you—and when YHWH your god gives them over to you and you defeat them, then you must utterly destroy them. Make no covenant with them and show them no mercy. Do not intermarry with them, giving your daughters to their sons or taking their daughters for your sons, for that would turn away your children from following me, to serve other gods. Then the anger of YHWH would be kindled against you, and he would destroy you quickly. But this is how you must deal with them: break down their altars, smash their pillars, hew down their sacred poles, and burn their idols with fire.
>
> For you are a people holy to YHWH your god; YHWH your god has chosen you out of all the peoples on earth to be his people, his treasured possession.

The reference in Deuteronomy to the seven nations who are living in Canaan when the Hebrews return to it from their slavery in Egypt is reflected in the officials' statement (Ezra 9:1) that "The people of Israel . . . have not separated themselves from the peoples of the lands whose abominations are like those of the Canaanites, the Hittites, the Perizzites, the Jebusites, the Ammonites, the Moabites, the Egyptians, and the Amorites."

This is clearly the writing of the biblical writer and does not belong to an authentic statement that Persian officials would make. It is loosely similar to Deuteronomy 7: 1–6, but, while Deuteronomy refers to the Hittites, the Girgashites, the Amorites, the Canaanites, the Perizzites, the Hivites, and the Jebusites, Ezra refers to the abominations of the Canaanites, the Hittites, the Perizzites, the Jebusites, the Ammonites, the Moabites, the Egyptians, and the Amorites. The first four nations that Ezra mentions are also mentioned in Deuteronomy 7, but Ammonites, Moabites, and Egyptians are not. Indeed, the first four nations that Ezra mentions had actually disappeared by the time of Ezra, but the last four were a constant presence. Regarding the last, the name of the Amorites had changed in meaning over the centuries. In the time of the Judean monarchy, the name in Assyrian texts referred to all the western peoples in Syria and the Levant. In Persian-period Babylonian texts, however, the term refers to the peoples of North Arabia.[75]

Indeed, these last three nations (or four, if we count the Arabs) were not forbidden according to other biblical writers. We see King David descended from a Moabite woman (Ruth 4:10–22). We see that Rehoboam, the first king of Judah after King Solomon, was the son of an Ammonite woman without affecting either his legitimacy or his ability to rule (1 Kings 14:21). This is in spite of the command in Deuteronomy 23:3: "No Ammonite or Moabite shall be admitted to YHWH's assembly. Even to the tenth generation, none of their descendants shall be admitted to YHWH's assembly." We also see that Abraham had married an Egyptian (Gen. 21:9–10).

Indeed, the command in Deuteronomy cannot be interpreted as a general prohibition against marriage with all non-Israelites, since we see that Moses himself marries a Midianite woman (Exod. 2:15–22), and he also marries an Ethiopian woman (Num. 12:1). Midianites and Ethiopians (Cushites) were evidently not forbidden since they were not among the seven Canaanite nations. Neither were the Egyptians. Joseph marries an Egyptian, and she bears him two sons, Manasseh and Ephraim, the eponymous ancestors of the two main tribes of the northern kingdom (Gen. 41:45, 50–52). "Pharaoh gave Joseph the name Zaphenath-paneah; and he gave him Asenath daughter of Potiphera, priest of On, as his wife. . . . Joseph had two sons, whom Asenath daughter of Potiphera, priest of On, bore to him. Joseph named the firstborn Manasseh. . . . The second he named Ephraim."

The marriage to the daughter of the high priest of On is given as proof of Joseph's valor and importance, and the biblical writer provides no condemnation of this marriage. Nor is there doubt about the status of the offspring, they are certainly Israelite and Hebrew. Those biblical writers saw nothing wrong with these unions per se. A problem occurs only if the foreign wife turns the heart of the Israelite's away from following God (1 Kings 11:1–3). "King Solomon loved many foreign women along with the daughter of Pharaoh: Moabite, Ammonite, Edomite, Sidonian, and Hittite women. . . . Solomon clung to these in love. Among his wives were seven hundred princesses and three hundred concubines; and his wives turned away his heart."

This fear that the foreign wives may turn the hearts of their husbands from YHWH may be what is behind the concern shown by the biblical writer, but it is never stated explicitly (except in Neh. 13:26). What is explicit, however, is the fear that violating God's commandments would result in the people's total destruction, leaving them without remnant or survivor (Ezra 9:14). Thus, to the biblical writer, it would not be the failure to remit the required tribute to Persia that could lead to their destruction but only their intermarriage with the peoples of the lands.

According to the biblical writer, the antidote to sin and to God's expected response to it is obedience to the law. To this end the people agree to form a new covenant with YHWH and to put away their foreign wives according to Torah (Ezra 10:3). This ability to change one's ways, to repent, to send away the foreign element, and to make a new covenant emphasizes God's patience and compassion as well as man's free will. Japhet points out that no event or situation in the narrative present is explained in Ezra-Nehemiah as a consequence of the sin of the intermarriages."[76] This may be because the mass divorce has averted the awful decree.

Conclusion

The story of Ezra in the biblical text is vastly different from the historical Ezra that we have constructed (see chapter 2). The historical Ezra was an official of the king, an outsider, with no real role in the Judean community except to spy on it. The biblical Ezra, in contrast, brings about a profound change in the people. He brings them the Law of God, purifies them of foreign influences according to the Torah, reads the Torah to them, and rededicates them to its precepts and to their God. It is this image of Ezra as the agent of change and rededication to Torah and to God that provided the impetus to all the stories of Ezra that we encounter in the subsequent chapters.

4

First, or Greek, Esdras—The Law Triumphant

The name Esdras is the Greek form of the Hebrew/English name Ezra. In the time of the Ptolemies, the third century B.C.E., the Hebrew Bible was translated into Greek by the Jewish community in Alexandria, Egypt. This Greek version is conventionally called the Septuagint, or LXX, because it is traditionally attributed to seventy-two translators.[1] In the Septuagint, our canonical Ezra-Nehemiah is considered as one book, a book that is called there 2 Esdras, or Esdras β. The Septuagint includes another book about Ezra, called there 1 Esdras, or Esdras α. This book was placed just before Esdras β, that is, before our Ezra-Nehemiah, when the books were placed into a codex, hence its name. The books that are in the Septuagint but not in the Hebrew Bible are known as the apocryphal books and together known as the Apocrypha. Unlike most books of the Apocrypha, 1 Esdras is not included in the Roman Catholic Old Testament.

First Esdras and Canonical Ezra-Nehemiah Compared

First Esdras (or 1 Esdras) overlaps in the gist (but not in every detail) with the end of canonical Chronicles, with parts of Nehemiah and with Ezra. It also adds a story about three bodyguards of King Darius, one of whom is Zerubbabel, the Davidic heir.[2] Because of the close similarity with the biblical book of Ezra, 1 Esdras has been labeled "rewritten Bible."[3] Josephus (writing between 70–95 C.E.) uses the text of 1 Esdras for this portion of his history of the Jews, rather than the canonical Ezra-Nehemiah, no doubt because the order of the chapters made better sense to him. The following chart illustrates the structure of 1 Esdras and the differences between it and the canonical Ezra-Nehemiah:

I Esdras	Chronicles, Ezra, Nehemiah	The Episode
1:1–33	2 Chron. 35:1–27	Josiah's celebration of the Passover, his battle with Pharaoh Necho, his death, and the national mourning for him.
1:34–58	2 Chron. 36:1–21	The last kings of Judah, the fall of Judah and Jerusalem to Babylon, and Jeremiah's prediction that the land will lay fallow for seventy years.

I Esdras	Chronicles, Ezra, Nehemiah	The Episode
2:1–15	Ezra 1:1–11	Cyrus, King of Persia, permits the Jews to return to Judah and to build a temple for YHWH in Jerusalem. Sheshbazzar (Gk Sanabassaros) brings the vessels from the original temple back from Babylon to Jerusalem.
2:16–30	Ezra 4:7–24a	A letter to King Artaxerxes from satrapal officials complaining that the Jews are rebuilding Jerusalem and its walls (1 Esdras adds "and laying the foundations for a temple"). The officials warn the king that if the city is rebuilt and the walls finished, they will not pay tribute. The king orders the building stopped, and all building is stopped until the second year of Darius.
3:1–5:6	No Parallel	Darius's three youthful bodyguards debate what the strongest thing in the world is. One picks wine, one picks the king, and one, Zerubbabel, says that a woman is stronger than a king, but truth is strongest of all. Darius then promises Zerubbabel anything that he wishes, and Zerubbabel wishes that Jerusalem be rebuilt and the temple within it. Darius thereupon orders that Zerubbabel lead the Jews back to Jerusalem and rebuild the temple and that funds be furnished from the satrapal treasury.
5:7–46	Ezra 2:1–70 (= Neh. 7:6–73a)	A list of the returnees who come up to Jerusalem with Zerubbabel and Joshua the priest.
5:47–65	Ezra 3:1–13	An altar is set up for sacrifices, and the temple foundations are laid.
5:66–73	Ezra 4:1–5	Enemies of Judah and Jerusalem offer to build the temple with them, but they are rejected. Thereupon they connive to prevent the completion of the building until the second year of Darius.
6:1–22	Ezra 4:24b–5:17	The prophets Haggai and Zechariah encourage the people to continue work on the temple. Sisinnes (Tattenai in Ezra), governor of Syria and Phoenicia, investigates the Jews who are building the temple and writes to Darius detailing his findings.
6:23–34	Ezra 6:1–12	Darius searches in the royal archives for proof that Cyrus has given permission rebuild the temple. Finding the document, Darius orders that the rebuilding continue and that funds be provided out of the tribute due the satrapy.

I Esdras	Chronicles, Ezra, Nehemiah	The Episode
7:1–15	Ezra 6:13–22	So the temple is built and rededicated in the sixth year of Darius. The Passover is celebrated.
8:1–27	Ezra 7:1–28	Ezra the scribe arrives in Jerusalem from Babylon in the seventh year of Artaxerxes. He comes bearing a letter from that king releasing cultic personnel from tribute or other taxes.
8:28–67	Ezra 8:1–36	This section includes a list of the people who went with Ezra up to Jerusalem. The priests are given responsibility to carry gold and silver vessels donated for use in the temple by the king and his friends.
8:68–90	Ezra 9:1–15	Soon after Ezra's arrival, the leaders come to him saying that the people Israel are marrying the foreign "peoples of the land." Ezra tears his garments and prays.
8:91–96	Ezra 10:1–5	The people Israel take an oath to separate from their foreign wives and their children.
9:1–36	Ezra 10:6–44	The men of the tribe of Judah and Benjamin assemble in Jerusalem, and all those with foreign wives separate from them. It is the ninth month.
9:37–55	Nehemiah 7:73b–8:13	On the new moon of the seventh month [of the following year], the people Israel gather before the East Gate of the temple, and Ezra reads them the law of Moses. The people rejoice and give gifts to one another and portions to those who have none.

Issues Surrounding 1 Esdras

The questions confronting readers of 1 Esdras are many: is this Greek text a translation from a Hebrew or Aramaic original, or was it originally written in Greek?[4] Is this the original version of Ezra, and is the order of the chapters the original order, or is the order in the canonical Ezra-Nehemiah the original? That is, did the author of Ezra-Nehemiah rewrite 1 Esdras, or did the author of 1 Esdras rewrite Ezra-Nehemiah?[5] When and why was it written? It ends in midsentence; what happened? Was the ending lost? Is the beginning the original beginning, or was that too lost? Is 1 Esdras simply a fragment of a much larger work that stretched from 1 Chronicles 1:1 to Nehemiah 13:31? The answer to all these questions as well as the purpose and theological import of the book must be sought in the order of the chapters, since that really is the only difference between the versions.

Work on the relationship between Ezra-Nehemiah and 1 Esdras has been ongoing for more than two hundred years. Ever since Pohlmann, however, scholars have been divided into two main camps.[6] One group considers 1 Esdras to be a fragment of a long history that includes Chronicles, Ezra, and Nehemiah.[7] According to this camp, except for the story of the three bodyguards, a late addition, 1 Esdras reveals the original form of the text of Ezra, with Nehemiah remaining a separate book. The story of Ezra and Nehemiah as told in Josephus supports this separation since in Josephus, Ezra dies before the story of Nehemiah even begins. According to this view, when Ezra and Nehemiah were merged into one book, the story of Ezra's reading the Torah was taken from the end of Ezra and plunked into the middle of Nehemiah. That author then added the long prayer and the *'Amānāh*-signing to form the covenant renewal ceremony often taken as the climax of the canonical story of the return.

A second group of scholars sees 1 Esdras as a compilation of various passages taken from the separate books of Chronicles and Ezra-Nehemiah, books that were already in their present form when the excerpts were taken from them.[8] According to this view, passages were compiled and rearranged just to accommodate the story of the three bodyguards, a story seen as integral to rewritten Ezra. Both groups recognize, however, that once that story is removed, not only is the order of events largely the same in the initial six or seven chapters of these books, but also the wording in the majority of passages is identical. Passages agree sentence for sentence. It must be concluded therefore either that 1 Esdras is a revision of Ezra-Nehemiah, or that Ezra-Nehemiah is a revision of 1 Esdras. Of course, they could both be revisions of an identical third source, but they cannot be independent accounts of historical events.

Date and Place of Composition

Although there is no consensus, the majority of scholars have concluded that 1 Esdras was based on the canonical texts of Chronicles, Ezra, and Nehemiah and that the story of Darius's three bodyguards, with Zerubbabel the Davidic heir among them, is intrinsic to rewritten Ezra.[9] If so, a general time period for its composition can be determined. Paul Harvey Jr. has shown that the author of the story of the bodyguards was acquainted with court titles that were used during the reign of Ptolemy II Philadelphus (283–246 B.C.E.) and not before.[10] This establishes a locale in Egypt, most probably Alexandria, and a general time period for the composition of the book. Thus, we have the same time and the same place of composition as the *Letter of Aristeas*. Indeed, that text exhibits the same attitude toward the law that we see in 1 Esdras:

> Our Lawgiver first of all laid down the principles of piety and righteousness and inculcated them point by point, not merely by prohibitions but by the use of examples as well, demonstrating the injurious effects of sin and the punishments inflicted by God upon the guilty.

> Working out these truths carefully and having made them plain he [Eleazar, the high priest] showed that even if a man should think of doing evil—to say nothing of actually effecting it—he would not escape detection, for he made it clear that the power of God pervaded the whole of the law. (*Letter of Aristeas* 131–34)

Purpose of 1 Esdras

Since recent research has come down on the side of the priority of the canonical Ezra-Nehemiah, we are able to ask about the purpose of the revision, and several theories have been proposed.[11] According to the text of our canonical Ezra, temple building was begun under the governorship of Zerubbabel, the Davidic heir, and under the high priesthood of Jeshua, grandson of the last high priest (Ezra 3:2). Samaritans offer to help build the temple (Ezra 4:2), but Zerubbabel and Jeshua refuse their help (Ezra 4:3). This rejection leads the Samaritans to write letters to the Persian kings, which ultimately puts a stop to the temple-building process. Building does not resume until the second year of Darius I (Ezra 4:24). In this canonical version, Zerubbabel and Jeshua are instrumental in causing temple building to be stopped, since it is they who have rejected Samaritan aid. (Of course, the letters incorporated into the text are actually to Xerxes [Ezra 4:6] and to Artaxerxes [Ezra 4:7], the kings who ruled *after* Darius I, so the letters have nothing to do with the temple. Historically speaking, there is no evidence of any stoppage in building the temple. It may actually have been only the city wall that was stopped for a while.)[12] In any case, in canonical Ezra, Zerubbabel and Joshua are responsible for work on the temple being stopped. By inserting the story of the three bodyguards into the story of Ezra (and by including Zerubbabel among them) and by moving the letters to the Persian kings so that they precede Zerubbabel's arrival in Jerusalem, the writer of 1 Esdras has given Zerubbabel a perfect alibi. He was not there when the altercation started, and he had nothing to do with stopping construction. Not only that, but it was his winning the contest in the presence of Darius that persuaded that king to permit temple building to resume.

While most scholars have focused on the first six chapters of Ezra and the purpose for their reordering and for including the story of the three bodyguards, Jacob Wright has focused on the reason for eliminating Nehemiah's story from 1 Esdras.[13] Wright argues that the author of 1 Esdras knew Ezra-Nehemiah as one book and that he purposely rewrote the story of Ezra to blot out Nehemiah's memory. Nehemiah's memoir offended the priestly writers who composed 1 Esdras because of its insinuation that the priesthood was corrupt and had made alliances with and even married into non-Israelite families. Moreover, Ezra-Nehemiah presents the city of Jerusalem in ruins until Nehemiah, a nonpriest and non-Davidide, comes and rebuilds it, rather than showing it built by the priests immediately upon their return. All this is rectified by a new and perfected version of the story of the return with the Davidide Zerubbabel and the priest Jeshua replacing Nehemiah as builders of both temple and city and as sole authorities in Judah and Jerusalem. This all seems right.

Coping with an Angry God: Torah as Antidote

One problem that has been overlooked, however, is that of coping with an angry god. While the solution is evident in Ezra-Nehemiah (remove foreign influences), 1 Esdras emphasizes Torah. First Esdras begins with the story of Josiah's Passover, which had not been celebrated in such a fashion before (1 Esdras 1:18 [English translation: 1:20]). Josiah is the epitome of the "good king" in both Kings and in Chronicles: "He did what was right in the sight of YHWH, and walked in all the way of his father David; he did not turn aside to the right or to the left" (2 Kings 22:2 = 2 Chron. 34:2). But 1 Esdras adds another verse that is not present in Kings: "The deeds of Josiah were upright in the sight of the Lord, for his heart was full of godliness. In ancient times the events of his reign have been recorded—concerning those who sinned and acted wickedly toward the Lord beyond any other people or kingdom, and how they grieved him deeply, so that the words of the Lord fell upon Israel" (1 Esdras 1:21–22 [English translation: 1:23–24]).[14] By emphasizing the people's sin, this additional verse in 1 Esdras foreshadows the fall of the kingdom to the Babylonians. It was only because of the people's sins and their wickedness that the kingdom fell, in spite of Josiah's righteousness.

First Esdras continues with the story of the fall of the kingdom (not told in canonical Ezra), the return of Judeans to Judah and Jerusalem, the immediate rebuilding of the city and the temple, opposition to the temple's construction, its final completion and dedication under Darius, and the celebration of the Passover (1 Esdras 7:10). This celebration forms an inclusio with Josiah's and indicates a return to Judah and Jerusalem not only in body but also in spirit.[15]

As in the canonical Ezra, Ezra arrives in Jerusalem immediately after the temple's dedication and the celebration of the Passover. He learns of the perfidy of the people in their intermarriages, and, as in canonical Ezra, he prays and mourns. As in canonical Ezra, the people undergo a mass divorce, but, in contrast to the canonical books, in 1 Ezra the narrative moves immediately to Ezra's reading the law. The entire story of Nehemiah is omitted. There is nothing in 1 Esdras about Nehemiah's building the wall or his reforms; nor is there anything resembling a covenant renewal ceremony. There is no public signing of an agreement. All that is gone. The only section included from Nehemiah is the story of the law reading, and, with that, Ezra's role ends. The book finishes with the completion of the reading and the people going forth in great rejoicing because they were inspired by the words that they had been taught.[16]

One must ask then, if the covenant renewal ceremony is the climax of Ezra-Nehemiah, as claimed (see chapter 3), why is it omitted from 1 Esdras? One answer offered is that we may not have 1 Esdras's actual ending. First Esdras ends with "and they were gathered together," a phrase possibly taken from Nehemiah 8:13 and possibly the beginning of the celebration of the Sukkot holiday.[17] The story of Nehemiah may have been lost from it. If 1 Esdras was actually intending to continue with the rest of Nehemiah 8, however, it would have begun as Nehemiah 8:13 does, with a reference to the second day. Nehemiah 8:13 begins "on the second day they gathered," a phrase not found in 1 Esdras. Indeed, Van der Kooij has shown that the ending of 1 Esdras is the original ending. He translates the final phrase not as the New Revised Standard Version does ("because they were inspired by the words which they had been taught. And they came together") but differently: "Then they all went their way, to eat and drink and enjoy themselves, and to give portions to those who had none, and to make great rejoicing; both because they were inspired by the words which they had been taught and because they had been brought together" (1 Esdras 9:54–55). This is one intelligible sentence, with the conjunction και, "and," meaning "both . . . and." We need to remember that the ancient Greek had no punctuation or capital letters to indicate the beginning and ending of sentences.

If the present ending is the original ending of 1 Esdras, one must seriously consider why the covenant renewal ceremony was omitted. It is not enough to argue for the *damnatio memoriae* of Nehemiah, since Nehemiah's title could have easily been substituted for his name throughout the book of Nehemiah, as it is in 1 Esdras 9:49.[18]

By ending with the law reading, by omitting the events of Nehemiah's governorship, and by omitting the covenant renewal ceremony, 1 Esdras presents a picture of the restoration period entirely different from that presented in the canonical books. According to 1 Esdras, the people of Judah had been removed from their land because of sin, but now Ezra has brought the law, he has cleansed the people from the impurities of their mixed marriages through the mass divorce, and has read the law in such way that the people now fully understand it. In 1 Esdras, the purified people hear and understand the law. They rejoice both because they have been inspired by it and because they have gathered together with their fellows. The picture is one of extreme optimism and relief. The world, or at least Judah and Jerusalem, has been set right, and as long as this course is kept all will go well. There is no possibility of backsliding because the people have truly understood the law. Understanding the law guarantees its observance. The world is in a perfected state.

This contrasts starkly with the ending of the present book of Nehemiah. In Nehemiah, the law reading is followed in Nehemiah 9 by a long confessional prayer in which it is admitted that God's gracious acts have been met only with disobedience and rebellion. The people then sign a promise and an oath to keep the commandments (Neh. 10), but the fact that this promise needs to be safeguarded by a curse (Neh. 10:30 [English translation: 29]) only emphasizes its fragility.

This fragility is brought home in Nehemiah 13. Nehemiah left Jerusalem, returning a few years later only to find that these wonderful promises made by the people in Nehemiah 10 were all for naught. The promise to bring the tithe to the Levites (Neh. 10:37 [36]) is broken as soon as Nehemiah leaves the city (Neh. 13:10). The promise to keep the Sabbath and not to buy grain or produce on the Sabbath (Neh. 10:32 [31]) is broken as soon as Nehemiah goes away (Neh. 13:15–16). To top it off, in spite of the mass divorce of the Judeans (Ezra 10) and in spite of their promise never to give their daughters to foreigners or to take their daughters for their sons (Neh. 10:31 [30]), Nehemiah returns after his short absence only to find that indeed Judeans had married the women of Ashdod, Ammon, and Moab (Neh. 13:23, 24). In contrast to the optimism and joy described in 1 Esdras, Ezra-Nehemiah ends in failure, the grand promises all broken. The value of simply understanding the law has proven to be nonexistent, the merriment only temporary. This may have been one reason why the author of 1 Esdras eliminated Nehemiah's memoir entirely and ended his story with Ezra's reading the law.

In 1 Esdras, the law reading is immediately preceded by a mass separation from foreign wives. In canonical Ezra-Nehemiah, the mass divorce is followed not by the law reading but by the story of Nehemiah's building the city wall. The divorce and law reading are separated by a good eight chapters. By directly preceding the law giving with the divorce, 1 Esdras highlights the holiness of the law—the entire community that hears the law is bound by it. Passive observers, those not under the strict command of the Mosaic covenant, are excluded from even listening to it. If the text of 1 Esdras had originally begun with Josiah's finding the law in the temple, then the story of Ezra reading the law to the assembled populace provides a nice conclusion. First Esdras depicts a return to a purified era in which God's will is done.

Josephus's Use of 1 Esdras in His Jewish Antiquities

Josephus Flavius (Joseph ben Mattatiyahu) was a Jewish writer of the first century C.E. who wrote a history of the Jewish war against Rome (*Jewish War*) following the fall of Jerusalem to Rome in 70. He wrote it first in Aramaic and then translated it into Greek five or ten years later.[19] He followed this with his larger work on the *History of the Jews* (*Jewish Antiquities*), which was probably finished around 90, and with his later works, *Contra Apion* (a defense against the man Apion and against anti-Semitism in general) and his autobiographical *Life*. He likely died around 100.

For his *History of the Jews,* Josephus used the story of Ezra from 1 Esdras, rather than from the canonical Ezra. Feldman suggests that this was because of its superior Greek style, its elimination of some chronological difficulties, and his romantic interest in the debate of the three bodyguards as to whether wine, the king, or women is the most powerful.[20] Even so, Josephus changes the king under whom both Ezra and Nehemiah arrive from Artaxerxes, Darius's grandson, to Xerxes, Darius's son (*J. Ant.* 11.120–21). He places the temple's dedication in the ninth year of Darius (*J. Ant.* 11.106–7) and then records Darius's death (11.120); Ezra's permission to go up to Jerusalem occurs immediately afterwards, in Xerxes's accession year. In this way his departure for Jerusalem follows immediately upon the dedication of the temple (as was probably intended by the author of the canonical Ezra), rather than 57 years later under Artaxerxes I or 117 years later under Artaxerxes II, as is historically most likely. Josephus then places Ezra's arrival during the high priesthood of Joiakim (*J. Ant.* 11.121), the son of Jeshua (the first high priest of the restoration) and the father of Eliashib (high priest during the governorship of Nehemiah; Neh. 12:10) all in an attempt to repair the chronology in Ezra and 1 Esdras. Josephus also omits Ezra's genealogy that makes him the son of the last high priest of the Judean monarchy, clearly preposterous even if he returns under Xerxes, not Artaxerxes (see chapters 2 and 3 for discussions of the date of Ezra). Feldman is astounded that Josephus does not include Ezra's pedigree, since it was customary for him to embellish the genealogies of his other biblical heroes.[21] He thinks that Josephus purposely diminished Ezra's stature by not relating his genealogy, but it was probably only Josephus's desire to clean up the chronology of the period that led him to omit it. If Ezra was born to the high priest of Judah who was killed in the conquest, as his genealogy demands, and if the return took place seventy years later under Cyrus (as Josephus surmises; *J. Ant.* 11:1), and if Cambyses (Cyrus's son) reigned six years (*J. Ant.* 11:30) and Darius at least nine (*J. Ant.* 11:107), and if Ezra did not leave for Judah until the seventh year of Xerxes's reign, as Josephus says (*J. Ant.* 11:135), then Ezra would have been at least ninety-two years old at the time of his return. If Josephus is trying to present Ezra as a vigorous young man, then he cannot include his genealogy and cannot have him be the son of the last high priest of the monarchic period.

Josephus thus attempts to smooth out the confusing chronologies that exist in both Ezra and 1 Esdras. First, he shows Ezra receiving permission to go to Jerusalem in Xerxes's accession year, the year that immediately follows the death of Darius I, Xerxes's father. Second, he postpones Ezra's departure until the seventh year of that king so that it conforms with the regnal year from the letter of Artaxerxes (although he has changed the name of the king to Xerxes, Artaxerxes's predecessor; *J. Ant.* 11:135; cf. Ezra 7:8–9; 1 Esdras 8:6). In so doing, however, Josephus causes a strange delay of seven years in Ezra's itinerary and makes him seem less eager to go up to Jerusalem than he appears in the biblical texts.

Other differences abound. In introducing him, Josephus states that Ezra enjoyed "a great reputation among the multitude" (*J. Ant.* 11:121). Admittedly, this is not necessarily a positive trait, for in the masses lay the seeds of rebellion.[22] However, it is certainly a trait that is necessary in a leader; one cannot lead if the masses do not follow. Second, according to Josephus (*J. Ant.* 11:122), Ezra requests a letter of introduction from the king to the various satraps of Syria, something absolutely necessary for travel but a phrase omitted in both Ezra and 1 Esdras but included in Nehemiah (2:7). Josephus may have included this not only to show Ezra's leadership qualities but also to explain the biblical verse that "the king honored all his requests" (1 Esdras 8:4; Ezra 7:6) when no requests from Ezra are actually recorded. Josephus also drastically reduces the amount that the king donates to the Judeans and to the Judean temple from the biblical "up to one hundred talents of silver, one hundred kors of wheat, one hundred baths of wine, one hundred baths of oil, and unlimited salt" (Ezra 7:22 = 1 Esdras 8:20) to "up to 100 kor of wheat" only (*J. Ant.* 11:127–28), although he does refer to the gold and silver gifts of the king elsewhere (*J. Ant.* 11:125–27). Josephus thus reduces the immense amounts of the royal expenditures recorded in the biblical books. This may be to mitigate the charge that Jews are greedy[23] or to make the amounts seem more realistic, since one hundred talents of silver may have amounted to 7,100 pounds![24]

As in the canonical Ezra and 1 Esdras, Josephus recounts that Ezra is told to appoint judges "who will hold court in all of Syria and Phoenicia," but, in contrast to the biblical books, Josephus specifies that these courts are for "your countrymen" (τῶν ὁμοεθνῶν σου), not for all the people in Beyond-the-River (Ezra 7:25–26 = 1 Esdras 8:23–24). These judges are to apply the Mosaic law code, but only for the Judeans living in Syria and Phoenicia, not for everyone. This may be not only in order to make the text seem more logical but also perhaps to emphasize the precedent that Jews were given permission by Persian kings to follow their own laws and were even punished by the royal apparatus for failure to do so. Further, in contrast to the biblical books, Josephus makes his text much more readable by omitting the several long lists of names that proliferate in these chapters.

Another difference between Josephus's Ezra and the Ezra in either canonical Ezra or 1 Esdras is the treatment of the mass divorce. After Ezra arrives in Jerusalem, according to Josephus "some men" approach Ezra to complain of intermarriages (*J. Ant.* 11:140): "But some time afterward there came to him [Ezra] some men, who accused some of the common people, as well as of some of the priests and Levites, of transgressing their constitution [τὴν πολιτείαν], and of breaking the laws of their ancestors [τοὺς πατρίους νόμους], by marrying foreign women, and of mixing the strain of the priestly families." This is in contrast to Ezra 9:1, where it seems to be Persian officials who approach Ezra, and in contrast to 1 Esdras 8:68, where it is the "leaders" who approach Ezra. Thus we see successive democratization of the men informing Ezra. More important, rather than violating Persian edicts, Josephus emphasizes that it is the Jews' own constitution and the laws of their own ancestors that they have broken. The remainder of this episode follows the biblical version, but, in stressing the Judeans' loyalty to their laws, Josephus adds: "The priests, Levites, and Israelites had a greater regard to the observation of the law than to their natural affection, and immediately cast out their wives, and the children who were born of them; and in order to appease God, they offered sacrifices, and slew rams, as oblations to him" (*J. Ant.* 11:152). Josephus's emphasis on the legal nature of the prohibition against mixed marriages—that intermarriage was a violation of their own constitution and ancestral laws—may have been intended to evoke in the mind of the reader a comparison to Pericles's similar citizenship laws of 451/450.[25] It also attempts to encourage the Roman kings to permit Judeans throughout their empire to follow their own customs and traditions.

As in 1 Esdras, Josephus follows the mass divorce with a greatly abbreviated account of Ezra's reading the law to the populace assembled in Jerusalem. In 1 Esdras (and in Nehemiah 8:1), Ezra reads it on the first day of the seventh month, whereas in Josephus it is on the first day of the Feast of Tabernacles (Sukkoth), which occurs on the fifteenth of that month (Lev. 23:24). This is in accordance with the Deuteronomic command to read the law to the assembled populace during the holiday of Sukkoth (Deut. 31:10–13). Moreover, in canonical Ezra, on the second day of the month, the elders come to Ezra to study the law and in it learn of the holiday of Sukkoth, which had not been celebrated since the days of Joshua son of Nun (Neh. 8:17). This is omitted from 1 Esdras and from Josephus. Neither text wants to assert that the returnees had not been following their ancestral customs.

After Ezra reads the law, Josephus records Ezra's death and burial in Jerusalem (*J. Ant.* 11:158), a detail not mentioned elsewhere (but see chapter 8 for rabbinic and Islamic traditions of Ezra's tomb), and only after Ezra's death is recorded does Josephus begin his story of Nehemiah. Thus, in Josephus, these two men do not appear together. Moreover, in contrast to his treatment of other biblical heroes and in stark contrast to the rabbinic treatment, Josephus does not exalt Ezra beyond what is written in the biblical passages. Indeed, Josephus does not mention Ezra in any of his works outside the single pericope in which the account of his activities occurs and apparently goes out of his way not to present Ezra as a second Moses.[26] Ezra did not write the laws, and no new laws were discovered in the book that Ezra read. Indeed, the reading itself followed the Deuteronomic law of Sukkoth. Ezra was learned in the laws of Moses and enforced those laws upon the people in establishing judges, in the divorce, and in his reading the law on the prescribed date. Josephus's goal was only to emphasize the Jews' adherence to their ancestral laws and customs in spite of all hardship. He does not need to go beyond this.

5

Fourth Ezra—The Ezra Apocalypse

We meet Ezra again in a late first-century-C.E. text, called 4 Ezra, or the Ezra Apocalypse. The protagonist in the text is our Ezra, who is living in Babylon among the exiles after the fall of the Jerusalem temple.

The Name of the Book

The spread of Roman Christianity necessitated a translation of the biblical text into Latin, so Latin translations were made of the Greek Septuagint. This Old Latin translation was the one used and commented on by the Church Fathers.[1] In 387 C.E. in Bethlehem, Jerome began a translation of the Old Testament based not on the Septuagint but on the Hebrew. Fourth Ezra, the book considered here, is not included in either the Hebrew Bible or the Septuagint Greek translation of it but was included in Jerome's Latin Vulgate with the title IV Esdras. In his translation, the canonical books Ezra and Nehemiah were separately designated I and II Esdras, with the book that is labeled 1 Esdras, or Esdras α, in the Septuagint being labeled III Esdras in the Vulgate. (Texts in the Latin version are designated by Roman numerals, texts in the Greek version are labeled according to Greek letters.) To make matters more confusing, later Latin manuscripts included Ezra and Nehemiah together in one book, which it called I Esdras; the book that is called 1 Esdras, Esdras α, in the Septuagint is called III Esdras, and the book discussed in the present chapter is called II Esdras. This new Latin version included two introductory and two concluding chapters that had been appended by later Christian authors. Since scholars still consider chapters 3–14 of II Esdras to be 4 Ezra, they conveniently label chapters 1–2 5 Ezra, while chapters 15 and 16 are called 6 Ezra. These Christian additions are discussed in chapter 6.

Although the original language of 4 Ezra was likely Hebrew, this Hebrew original and the early Greek translations made from it do not survive. All that survives are medieval copies of the Latin Vulgate and Syriac, Ethiopic, Arabic, and Armenian translations of the Greek. These translations are discussed in Appendix 2. Since these latter translations are of the Greek, they do not include the first two chapters (5 Ezra) or the last two (6 Ezra). This chart will clarify matters:

Labels of Various Texts according to the Different Versions

	Ezra	**Nehemiah**	**2 Chron. 35–36; Ezra; Neh. 8:1–12**	**Ezra Apocalypse**
English	Ezra	Nehemiah	1 Esdras	4 Ezra (chapters 3–14 of II Esdras)
Hebrew Bible	Ezra, chapters 1–10	Ezra, chapters 11–23		
Septuagint	Esdras β (2 Esdras)		Esdras α (1 Esdras)	
Vulgate	I Esdras	II Esdras	III Esdras	IV Esdras (chapters 3–14)
Later Latin Manuscripts	I Esdras		III Esdras	II Esdras (chapters 1–2 = 5 Ezra; chapters 3–14 = 4 Ezra; chapters 15–16 = 6 Ezra)

This present discussion is based on chapters 3–14 of II Esdras, that is, 4 Ezra. The two initial chapters and the two final chapters of II Esdras are discussed in chapter 6.

Fourth Ezra, the Ezra Apocalypse

The date of 4 Ezra's composition can be fixed to the end of the reign of Domitian, the last decade of the first century C.E. The place of composition is very likely in Judea since the original language appears to be Hebrew.[2]

Fourth Ezra is an apocalypse. That is, the genre of 4 Ezra is apocalyptic. Apocalyptic writing is literature and does not reveal actual visionary experiences by a mystical author.[3] Fourth Ezra does not come labeled as an apocalypse by its author, however; it is so labeled only by scholars. The term "apocalypse" is the Greek word for "revelation." The title derives from the New Testament Book of Revelation (the Apocalypse of John) and is used by scholars to denote texts that are similar to it. The definition of apocalypse proposed in 1979 has held sway: "Apocalypse is a genre of revelatory literature with a narrative framework, in which a revelation is mediated by an otherworldly being to a human recipient, disclosing a transcendent reality which is both temporal, insofar as it envisages eschatological salvation, and spatial, insofar as it involves another supernatural world."[4] This definition is unpacked further in the following section, but we have all of this in 4 Ezra.

Narrative Framework

Analyzing our definition, we see that an apocalypse contains a narrative framework: "Apocalypse is a genre of revelatory literature with *a narrative framework*,

"When the sacred books had been consumed in the fires of war, Ezra repaired the damage." Frontispiece, *Codex Amiatinus*, Biblioteca Medicea Laurenziana (Cat. Sala Studio 6), Florence, eighth century

in which a revelation is mediated by an otherworldly being to a human recipient, disclosing a transcendent reality which is both temporal, insofar as it envisages eschatological salvation, and spatial, insofar as it involves another supernatural world [emphasis added]."

Fourth Ezra is first and foremost a story. It is told in the first person and begins with the protagonist introducing himself and providing the date and place of his writing and the reason for it: "In the thirtieth year after the destruction of the city, I was in Babylon—I, Salatiel [Hebrew: Shealtiel], who am also called Ezra. I was troubled as I lay on my bed, and my thoughts welled up in my heart, because I saw the desolation of Zion and the wealth of those who lived in Babylon" (4 Ezra 3:1–2).[5] This speaker is the Ezra of the canonical book, and so the destroyed city is Jerusalem, the date is 556 B.C.E. (thirty years after its destruction), and Ezra is in Babylon, where he had evidently been deported after the destruction. This is the setting of the story. He has taken the name Shealtiel, which in Hebrew means "I asked God" or "I importuned God," because importuning God has become the crux of his new identity. He is "the one who importunes God" about the destruction of both his holy city and his covenanted people by a foreign race that does not know God.

A Shealtiel appears elsewhere in the Hebrew Bible both as the son of Jeconiah/Jehoiachin, the penultimate king of Judah who had been exiled to Babylon at the age of 18 (1 Chron. 3:17; 2 Kings 24:8–12), and as the father of Zerubbabel, the governor of Judah during the restoration period (Ezra 3:2). Several scholars have advocated the view that the two names for the protagonist (Shealtiel and Ezra) indicate that two separate sources have been combined in 4 Ezra, a Shealtiel source and an Ezra source.[6] If the author of the Shealtiel source intended the protagonist to be the son of the eighteen-year-old exiled king, then Shealtiel would have been born in Babylon and would have spent his life there. If that is the case, this would have been an attempt to place him in the period of the Babylonian exile (586–538 B.C.E.), whereas the historic Ezra lived much later, probably in the reign of Artaxerxes II (398 B.C.E.; see chapter 2). More likely, however, there is only one source and Ezra is given the additional name because of his role as the one who importunes God.[7]

Ezra's major complaint is that God has treated his own covenanted people, the people Israel, unjustly. He asks God:

> Are the deeds of those who inhabit Babylon any better? Is that why it has gained dominion over Zion? For when I came here [to Babylon], I saw ungodly deeds without number, and my soul has seen many sinners during these thirty years. And my heart fails me, because I have seen how you endure those who sin, and have spared those who act wickedly, and have destroyed your people, and protected your enemies, and have not shown to anyone how your way may be comprehended.
>
> Are the deeds of Babylon better than those of Zion?
>
> Or has another nation known you besides Israel? Or what tribes have so believed the covenants as have these tribes of Jacob?
>
> Yet their reward has not appeared and their labor has borne no fruit. For I have traveled widely among the nations and have seen that they abound in wealth, though they are unmindful of your commandments. Now therefore weigh in a balance our iniquities and those of the inhabitants of the world; and it will be found which way the turn of the scale will incline.
>
> When have the inhabitants of the earth not sinned in your sight? Or what nation has kept your commandments so well?
>
> You may indeed find individuals who have kept your commandments, but nations you will not find. (4 Ezra 3:28–36)

The story thus begins with Ezra accusing God of injustice. The story ends in chapter 14 with Ezra's receiving God's blessings plus the key to all knowledge and wisdom. This knowledge and wisdom are contained in the twenty-four revealed books that constitute the Hebrew Bible and the seventy books of secret lore to be held in reserve for the wise among the Jews. In between, Ezra receives a revelation of the destiny of mankind. This is the narrative framework, but there is much more to 4 Ezra than the narrative.

Revelations Mediated by an Otherworldly Being to Ezra

Unpacking the definition of apocalypse further, we have: "Apocalypse is a genre of *revelatory literature* with a narrative framework in which a *revelation is mediated by an otherworldly being* to a human recipient disclosing a transcendent reality which is both temporal, insofar as it envisages eschatological salvation, and spatial, insofar as it involves another supernatural world [emphasis added]."[8]

The First Three Episodes—Three Conversations with the Interpreting Angel, Uriel

The definition of apocalyptic literature includes a revelation by an otherworldly being, and this we have in 4 Ezra. The story opens with Ezra praying to God, asking him to explain why he has allowed his covenanted people and his holy temple to fall to the Babylonians. His prayer is answered in a dream vision not of God himself but of the angel Uriel. Uriel is not introduced but is referred to only as the "angel who has been sent to me." In fact, the angel Uriel may have been well known to the readers of 4 Ezra. He is the archangel who gives a tour of heaven and hell to Enoch in a well-known third-century-B.C.E. text of that name (for example, 4Q Enoch; Jude 1:14).

Ezra asks Uriel the most profound of questions: "Why has Israel been given over to the Gentiles in disgrace? Why has the people whom you loved been given over to godless tribes, and the law of our ancestors has been brought to destruction and the written covenants no longer exist?" (4 Ezra 4:23). Ezra lays the blame on God. God gave Israel the law but not the ability to follow it. Since God has infinite power, even the power to pass through the four gates of fire and ice to descend on Mount Sinai, he has the power to make Israel capable of following the law. Ezra complains, "Your glory passed through the four gates of fire and earthquake and wind and ice, to give the law to the descendants of Jacob, and your commandment to the posterity of Israel. Yet you did not take away their evil heart from them, so that your law might produce fruit in them" (4 Ezra 3:19–20). The fault lies with God. He created man weak and then punishes him for it.

The answer that the angel gives to Ezra, however, is the same answer that God gives to Job when he speaks out of the whirlwind (Job 38–41), essentially "Who are you to question God?"

> Then the angel that had been sent to me, whose name was Uriel, answered and said to me, "Your understanding has utterly failed regarding this world, and do you think you can comprehend the way of the Most High?"

> "Go, weigh for me the weight of fire, or measure for me a blast of wind, or call back for me the day that is past."
>
> He said to me, "You cannot understand the things with which you have grown up; how then can your mind comprehend the way of the Most High?" (4 Ezra 4:1–2, 5, 10–11)

But unlike Job, who responds (42:6), "I despise myself, I repent in dust and ashes," Ezra stands his ground and continues to importune God. Although the revelation occurs in a dream, when Ezra awakes the angel is still there, holding him, strengthening him, and setting him on his feet (4 Ezra 5:15).

His prayer to God, the appearance of the angel Uriel, his dialogue or, rather, his dispute with the angel, and his awakening occur twice more, the three encounters separated by seven-day fasts. After the third encounter, Uriel bids Ezra not to fast but to go into a field onto which no building has been built and to eat only the flowers of the field and to pray to the Most High continually (4 Ezra 9:23–25).

The Fourth Episode: A Vision of a Woman and a City

This fourth episode is the midpoint of the seven encounters with the supernatural that Ezra has, and it is the climax of the book. Ezra obeys Uriel's command, and, after seven days of eating only the flowers of the field, he complains again to the Most High:

> Now this is the general rule that when the ground has received seed, or the sea a ship, or any dish food or drink, and when it comes about that what was sown or what was launched or what was put in is destroyed, they are destroyed, but the things that held them [the ground, the sea, and the dish] remain; yet with us it has not been so.
>
> For we, who have received the law and have sinned, will perish, both we as well as our hearts that received it; the law, however, does not perish but survives in its glory. (4 Ezra 9:34–37)

Unlike the seed, the ship, or the food that may perish though the container survives, with us it is the opposite. The containers, our hearts, which have received the Torah but which have sinned, perish. The Torah, the law, the object put into the containing heart, survives eternally. Only the container dies. That the body perishes is not the fault of the Torah, however, since it survives forever. This presages the conclusion in chapter 14 in which salvation and hope lie not in God's mercy (which as we will see does not exist) but in Torah.

After he says these words, Ezra sees a woman standing in the field weeping and mourning, her clothes rent and ashes on her head (4 Esdras 9:38). She is mourning her only son, who died on his wedding night (10:1). Ezra chastises the woman for mourning only one person, when all Israel is mourning her mother, Jerusalem:

> You most foolish of women, do you not see our mourning, and what has happened to us?
> [7] For Zion, the mother of us all, is in deep grief and great distress.
> [8] It is most appropriate to mourn now, because we are all mourning, and to be sorrowful, because we are all sorrowing; you are sorrowing for one son, but we, the whole world, for our mother. (4 Ezra 10:6–8)

> [15] Now, therefore, keep your sorrow to yourself, and bear bravely the troubles that have come upon you.
> [16] For if you acknowledge the decree of God to be just, you will receive your son back in due time, and will be praised among women. (4 Ezra 10:15, 16)

In this last verse, Ezra urges that God's justice be acknowledged, even if it cannot be understood. Moreover, if the woman acknowledges God as just, even if she does not understand God's ways completely, she will receive her son back again. This is the turning point of the book, for with this statement Ezra begins to console himself and to forgive God. With this statement, however, Ezra relinquishes hope in this world for those who suffer and begins to rely on an ultimate reward in the world to come. He sacrifices present reality for a future that cannot be verified and that is impervious to empirical verification.[9]

He speaks to her again: "Let yourself be persuaded—for how many are the adversities of Zion?—and be consoled because of the sorrow of Jerusalem. Shake off your great sadness and lay aside your many sorrows, so that the Mighty One may be merciful to you again, and the Most High may give you rest, respite from your troubles" (4 Ezra 10:20, 24). These words, while ostensibly directed at the mourning woman, are really directed at himself and at all Israel. They are miraculously answered, for as soon as he says them the mourning woman utters a loud cry (10:26) and disappears, to be replaced by the scene of a city being built. The angel Uriel comes to him again and explains that the mourning woman is Zion mourning for her only son. She had been barren for thirty years, representing the three thousand years until Solomon built the city and presented offerings in it (4 Ezra 10:46). The city was thus not considered occupied until Solomon had built his temple and commenced the sacrifices. The woman's only son is therefore either the temple itself or the offerings performed within it. She (the city) has tended her son (that is, the temple and the offerings) with great care, but when he matured and entered his wedding chamber he fell down and died (10:1), that is, the temple was destroyed. The woman and her neighbors put out their lamps in mourning for the destroyed temple and for the offerings that had ended (10:2). She then goes into the barren field to weep, mourn, and fast for her only son (10:4).

The angel does not interpret for Ezra the meaning of the son or the significance of the wedding chamber. Perhaps he does not need to. Perhaps the passage refers to a saying, already well known among Judeans, about the bridegroom symbolizing the temple, as well as of the importance of fasting for the fallen temple:

> 19 Jesus said to them,
> The wedding guests cannot fast while the bridegroom is with them, can they? As long as they have the bridegroom with them, they cannot fast.
> 20 The days will come when the bridegroom is taken away from them, and then they will fast on that day" (Mark 2:19–20 = Matt. 9:15, Luke 5:34–35).[10]

These two verses may reflect a common saying in post-70 Jerusalem that referred to the fall of the temple, a saying later appropriated by Christians to refer to Jesus's body, the temple not made with hands (Mark 14:58). As long as the temple was with us, we did not need to fast, as we had the bridegroom with us. Now that the temple is no longer with us, we must fast. Thus, in 4 Ezra, the temple, that is, the woman's son, the bridegroom, is no longer with her, and so she fasts.[11]

As Ezra consoles and chastises the woman for mourning only one son when all the world has lost its mother, she is transformed before his eyes into a city in the process of being built, with its foundations being laid. The interpreting angel, Uriel, tells Ezra that the city is Zion and that he should not be afraid and to go inside the building and see its splendor (10:55). He is told not to go inside the city but to go into the building. This building is the physical temple, the son that had been within the woman, that is, within the city. The temple is the dwelling of God. Ezra is thus called here to be in the presence of the Most High (10:57).[12]

The Fifth Episode: A Vision of an Eagle with Twelve Wings and Three Heads and a Vision of the Anointed One

Uriel tells Ezra to sleep "there" that night and the following one. It is not specified, but "there" must be within the rebuilt earthly/heavenly temple. He does so and on the second night has a dream (11:1). (Temples are perfect incubators for dreams; cf. 1 Sam. 3:1–8.)

In his dream Ezra sees an eagle rising from the sea. It has twelve wings and three heads (11:1; cf. Rev. 13:1). While staring at all the manifold changes that the creature undergoes, he hears a voice telling him to look and to consider what he sees (11:36). A lion then comes roaring out of a forest and, speaking in a human voice, condemns the eagle (11:37):

> You have judged the earth, but not with truth,
> 42 for you have oppressed the meek and injured the peaceable; you have hated those who tell the truth, and have loved liars; you have destroyed the homes of those who brought forth fruit, and have laid low the walls of those who did you no harm.

43 Your insolence has come up before the Most High, and your pride to the Mighty One.
44 The Most High has looked at his times; now they have ended, and his ages have reached completion.
45 Therefore you, eagle, will surely disappear, you and your terrifying wings, your most evil little wings, your malicious heads, your most evil talons, and your whole worthless body,
46 so that the whole earth, freed from your violence, may be refreshed and relieved, and may hope for the judgment and mercy of him who made it. (4 Ezra 11:41–46)

Ezra looks and sees the eagle and all its parts vanishing, and when he looks again the whole body of the eagle is burned, and the earth exceedingly terrified (12:1–3). As is explicitly stated (4 Ezra 12:11), the eagle is the fourth beast and the fourth kingdom in the book of Daniel (Dan. 7:7–8). This fourth beast is not described in Daniel but is described in Ezra's dream as an eagle coming up out of the sea, an eagle with twelve wings and three heads (4 Ezra 11:1; 12:10). The interpretation of the kingdom and of the three heads of the eagle allows the date of 4 Ezra to be decided. The three heads have been determined to be Vespasian, Titus, and Domitian (81–96 C.E.), and the composition of 4 Ezra may be dated toward the end of the latter's reign.[13]

Upon seeing this horrible vision, Ezra wakes and prays to God for an explanation of the dream (12:7–9). Although this is not stated explicitly, it must be the angel Uriel who explains the vision, since he refers to the Most High in the third person (12:36). The three heads are three kings who will rule the earth more oppressively than any before them (12:22–25). As for the lion who condemns and destroys them, he is the Anointed One, the Messiah. He will destroy the evil rulers and will set "my people" free, that is, the people Israel who will be alive at that time:

[The lion] is the Anointed One whom the Most High has kept until the end of days, who will arise from the offspring of David, and will come and speak with [those kings]. He will denounce them for their ungodliness and for their wickedness, and will display before them their contemptuous dealings.
33 For first he will bring them alive before his judgment seat, and when he has reproved them, then he will destroy them.
34 But in mercy he will set free the remnant of my people, those who have been saved throughout my borders, and he will make them joyful until the end comes, the day of judgment, of which I spoke to you at the beginning. (4 Ezra 12:32–34)

The Anointed One, the Messiah, described here has the traditional political role of the Anointed One that we see in Isaiah's description of Cyrus.[14]

> Thus says YHWH, your Redeemer, who formed you in the womb: I am YHWH, who made all things, who alone stretched out the heavens, who by myself spread out the earth; who frustrates the omens of liars, and makes fools of diviners; who turns back the wise, and makes their knowledge foolish; who confirms the word of his Servant, and fulfills the prediction of his Messengers; who says of Jerusalem, "It shall be inhabited," and of the cities of Judah, "They shall be rebuilt, and I will raise up their ruins"; who says of Cyrus, "He is my Shepherd, and he shall carry out all my purpose"; and who says of Jerusalem, "It shall be rebuilt," and of the temple, "Your foundation shall be laid."
>
> Thus says YHWH to his Anointed, to Cyrus, whose right hand I have grasped to subdue nations before him and strip kings of their robes, to open doors before him—and the gates shall not be closed. (Isaiah 44:24–45:1)

The role of the Messiah in Isaiah and here in 4 Ezra is to destroy oppressive kings, restore the cities of Judah, especially Jerusalem, rebuild the temple, and bring the Judean people back home.

At the end of the dream and of the explanation, Uriel bids Ezra to write down everything he has seen in a book, put the book in a hidden place, and teach his writings to the wise among his people. Then he is told to wait in the field seven more days, eating only the flowers of the field. He does so, and dreams again.

The Sixth Episode—A Vision of a Man Flying out of the Sea

In this vision or dream, Ezra sees a man come up out of the sea, flying with the clouds of heaven (13:1–3). A great multitude rushes to make war against him, but he destroys them all with the breath of his mouth (13:10–11). Then a peaceful multitude approaches him, and he gathers them to him (13:12–13). Ezra awakes in great terror, and the interpreting angel explains that this man also is the Anointed One, the Servant[15] of the Most High, the one whom God has been keeping back for many ages. When all the nations go to war against one another, then this man will be revealed as the one you saw coming out of the sea. He will destroy the warring multitudes by means of the Law, symbolized by the fire of his mouth (13:38). The second, peaceful multitude that approaches him comprises the nine tribes taken into exile by Assyria and made captive there (13:39–40). This is again a prediction of the coming of the Messiah, God's Servant, who will crush the warring nations, restore the cities of Judah, and bring the exiled people of Israel home again. This image of a political messiah is again based on Isaiah's description of Cyrus as God's Servant and his Anointed (Isaiah 44:26–45:1). Upon hearing all this, Ezra gets up and walks in the field and stays there three days.

The Seventh Episode—The Voice out of the Bush

In this final vision God himself speaks to Ezra out of the bush, as he spoke with Moses (4 Ezra 14:1–3; cf. Exod. 3:2). Ezra is told to take five men who write quickly and to dictate to them all the words that come out of his mouth. Over a forty-day period he dictates to them ninety-four books, twenty-four of which (that is, the twenty-four books of the Hebrew Bible) he is to make public to both the "worthy and the unworthy." The other seventy he shall give only to the wise among his people, "for in them is the spring of understanding, the fountain of wisdom, and the river of knowledge" (4 Ezra 14:47), as well as the key to surviving the judgment at the end of the present age. This forty-day period is reminiscent of the number of days in which Moses is on the mountain receiving the books of the Torah (Exod. 34:28). Most scholars assume the seventy books to be apocalyptic books, including the present one.[16]

The Angel Discloses a Transcendent Reality

The Angel Tells of Another Age

According to the definition of apocalypse proposed earlier, the interpreting angel discloses a transcendent reality, another time and another place. The postponement of salvation to another time and another place suggests despair about God's ability to create a just world in this present place and at this present time. Indeed, in Ezra's first dispute with the angel Uriel, Uriel tells him that "this age is hurrying swiftly to its end," and "if you are alive then, you will see" (4 Ezra 4:26). The current age is the age in which the evil seed that was sown first in Adam's heart and that caused him to sin must be reaped and pass away in order to make room for the harvest of the good seed (4 Ezra 4:29–30).

That this evil age was nearing its end was a common form of reassurance in the first century C.E., as seen in Paul's letter to the Corinthians (1 Cor. 7:29–31): "I mean, brothers, the appointed time has grown short; from now on, let even those who have wives be as though they had none, and those who mourn as though they were not mourning, and those who rejoice as though they were not rejoicing, and those who buy as though they had no possessions, and those who deal with the world as though they had no dealings with it. For the present form of this world is passing away."

This notion of a present evil age and a future age without pain or suffering may derive originally from the words of the prophet Isaiah:

> For I am about to create new heavens and a new earth; the former things shall not be remembered or come to mind.
>
> 18 But be glad and rejoice forever in what I am creating; for I am about to create Jerusalem as a joy, and its people as a delight.
>
> 19 I will rejoice in Jerusalem, and delight in my people; no more shall the sound of weeping be heard in it, or the cry of distress.
>
> 20 No more shall there be in it an infant that lives but a few days, or an old person who does not live out a lifetime; for one who dies at a hundred years will be considered a youth, and one who falls short of a hundred will be considered accursed.

> 21 They shall build houses and inhabit them; they shall plant vineyards and eat their fruit.
> 22 They shall not build and another inhabit; they shall not plant and another eat; for like the days of a tree shall the days of my people be, and my chosen shall long enjoy the work of their hands.
> 23 They shall not labor in vain, or bear children for calamity; for they shall be offspring blessed by YHWH—and their descendants as well.
> 24 Before they call I will answer, while they are yet speaking I will hear.
> 25 The wolf and the lamb shall feed together, the lion shall eat straw like the ox; and the serpent—its food shall be dust! They shall not hurt or destroy on all my holy mountain, says YHWH. (Isaiah 65:17–25)

The Time of the Present Age Is Fixed

According to the angel Uriel, this present age will pass away, but not until all the evil that has been sown in it is harvested (4:29). The place where it has been sown is, of course, the human heart (4:30). Ezra asks how long this present age will last (4:33), and Uriel answers in reference to all those righteous who have already died and all the souls who have not yet been born: "Did not the souls of the righteous in their treasuries ask about these matters, saying, 'How long are we to remain here? And when will the harvest of our reward come?' And the archangel Jeremiel answered and said, 'When the number of those like yourselves is completed,' for he [God] has weighed the age in the balance" (4 Ezra 4:35–36).

Thus, the present age will last until all the righteous have been born, and moreover, the number of people to be born has been predetermined. Because of the use of the past tense in the question ("did" rather than "do"), Uriel likely refers to a well-known document, now lost, in which the souls of the righteous ask this of the archangel Jeremiel, יְרַחְמְאֵל ("God will have compassion").[17] Apparently, the souls of the dead languish in Hades in an intermediate state until the end of this present evil age. There is no reward or punishment for the souls at this point. They simply await the judgment.[18] According to *The Apocalypse of Zephaniah,* Eremiel (Jeremiel) is in charge of the souls of the dead while they are waiting: " I am the great angel Eremiel, who is over the abyss and Hades, where all of the souls [of the dead] are imprisoned from the end of the Flood which came upon the earth, until this day. Then I [Zephaniah] inquired of the angel with me, 'What is this place to which I have come?' He said to me, 'It is Hades.' Then I asked him, 'Who is that great angel who stands thus, whom I saw?' He said, 'This is the one who accuses men in the presence of the Lord'" (*Apoc. of Zephaniah* 6:16–17).

Here, in 4 Ezra, Uriel tells Ezra that the times are fixed until the end of this present age, just as the time of an infant in his mother's womb is fixed. He then adds, "and he will not move or arouse them until that measure is fulfilled" (4 Ezra

4:37). This refers to the resurrection of the souls of the dead from their internment in Hades until the present age ends. Uriel does provide information on how the end of the present age can be recognized, however. The end of the present age will be signaled by what was then known as "the birth pangs of the Messiah" (Matt. 24:6–13; Mark 13:8; *Sanhedrin* 98b).

> 4 If the Most High grants that you live, you shall see it [the present age] thrown into confusion after the third period; and the sun shall suddenly begin to shine at night, and the moon during the day.
> 5 Blood shall drip from wood, and the stone shall utter its voice; the peoples shall be troubled, and the stars shall fall.
> 6 And one shall reign whom those who inhabit the earth do not expect, and the birds shall fly away together;
> 9 . . . reason shall hide itself, and wisdom shall withdraw into its chamber,
> 10 it shall be sought by many but shall not be found, and unrighteousness and unrestraint shall increase on earth. (4 Ezra 5:4–6, 9–10)

The unexpected king (vs. 6) is part of the confused and evil conditions that will prevail at the end times. In the fifth vision (described earlier) this king is the fourth beast in the series of beasts that Daniel (Dan. 7) saw in his dream and therefore the fourth kingdom of the kingdoms that rule the earth. Everyone who remains alive after the confused and evil conditions that presage the end of time shall be saved and taken up to be with God, and evil shall be no more. "It shall be that whoever remains [alive] after all that I have foretold to you shall be saved and shall see my salvation and the end of my world. And they shall see those who were taken up, who from their birth have not tasted death; and the heart of the earth's inhabitants shall be changed and converted to a different spirit. For evil shall be blotted out, and deceit shall be quenched" (4 Ezra 6:25–27).

The end of the present age will be characterized by confused and evil times, but whoever remains alive through that time shall be saved along with those who have already been taken up (from the earth to the sky?) and who have never tasted death. This would presumably include Enoch: "Enoch walked with God; then he was no more, because God took him" (Gen. 5:24), and Elijah:

> When they had crossed, Elijah said to Elisha, "Tell me what I may do for you, before I am taken from you." Elisha said, "Please let me inherit a double share of your spirit."
> 10 He responded, "You have asked a hard thing; yet, if you see me as I am being taken from you, it will be granted you; if not, it will not."
> 11 As they continued walking and talking, a chariot of fire and horses of fire separated the two of them, and Elijah ascended in a whirlwind into heaven (2 Kings 2:9–11).

Some who are currently alive will also be saved, as assumed by the author of Matthew: "Truly I tell you, there are some standing here who will not taste death before they see the Son of Man coming in his kingdom" (Matt. 16:28). According to Matthew, when the present evil age has ended, everyone who is delivered from these evils and is still alive will be taken up. So too in 4 Ezra. Everyone who survives the period of evil and confusion will see all the signs and be delivered.

Signs of the End

The first sign of the end is the appearance of the city: "For indeed the time will come, when the signs that I have foretold to you will come to pass, that the city that now is not seen shall appear, and the land that now is hidden shall be disclosed" (4 Ezra 7:26). This city is either the rebuilt earthly Jerusalem or the heavenly Jerusalem, which becomes reified, or—what is more likely—both—that they are in fact the same city. The physical Jerusalem that holds the temple is actually the heavenly Jerusalem, since the temple houses the deity. The fact that Ezra sees this city (fourth vision, 4 Ezra 10:27) indicates that the end of times is indeed at hand.

The second sign for those still alive is the appearance of the Anointed One, the Messiah: "Everyone who has been delivered from the evils that I have foretold shall see my wonders. For my Servant the Messiah shall be revealed with those who are with him, and those who remain shall rejoice four hundred years. After those years my Servant the Messiah shall die, along with all who draw human breath" (4 Ezra 7:27–29).

That the Messiah is to be revealed (and not born or created) suggests that he is preexistent.[19] The Messiah rejoices with those alive, and he too dies with them at the end of the four hundred years of the Messianic Age. He first appears to Ezra in the form of a lion announcing that with the destruction of the eagle's third head the current age is ended and that the ages are complete (4 Ezra 11:36–45). The lion warns the eagle: "Your insolence has come up before the Most High, and your pride to the Mighty One. The Most High has looked at his times; now they have ended, and his ages have reached completion" (4 Ezra 11:43–44). After the lion has finished speaking, the eagle's heads and all its parts burn up and vanish: "When I looked again, they were already vanishing. The whole body of the eagle was burned, and the earth was exceedingly terrified. Then I woke up in great perplexity of mind and great fear" (4 Ezra 12:1–3).

The eagle represents the Roman Empire, perhaps chosen because of the image found on the standards of the Roman legions.[20] Uriel tells Ezra that the lion is the Anointed One, of the line of David, whom the Most High has preserved until the end of days (12:31). This again suggests that, even though of the line of David, he is preexistent (cf. 7:28), an apparent anomaly also grappled with in the works of Paul and the Gospels.[21] Uriel explains that the Anointed One will judge and condemn the wicked kings and then destroy them (12:33), although this is not included in the vision. In the vision, the eagle simply fades away. This destruction (or fading away) is followed by the Messianic Age, four hundred years of rejoicing. "But in mercy he will set free the remnant of my people, those who have been saved throughout my borders, and he will make them joyful until the end comes, the day of judgment, of which I spoke to you at the beginning" (4 Ezra 12:34; cf. 4 Ezra 7:28).

This is certainly based on Daniel 7 in which the fourth beast burns up, most probably from the stream of fire that flows out from the presence of the Most High (Dan. 7:10). In Daniel, the beast is then replaced by "one like a Son of Man coming with the clouds of heaven" (Dan. 7:13), implying the dominion of this last figure, who reigns in place of the beasts. This is also the image in 4 Ezra, when the rule of the Lion (the Lion of Judah) reigns in place of the eagle but also when one in the form of a man rules as the Messiah in Ezra's next vision.

Those who have been saved, the remnant of God's people (presumably the Jewish people), are those who are still alive at the end of days. This is also the view in Mark 13:13, where it is stated that "the one who endures to the end [of the present age] will be saved." In 4 Ezra, those who have survived will experience a great joy for four hundred years (12:34; 7:28).

A second Redeemer is revealed to Ezra in a second dream vision (13:1–12). In this vision he comes out of the sea as "something like the figure of a man . . . flying with the clouds of heaven (13:2–3)." This is strongly reminiscent of "one like a son of man coming with the clouds of heaven" in Daniel 7:13. It is also reminiscent of the figure of YHWH himself, who appears to Ezekiel in "the appearance of a man" in Ezekiel (8:2)[22] and who rides on the clouds of heaven (Isa. 19:1), and, most closely, of YHWH as he is described in Psalm 104:3: "you set the beams of your chambers on the waters, you make the clouds your chariot, you ride on the wings of the wind." According to the interpreting angel, the man who comes out of the sea is "my Servant" (13:37), "the one whom the Most High has been keeping for many ages, through whom he will deliver his creation" (13:26). In Ezra's dream, a multitude comes from the four winds of heaven to make war against this one who is "something like a figure of a man" (13:8). The man has no weapon of war with him, but out of his mouth comes a stream of fire that turns the multitude into ashes and smoke (13:9–11). This fire is the law, which alone incriminates and destroys them (13:38). After this another multitude comes to him, this time in peace (13:12): "Many people came to him, some of whom were joyful and some sorrowful; some of them were bound, and some were bringing others as offerings" (4 Ezra 13:13).

The interpreting angel (or is it the Most High himself?) explains that this multitude consists of the nine and one-half tribes that were led into captivity in the days of King Hoshea (that is, the northern tribes) and who escaped from Assyria to a distant land that they might be able to keep the commandments (13:40–42). With them come those "of your people" who are still within "my holy borders"

(13:48). These are the people who will be saved, those who are still alive and who will survive the tumult preceding the end of the current age. This expectation is also expressed in the Psalms of Solomon:

> Behold, O Lord, and raise up to them their King, the son of David, at the time, which you choose, O God, that he may reign over Israel your servant.
> 22 And gird him with strength, that he may shatter unrighteous rulers. And that he may purge Jerusalem from nations that trample [her] down to destruction.
> 23 In the wisdom of righteousness he will thrust out sinners from [the] inheritance, he will destroy the pride of the sinner as a potter's vessel.
> 24 With a rod of iron he will break in pieces all their substance. He will destroy the godless nations with the word of his mouth.
> 25 At his rebuke nations will flee before him. And he will reprove sinners for the thoughts of their heart.
> 26 And he will gather together the holy people, whom he will lead in righteousness. And he will judge the tribes of the people that has been sanctified by the Lord his God.
> 27 And he will not suffer unrighteousness to lodge any more in their midst, nor will there dwell with them any man that knows wickedness. For he will know them, that they are all sons of their God.
> 28 And he will divide them according to their tribes upon the land. And neither sojourner nor alien will sojourn with them any more.
> 29 He will judge peoples and nations in the wisdom of his righteousness. Selah.
> 30 And he will have the heathen nations to serve him under his yoke. And he will glorify the Lord in [a place] well known [above] all the earth. And he will purge Jerusalem, making it holy as of old,
> 31 so that nations will come from the ends of the earth to see his glory, bringing as gifts her sons who had fainted, and to see the glory of the Lord, with which God hath glorified her. (Psalms of Solomon 17:21–31)

Those who survive the period of evil and confusion "will live in joy with the Messiah for four hundred years." After this, everything dies, including the Messiah himself, and the world reverts for seven days to the quiet existence it had at the beginning of creation. This seven-day period will be followed by the resurrection of the dead. "The earth shall give up those who are asleep in it, and the dust those who rest there in silence; and the chambers shall give up the souls that have been committed to them" (4 Ezra 7:32). The resurrection is followed by universal judgment, with no compassion: "The Most High shall be revealed on the seat of judgment, and compassion shall pass away, and patience shall be withdrawn. Only judgment shall remain, truth shall stand, and faithfulness shall grow strong. Recompense shall follow, and the reward shall be manifested; righteous deeds shall awake, and unrighteous deeds shall not sleep. The pit of torment shall appear, and opposite it shall be the place of rest; and the furnace of hell shall be disclosed, and opposite it the paradise of delight" (4 Ezra 7:33–36).

Ezra then asks the angel Uriel what happens when we die. He answers that the souls of those who have despised the law will not enter the treasuries but will wander about in shame and torment (7:80), whereas those who have kept the ways of the Most High shall see God's glory (7:91) and will be ushered into a rest of profound quiet (7:95). They will be incorruptible; their faces will shine like the sun, and they will be made like the light of the stars (7:97).

In the passage quoted earlier (7:32) it is implied that all the souls sleep in the chambers or "treasuries" until the day of judgment. Here (7:80) it is stated that only those who have kept the law or at least have not despised it will rest in the treasuries. The others will wander the earth. This apparent conflict is resolved in 7:101, where it is stated that after seven days of wandering and torment, those souls too shall be gathered into their treasuries. Moreover, the Day of Judgment is decisive; there is no intercession by the righteous for the ungodly, and "all shall bear their own righteousness and unrighteousness" (7:104–5).

It should be pointed out as an aside that in many manuscripts of the Latin Vulgate the entire section of 4 Ezra 7:36–105 is missing. This is the section that Michael Stone dubs "the divine address to the wicked."[23] In this section it is emphasized that the day of judgment is decisive, that the righteous cannot pray for the deceased, and that there is no substitutiary atonement. Each one suffers for his own sins. "Just as now a father does not send his son, or a son his father, or a master his servant, or a friend his dearest friend, to be ill or sleep or eat or be healed in his place, so no one shall ever pray for another on that day, neither shall anyone lay a burden on another; for then all shall bear their own righteousness and unrighteousness" (4 Ezra 7:104–5). Although missing from the Latin Vulgate, this long section is present in all the versions translated from the Greek (see Appendix 2). In 1865 J. Gildemeister discovered that the Latin Codex Sangermanensis (822 C.E.) contained the stub of a leaf that had been intentionally cut out. The pages before and following this excision ended and began with the words included in the Vulgate, so all subsequent Latin manuscripts must go back to this one with the excised page.[24]

The Angel Tells of Another World

In addition to foretelling the end of days and another time, Uriel also discloses another place. In the fourth episode, discussed earlier, Ezra is shown a city, and the Angel Uriel tells him that he may enter it:

> I told you to go into the field where there was no foundation of any building,
> 54 because no work of human construction could endure in a place where the city of the Most High was to be revealed.

> 55 "Therefore do not be afraid, and do not let your heart be terrified; but go inside and see the splendor or the vastness of the building, as far as it is possible for your eyes to see it,
> 56 and afterward you will hear as much as your ears can hear.
> 57 For you are more blessed than many, and you have been called to be with the Most High as few have been. (4 Ezra 10:53–57)

The city that he sees is the dwelling-place of the Most High. It is a physical entity, the earthly Jerusalem, since Ezra sees it not in a dream but while awake and he is told to enter it and look around. At the same time, it describes another world since the heavenly Jerusalem is the abode of God.[25] Ezra is more blessed than many since he has been called to enter the divine dwelling place and to be with God (10:57; cf. Rev. 21:1–4).

Fourth Ezra as Theodicy

Fourth Ezra has achieved its popularity not only for its apocalyptic visions of the end times but also because of Ezra's discourse with the angel Uriel on God's justice, which occurs in the first three episodes of the book. It is worthwhile exploring these issues in more detail.

Vision 1. First Conversation with Uriel

This vision begins with Ezra's prayer to God in Babylon in the "thirtieth year after the destruction of the temple" (3:1). It is motivated by Ezra's agitation over the desolation of Zion and the wealth of those who live in Babylon (3:2). Ezra states:

> You handed over your city to your enemies.
> 8 "So I said in my heart, Are the deeds of those who inhabit Babylon any better? Is that why it has gained dominion over Zion?
> 29 For when I came here I saw ungodly deeds without number, and my soul has seen many sinners during these thirty years. And my heart failed me,
> 30 because I have seen how you endure those who sin, and have spared those who act wickedly, and have destroyed your people, and protected your enemies,
> 31 and have not shown to anyone how your way may be comprehended. Are the deeds of Babylon better than those of Zion?
> 32 Or has another nation known you besides Israel? Or what tribes have so believed the covenants as these tribes of Jacob?
> 33 Yet their reward has not appeared and their labor has borne no fruit. For I have traveled widely among the nations and have seen that they abound in wealth, though they are unmindful of your commandments.
> 34 Now therefore weigh in a balance our iniquities and those of the inhabitants of the world; and it will be found which way the turn of the scale will incline.

35 When have the inhabitants of the earth not sinned in your sight? Or what nation has kept your commandments so well?
36 You may indeed find individuals who have kept your commandments, but nations you will not find. (4 Ezra 3:27–36)

This indeed is the age-old question of God's justice. The people of Babylon behave no better than the people of Israel, yet the Babylonians are triumphant and the Judeans banished from their homeland. God condemns Israel for not following Torah, yet does not condemn the other peoples to whom he has not given it. Nevertheless, he did not create Israel with the ability to follow the laws. The fall of the temple and the city was caused not by Judah's rebellion against Rome but by their failure to keep the commandments of Torah. God is in charge, not Rome. Behind this assumption of God's power is the assumption of human ability to control the deity. God marches in lockstep with human behavior. Had the Judeans only kept Torah to the degree that God demanded, the divine quid pro quo would have given them victory over Roman legions.[26]

Ezra complains again that God did not make Israel capable of keeping the law: "You gave the law to the descendants of Jacob, and your commandments to the posterity of Israel. Yet you did not take away their evil heart from them, so that your law might produce fruit in them" (4 Ezra 3:19–20). God created the people Israel, he gave them commandments, but at the same time he did not take away from them the evil heart that they had inherited from Adam. God did not create them capable of following the laws, and now he punishes them for it.

Ezra asks: "Should not the God of Justice do what is just? Was there no one righteous in the city that you might have spared it for his sake?"[27] This is a reference to Abraham's argument with God prior to his destruction of Sodom. God assures Abraham that he would spare Sodom if there were ten righteous people in it:

Then Abraham came near and said, "Will you indeed sweep away the righteous [of Sodom] with the wicked?
24 Suppose there are fifty righteous within the city; will you then sweep away the place and not forgive it for the fifty righteous who are in it?
25 Far be it from you to do such a thing, to slay the righteous with the wicked, so that the righteous fare as the wicked! Far be that from you! Shall not the Judge of all the earth do what is just?"
26 And YHWH said, "If I find at Sodom fifty righteous in the city, I will forgive the whole place for their sake."
27 Abraham answered, "Let me take it upon myself to speak to my Lord, I who am but dust and ashes.
28 Suppose five of the fifty righteous are lacking? Will you destroy the whole city for lack of five?" And he said, "I will not destroy it if I find forty-five there."

> 29 Again he spoke to him, "Suppose forty are found there." He answered, "For the sake of forty I will not do it."
> 30 Then he said, "Oh do not let the Lord be angry if I speak. Suppose thirty are found there." He answered, "I will not do it, if I find thirty there."
> 31 He said, "Let me take it upon myself to speak to the Lord. Suppose twenty are found there." He answered, "For the sake of twenty I will not destroy it."
> 32 Then he said, "Oh do not let the Lord be angry if I speak just once more. Suppose ten are found there." He answered, "For the sake of ten I will not destroy it."
> 33 And YHWH went his way, when he had finished speaking to Abraham; and Abraham returned to his place. (Gen. 18:23–33)

Could it be that there were not even ten righteous people in all of Jerusalem, or is God harsher on his own people than on the Sodomites? The angel Uriel tells Ezra that mankind can only know the ways of the earth; it cannot know the ways of heaven (4:21). This is a common response when defending God—an appeal to human ignorance. God's ways are just, but human understanding of God is limited.[28] Ezra responds that he is inquiring not about the ways of heaven but only about those things on earth that we experience daily. In particular he asks about God's covenant with Israel:

> For I did not wish to inquire about the ways above, but about those things that we daily experience: why Israel has been given over to the Gentiles in disgrace; why the people whom you loved has been given over to godless tribes, and the law of our ancestors has been brought to destruction and the written covenants no longer exist.
> 24 We pass from the world like locusts, and our life is like a mist, and we are not worthy to obtain mercy.
> 25 But what will he do for his name that is invoked over us? It is about these things that I have asked. (4 Ezra 4:23–25)

God has seemingly abolished his covenant with his people, and now what will become of his great name? Shall it be bruited about that God is not able to keep his promises?[29]

The only answer that the angel can give is that the present age is hastening to its end and that the end time will be preceded by calamities. Until these calamities are fulfilled, the reward for the righteous cannot appear (4:26–29; 5:1–12).

Vision 2. Second Conversation with Uriel

This is no answer at all, so Ezra returns in his second vision to his original complaint:

> From all the multitude of peoples you have gotten for yourself one people; and to this people, whom you have loved, you have given the law that is approved by all.

> 28 And now, O Lord, why have you handed the one over to the many, and dishonored the one root beyond the others, and scattered your only one among the many?
> 29 And those who opposed your promises have trampled on those who believed your covenants.
> 30 If you really hate your people, they should be punished at your own hands. (4 Ezra 5:27–30)

Why do you give your people, whom you love, over to the heathen nations who do not know you? If you hate your people so much, then punish them by yourself; don't send a proxy!

In this vision, the angel responds similarly to his previous response: "You cannot discover my judgment or the goal of the love that I have promised my people" (5:40). You cannot understand God. Ezra pleads for reassurance, and he hears a voice like the sound of "many waters" saying that the time is coming when "evil shall be blotted out, and deceit shall be quenched; when faithfulness shall flourish, and corruption shall be overcome, and the truth, which has been so long without fruit, shall be revealed" (4 Ezra 6:27–28). This is a statement that the end of present age is upon us and a new age is being ushered in. It is intended to provide a feeling of hope.

Vision 3. Third Conversation with Uriel

Nevertheless, again, this is no answer, so Ezra persists:

> All this I have spoken before you, O Lord, because you have said that it was for us that you created this world.
> 56 As for the other nations that have descended from Adam, you have said that they are nothing, and that they are like spittle, and you have compared their abundance to a drop from a bucket.
> 57 And now, O Lord, these nations, which are reputed to be as nothing, domineer over us and devour us.
> 58 But we your people, whom you have called your firstborn, only-begotten, zealous for you, and most dear, have been given into their hands.
> 59 If the world has indeed been created for us, why do we not possess our world as an inheritance? (4 Ezra 6:55–59)

God has promised a special relationship between him and the people Israel, but where is the evidence of it? Again the only answer is that mankind must travel through the difficult experience of this life in order to enter the world of immortality and receive the things that have been reserved for us (7:14). The calamity that the Judeans faced has convinced the author that the reward of the covenantal relationship between God and Israel can lie only in the world to come, not in this world.[30] Only those who survive the last days will see the City (the physical and heavenly Jerusalem, the abode of God), the Messiah, and the final judgment (7:26–34). This response too is not enough for Ezra, who persists and asks after the sinners, since there is no one who has not sinned: "But what of those for whom I prayed? For who among the living is there that has not sinned, or who is there among mortals that has not transgressed your covenant" (4 Ezra 7:46)?

Uriel answers that God rejoices over the few who will be honored and does not grieve over the multitude who will perish (7:60–61). Ezra tries again to persuade God to have mercy on those who have sinned because God created man but did not teach him how to avoid sin. All man can do now is live in sorrow and hardship on this earth and expect nothing but punishment after it (7:117, 119). Ezra tries for the last time to persuade God to be God and to live up to his names and his reputation as "the Gracious One," "the Patient One," "the Merciful One," "the Compassionate One":

> I answered and said, "I know, O Lord, that the Most High is now called the Gracious One, because he is gracious to those who turn in repentance to his law;
> 134 and the Patient One, because he shows patience toward those who have sinned, since they are his own creatures;
> 135 and Bountiful, because he would rather give than take away;
> 136 and Abundant in Compassion, because he makes his compassions abound more and more to those now living and to those who are gone and to those yet to come—
> 137 for if he did not make them abound, the world with those who inhabit it would not have life—
> 138 and he is called the Giver, because if he did not give out of his goodness so that those who have committed iniquities might be relieved of them, not one ten-thousandth of humankind could have life;
> 139 and the Judge, because if he did not pardon those who were created by his word and blot out the multitude of their sins, 140 there would probably be left only very few of the innumerable multitude. (4 Ezra 7:133–40)

In point of fact, however, Uriel responds to Ezra that God is neither Gracious, nor Patient, nor Abundant in Compassion, nor Giving, nor a Merciful Judge, since God neither forgives nor blots out the sins of the sinner and only a very few of the innumerable multitude will survive (8:1–3).

Ezra then asks Uriel, if life is so short and eternity so dreadful, "for what purpose was man made?" (8:15). Ezra complains to God that he cannot be called Merciful if he rewards only the righteous, since rewarding only the righteous is not mercy. It is mercy only if clemency is granted the sinner:

> For [only] if you have desired to have pity on us, who have no works of righteousness, [only] then you will be called Merciful.

> [33] For the righteous, who have many works laid up with you, shall receive their reward in consequence of their own deeds.
> [34] But what are mortals, that you are angry with them; or what is a corruptible race, that you are so bitter against it?
> [35] For in truth there is no one among those who have been born who has not acted wickedly; among those who have existed there is no one who has not done wrong.
> [36] For [only] in this, O Lord, will your righteousness and goodness be declared, when you are merciful to those who have no store of good works. (4 Ezra 8:32–36)

Ezra is indeed a wonderful champion for humanity before God, but it is to no avail—only a few will be saved. God is recorded as saying that he has no pity for the sinners.

> I considered my world, and saw that it was lost. I saw that my earth was in peril because of the devices of those who had come into it.
> [21] And I saw and spared some with great difficulty, and saved for myself one grape out of a cluster, and one plant out of a great forest.
> [22] So let the multitude perish that has been born in vain, but let my grape and my plant be saved, because with much labor I have perfected them. (4 Ezra 9:20–22)

So ends Ezra's conversations with the angel Uriel. Although he continues to see visions of the heavenly Jerusalem and of the world to come, none of this can reassure him of God's mercy on his creation. God made man fallible and then punishes him for failing. The visions reassure Ezra only that the end of the present age of suffering is near.

The author of 4 Ezra has thus abandoned the Deuteronomic theology (Deut. 28) that promises good things in this life to those who obey God's commandments and bad things in this life to those who do not, a theology also regnant in canonical Ezra-Nehemiah and in 1 Esdras.[31] In 4 Ezra this faith in a divine quid pro quo that is enacted in the present time and on the present stage is gone. God has stacked the deck against us. He has created us with a nature that makes the commandments impossible for all but a few to keep. Moreover, the reward for the few who do keep the law is postponed to a far-off future life and future age. Because on earth the innocent must share in the punishment of the many, their suffering in the present age is not mitigated. The punishment for the many, on the other hand, takes place not only in the present life in the form of disease, exile, and death but also in the hideous future life that awaits them at the end of time. God's ultimate reward is only for the few and is postponed onto a future time and a future place.[32]

The Only Possible Response

The writer finds only one possible response to God's implacability and that is to call his bluff. After being shown how the world will end and the disasters meted out for those who fail to comply with God's desires, Ezra asks to be imbued with the spirit of holiness that he might write down the law, God's Torah. Ezra wants "people to be able to find the path, so that those who want to survive the last days may do so" (4 Ezra 14:22). The only answer offered to the issue of God's justice is to have faith that even though both the bad and the good suffer in this life, the good will receive their reward eventually. The struggle is worth the cost, for it is possible to be good. "If you will rule over your minds and discipline your hearts, you shall be kept alive, and after death you shall obtain mercy (4 Ezra 14:34).

Ezra is granted his desire and is given a magic potion to drink; after he drinks it, his heart pours forth understanding, and wisdom increases in his breast, and his spirit retains its memory (4 Ezra 14:40). During the ensuing forty days and forty nights Ezra is able to dictate not only the twenty-four books that are to be made public but also the seventy books that are to be given only to the "wise among your people, for in them is the spring of understanding, the fountain of wisdom, and the river of knowledge" (4 Ezra 14:47). Ezra is thus granted the ability to save his people, for if survival depends on obeying God's law, then the only recourse is to learn what it is and to follow it. There is no other choice. God has not left us blind and flailing about in the dark but has given us a path and has lighted it. The path is lit by the twenty-four books that are made public. The seventy secret books are most likely those that present the secret knowledge of the end times, including perhaps the book we have just read.[33] The fact that the author has selected Ezra as the protagonist in this apocalypse, rather than any other Old Testament figure, indicates the faith that he puts in Torah as the only hope for Israel's salvation.

6

The Christian Additions to the Ezra Apocalypse

As noted in chapter 5, the Jewish work known as 4 Ezra or the Ezra Apocalypse has had a Christian introduction (5 Ezra = chapters 1 and 2) and ending (6 Ezra = chapters 15 and 16) added to it. The entire work, 5 Ezra + 4 Ezra + 6 Ezra, is confusingly known as II Esdras. That Christians have found great meaning in Apocalyptic or 4 Ezra is amply demonstrated in these Christian additions, in the many Christian translations of 4 Ezra (discussed in appendix 2), and the many other Christian apocalypses that have spun off from it (discussed in chapter 7).

Fifth Ezra—A Christian Introduction to 4 Ezra (Chapters 1 and 2)

Purpose of These Chapters

Fifth Ezra (chapters 1 and 2) proclaims the Christian message of supersessionism (from English "supersede," "to supplant"): Because of their sins, God has replaced the people Israel with a new people who had not previously known him. These two introductory chapters must be dated to the second century C.E., since it must have been written after the time that the text of 4 Ezra was written (around 100 C.E.) and after it had been translated into Greek. It also must have been written after the Bar Kokhba Revolt (132–135 C.E.), since it was only then that Judeans were forcibly removed from Judea and driven into Egypt and Europe. This is referred to in the curse upon the Jews, uttered in 5 Ezra 2:7: "Let them be scattered among the nations; let their names be blotted out from the earth."

The book 5 Ezra begins with a genealogy of Ezra, a genealogy that, although not completely identical to that provided in either canonical Ezra 7 or 1 Esdras 8, does stretch back to Aaron, the first high priest, and designates Ezra as son of Seraiah, the last high priest of the Judean monarchy. Thus the author clarifies what may have been unclear to the reader of 4 Ezra, that we are reading about the same Ezra whose story is told in the Hebrew Bible. He is called here "the prophet," and, although he is not explicitly labeled such elsewhere, the label picks up on 4 Ezra 12:42, in which the people plead with Ezra that he not leave them: "For of all the prophets you alone are left to us, like a cluster of grapes from the vintage, and like a lamp in a dark place, and like a haven for a ship saved from a storm" (4 Ezra

12:42). Accordingly, 5 Ezra begins with Ezra's statement, in prophetic language, that "the word of the Lord came to me, saying. . . ." Thus, for most (but not all) of 5 Ezra, God speaks to Ezra directly, not through an angelic intermediary as in 4 Ezra.

That these first two chapters are written by an author distinct from the author of chapters 3–14 is easily seen. To begin with, in 4 Ezra, Ezra proclaims over and over again that the people Israel has kept the covenant and the laws to the best of its ability. If Israel has not been perfect in obedience, only God is at fault, for God has given it laws and commandments but not the ability to keep them:

> 19 Your glory passed through the four gates of fire and earthquake and wind and ice, to give the law to the descendants of Jacob, and your commandments to the posterity of Israel.
> 20 Yet you did not take away their evil heart from them, so that your law might produce fruit in them.
> 21 For the first Adam, burdened with an evil heart, transgressed and was overcome, as were also all who were descended from him. (4 Ezra 3:19–21)

Even so, the people Israel has kept the laws far better than any other nation, yet they are not rewarded for it:

> 32 Has another nation known you besides Israel? Or what tribes have so believed the covenants as these tribes of Jacob?
> 33 Yet their reward has not appeared and their labor has borne no fruit. For I have traveled widely among the nations and have seen that they abound in wealth, though they are unmindful of your commandments.
> 34 Now therefore weigh in a balance our iniquities and those of the inhabitants of the world; and it will be found which way the turn of the scale will incline. (4 Ezra 3:32–34)

In contrast, the author of chapters 1 and 2 describes Israel's sins as so calamitous that God has rejected Israel and has turned to another people, the Gentiles:

> What shall I do to you, O Jacob? You, Judah, would not obey me. I will turn to other nations and will give them my name, so that they may keep my statutes.
> 25 Because you have forsaken me, I also will forsake you. When you beg mercy of me, I will show you no mercy.
> 26 When you call to me, I will not listen to you; for you have defiled your hands with blood, and your feet are swift to commit murder.
> 27 It is not as though you had forsaken me; you have forsaken yourselves, says the Lord. (5 Ezra 1:24–27)

Because of their sins, the people Israel will be driven out to be replaced by others deemed more worthy:

> I gathered you as a hen gathers her chicks under her wings.
> But now, what shall I do to you? I will cast you out from my presence.
> [31] When you offer oblations to me, I will turn my face from you; for I have rejected your festal days, and new moons, and circumcisions of the flesh. . . .
> [33] "Thus says the Lord Almighty: Your house is desolate; I will drive you out as the wind drives straw;
> [35] I will give your houses to a people that will come, who without having heard me will believe. Those to whom I have shown no signs will do what I have commanded.
> [36] They have seen no prophets, yet will recall their former state.
> [37] I call to witness the gratitude of the people that is to come, whose children rejoice with gladness; though they do not see me with bodily eyes, yet with the spirit they will believe the things I have said. (5 Ezra 1:31, 33, 35–37)

This passage relies on Matthew 23:37 (= Luke 13:34): "How often have I desired to gather your children together as a hen gathers her brood under her wings, and you were not willing!" (Matt. 23:37) The ultimate punishment for this Christian author is for ethnic Israel to lose its homeland and to be scattered among the nations with pariah status: "Let them be scattered among the nations; let their names be blotted out from the earth, because they have despised my covenant" (5 Ezra 2:7).

The relationship that God had with Israel is now to be replaced by a relationship with a new people. Everything that had been Israel's is taken from them and given to these others, now called "my people," a people that is not Israel. "Thus says the Lord to Ezra: "Tell *my people* that I will give them the kingdom of Jerusalem, which I was going to give to Israel. Moreover, I will take back to myself their glory, and will give to these others the everlasting habitations, which I had prepared for Israel" (5 Ezra 2:10–11, emphasis added).

In this text, Ezra does not lament or argue with God to prevent the covenant with Israel from being annulled. He says not a word, since to this author Ezra is a member of this new people. Ezra warns God's new people that the end of the present world is at hand, that the material world is passing away, and that a new world is upon them. Give up the joys of the present age, he says, and turn to the joys of the new age. "Therefore I (= Ezra) say to you, to you nations that hear and understand, 'Wait for your shepherd; he will give you everlasting rest, because he, who comes at the end of the age, is close at hand. Be ready for the rewards of the kingdom, because perpetual light will shine on you forevermore. Flee from the shadow of this age, receive the joy of your glory; I publicly call on my savior to witness'" (5 Ezra 2:34–36). This notion that the end of the present age is close at hand as indicated by the savior's (Jesus's) immanent return is a common New Testament message:

> The end of all things is near, therefore be serious and discipline yourselves for the sake of your prayers. (1 Peter 4:7)

> The time is fulfilled, and the kingdom of God has come near; repent, and believe in the good news. (Mark 1:15)

> And he said to them, "Truly I tell you, there are some standing here who will not taste death until they see that the kingdom of God has come with power." (Mark 9:1 = Matt. 16:28 = Luke 9:27)

Ezra then sees a vision of a crowd of people praising the Lord with song. In the middle of the throng is a young man who puts crowns on the head of each of them.

> I, Ezra, saw on Mount Zion a great multitude that I could not number, and they all were praising the Lord with songs.
> 43 In their midst was a young man of great stature, taller than any of the others, and on the head of each of them he placed a crown, but he was more exalted than they. I was held spellbound.
> 44 Then I asked an angel, "Who are these, my lord?"
> 45 He answered and said to me, "These are they who have put off mortal clothing and have put on the immortal, and have confessed the name of God. Now they are being crowned, and receive palms."
> 46 Then I said to the angel, "Who is that young man who is placing crowns on them and putting palms in their hands?"
> 47 He answered and said to me, "He is the Son of God, whom they confessed in the world." (5 Ezra 2:42–47).

Those being crowned with victory are not the "dead in Christ" (1 Thess. 4:16) but those who are still alive, since they still have the choice to flee from the shadow of this age (5 Ezra 2:36). These are the ones who have put off their mortal bodies and put on immortality, not as a consequence of dying but as a consequence of baptism into the immortal body of Christ.[1] This reflects the words of Paul:

> 53 This perishable body must put on imperishability, and this mortal body must put on immortality.
> 54 When this perishable body puts on imperishability, and this mortal body puts on immortality, then the saying that is written will be fulfilled: "Death has been swallowed up in victory."
> 55 "Where, O death, is your victory? Where, O death, is your sting?"
> 56 The sting of death is sin, and the power of sin is the law.
> 57 But thanks be to God, who gives us victory [over death] through our Lord Jesus Christ. (1 Cor. 15:52–57)

The moment being celebrated in this scene in 5 Ezra is this victory. The people have not tasted death but are seeing the kingdom of God, Christ's return to earth.

Kraft suggests that 5 Ezra is at base a Jewish work with only slight Christian additions.[2] He finds it similar to material found in the prophetic writings of Jeremiah, Isaiah, and Hosea in which God states that he is going to abandon his people because they have abandoned him and that he will turn them over to another.[3] Certainly Hosea and Amos predict that God will turn his people over to the conquering Assyrians, while Jeremiah predicts it will be to the conquering Babylonians. Never, however, does God declare that he is going to place his name on another people or that he will replace his covenant with the Jewish people with a new people. As Bergren states, "It is a *sine qua non* of Jewish biblical ideology that God's people are not abandoned [in spite of all their punishments and humiliations] and that the promise made to them by God is irrefutable."[4] This is certainly not the case in 5 Ezra, where God's name is placed on another people and the covenantal promises transferred to them. This is standard Christian supersessionism.

Bergren points out the long tradition of intra-Jewish polemic both within the Bible and outside it.[5] Jeremiah 24 and Ezekiel 11 distinguish the remnant in Babylon from those in Judah who will be destroyed in the Babylonian conquest. Nevertheless, as Bergren shows, both groups, the saved and the destroyed, are part of the same people Israel. There is no "new people" who did not know God and had not participated in the Exodus to whom the covenant is now being transferred as we see in 5 Ezra. Thus we may conclude that 5 Ezra is a thoroughly Christian document, whose purpose is to encourage the new Christians that they are the new people of God and have replaced ethnic Israel in God's covenant.

Date and Provenance

This text must be seen as part of a general polemic against Judean self-understanding, so it is fruitful to ask when such a polemic would have been most helpful to the nascent Christian community. The fact that the Christian author of these chapters has clearly piggybacked onto 4 Ezra demands a date in the second century C.E. at the earliest. It is striking that this author would appropriate 4 Ezra when the image of the Messiah in it is so starkly different from that presented in the Gospels. The first half of the second century C.E. seems to have been a time when Christian theologians were fiercely debating the nature of the Messiah and the divinity of Christ.[6] The acceptance of this work into Christian literature could not have been maintained once the character of the Messiah was solidified. Moreover, the second century was the time of a steadily emerging sense of Christians as a "third race," neither Jews nor Gentiles.[7] While certainty cannot be possible, this work seems to belong to the second quarter of the second century.

Sixth Ezra—A Tumultuous Conclusion

Author

Whereas 4 Ezra was clearly written by a Jew and 5 Ezra by a Christian, the identity of 6 Ezra's author is not so clear.[8] There is a reference to "my people" (15:1, 10; 16:40), to "my elect" (15:21; 16:73, 74), and to "my chosen" (15:53, 56), but it is not certain whether this refers to Jews or to Christians who have appropriated the title. Sixth Ezra relates a warning given by God apparently to Ezra against all the unbelievers (15:4) and against the sinners who spill innocent and righteous blood (15:8). God states that "my people" are being led like a flock to the slaughter in the land of Egypt (15:10) and that he himself will bring them out and will destroy all its land (15:11). Moreover, just as all "the kings of the earth" do to "my elect," so will he do to these sinners to repay them (15:21). God will hand over to death and slaughter all who sin against him and who do not observe his commandments (15:24–26).

The rest of these two chapters describes impending wars, bloodshed, destruction, and death in Babylon and Asia, Egypt and Syria (16:1), followed by famine for those who remain alive. These are the punishments for the sinful "kings of the earth" who persecute "my elect." This persecution may refer to the edicts of the Roman emperors Decius (249–251 C.E.) and Valerian (253–259 C.E.). Decius ordered everyone to sacrifice to the old Roman gods, an order rigorously enforced by local commissioners chosen for the purpose from local city councils.[9] Compliant participants received a certificate that they had obeyed the order. These certificates attested to the bearer's lifelong piety to the gods and his act of sacrifice in the presence of the commissioner. One such certificate reads as follows: "To those appointed to see to the sacrifices: From Aurelia Charis of the Egyptian village of Theadelphia. I have always continued to sacrifice and show piety to the gods and now, in your presence, I have poured a libation and sacrificed and eaten some of the sacrificial meat. I request you to certify this for me below."[10]

Executions followed for those unwilling to comply. Pope Fabian was among the first to be killed, on January 20, 250.[11] Trials and executions of Christians followed throughout the empire. While the persecutions lapsed for a couple of years after Decius's death, they resumed again under Valerian. In the years 257–258, Valerian and Gallienus, his son and co-regent, sent letters to all the provincial governors ordering that bishops and elders of the Christian churches be punished and that no Christians be allowed to hold a meeting or enter a cemetery. If they did, they were to be executed. A second letter ordered death, exile, or forced labor for Christians of various classes.[12] This period very likely forms the backdrop of the cries for vengeance on the kings of the earth that we read in 6 Ezra. Since Judeans were grandfathered in and exempt from these draconian laws, the author would have been a Christian.

Date

One passage in particular has been seized upon by scholars as a key to the book's date (15:28–33):[13]

> For God knows all who sin against him; therefore he will hand them over to death and slaughter.
>
> Already calamities have come upon the whole earth, and you shall remain in them; God will not deliver you, because you have sinned against him.
>
> See the terrifying sight, appearing from the east!
>
> The nations of the dragons of Arabia shall come out with many chariots, and from the day that they set out, their hissing shall spread over the earth, so that all who hear them will fear and tremble.
>
> The Carmonians, raging in wrath, shall go forth from the forest, and with great power they shall come and engage them in battle, devastating a portion of the land of the Assyrians with their teeth.
>
> And after that the dragons, remembering their nature, shall become still stronger; and when they combine in great power and turn to pursue them [the Assyrians], then these [the pursued] shall be disorganized and silenced by their [the dragons'] power, and shall turn and flee.
>
> And in the land of the Assyrians a waylayer shall lurk in ambush and devour one of them, and fear and trembling shall come upon their army, and indecision upon their kings.

According to von Gutschmid, this refers to one and only one possible series of historical events, the battles between Odenathus of Palmyra and Shapur I, the Sassanid (Persian) king, which took place between 260 and 267 C.E.[14] To von Gutschmid, the dragons of Arabia refer to Odenathus, since he was called "Prince of the Saracens [of the Arabs]" by the historians Procopius and Malalas, both writing in the sixth century.[15] The Carmonians, on the other hand, represented to von Gutschmid the Sassanid king Shapur I. Carmania or Carmonia (Kermān) lay directly east of the Persian province of Fars, on the Gulf of Oman, and was among the first provinces, after Fars itself, that Ardashir, Shapur's father, captured in his rebellion against the Parthians in 224.[16]

Although von Gutschmid's dating may be correct, his reasons may not be. To begin with, inscriptions recently found show Odenathus to have been the grandson of one Vaballathus Nasor and the son of one Hairan. Judging by these names, we can conclude that he was of Aramean, not Arab, descent.[17] Second, the hissing dragons and their chariots most likely refer to the Sassanid Persians themselves, not Palmyra. According to the historian Ammianus Marcellinus (ca. 325–391), Ardashir, the son of Sassan, founder of the Sassanid Empire, went to war "surrounded by dragons, woven out of purple thread and bound to the golden and

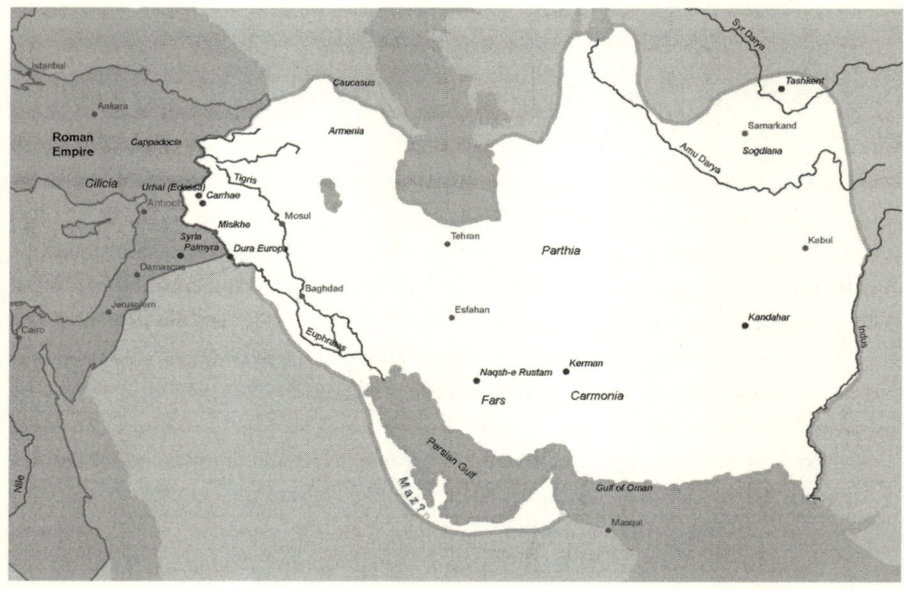

Map of the Sassanid Empire under King Shapur I. Map courtesy of Karl Longstreth, University of Michigan, Map Library.

jeweled tops of spears, with wide mouths open to the breeze and hence hissing as if roused by anger, and leaving their tails winding in the wind."[18]

In fact, the Persian Empire included Arabs even from the beginning of the conquest by Cyrus the Great. The satrapy Maka of the Achaemenid Empire is listed in the Behistun inscription among those kingdoms already subject to Darius when he first claimed the throne (I:6). It was included in the later Parthian and Sassanian Empires as Mazun and corresponds to modern Bahrain, Qatar, and United Arab Emirates, plus the northern half of Oman.[19] The "nations of the Dragons of Arabia" (15:29) must therefore refer to the Sassanid Persians of Fars and Mazun, and the Carmonians coming out of the forest must also have been part of the Sassanid Empire, fighting alongside the Persian dragons, not against them.

The land of Assyria that the Persian forces are said to have devastated is the upper Euphrates valley taken from Rome by Ardashir. In 241 Ardashir died, leaving the empire to his son Shapur I, who, after a series of battles, extended the Sassanid Empire north to the Caucasus, east to Kandahar, Sogdiana, and Tashkent, west to Syria and even to Cappodocia. From Shapur's own inscription at Naqsh-e Rustam, we have a description of his first campaign against Rome in 244 and a reference to the death of the Roman emperor Gordion III in battle: "When at first we had become established in the empire, Gordian Caesar raised in all of the Roman Empire a force from the Goth and German realms and marched on Babylonia [Asuristan] against the Empire of Iran and against us. On the border of Babylonia at Misikhe, a great 'frontal' battle occurred. Gordian Caesar was killed and the Roman force was destroyed. And the Romans made Philip, Caesar. Then Philip Caesar came to us for terms, and to ransom their lives, gave us 500,000 denars, and became tributary to us. And for this reason we have renamed Misikhe Peroz-Shapur [Shapur bursts out]."[20]

Shapur's second campaign, probably in the early 250s, is described in the same inscription. In this campaign the Persians reached the very shores of the Mediterranean Sea and marched up into Armenia and Cappadocia: "And Caesar lied again and did wrong to Armenia. Then we attacked the Roman Empire and annihilated at Barbalissos a Roman force of 60,000. Syria and the environs of Syria we burned, ruined and pillaged all. In this one campaign we conquered of the Roman Empire fortresses and towns: [town list], a total of 37 towns with surrounding villages." This assault into Asia Minor is reflected in the oracle against Asia that is described in 6 Ezra as participating in Rome's deceitful acts (referred to as Babylon in these post-70 texts):

> And you, Asia, who share in the splendor of Babylon and the glory of her person,
> 47 woe to you, miserable wretch! For you have made yourself like her; you have decked out your daughters for prostitution to please and glory in your lovers, who have always lusted after you.
> 48 You have imitated that hateful one in all her deeds and devices. Therefore God says,
> 49 I will send evils upon you: widowhood, poverty, famine, sword, and pestilence, bringing ruin to your houses, bringing destruction and death. (6 Ezra 15:46–49)

The evils predicted for Asia here are a description of Shapur's onslaught into Armenia and Cappadocia.

Shapur's description of his third campaign notes the capture of the emperor Valerian himself in 259.

> In the third campaign, when we attacked Carrhae and Urhai [Edessa] and were besieging Carrhae and Edessa, Valerian Caesar marched against us. He had with him a force of 70,000. . . .
>
> And beyond Carrhae and Edessa we had a great battle with Valerian Caesar. We made prisoner ourselves with our own hands Valerian Caesar and the others, chiefs of that army, the praetorian prefect, senators; we made all prisoners and deported them to Persis.
>
> And Syria, Cilicia and Cappadocia we burned, ruined and pillaged.

These conquests of Shapur deep into what had been Roman territory, culminating in the ignominious defeat of the vaunted Roman army and the capture of the emperor himself, must have thrilled Christians (and Jews) everywhere and sparked within them the certain knowledge of God's justice.

The rest of 6 Ezra predicts the fall of Rome:

> 34 See the clouds from the east, and from the north to the south! Their appearance is exceedingly threatening, full of wrath and storm.
> 35 They shall clash against one another and shall pour out a heavy tempest on the earth, and their own tempest; and there shall be blood from the sword as high as a horse's belly. . . .
> 40 Great and mighty clouds, full of wrath and tempest, shall rise and destroy all the earth and its inhabitants, and shall pour out upon every high and lofty place a
> terrible tempest, 41 fire and hail and flying swords and floods of water, so that all
> the fields and all the streams shall be filled with the abundance of those waters.
> 42 They shall destroy cities and walls, mountains and hills, trees of the forests, and grass of the meadows, and their grain. (6 Ezra 15:34–35, 40–42)

Most important is the last verse of this passage (15:43), which states: "*et transibunt constanter usque Babylonem et exterent eam*" (They shall go on steadily to Babylon and blot it out). Babylon is the code word for Rome in Jewish and Christian texts after the destruction of the second temple in 70 C.E. This verse describes an expectation that the Sassanid armies will march up to Rome itself and destroy it, that God will avenge his people (6 Ezra 16:8–13):

> The Lord God sends calamities, and who will drive them away?
> 9 Fire will go forth from his wrath, and who is there to quench it?
> 10 He will flash lightning, and who will not be afraid? He will thunder, and who
> will not be terrified? 11 The Lord will threaten, and who will not be utterly shattered at his presence?
> 12 The earth and its foundations quake, the sea is churned up from the depths, and its waves and the fish with them shall be troubled at the presence of the Lord and the glory of his power.
> 13 For his right hand that bends the bow is strong, and his arrows that he shoots are sharp and when they are shot to the ends of the world will not miss once.

This was not to be. In 267 Odenathus of Palmyra pushed the Sassanids back to the Tigris, where they remained.[21] We can thus agree about the date of 6 Ezra and fix it to between 259, the year of Valerian's capture, and 267, the year of Shapur's defeat, when hope still bloomed for God's justice and Rome's demise.

It is difficult to say why the author chose to append his two chapters to 4 Ezra, except that it may reflect the prediction in it of the demise of Rome and the rule of one whom those who inhabit the earth do not expect, though this prediction itself is not repeated in 6 Ezra:

> Now concerning the signs: lo, the days are coming when those who inhabit the earth shall be seized with great terror, and the way of truth shall be hidden, and the land shall be barren of faith.

> 2 Unrighteousness shall be increased beyond what you yourself see, and beyond what you heard of formerly.
>
> 3 And the land that you now see ruling shall be a trackless waste, and people shall see it desolate.
>
> 4 But if the Most High grants that you live, you shall see it thrown into confusion after the third period; and the sun shall suddenly begin to shine at night, and the moon during the day.
>
> 5 Blood shall drip from wood, and the stone shall utter its voice; the peoples shall be troubled, and the stars shall fall.
>
> 6 And one shall reign whom those who inhabit the earth do not expect, and the birds shall fly away together. (4 Ezra 5:1–6)

The possibility of Rome's immanent destruction has made other views of God's justice irrelevant. The author assumes that the evil empire will receive its just reward right here on earth, in the present time, and in the present place.

7

Ezra Ascends to Heaven and Goes to Hell

As is witnessed by the many translations of 4 Ezra and by its Christian additions at the beginning and at the end of the book, the character of Ezra in 4 Ezra has resonated with a good many Christian writers throughout antiquity. The attraction may have been in the way in which he pleads for sinners. In 4 Ezra, Ezra asks, for example:

> "O sovereign Lord, I said then and I say now: Blessed are those who are alive and keep your commandments!
> 46 But what of those for whom I prayed? For who among the living is there that has not sinned, or who is there among mortals that has not transgressed your covenant?
> 47 And now I see that the world to come will bring delight to few, but torments to many.
> 48 For an evil heart has grown up in us, which has alienated us from God, and has brought us into corruption and the ways of death, and has shown us the paths of perdition and removed us far from life—and that not merely for a few but for almost all who have been created." (4 Ezra 7:45–48)

It is not only a few who have sinned but almost all who have been created. "What of them?" Ezra asks. It may have been the inadequacy of the answers given to Ezra's questions in 4 Ezra that led later Christian writers not only to make the various translations and rewritings that are discussed in Appendix 2 but also to employ the Ezra figure to speculate further on the nature of God's justice. Among their works are the *Greek Apocalypse of Ezra,* the Latin *Vision of the Blessed Ezra,* the Armenian *Questions of Ezra,* the *Apocalypse of Sedrach,* two additional political apocalypses, one in Syriac and one in Ethiopic, and a *kalandologion,* or almanac, attributed to Ezra, called *The Revelation of Ezra.* These are the focus of this chapter.

The Greek Apocalypse of Ezra

The Greek Apocalypse of Ezra was written in Greek sometime between the fourth and ninth centuries.[1] It is, according to Stone, a Christian work of the Byzantine apocalyptic tradition.[2] In it, Ezra, now called the Holy Prophet and Beloved of God (*Gk. Apoc. Ezra* 1:1), prays to be shown the divine mysteries. The archangel

Hell in the Garden of Delights. From the *Hortus deliciarum,* Herrad of Landsberg (about 1180).

Michael and Raphael, the commander of the heavenly host, appear to Ezra at night and bid him fast, which he does, first for 70 weeks and then for an additional 120, and he sees the mysteries of God and all his angels. He tells the angels that he wishes to enter a [legal] plea on behalf of the "Christian race": "And I said to them: 'I wish to plead before God about the race of the Christians. It is better for a man not to be born rather than to come into the world'" (*Gk. Apoc. Ezra* 1:6). This plea is drawn from 4 Ezra, where it occurs many times (for example, 5:35; 7:63, 65). Accordingly, Ezra is taken up into the first heaven and is shown the place of judgments. This transport to the divine realms differs completely from the story as told in 4 Ezra. In 4 Ezra, Ezra is either in his house (chapters 1–6) or in an empty field (chapters 7–14). He has a vision of the heavenly Jerusalem, and in his vision he enters the temple and the abode of God, but physically he remains in the field. However, here in the *Greek Apocalypse of Ezra* and in the subsequent apocalypses, Ezra is actually taken first into the upper and then into the lower realms. These detailed tours of heaven and hell were apparently heavily influenced by the *Apocalypse of Paul,* a late-fourth-century text.[3]

In the first heaven Ezra sees a great host of angels, and they show him the trials and the judgments. There he hears a voice crying out: "Have pity on us, Ezra elect of God." Ezra replies: "Woe to sinners when they see the righteous one elevated above angels and they themselves are headed for the Gehenna of fire!" (*Gk. Apoc. Ezra* 1:9). Part of the punishment of those bound for the fires of Gehenna includes seeing the righteous bound for heaven, while they themselves are bound for hell. Indeed, in 4 Ezra (7:83) this is one of the ways that souls suffer after being separated from the body and before entering into their habitations to wait for the final judgment.

Although 4 Ezra (7.93) predicts that the righteous will feel joy when they compare their own fortune to the punishment awaiting the ungodly, Ezra himself feels no joy. Rather, he is moved to pity. Then follows the same themes as we have seen in 4 Ezra, for Ezra replies that it is not merciful of God to reward only the righteous. True mercy is pardoning the iniquitous. Ezra pleads with God to pity the sinners, for they too are God's handiwork. "And Ezra said: 'Have mercy on the works of your hands, you who are compassionate, and of great mercy'" (*Gk. Apoc. Ezra* 1:10).

This alludes to another of the main themes of 4 Ezra: God made mankind, hemmed him in with laws and commandments, yet did not give him the strength to observe them. Out of his great pity for the sufferers, Ezra offers himself as a substitute (*Gk. Apoc. Ezra* 1:11): "Condemn me rather than the souls of the sinners; for it is better that one soul should he punished, than that the whole world should come to destruction." God answers (*Gk. Apoc. Ezra* 1:12) that he is indeed merciful but only to the righteous: "And God said: 'I will give rest in paradise to the righteous, for I am merciful.'" But Ezra complains again that it is not mercy to confer benefits on the righteous, since they have earned their benefits. "And Ezra said: 'Lord, why do you confer benefits [only] on the righteous? Have mercy on the sinners, for we know that you are merciful'" (*Gk. Apoc. Ezra* 1:10–15). God answers: "I do not see how I can have mercy upon them" (1:16), and Ezra laments: "It is good for a man not to be born. It is good not to be in life. The irrational [animals] are better than man, because they have no punishment; but you have taken us, and given us up to condemnation" (*Gk. Apoc. Ezra* 1:21–23). Ezra continues: "Woe to the sinners in the world to come, because their punishment is endless, and the flame unquenchable" (*Gk. Apoc. Ezra* 1:24).

These are the same themes as in 4 Ezra—the animals are better off than mankind, since they are not judged, and it would have been better for man if he had not been born (4 Ezra 7:65–66). God is not merciful if he accepts only the righteous; true mercy is pardoning the sinner. It is notable that in this patently Christian work there is no reference to the role of Christ in saving the sinner. Ezra offers himself as a substitute for the sinners (1:11), and he is turned down, but the notion of Christ's substitutionary atonement for Christians who are languishing in hell is not a feature of this author's theology.

Ezra asks God: "Where is your long-suffering [nature]"? And God answers: "As I have made night and day, I have made the righteous and the sinner; and the sinner should have lived like the righteous" (*Gk. Apoc. Ezra* 2:9). This is like saying that the night should act like the day, an impossibility. So again God creates man's sinful nature and then punishes him for it.

Ezra cries out: "Have mercy, O Lord, upon sinners; have mercy upon your own creatures; have pity upon your own work" (*Gk. Apoc. Ezra* 2:23). God answers: "How can I have mercy upon them, when they gave me vinegar and gall to drink?" (*Gk. Apoc. Ezra* 2:24–25). God in this text is Jesus; nevertheless, we have here in the *Greek Apocalypse of Ezra,* as in 4 Ezra, a god without mercy who condemns those who have sinned. This attitude toward the sinner is not unknown in New Testament texts, such as 2 Peter 2:20–22: "For if, after they have escaped the defilements of the world through the knowledge of our Lord and Savior Jesus Christ, they are again entangled in them and overpowered, the last state has become worse for them than the first. For it would have been better for them never to have known the way of righteousness than, after knowing it, to turn back from the holy commandment that was passed on to them. It has happened to them according to the true proverb, 'The dog turns back to its own vomit,' and, 'The sow is washed only to wallow in the mud.'" Similarly in 1 John 3:8–9:

> Everyone who commits sin is a child of the devil; for the devil has been sinning from the beginning. The Son of God was revealed for this purpose, to destroy the works of the devil.
>
> 9 Those who have been born of God do not sin, because God's seed abides in them; they cannot sin, because they have been born of God.
>
> 10 The children of God and the children of the devil are revealed in this way: all who do not do what is right are not from God, nor are those who do not love their brothers and sisters. (1 John 3:10)

While prevalent in early Christian thought, the image of an unforgiving god in the *Greek Apocalypse of Ezra* is certainly taken over from 4 Ezra. In 4 Ezra, however, the view that God is unforgiving was a response to the Roman destruction of Jerusalem in 70 C.E. What calamitous Byzantine event could have occurred in the early Middle Ages that would have encouraged a vision of a god so totally lacking in mercy? It may have been the Plague of Justinian, the bubonic plague, which began in 542 C.E. Named after the Byzantine emperor Justinian I, it is reputed to have killed up to ten thousand people a day in Constantinople alone. Tombs already in existence were full, and so great pits were dug that could hold 70,000 corpses each. Then Justinian hired men to collect the dead. When the pits overflowed, corpses were heaped inside the towers on the walls where they putrefied with a stench that pervaded the whole city.[4] This horror certainly would have evoked the conviction of a revengeful and unmerciful god. Martha Himmelfarb conjectures that, "As for natural disaster, the contemporary historian Agathias describes the widespread fear and sense of eschatological doom in response to the earthquakes that shook Constantinople in 557 and 558, causing the collapse of the main dome of the great church of Hagia Sophia."[5] The confluence of the plague and the earthquake could certainly have inspired apocalypses in mid-sixth-century Constantinople.

Ezra asks when the day of judgment will come (*Gk. Apoc. Ezra* 3:5). God answers: "When you see that brother gives up brother to death, and that children will rise up against their parents, and that a woman forsakes her own husband, and when nation will rise up against nation in war, then will you know that the end is near. For then neither brother pities brother, nor man wife, nor children parents, nor friends friends, nor a slave his lord; for he who is the Adversary of men will come up from Tartarus, and will show men many things" (*Gk. Apoc. Ezra* 3:12–15).[6]

This description of the end of the present age is similar to that seen in 4 Ezra (6:24; 9:1–3), except for the Christian notion of the Adversary, the Antichrist, which does not appear in it. At this point in the *Greek Apocalypse of Ezra,* God says: "I will stretch forth my hand, and lay hold of the world by the four quarters, and bring them all together into the valley of Jehoshaphat, and I will wipe out the race of men, so that the world will be no more" (*Gk. Apoc. Ezra* 3:6). In contrast to 4 Ezra, in the *Greek Apocalypse of Ezra* this final annihilation of the race of men is not prefigured by the Anointed One who destroys only the wicked but saves the righteous. Rather, here it is God himself who is the Destroyer, and it is all of mankind that he destroys; no one is saved. Ezra asks, if so, if everyone is dead, "how will your right hand be glorified," and God answers: "I will be glorified by my angels" (3:8). "If this was your plan," Ezra asks, "why did you create mankind?" (3:9), but to this he receives no answer.

Ezra asks next to see those sinners suffering in the lowest parts of Tartarus, the lowest parts of the underworld (4:5). Accordingly, Michael, Gabriel, and thirty-four other angels guide Ezra down 585 steps into the underworld. At this point Ezra sees an old man sitting on a fiery throne. It is Herod, who ordered the murder of infants two years old and younger (4:9–12). Ezra is led down another thirty steps to see sinners in boiling fire (4:13) and then descends many more steps to see old men, eavesdroppers, with fiery axels on their ears (4:16). Another five hundred steps down leads to more sinners suffering in the consuming fire (4:20), and down further still Ezra sees a man hanging by his eyelids, with an angel beating him, because he had looked lustfully at a member of his own family.

In contrast to 4 Ezra, here we see punishments of the souls prior to the final Judgment Day. Rather than, as in 4 Ezra (7:29–36), their punishment right after death being limited to a vision of their own prospective suffering and the reward of the righteous after the Day of Judgment, here the souls are punished immediately upon dying. Bauckham suggests that sometime over the first and second centuries C.E. the view toward the fate of the dead changed, so that their punishments (or rewards) begin right away, rather than their waiting in quiet habitations for the Judgment Day.[7] This may have resulted from the fact that Judgment Day was so long in coming after Jesus's death and resurrection.

After reaching the lowest level of hell, the angels lead Ezra to the north, where he sees a man restrained by iron bars (*Gk. Apoc. Ezra* 4:25). He is told that this is the Antichrist (4:31), who claims to be the Son of God (4:27). He wears an inscription: "Antichrist: This one had been exalted up to heaven, but he will descend as far as Hades" (*Gk. Apoc. Ezra* 4:32). The reference to restraining the Antichrist may be a reference to 2 Thessalonians 2:3–8:

> Let no one deceive you in any way; for that day will not come unless the rebellion comes first and the Lawless One is revealed, the one destined for destruction. He opposes and exalts himself above every so-called god or object of worship, so that he takes his seat in the temple of God, declaring himself to be God.
>
> [5] Do you not remember that I told you these things when I was still with you? [6] And you know what is now restraining him, so that he may be revealed when his time comes. [7] For the mystery of lawlessness is already at work, but only until the one who now restrains it is removed. [8] And then the lawless one will be revealed. (2 Thess. 2:3–8)

In the *Greek Apocalypse of Ezra,* the revelation of the Antichrist is followed by the resurrection of the dead: "And after this a trumpet, and the tombs will be opened, and the dead will be raised incorruptible [ἄφθαρτοι]" (*Gr. Apoc. Ezra* 4:36).

The reference to the trumpet is likely based on Paul's First Letter to the Thessalonians: "For the Lord himself, with a cry of command, with the archangel's call and with the sound of God's trumpet, will descend from heaven, and the dead in Christ will rise first. Then we who are alive, who are left, will be caught up in the clouds together with them to meet the Lord in the air; and so we will be with the Lord forever" (1 Thess 4:16–17).

The notion of being raised in an incorruptible body, on the other hand, is found in Paul's First Letter to the Corinthians: "So it is with the resurrection of the dead. What is sown is corruptible, what is raised is incorruptible [ἀφθαρσίᾳ]. It is sown in dishonor, it is raised in glory. It is sown in weakness, it is raised in power. It is sown a physical body, it is raised a spiritual body. If there is a physical body, there is also a spiritual body" (1 Cor. 15:42–44) . The Adversary, seeing the resurrection of the dead, will hide himself in darkness (*Gr. Apoc. Ezra* 4:37). Then the heaven and the earth and the sea will perish (4:39) because they had hidden him.

After seeing more sinners in torments, a cloud comes and seizes Ezra, and he is taken up into heaven, where he sees God pronouncing many more judgments and condemnations (*Gk. Apoc. Ezra* 5:1–9). He protests, asking God: "Where is your goodness?" God answers that he has prepared everything for man, but man does not keep his commandments (*Gk. Apoc. Ezra* 5:18–19). He will not pardon the sinners, those who transgress.

Finally it is time for Ezra too to die. The angels come for his soul (*Gk. Apoc. Ezra* 6:3), but he resists. God finally tells his only begotten Son to go with a host of angels and receive Ezra's soul (6:16). When it becomes clear to Ezra that he is about to die, he breaks into tears: "Woe is me, woe is me, that I am going to be consumed by worms! Weep, all you holy ones and you righteous ones for me, who have pleaded much, and who am delivered up to death. Weep for me, all you saints and you righteous, because I have gone to the pit of Hades" (*Gk. Apoc. Ezra* 6:23–26). It is clear that Ezra fears the torments that he has seen. He knows that he too has sinned and that there is no respite or safety for him in the grave.

God tries to reassure him and describes his experience in this life: "And God said to him: 'Listen, Ezra, my beloved. I, who am immortal, endured a cross; I tasted vinegar and gall; I was laid in a tomb, and I raised up my chosen ones; I called Adam up out of Hades, that [I might save] the race of men. Do not therefore be afraid of death: for that which is from me—that is to say, the soul—goes to heaven; and that which is from the earth—that is to say, the body—goes to the earth, from which it was taken'" (*Gk. Apoc. Ezra* 7:1–3). This is a clear statement of the separation of body and soul: the body lies in the dust, while the soul receives its award or punishment immediately and endures it until the time of the resurrection of the body (*Gk Apoc. Ezra* 4:36). We are not told, however, who is to be resurrected—everyone or only those who have escaped the predicted total destruction (*Gk. Apoc. Ezra* 3:6).

But Ezra is still terrified: "And the prophet said: 'Woe is me! Woe is me! What will I set about? What will I do? I know not'" (*Gk. Apoc. Ezra* 7:4). Ezra pleads again for God to give his blessing to all who read and copy and preserve this book and to forget the sins of each on the day of his judgment, and God relents, promising that their sins will be forgotten but that the souls of those who do not believe this book will be burned like those in Sodom and Gomorrah (7:5–13).

What must be believed in this book, evidently, is not necessarily the precise description of hell that Ezra sees but rather that he who sins will be punished for his sins. Perhaps to the author, believing this may be enough to redeem his soul, even though, being mortal, he will sin.

While the text is obviously Christian as it now exists, several scholars find evidence of a Jewish original. They argue that the obvious Christian sentences or paragraphs are simply Christian insertions into an original Jewish text. Denis states that "certain typically Judeo-Hellenistic themes cannot be Christian, for example God's lack of mercy."[8] This is certainly an odd statement in view of the quotations cited earlier from 2 Peter and 1 John, in view of the fact that the pessimism in all these tours of hell of the Ezra cycle likely go back to the Apocalypses of Peter and of Paul,[9] and when we consider that 4 Ezra itself was absorbed into Christian literature and so into Christian thought (demonstrated by the existence of 5 and 6 Ezra and the numerous translations). These Christian additions and translations indicate that the themes of God's lack of mercy could not have been considered foreign or alien to their Christian authors. Indeed, the other themes too that Denis points to as "not possibly Christian" are all in 4 Ezra—predestination, the necessity of fulfilling the times before the end can come, the interrogation and the suit against God, as well as the claim that it would be better for man not to be born—and so have become Christian with the absorption of 4 Ezra. Kraft cautions us against excluding from the category "Christian" materials in a Christian text that do not betray "characteristically Christian" traits as if we knew exactly what those traits were.[10] To do so is to engage in circular reasoning.

The Vision of the Blessed Ezra

Another Christian work that grew out of the biblical character of Ezra and out of the apocalyptic seer of 4 Ezra is *The Vision of the Blessed Ezra,* extant only in Latin but very likely originally written in Greek sometime between the fourth and the end of the sixth centuries C.E.[11] Yarbro Collins sees this text as simply a shorter Latin version of the *Greek Apocalypse of Ezra,* so we should perhaps date it a little later.[12] This shorter version is only one chapter long. It begins abruptly with Ezra's pleas that he might not be frightened when he sees the judgments of the sinners. He is then granted seven angels to lead him down to Tartarus. As in the *Greek Apocalypse,* they lead him down by stages. At each stage Ezra witnesses people suffering frightful torments, and at each stage Ezra pleads that God might have mercy on their souls. Unlike the previous apocalypses discussed, the just are seen striding easily through the gates of hell on their way to heaven, while the sinners are ensnared in them, attacked by dogs or lions. God responds to Ezra's pleas by saying that the sinners are receiving justice according to their deeds. Finally Ezra is lifted into heaven and sees a multitude of angels, and they too ask him to pray to the Lord on behalf of the sinners. Ezra does so, but God again replies that they are requited according to their works. As elsewhere in these apocalypses, Ezra complains that God shows more clemency to the animals that eat the grass and do not praise God than to mankind, whom God tortures eternally (*The Vision of the Blessed Ezra* 60). God replies that sinners may be saved on account of their confession of sins, their penitence, and their almsgiving. There is no reference to either the Christ or the Antichrist in this text,[13] but we do see a first inkling that the sacraments of the Church may be a way to avoid the eternal torments.[14]

The Questions of Ezra

The *Questions of Ezra* is another short Christian work (also only one chapter) clearly derived from 4 Ezra, from the *Greek Apocalypse of Ezra,* and from the Armenian version of 4 Ezra (see Appendix 2).[15] It is extant in two Armenian recensions, dubbed A and B.[16] Although Recension B is much shorter, each version can be used to fill in lacunae in the other. B lacks verses 11–30 of A but preserves verses missing in A (those following verses 10 and 40 in B). It cannot be determined whether Armenian is the original language or if the two recensions were translated from Greek or Latin.

In *The Questions of Ezra,* Ezra asks the Angel of God what happens to man's soul "at the consummation," that is, "the day of the end," the final Day of Judgment. He is told that "great joy and eternal light" await the righteous but that "outer darkness and eternal fire" await the sinner. As in 4 Ezra, Ezra argues that there is no one among the living who has not sinned, and, as in the other books of the Ezra cycle, Ezra declaims that the animals have it far better than mankind—they eat grass, have no expectation of the resurrection, and are not judged at the end. The Angel replies that Ezra sins in saying this, for God made everything for the sake of man, and he made man for the sake of God. God judges man only by the things he finds in him.

Ezra asks where the angel takes the souls of men when it takes them. He is told that when the end arrives, an angel takes the soul and guides it to its recompense, a good angel taking the good soul and an evil one the evil. (This has certain resemblances to Zoroastrianism, in which the personification of the deceased—either as a beautiful woman or as an ugly one—leads the soul to the place of its reward.)[17] The good soul is brought to worship God; the souls of the sinners are seized by demons and are imprisoned in the atmosphere.

Ezra complains that we are all sinners and asks what will become of us. How can the soul that is seized by Satan be saved? The angel answers that if the sinner's soul has a good memorial in this world, father, mother, sister, son, or daughter or any other Christian to offer prayers with fasts for him, then the soul is released from Satan's power. For Christ was sacrificed for our sake upon the cross. If the friend of the sinner will stay in the church, reciting the psalms of David, and giving alms to the poor, then there will be rest and mercy for the deceased through the sacrifice of Christ, and he will be saved from Satan's hands.

This type of intercession is explicitly denied in 4 Ezra, but the section that contains the denial was excised from many Latin copies (see chapter 5). Moreover, this is the first in the Ezra cycle to specifically mention Christ's atoning sacrifice on behalf of the sinner, but it is possible only if the sinner has friends or family members to pray for him. According to Recension B, if there is no one to pray for the sinner, he remains in the hands of Satan until the Parousia. Then, at Christ's second coming, a trumpet will be sounded and all the souls will be freed from Satan's power. Each soul will be united with its body, raised, and judged by Christ, who will requite each for his deeds.

The Christology in this text is much more developed than in the ones discussed previously. It appears, however, that the end time in which the soul is taken to either Satan or to God is not the same as the time of the second coming, when souls are reunited with their bodies and they rise to be judged again, this time by Christ. This double day of judgment occurs only in Recension B, although Stone assumes that it is also the original ending, now lost, of A.[18]

The Apocalypse of Sedrach

A further composition in this series is the full-length *Apocalypse of Sedrach,* composed in Greek.[19] Although the seer in it is named Sedrach, he is likely not the companion of Daniel (1:7, Shadrach in Hebrew); rather, the name is more likely a corruption of Esdras. This apocalypse has strong affinities with 4 Ezra and with the other texts of the Ezra cycle. According to the title, this is "The word of the holy and blessed Sedrach concerning love and concerning repentance and Orthodox Christians, and concerning the Second Coming of our Lord Jesus Christ" (*Apoc. Sedrach* 1:1). The first chapter is a sermon on the importance of love, maintaining that love of God and love of one's brother fulfills all the law and all the prophets (*Apoc. Sedrach* 1:13). It is God's love that brought down the Son of God and by which "death was trampled down, Hades made captive" (*Apoc. Sedrach* 1:21).

The story proper begins with Sedrach hearing a voice after noting that Sedrach has asked to speak with God (*Apoc. Sedrach* 2:1), although the request itself is lacking in the present text. The voice is evidently that of an angel who stretches out his wings and carries Sedrach up to the third heaven, where he sees the flame of the divinity standing there (2:5). Sedrach, like Ezra, complains to God that it would have been better for man not to have been born (4:1). He asks God why he created mankind if he did not intend to have mercy on him (4:3). God replies that he created Adam and placed him in Paradise. He gave him only one commandment, but, having been deceived by the devil, he disobeyed it (4:5). Sedrach replies that it was only by God's will that Adam was deceived. If God really loved mankind, why did he not kill the devil, the creator of all iniquity (5:3)? God created the devil, and man is powerless against him. "If you loved man, why did you not slay the devil, the worker of unrighteousness? Who is able to fight an invisible spirit? Who as smoke enters into the hearts of men and teaches them every sin. He fights against you, the immortal God, and what can wretched man then do to him?" (*Apoc. Sedrach,* 5:3–6). This type of argument we see only in the Armenian 4 Ezra (see Appendix 2). It is the true problem of evil: why does a presumably good and all-powerful god allow evil to exist? "Where is your mercy?" Sedrach, like Ezra, pleads for mercy: "True mercy is mercy shown on the sinner, not the righteous"

(*Apoc. Sedrach* 5:7). "But have mercy, O Master, and stop the punishments: but if not, count me also with the sinners. If you will have no mercy on the sinners, where are your mercies, where is your compassion, O Lord?" (*Apoc. Sedrach* 5:7).

Unlike the Latin of 4 Ezra, God responds that all of man's commandments are within his reach (*Apoc. Sedrach* 6:1; cf. Deut. 30:11–14). He had given man everything he needs to live, but man took those things and went away and sinned (*Apoc. Sedrach* 6:3–6). Again, this line of argument is similar to that expressed in the Armenian translation of 4 Ezra. Sedrach asks whether, since everyone sins, he is to be alone in the celestial realm and whether he is to fill the space by himself (*Apoc. Sedrach* 7:2). You commanded that we not repay evil for evil (cf. Rom. 12:17; 1 Thess. 5:15; 1 Pet. 3:9), yet this is how you yourself repay man, evil for evil (*Apoc. Sedrach* 7:10). Moreover, mankind sins by your will; if you did not allow him to sin, he could not sin. In agreement with the Armenian 4 Ezra (discussed in Appendix 2), God responds that it was because he loved mankind that he gave him free will (*Apoc. Sedrach* 8:1). Ezra does not ask why this free will is so valuable that innocent people should be allowed to fall victim to it.

Finally, God gets exasperated and asks Sedrach if he knows how many people have been born and died since he created the world and how many hairs each one has? How many waves are there in the sea and how many winds near the shore? If Sedrach knows so much, how many drops of rain have fallen on the earth since the world was created (*Apoc. Sedrach* 8:3–9)? This is the argument we see in 4 Ezra and in Job: Man cannot know the ways of God. Sedrach replies that he does not know [nor does he care to know] the answer to any of these questions; he asks only that man be free from punishment. Unless mankind is freed, Sedrach continues, he is going to accept punishment so as not to be separated from the rest of his race (*Apoc. Sedrach* 8:10).

God then tells his only begotten Son to take the soul of his beloved Sedrach and bring it into Paradise (9:1), but Sedrach refuses to give it to him (9:3–5). When God insists that his soul be taken from him, Sedrach laments and mourns his body with a paean worthy of Walt Whitman (11:1–13). Christ tells him to stop carrying on like this, as Paradise has been opened to him.

The climax of the piece follows, with Sedrach asking, if a man who has sinned all his life later repents, how many days of repentance would he need to do in order for God to forgive his sins? Christ replies: "Three years." Sedrach responds that that is too many, so God lowers it to one year. Sedrach says that a year is also too long; a person could die before the year is up. How about forty days? God (or Christ?) responds that if a man repents for [only?] forty days, he will remember all his sins (*Apoc. Sedrach* 13:6).

Sedrach then approaches the archangel Michael and asks how mankind can be saved (14:1). (The transition to the archangel is abrupt. Michael may have been the one originally sent to retrieve Sedrach's soul, with Christ substituted by a later author, perhaps the one who prefaced the text with his sermon.)[20] Both Sedrach and Michael fall on their faces, asking God how man may be saved (14:2). God answers that by repentances, supplications, and liturgies, man may be saved (14:3). Repentance is available to those who have been baptized and to those who have not (14:5–9). Those who have repented will not see punishment (14:9). Then the Lord says to Sedrach, I will have compassion on a sinner for even less than forty days, if he repents for twenty days, and upon whoever reads and copies this book, or who performs a liturgy in your honor, him I will rescue from evil (16:3–5). Again, repentance averts the evil decree, as does reading and copying the book or performing liturgies. The point is likely that the belief that sin is punished and that one must do something to avoid the punishment is enough to save one's soul.

Agourides sees a Jewish original in this text, which was written between 150 and 500 C.E. and then redacted by a Christian writing in the Byzantine period, around 1000.[21] Agourides argues first that in Christian tradition the role of intercessor on behalf of sinners languishing in hell has been given to Mary, who then pleads with her son on their behalf (cf. *The Apocalypse of Mary*). Assigning this role exclusively to Mary belies the prominence of Ezra in all these texts discussed earlier and in Appendix 2 that have been taken up and into the Christian tradition. Agourides argues second that settling on the short period of only twenty days of repentance conflicts with later Church discipline, which requires several years of penitence. This is interesting and suggests that a Christian author may be arguing with exactly that Church tradition, stating that he has it on divine authority that only twenty days are necessary. A longer period would be unfair, since a person might die before it was completed, even though he had every intention of completing it. In his third argument, Agourides appeals to the lack of Christian elements, such as the incarnation or the cross. This lack has been noted in the Christian apocalypses discussed earlier and suggests an avowedly non-Pauline, pre-Lutheran Christianity in which good works and repentance, not Jesus's sacrifice, are the only things that ensure safety in the afterlife. The profound effect of Luther and his reliance on faith in Jesus's sacrifice as sufficient for a beneficent afterlife and as the only atonement necessary has prevented us from seeing exactly what pre-Lutheran Christianity had been. This is the Christianity revealed in these medieval apocalypses.

The basic assumption underlying all these apocalypses is that mankind receives according to his deeds. This recompense is necessarily pushed into the afterlife, since it is certainly not evident on earth. If men are divided into the righteous and the sinner, then only very few people will obtain the reward of the righteous, while the rest of us will suffer eternal torments, for who among the living has not sinned? Christ's death is not presented as having atoning power in these texts, for each person is requited according to his works, yet, as in Judaism, repentance does turn aside the evil decree. Besides the character of Ezra, these apocalypses share the hope that belief in punishment after death for sin may be enough to turn the sinner away from his sin.

Political Apocalypses

Two additional apocalypses of Ezra may be said to be political rather than personal.[22] The first, written in Syriac, predicts the destruction of the Ishmaelites, or Muslims, and the recapture of Jerusalem by the (Christian) Messiah. The second is the Ethiopic Book of Ezra, composed in Ge'ez. These works pick up on the political predictions in 4 Ezra, particularly Vision 5, the Vision of the Eagle, and the description of the sequence of kingdoms on the earth and of the ultimate destruction of the evil empire.

The Syriac Apocalypse of Ezra

The Syriac Apocalypse of Ezra, a brief text (one chapter), written in Syriac, is a polemic against the Muslim invasion.[23] It begins with the third-person statement of its title: "The question that Ezra the Scribe posed when he was in the desert with his disciple, one named Qarpos. He asked God to reveal to him the things that must occur at the end of time." Then begins a first-person account in which Ezra describes to his disciple the "terrible vision" that he saw when he asked God to show him what will happen to the children of Ishmael at the end of time (vs. 3). (Ishmaelite was the term used by Christians to refer to Arabs and to those who professed Islam.)[24] The author describes the bull (representing the children of Ishmael) who strikes and abuses whoever falls under his power (vs. 29). The bull has an evil design against both the "seven hills" (Rome?) and against "the great city of Constantinople," a design referring perhaps to the ultimately unsuccessful Arab siege of Constantinople (674–678 C.E.). The text predicts the demise of those areas that submitted to the Arab conquest and says that Egypt will become a desert (vs. 36), that Damascus (vs. 38) and Antioch will be annihilated (vs. 39), and that the land all the way to the Euphrates River will be trampled first by the Ishmaelite bull, which pillages and destroys all that it touches (vs. 43), and then by a young lion (representing the Messiah), which will come out against the bull and all his armies and annihilate them. He will destroy the cities of the Ishmaelites, and they will remain empty for centuries upon centuries because they have scorned God and transgressed his commandments (vss. 45–47). Damascus receives special attention; it alone will be torn down to its foundations because it has rebelled against the Most High (vs. 52). Then, after destroying Damascus, the young lion will go up to Jerusalem in great ceremony and go into his royal city and extend his reign over the promised land (vs. 54), and great peace will reign over the entire earth for three years and seven months (vs. 55). At the end of this time God will send an angel to destroy the rebellious race without pity (vs. 64). Gog and Magog will come out of the mountains of the north and cast down the race of Ishmaelites (vs. 67), the angel Michael will destroy the rebellious race without pity, and all the sons of perdition will be cast into Gehenna (vs. 73).

Although the book draws its setting from 4 Ezra, it is heavily dependent on the visions of Ezekiel and Daniel and on those in the Book of Revelation, all according to the language in the Peshitta.[25] It was likely written in the last quarter of the seventh century. It is an apocalypse because it speaks of another time, yet it differs from those already considered in that there is no thought of another world. The Christian god will wreak his vengeance on the very real cities of the Muslims.

An Ethiopic Apocalypse of Ezra

The Ethiopic Apocalypse of Ezra is also a polemic against the Muslim invasion but a rather muted one compared to the Syriac text.[26] The manuscript from which the translation was made was written in Ge'ez and was acquired by Joseph Halévy in 1867 from a "*Falashan debtera,*" that is, a scholar (*debtera*) from the people of Ethiopia known today as Beta Israel. The manuscript contains seven writings, all in Ge'ez, and all recognized as sacred by the Beta Israel (at least in 1867). These are (1) a text entitled *Te'ezâza Sanbat* (The Commandments of the Sabbath); (2) *Abba Eliyahu,* the words of Father Eliyahu, a priest or *kohen,* of the Beta Israel; (3) *The Book of the Angels,* which treats of the two rival angels that accompany a person from his birth to his death, the good angel, which sits at his right hand, and the bad angel, which sits at his left; each registers the deeds with which he is concerned, and each brings his book before God at the person's death; (4) *The Ethiopic Apocalypse of Ezra,* with which we will deal further below; (5) *The Revelations That God Made to the Holy and Blessed Father Baruch;* (6) *The Words of Gorgorios the Prophet;* and (7) a group of unrelated prayers, blessings, and invocations, which may have been a school text.[27]

All but one of these texts are clearly Jewish, with no overtly Christian references. Several texts refer to the commandments of the law, for example the law of unleavened bread on Passover. Others refer to the Day of Atonement and its twenty-five-hour fast, as well as the fast of Ab, commemorating the destruction of the temple in Jerusalem.[28] These last indicate rabbinic rather than biblical influences. Halévy suggests that *Abba Eliyahu* was originally a Christian text, since it refers to a demon called "Legion" that does not appear outside the Gospels, although there are no other Christian references in it.[29] Halévy also considers the books of Baruch and Gorgorios to be versions of Christian texts rewritten by a scribe of the Beta Israel.[30]

The Ethiopic Apocalypse of Ezra consists of two separate parts, the first of which describes the last judgment and the resurrection of the dead. The second part includes a history of the world from the time of Adam up to the end of time, including an evaluation of a series of Ethiopian kings. Although the names of the kings are not given and are indicated by only one letter, one is recognizable—Lalibela (1182–1225), who carved whole churches out of rocks. During the course of the recitation of the (future) history of the world, we learn that the children of Ishmael will "oppress the faithful and ravage their country," but after seven hundred years they will be destroyed by a man, the son of a lion (the Messiah), whom God has preserved until then.

Christian influences abound in the text. Although it begins with the benediction "Blessed be God, Lord of Israel," the first passage reads: "This is what God said to Ezra, 'When I will come in order to judge the living and the dead, on that day he will come who is named Word, who resembles a flash of light that comes out of the east and shines up to the west. Thus will be the coming of God'" (folio 68 recto). According to Halévy, the name Word is the name of the Messiah in the Ethiopic book of Enoch, but he does not provide a reference to it, and I do not find it in the translation by Isaac.[31] There are, however, other antecedents of this name of Word as the title of the Messiah, prominent among them the Gospel of John 1:1–5, 14. There are other Christian influences in this passage. A reference to the Messiah as the "judge of the living and the dead" is found, to my knowledge, only in Christian works—for example, Acts 10:42; 2 Timothy 4:1; and 1 Peter 4:5.

This passage also reflects other Christian texts. In Matthew 24:27 (= Luke 17:24), we read: "For as the lightning comes from the east and flashes as far as the west, so will be the coming of the Son of Man"(Matt. 24:27). The difference is that in the *Apocalypse,* it is not the Messiah, nor the Son of God, nor the Son of Man who comes in a flash of light but God himself. In the next verse of the *Apocalypse* we read: "Then the sun will be darkened, the moon will no longer give its light, and the stars will fall from the sky, and the powers in the sky will tremble" (*Ethiop. Appoc. Ezra,* fol. 68 r.; cf. 4 Ezra 5:5), which appears to be a quotation from Mark 13:24–25: "But in those days, after that suffering, the sun will be darkened, and the moon will not give its light, and the stars will be falling from heaven, and the powers in the heavens will be shaken." The author of the *Ethiopic Apocalypse* is clearly familiar with the Christian scriptures.

The *Ethiopic Apocalypse* next announces that "at that moment the angel Raphael will sound his horn and in a twinkling of an eye, those who are dead will rise, both the sinners and the just" (fol. 68 v.). This is right out of Paul (1 Cor. 15:51–52): "We will all be changed, in a moment, in the twinkling of an eye, at the last trumpet. For the trumpet will sound, and the dead will be raised imperishable, and we will be changed." Moreover, "an appearance of God will show itself in a cloud of the sky to the peoples on the earth" (fol. 68 v.). This too is from Paul: "Then we who are alive, who are left, will be caught up in the clouds together with them to meet the Lord in the air; and so we will be with the Lord forever" (1 Thess. 4:17). The difference between *The Ethiopic Apocalypse* and Paul is that it is God himself, neither Jesus nor a Messiah, who appears in the cloud. The *Apocalypse* continues that God will assemble his elect from the four corners of the earth, and in Matthew (24:31), we read: "And he will send out his angels with a loud trumpet call, and they will gather his elect from the four winds, from one end of heaven to the other."

According to this *Apocalypse,* the just who have been raised will jump with joy, for they will see face to face their Lord whom they had worshipped in their life (fol. 69 r.). All the creatures will be raised as from a deep sleep, they will rise naked as Adam, and they will be neither male nor female, all will have the same body, the same form. The evil ones, on the other hand, will be full of groanings, fears, terrors, and shame, and they will not be able to look upon the one who created them. Then the destructive angels will come to separate the sinners from the just (fol. 69, v.). Bernâ'el will drag the sinners with chains of fire up to the glorious throne for judgment. There they will weep and groan, but there will be no pity for them. The sinners are those who neglected the laws of God, abandoned the commandments, and did not rest on the Sabbath or during the festivals. They will be consigned to Gehenna for one thousand years where they will be subjected to a sea of fire (fol. 71 r.). They will be delivered to Temlyakos, the angel of Gehenna, who will distribute fiery punishments to them according to their deeds (fol. 71 v.). "On that day [the Day of Judgment], God will ask: 'Why have you rejected my law, my prescriptions, my Sabbaths, and my feast days by which I have sanctified myself in the midst of you, in order that you yourselves will be sanctified to me, so that you will become my elect in all your works and your travails'" (fol. 72 v.)? The focus on the laws differentiates this text from the obviously Christian texts already discussed.

When the resurrected and the living approach the throne of God, Enoch will read aloud the scroll of their deeds. They will not be able to deny what is written there (fol. 73 r.), "and the father will not be able to save his son, nor the son the father, nor the servant his master, nor the maidservant her mistress, nor the mother her daughter, nor brother his brother, nor friend his friend." This passage seems to be borrowed from 4 Ezra and from a version which existed before the section in which one cannot pray for the deceased (4 Ezra 7:102–15) was removed in the medieval period.

Finally the just will approach the throne, those who have scorned the perishable world and who have kept the laws and the Sabbaths. They will have joy without end; they will live forever without fear of scarcity, sickness, or death. They will live in the celestial city until the end of time.

At this point, the historical portion of *The Ethiopic Apocalypse* begins. Ezra goes into the desert to fast and pray, asking God to reveal his secrets (fol. 75 v.). God sends to Ezra the archangel Uriel, who tells Ezra that the secrets that Ezra wants to know have not been revealed to any man, even to those as good and as saintly as he (fol.76 r.). Ezra begs, saying that he needs to know, as his "kidneys burn within him." Uriel tells him to go into the desert where no one lives and that no one ever frequents, and the mysteries of God will be revealed to him (fol. 76 r.). He is told to fast for three complete weeks, so he fasts as he is told. At the end of this period, the angel Uriel comes to him and gives him a drink whose color resembles that of fire (cf. 4 Ezra 14:39). Immediately Ezra knows all the mysteries, all the sciences, all the history of all the periods of mankind since Adam, as well as everything that must occur on earth up until the day of judgment.

Evil kings will reign, but they and their armies will perish (fol. 83 r.). Then will come a good king who will be killed on his bed. His kingdom will pass to another race, which will respect in its heart the will of God (fol. 83 v.). A powerful king will arise who will fear God, loving the law and giving charity. He will walk according to the law of God. He will construct many churches carved into the rock (evidently King Gebre Mesqel Lalibela [1189–1229]). He will subject the powerful to him and exterminate them. All the earth will belong to him, and there will be an abundance of wheat and of clothing, the poor will rejoice, and everyone will live in perfect accord (fol. 84 r.). After him, one of his relatives, named Ye, will seize the kingdom (perhaps his son Yetbarak or the cousin who preceded Yetbarak, Na'akueto La'ab, who ruled for about eighteen months). Under this king no one will walk according to justice or right, and everyone will swear false oaths. Slaves will be sold to the children of Ishmael. There will be famine and pestilence, and mankind will perish (fol. 83 v.).

The children of Ishmael will reign for seven hundred years (fol. 87 r.). Then the son of a lion will raise himself, like someone who has just awakened from a sleep. He is he, of the family of David, whom the Most High has preserved for the end time. He will take vengeance on the children of Ishmael. Out of his mouth will come fire, and with the rapidity of a hurricane he will kill them and disperse them to all sides (fol. 87 v.). Along with him will come the nine tribes that were exiled to the other side of the Euphrates by King Shalmaneser (4 Ezra 13:39–46; cf. 2 Kings 17:1–6). These tribes remained by themselves in order to keep the law. This man, the son of the lion, will bring them with him and with God to give them a heritage in the blessed city (fol. 88 v.). The son of the lion will reign in peace for forty years, and then he will hide himself and remain unknown (fol. 90 v.). The kingdoms of the earth will become corrupt after that. Gog, Magog, and Guga, who are to come at the end of days, will devastate the earth (fol. 91 v.). They will be followed by a false messiah, who will reign for three years, six months, and three days. Then God will strike him with the rod of his anger and bring him down to Sheol (fol. 92 r.), where he will live until the end of time. The false messiah is here termed not the Anti-Christ, as he is in the Christian texts discussed earlier, but rather "the devil."

What is most noticeable about these two political apocalypses seen in comparison with 4 Ezra and the Christian apocalypses of Ezra discussed earlier is the attitude toward the sinner. Here there is no pleading with God to forgive them. Rather, their destruction and their banishment to Gehenna are viewed as their just desserts. The reason for this is of course the concern with the hostile Muslim conquest and not with individual sinners who may have simply gossiped. The dichotomy between God's justice and God's mercy is not approached here. These texts reassure us that however much we suffer now, God will eventually awaken his Messiah, whom he has kept in reserve, and will wreak justice on the evil of the earth.

The Revelation of Ezra

In addition to the Apocalypses of Ezra, I include here a *kalandologion,* or almanac, attributed to Ezra.[32] Written in Latin and dated to the ninth century, it describes the nature of the year as a function of the day of the week on which the year begins. The use of Ezra in this regard testifies to the importance he achieved as a prognosticator. The text begins: "The revelation which was made to Ezra and the children of Israel concerning the nature of the year by means of the beginning of January." Seven paragraphs ensue, each beginning with a day of the week, starting with "the Lord's Day." Sunday is "the Lord's Day," Monday is named after the Moon, Tuesday is the "Day of Mars," Wednesday is the "Day of Mercury," Thursday is the "Day of Jupiter," Friday is the "Day of Venus," and Saturday is the "Day of Saturn." Temperatures, rainfall, floods, plagues, wars, and crop failures and prices, as well as sailing conditions, can all be predicted. This text has strong similarities to the Jewish Treatise of Shem, preserved in Syriac but probably composed in Aramaic in Alexandria in the last third of the first century B.C.E.[33] That text describes the character of the year depending on the sign of the zodiac under which it begins. Like the *Revelation of Ezra,* it too predicts the amount of rainfall and so on, as well as the personal character and fate of anyone born under its sign. We also see this type of work at the Dead Sea. The fragmentary text 4QCryptic, *olim* 4Q186, asserts that a person's physical characteristics are determined by the sign of the zodiac under which he was born.

8

Ezra among Christians, Samaritans, Muslims, and Jews of Late Antiquity

In 4 Ezra, we are told that because of Ezra's faith and his merit before God, God provided him with a potion that enabled him to dictate to "ready scribes" the twenty-four books of the Hebrew Bible that he was to make public, as well as seventy secret texts that were to be revealed only to the wise among his people. The twenty-four biblical books included, of course, the five books of Moses, the Torah. Samaritan and Islamic scholars, as well as several of the Church Fathers, argue that Ezra falsified the Bible when he rewrote it and that the Torah we have now could not be the same as the one that Moses dictated. Several Church Fathers claimed that if we had the original Torah of Moses, Jesus's coming and resurrection would have been more clearly revealed in it than they are now. Samaritan writers claimed that Ezra falsified the Torah on the grounds that it does not mention Mount Gerizim as the place where God caused his name to be placed and which Samaritans venerate as the holiest site on earth. Muslim scholars claimed that had we the original Torah of Moses, Mohammed would surely have been mentioned in it.

In sharp contrast to Christian, Samaritan, and Islamic scholarly traditions, the rabbis hail Ezra as a second Moses. To the rabbis, Ezra is a hero, the last prophet—namely the prophet Malachi. They consider him to have been one of the founders of the Great Assembly, the assembly that they say governed Judah under the Romans. It is to these different traditions regarding Ezra that we now turn.

Ezra in Early Christian Tradition

Ezra appears in Christian tradition as the leader of the Judeans at the time of the return from Babylonian captivity. A problem for the early Christians was the differences between the Greek translation of the Hebrew Bible (the Septuagint), which was the translation of the Old Testament that they relied upon, and the Hebrew Bible used by the Jews. Nevertheless, most early Christians viewed Ezra positively. Irenaeus (d. 202) writes: "And there was nothing astonishing in God having done this [created the perfect Greek translation, that is, the Septuagint]. He who, when, during the captivity of the people under Nebuchadnezzar, the Scriptures

Ezra Reads the Law. Painting from the Synagogue of Dura Europos, 244 C.E. Michael Rostovtzeff, *Excavations at Dura Europas,* vol. 8 (1943), Plate 77. Courtesy of Yale University Press, New Haven, CT.

had been corrupted, and when, after seventy years, the Jews had returned to their own land, then, in the time of Artaxerxes, king of the Persians, He [God] inspired Esdras the priest, of the tribe of Levi, to recast all the words of the former prophets, and to re-establish with the people the Mosaic legislation" (*Adversus haereses* 3.21.2).[1] Since God caused the Septuagint to be a perfect translation, it is reasonable to suppose that he would have allowed Ezra to recast a perfect version of the Torah as well after it had been destroyed by Nebuchadnezzar. Thus, to Irenaeus, both are perfect, the Septuagint and Ezra's Hebrew version of the Bible.

Clement of Alexandria (d. 215) agrees: "Zorobabel . . . obtained from Darius permission to rebuild Jerusalem and with Esdras he returned to the ancestral land. Through him [that is, through Ezra] came about the redemption of the people and the recognition and restoration of the divinely inspired oracles, and the Passover peace-offering took place and the dissolution of foreign marriages" (1.124:1–2).[2]

Clement also reports that "in an inspired state he [Ezra] prophesied by renewing again all the ancient scriptures," which had been destroyed at the time of Nebuchadnezzar (*Stromata* 1.[22]149.3).[3] Similarly, the third-century Christian theologian Hippolytus of Rome (d. 235) refers to Ezra the scribe, who, along with Zerubbabel son of Salathiel, led the people back from Babylon in the seventieth year.[4]

The Coptic Apocryphon of Jeremiah inserts a story about Ezra in its narrative about Jeremiah. The manuscript, presently housed in the Pierpont Morgan Library in New York, is dated by the paleography to the ninth century.[5] The text was apparently prepared for the Monastery of the Archangel Saint Michael at Hamouli in Fayyum, Egypt, and the numerous Christian passages indicate that the work is at present a Christian text.[6] The work may be of Jewish origin, however, since the Christian elements can be easily detached.[7] Fragments of other copies of this Apocryphon exist, and all can be dated to the ninth century, except for one page presently in the British Museum, which is dated to the seventh century. The work appears to be dependent on the *Paralipomena Ieremiae,* which scholars assign to the second century, so the work may be dated any time between the second and seventh centuries.

The Coptic Apocryphon of Jeremiah is generally about the prophet Jeremiah, but, instead of his fleeing to Egypt as in the biblical text, he is taken to Babylon. While Jeremiah is there, praying for his people, we read of Ezra as a schoolboy attending a school that both Hebrew and Chaldean children attend. Thus, to this author, Ezra is a younger contemporary of Jeremiah:

> Now there were some of the little children of the Hebrews in the school of the Chaldeans receiving instruction, and they totaled seventy children. And there was a child among them whose name was Ezra who was in his mother's arms and who did not yet know good from evil.
>
> When he had reached the proper age, they sent him to the school, and the spirit of the Lord was upon him. The children of the Hebrews and of the Chaldeans went to the river at eventide to draw water and sprinkle the school.
>
> [When they had reached the river], they filled their vessels with water, but the vessel that was in Ezra's hand broke.
>
> The children of the Chaldeans turned on him, saying, "O Hebrews, you are people whose bones are feeble, but they will teach you here."
>
> But Ezra lifted up his eyes and wept, saying, "God of Abraham, and Isaac, and Jacob, see what they do to us."
>
> When Ezra finished speaking, he went down to the water, filled his robe like a vessel with water, raised it upon his shoulder, and went with the children. When he reached the school, he put his robe down full of water like a vessel, and he sprinkled the school. When he had finished sprinkling it, he took his robe which was dry and put it on.

> When the teacher of the school saw this, he bowed down and paid reverence to Ezra, saying, "You shall deliver this people from captivity." (*Coptic Apocryphon of Jeremiah* 32)[8]

The *Coptic Apocryphon of Jeremiah* continues to relate several more wonders and miracles of Ezra. In particular we read in a prayer of Ezra a reference to the covenant, which supports the claim of a Jewish origin to the text:

> I beseech you, my Lord, hear my prayer, listen to my weeping. Remember the covenant which you did make with our fathers, saying, "If your sons keep the covenant, I shall humble their enemies" [Exod. 23:22]. So now we confess your covenant, we are ready to die for your mercy. Hear us in thy holy heaven and accept our sacrifice from us and have mercy on your people.
>
> Now when Ezra had said this, his prayer entered the ears of the Lord. He sent his angels and he accepted Ezra's sacrifice from him. The angel Eremiel came and stood by Ezra's sacrifice. He set the sheep and the wood on fire. The fire came out of heaven and devoured them. The angel stood in the air and made himself manifest to the youths [with Ezra]. (*Coptic Apocryphon of Jeremiah* 34)[9]

We saw Eremiel in 4 Ezra as one of the angels who guarded the souls in their habitations until the arrival of the Day of Judgment. Having absolute faith in God's mercy and reminding God of his part in the covenantal bargain are apparently effective in guaranteeing that Ezra will indeed lead his people back from captivity.

Not all the Christian references to Ezra are positive, however. From as early as the beginning of the second century, Christians accused the Jews of falsifying their own scriptures.[10] This was apparently to defend the purity of the Septuagint against rival Christian groups with rival translations. Justin Martyr (d. 165), in his (fictitious) *Dialogue with Trypho the Jew*, writes that the Jews removed references to the coming of Jesus from their texts, not Ezra specifically but rather a nameless "they": "From the statements which Ezra made in reference to the law of the Passover, they have taken away the following [phrase]: 'And Ezra said to the people, 'This Passover is our Savior and our refuge. And if you have understood, and your heart has taken it in, that we shall humble Him on a standard, and thereafter hope in Him, then this place [the temple] shall not be forsaken forever, says the God of hosts. But if you will not believe Him, and will not listen to His declaration, you shall be a laughing-stock to the nations'" (*Justin's Dialogue with Trypho*, chapter LXXII). He also claims that:

> From the sayings of Jeremiah they have cut out the following: 'I[was] like a lamb that is brought to the slaughter: they devised a device against me, saying, Come, let us destroy the tree with the fruit, and let us blot Him out from the land of the

> living; and His name shall no more be remembered.' And this passage from the sayings of Jeremiah is still written in some copies [of the scriptures] in the synagogues of the Jews [for it is only a short time since they were cut out]. (*Justin's Dialogue with Trypho,* chapter LXXII)

> Trypho remarked, "Whether[or not] the rulers of the people have erased any portion of the Scriptures, as you affirm, God knows; but it seems incredible."
>
> "Assuredly," said I, "it does seem incredible. For it is more horrible than the calf which they made, when satisfied with manna on the earth; or than the sacrifice of children to demons; or than the slaying of the prophets. But," said I, "you appear to me not to have heard the Scriptures which I said they had stolen away. For such as have been quoted are more than enough to prove the points in dispute, besides those which are retained by us, and shall yet be brought forward." (*Justin's Dialogue with Trypho,* chapter LXXIII)

Justin accuses the Jews of having removed portions from their Bible that predict the coming of Jesus and compares this removal to other heinous acts such as building the golden calf. There is no evidence for Jewish sacrifice of their children to demons or for the New Testament charge that the Jews killed their prophets (Matt 23:34; Luke 11:49). These accusations were used by New Testament authors to increase the credibility of their libelous charge that the Jews killed Jesus.[11]

Although Justin does not explicitly blame Ezra, Porphyry of Tyre (d. 305) does in his *Adversus Christianos* (Frag. 465e). He writes that nothing remains of the true Torah. All we have is the one created by Ezra, which is false: "Nothing has been preserved of Moses, as all his writings are said to have been burnt together with the temple. And all those which were written under his name afterwards were composed *inaccurately* one thousand one hundred and eighty years after Moses' death by Ezra and his followers."[12] The monk, historian, and theologian Tyrannius Rufinus or Rufinus of Aquileia (Rufinus Aquileiensis, 340/345–410) agrees. He states that Origin wrote the Hexapla only to refute the Jews "because they lied, since in our Scriptures a considerable number of passages had been changed, or lacking, or added on."[13]

The very early charge that the Jews falsified their text even entered disputes between Muslims and Christians, as witnessed in an exchange of letters between Omar II, Umayyad caliph (717–720 C.E.), and the Byzantine Emperor Leo III (717–741 C.E.). In disputes with Muslims, Christians found themselves defending the authenticity of the text, even the edition of Ezra.

The Caliph writes:

> How, indeed, are you able to justify these same Scriptures, and follow them in what suits your intentions? You declare that the

> Code was more than once written by the Children of Israel who read it and understood it, and that it was many times lost, so that for a long time there was nothing of it remaining among them, till at a later period some men recomposed it out of their own heads. You admit that it was handed down from generation to generation, from people to people, by fleshly creatures, who inasmuch as they were sons of Adam, were forgetful, subject to error, and perhaps acting under the inspiration of Satan, and those who, by their hostile acts, resemble him.[14]

The Patriarch responds:

> You pretend that the Old Testament was composed by human genius, and I know that you attack the second edition that Esdras composed. Yet this man possessed the grace of the Holy Spirit, and all that he composed has the cachet of infallibility, as is proved by the fact that when all the people, delivered from captivity, came back to Jerusalem, bringing with them the Testament, there was seen the marvelous work of God, for when it was compared with the edition of Esdras, this was found completely in conformity with the former.[15]

Here Leo defends the authenticity of Ezra's edition because the Old Testament is part of the Christian canon. His basic proof that the Old Testament had not been falsified is the numerous references in it to the coming of Christ. If the Jews were going to falsify their scriptures, would they have left those intact?[16]

Ezra in Samaritan Tradition

The Samaritans (Hebrew: שומרונים *Shomronim,* Arabic: السامريون *as-Sāmariyyūn*) are a people who at the close of 2011 C.E. numbered fewer than eight hundred individuals, half of whom resided at Kiryat Luza on Mount Gerizim near Nablus (Shechem) and the rest of whom lived in the city of Holon, just outside Tel Aviv. They consider themselves to be the direct descendants of those of the northern Israelite tribes of Manasseh and Ephraim who survived the Assyrian conquest, were not deported, and did not intermarry with those who were brought in by the Assyrians from abroad. The traditional Jewish view of the Samaritans, which stems from the statement in 2 Kings 17:5–6, 24, is just the opposite:

> Then the king of Assyria invaded all the land and came to Samaria; for three years he besieged it. In the ninth year of Hoshea [the king of Israel], the king of Assyria captured Samaria [the capital, and another name for the whole area]; he carried the Israelites away to Assyria. He placed them in Halah, on the Chabor, the river of Gozan, and in the cities of the Medes. (2 Kings 17:5–6)

> The king of Assyria brought people from Babylon, Cuthah, Avva, Hamath, and Sepharvaim, and placed them in the cities of Samaria in place of the people of Israel; they took possession of Samaria, and settled in its cities. (2 Kings 17:24)

This view is supplemented and supported by the statement in Ezra 4:1–2: "When the rivals of Judah and Benjamin heard that the returned exiles were building a temple to YHWH, the God of Israel, they approached Zerubbabel and the heads of families and said to them, 'Let us build with you, for we worship your God as you do, and we have been sacrificing to him ever since the days of King Esarhaddon of Assyria who brought us here.'"

This statement, apparently in their own words, has cemented the Jewish view that the Samaritans were not actually descended from the northern tribes but were only brought to the region by Assyrian kings. According to these biblical texts, the Samaritans are not descendants of the tribes of Israel. This view is upheld in the New Testament, which reveals a profound split between the Jewish and the Samaritan communities even though both communities worshipped YHWH according to the Torah of Moses. This split can readily be seen in the Gospel of Matthew: "These twelve Jesus sent out with the following instructions: 'Go nowhere among the Gentiles, and enter no town of the Samaritans, but go rather to the lost sheep of the house of Israel'" (Matt. 10:5–6). The author of this passage does not see the Samaritans as Gentiles, but neither does he see them as members of the house of Israel. So, while the Samaritans consider themselves as constituting the true house of Israel, the Jews (and then the Christians) saw them as interlopers. According to Samaritan tradition, however, the Judeans (Jews) split off from the central stream of Israelite tradition in the time of the priest Eli in the eleventh century B.C.E.

The major dispute between Samaritans and Jews or Judeans has to do with the location of the temple. Whereas the Judeans built their temple in Jerusalem, the Samaritans still today regard the peak of Mount Gerizim, the mount of blessing (Deut. 11:29; 27:12; see also Josh. 8:33; Judges 9:7), as the sacred place upon which God commanded Moses to build his altar. This difference in the location of the temple is reflected in the difference in various verses between the Samaritan and Jewish Torahs. For example, the Masoretic Text (the canonical version) reads: "So when you have crossed over the Jordan, you shall set up these stones, about which I am commanding you today, on Mount Ebal, and you shall cover them with plaster. And you shall build an altar there to YHWH your God, an altar of stones on which you have not used an iron tool" (Deut. 27:4–5). The Samaritan text, however, reads "Mount Gerizim" instead of "Mount Ebal," which actually makes more sense, since Gerizim is the mount of blessing and Ebal the mount of cursing (Deut. 11:29).

The Samaritans claim that the Israelites built an altar on Mount Gerizim when they first entered the land and that they, as descendants of the first Israelites, have been worshipping YHWH there ever since. In contrast, the Masoretic text states that the first altar was built on Mount Ebal (Josh. 8:30–32): "Then Joshua built on Mount Ebal an altar to YHWH, the God of Israel, just as Moses, the servant of YHWH, had commanded the Israelites, as it is written in the book of the law of Moses, 'an altar of unhewnstones, on which no iron tool has been used'; and they offered on it burnt offerings to YHWH, and sacrificed offerings of well-being. And there, in the presence of the Israelites, Joshua wrote on the stones a copy of the law of Moses, which he had written."

According to the medieval Samaritan book of Joshua [SJ], however, Joshua built the altar on Mount Gerizim, as well as a synagogue to house the ark. "He [Joshua] built a synagogue on the summit of the Blessed Mount [Mount of Blessing, Mount Gerizim] and collected and kept in it the tabernacle of YHWH and no one after him touched it except the priests and Levites" (chapter 24).[17]

There are other differences between the Samaritan Pentateuch and the Masoretic Text used by Jews. Numerous verses in the Masoretic Text which command an altar on "the place that God *will choose,*" command in the Samaritan Pentateuch an altar on "the place that YHWH *has chosen.*" For example, Deuteronomy 12:13–14 of the Masoretic Text reads:

> But you shall seek the place that YHWH your God will choose [Samaritan Pentateuch: "has chosen"] out of all your tribes as his habitation to put his name there. You shall go there, bringing there your burnt offerings and your sacrifices, your tithes and your donations, your votive gifts, your freewill offerings, and the firstlings of your herds and flocks. (Deut. 12:5–6)

> Take care that you do not offer your burnt offerings at any place you happen to see. But only at the place that YHWH will choose [Samaritan Pentateuch: "has chosen"] in one of your tribes—there you shall offer your burnt offerings and there you shall do everything I command you. (Deut. 12:13–14)

The Samaritan Pentateuch reads "has chosen" wherever the Masoretic Text reads "the place that YHWH will choose," because to the Samaritans, Deuteronomy 11:29 has already indicated the chosen place, that is, Mount Gerizim: "When YHWH your God has brought you into the land that you are entering to occupy, you shall set the blessing on Mount Gerizim and the curse on Mount Ebal" (Deut. 11:29). To the Samaritans, the "blessing" is the tabernacle and the Torah of Moses. The Samaritans accuse the Judeans of having altered the text by substituting "will choose" for "has chosen" and of having built a rival site to Mount Gerizim in Jerusalem. According to Jewish tradition, "the place that YHWH will choose" is Jerusalem, and the site was not chosen until much later, when King David conquered it and brought the ark there (2 Sam. 6–7). In any case, at least by the early Persian period there were two competing temples, a Jewish one in Jerusalem and a Samaritan one on Mount Gerizim.[18]

The Samaritan accusation that the Jews falsified the text goes back at least to the early Middle Ages. According to the Islamic historian and geographer al-Mas'udi, writing in the tenth century (896–956 C.E.), the Samaritans claimed that the Jews falsified their Torah: "Now the Samaritans allege that the Torah that is in the hands of the Jews is not the Torah that Moses, son of Amram, brought, but that it is forged, altered, and changed, and that the one who produced the version that is in their possession is the king just mentioned [Zerubbabel, the Persian governor of Judah and the Davidic heir], because he assembled it from what certain Israelites had remembered. [The Samaritans claim] that the real Torah is in the possession of the Samaritans and no one else."[19] The "certain Israelites who remembered the Torah" in the passage would certainly include Ezra, who is said (in 4 Ezra) to have dictated the Torah from memory upon his return to Judah from Babylon.

This accusation is reiterated in *The Kitāb al-Tarīkh of Abu 'l-Fatḥ,* or *The Chronicle of Abu 'l-Fatḥ,* a Samaritan work written in Arabic in 1355 by Ibn Abi al-Hasan al-Samiri al-Danafi, also known as Abu 'l-Fatḥ.[20] The work gives a history of the Samaritans from Adam to Mohammed. According to this chronicle, at the time of the return from exile at the beginning of the Persian period, the leaders of both the Judeans and the Samaritans were gathered in front of King Šūrdī (probably Darius)[21] to discuss where the temple should be built and where sacrifices should be presented:

> Šūrdī the king then said, "Let us offer sacrifices on Mount Gerizim!"
>
> Thereupon Zerubbabel became enraged in the presence of the king, and said, "The writings which we possess prophesy that sacrifices will [only] be offered in Jerusalem."
>
> To this Sanballat retorted, saying to Šūrdī the king, "The books which are in the possession of Zerubbabel are forgeries, deceits, and lies. Order me to, and I will throw them into the fire. But as for this Scroll of the Torah [of ours] let him throw it in if he can."
>
> So Šūrdī the king ordered Sanballat to throw the Books of David[22] into the fire. He threw them into the fire, and they were burnt up. Then Šūrdī commanded Zerubbabel to throw the Samaritan Book of the Torah [into the fire].
>
> He took it, opened it, looked in it and then said, "I cannot throw it. For my Book was mine alone; but this Book is mine and his, because the one who wrote it is the Lord, the Messenger [of God], Moses, upon whom be perfect peace.
>
> Šūrdī the king, in reply, said to Zerubbabel, "I consider your books to be nothing but forgeries and lies. Why did Sanballat throw your Books into the fire, while you do not throw his Books?"
>
> Out of fear, Zerubbabel then took the [Samaritan] Scroll of the Torah and threw it into the fire. It leapt into the air and came out of the fire.

> Then Zerubbabel asked permission to throw it a second time; so he ordered him to throw it.
>
> He threw it a second time, but it flew and came out of the fire again.
>
> So he asked permission to throw it a third time. He took hold of it, opened it, spat upon it, and then threw it into the fire.
>
> The place where he spat was burnt, but the Book leapt out of the fire and flew into the presence of Šūrdī the king.
>
> The nations thus learned that the [Samaritan] Book of the Torah, which God had revealed by means of Moses, upon whom be peace, was the only perfect one. (*Chronicle of Abu 'l-Fatḥ* 77)[23]

According to *The Chronicle of Abu 'l-Fatḥ,* Šūrdī then orders Sanballat to appoint for himself leaders and to go up to Jerusalem to stop its rebuilding (*Chronicle of Abu 'l-Fatḥ* 78).[24]

This last passage has clear similarities with the story in Ezra 4 in which the Samaritans write a letter to the king to try to prevent the rebuilding of Jerusalem. It also echoes the story in Nehemiah in which Sanballat, the Samaritan governor, attempts to prevent Nehemiah from rebuilding Jerusalem's city wall.[25] Here in the Samaritan chronicle the king agrees that the temple in Jerusalem is illegitimate and that only the temple on Mount Gerizim is ordained by God. The king then initiates the activity against Jerusalem by ordering Sanballat to gather some leaders and go to that city and prevent its rebuilding.

Is this story in *The Chronicle of Abu ʿal-Fataḥ* simply a tendentious rewriting of the one in the Book of Ezra (or 1 Esdras), or does it go back to an earlier, more authentic version of the events? Should we see the Samaritan hostility described in Ezra-Nehemiah as historic and as opposition to a temple in Jerusalem?

The Chronicle of Abu 'l-Fataḥ was written in 1355, as he states (*The Chronicle of Abu 'l-Fatḥ* 190). His major source was the so-called Book of Joshua, not the biblical book of Joshua but a thirteenth-century text written in the Arabic script and language (*Chronicle of Abu 'l-Fatḥ* 3).[26] The major source for the Samaritan Book of Joshua could only have been the Hebrew Bible, however, since the only governor of Samaria mentioned for the period of the return to Zion is Sanballat, who alone is mentioned in the Masoretic Text. This is in spite of the fact that Samaritan coins from the period of the return reveal the names of many more governors, including an early one named Jeroboam.[27] Had the author authentic historic sources, some of these governors would certainly have been named in them.

After Zerubbabel's Torah is burnt up, *The Chronicle of Abu ʿal-Fataḥ* continues: "Because of all this, Ezra and Zerubbabel set about making up an alphabet of their own, different from the [paleo-]Hebrew alphabet [that had been in use before the exile]; they made it of 27 letters.[28] They tampered with the Holy Law, copying it out in the alphabet they had newly created. They cut out many passages of the Holy Law, because of the fourth of the ten commandments, and [they cut out] the references to Mount Gerizim and its boundaries" (*Chronicle of Abu 'l-Fatḥ* 81).[29]

According to the Samaritan reckoning, the fourth commandment is "Honor your father and your mother that your days may be long in the land that YHWH your god has given you." That is, the Jews altered their Torah to honor their fathers. The reference to the ten commandments refers to the commandments as they are written in the Samaritan Pentateuch. As its tenth commandment, the Samaritan Pentateuch includes a passage taken from Deuteronomy 27:2–7 with Samaritan additions to it:

> And when YHWH your god brings you into the land of the Canaanites, which you are entering to take possession of, you shall set up these stones and plaster them with plaster, and you shall write upon them all the words of the law. And when you have passed over the Jordan, you shall set up these stones, concerning which I have commanded you this day on Mount Gerizim. And there you shall build an altar to YHWH your god, an alter of stones, you shall lift no iron tool upon them. You shall build an altar to YHWH your God; and you shall sacrifice peace offerings and shall eat there; and you shall rejoice before YHWH your god. That mountain is beyond the Jordan, west of the road, toward the going down of the sun, in the land of the Canaanites who live in the Arabah, over against Gilgal, beside the oak of Moreh in front of Shechem.[30]

The Chronicle of Abu 'al-Fataḥ continues further with a curse upon Ezra: "They [the Judeans] added to [the Torah], cut things out from it, changed it and misconstrued it. May God oppose them. In the morning of the Day of Days, Ezra, may he be cursed, called the Jews together and said to them, 'God said to me yesterday when he gave me this Book, "This is the Book of God, the authentic truth. Put your faith in it and make copies of this one alone"'" (*Chronicle of Abu 'l-Fatḥ* 81).

Whereas the story describing Zerubbabel and Sanballat throwing each other's Torahs into the fire is told in chapter 45 of the *Book of Joshua*, Abu 'al-Fataḥ's source, this passage describing Ezra as having falsified the Torah is not. It is likely 'al-Fataḥ's own composition, since to Abu 'al-Fataḥ the differences between the Samaritan Pentateuch and the Jewish Torah prove that someone falsified the Torah and that it must have been Ezra. He also could have learned it from Islamic texts or from conversations with Muslims. These ideas have been prevalent in Islamic writings since at least the eleventh century and the writings of Ibn Ḥazm (see the following).

Ezra in Islamic Traditions

In Islamic tradition, Ezra is known in three separate ways. Two of these are based on verses in the Koran, and the third appears in Islamic tradition only. According to the first, Ezra is said to be referred to by Jews as the son of God (Sura 9:30); according to the second, Ezra is condemned for questioning predestination and God's ability to revive the dead (Sura 2:259); and in the third, which is not in the Koran itself, Ezra is condemned for having distorted the Torah when he rewrote it during the period of the return of the Jews to Israel.

The name Ezra does not appear anywhere in the Koran, but in Sura 9:30 the name ʿUzayr is used, which is taken, according to most (but not all) Islamic scholars, to refer to Ezra.[31] In Sura 2:259, no name appears at all, but tradition applies it to ʿUzayr (i.e, to Ezra). Each of these is discussed in turn.

Ezra as the Son of God

We read in the Koran:

> [9:29] Fight those who do not believe in God, nor in the Last Day, or who do not prohibit what God and His Apostle [Mohammed] have prohibited, or who do not follow the religion of truth; and among those, those who have been given the Book [Jews and Christians], fight them until they pay the *jizya* tax [poll tax or *dhimmi* tax] in acknowledgment of [Muslim] superiority and that they [Jews and Christians] are in a state of subjugation.
>
> [9:30] The Jews say: ʿUzair is the son of God; and the Christians say: the Messiah is the son of God; these are the words of their mouths; they imitate the saying of those who disbelieved before; may God destroy them; how perverse are they!
>
> [9.31] They have taken their doctors of law and their monks for Lords besides God, and [also] the Messiah son of Marium and they were enjoined that they should serve one God only, that there is no god but He; far from His glory be what they set up [with Him].

These verses, intending to condemn both Jews and Christians as idol worshippers, apparently belong to the later Medinese period of Mohammed's life, a period that produced numerous polemics against the Jews since they did not accept him.[32] Indeed, according to Islamic tradition, this Sura (Sura 9) was one of the last of the Koran to be revealed.[33] The charge of idolatry, leveled here (9:30) against Jews and Christians, is the most serious that Muslims can make against any person or group.[34] The verse preceding this one includes the obligation either to make war against them or to impose the *jizya* tax upon them. It thus defines once and for all the permissible relations between the community of Muslims and their non-Muslim Jewish and Christian subjects or neighbors.[35] That Jews denied (and deny) that they ever viewed Ezra as the son of God is irrelevant. Al-Thaʿālibī (1384–1468) reiterates the view that there were in his day no longer any Jews who made this claim, but "even if only one of their chiefs said it, the evil of this claim would apply to them all."[36] Most Islamic writers try to minimize the accusation by saying that only a small sect made it and that this sect has disappeared.[37] However, Ayoub, writing in 1986, states that this came into Islamic tradition through Jews, that is, through "the famous Rabbi Ka'b al-Aḥbār (d. 652) and the Yemenite Jewish savant Wahb b. Munabbih (d. 728 or 732)," so it must have "come into Islamic tradition after a long period of Jewish development."[38] In other words, Ayoub assumes that the claim has a basis in fact. Rabbi Ka'b al-Aḥbār was evidently a convert to Islam, while Wahb b. Munabbih, though of Jewish descent, was likely born a Muslim.[39] In spite of his apparent Jewish ancestry, there are many spurious passages that Wahb b. Munabbih asserts are from the Torah, including the statement that everything is made from earth, fire, air, and water.[40]

The Syrian traditionalist and commentator Ibn Kathīr (1300–1373) states of Sura 9:30: "This is [reported] by way of enticement by God of the people of faith [that is, the Muslims] to fight the rejecters of the faith, the Jews and Christians, because of the ugly battle which they [the Jews and Christians] fought against the people of faith [the Muslims]. It is also because of the lie which they [the Jews and Christians] invented about God. As for the Jews, it was their saying, 'Uzayr is the son of God.'"[41] In other words, it may not be true that the Jews do say this, but God put it in the Koran anyway to entice Muslims to fight against Jews and Christians because of their rejection of Islam. Fakhr al-Dīn al-Rāzī (1149–1209) also asserts that the association of a son with God by Jews and Christians is no different from idol worship: "The fact that the Jews deny such a belief proves nothing because God's report concerning them is more true [than their denial]."[42] Sunni tradition reports a dispute between the Jews and Mohammed about whether 'Uzayr is the son of God.[43] According to the reported dispute, Mohammed asks the Jews what makes them say this. They report that it was because he revived the Torah for them after it had disappeared. Mohammed refutes this by asking them why then Moses was not called the son of God; he should have had an even more exalted status since he had written the Torah in the first place.

The Persian theologian Ṭabaṭabā'ī (1892–1981) wrote that Ezra may have been called "son of God" as an honorific only.[44] Ṭabaṭabā'ī states: "Because of the great services which he [Ezra] rendered to them, they exalted his status, greatly respected him and called him 'son of God.' We do not know whether this claim of sonship was meant in the same sense in which Christians used it when they call Christ the son of God. What is intended is that there was in him something of the divine substance, or that he was derived from it, or that he was synonymous with it." He continues: "In God's word [in the Koran] it is attributed to all of them [all of the Jews] because some said it and the others consented to what they said. They were all of one opinion and general view." Elsewhere he writes: "God's wrath increased toward the Jews when they said, 'Uzayr is the son of God.' Likewise it increased toward the Christians when they said, 'Jesus is the son of God.'" That this verse (9:30) continues to be used as a prooftext for attacks against Jews and Christians is seen in the writings of Sayyid Qutb (1906–1966), a leading thinker of the Egyptian Muslim Brotherhood. He saw the verse as the justification for the *jizya* on Jews and Christians and as the basis of the command to fight against them, since the verse commanding the *jizya* (9:29) and the command to fight against even those who have the Book (Jews and Christians) appears right before the verse that asserts that the Jews believe that ʿUzayr is the son of God.

Al-Ṭabarī (d. 923) explains how it came about that the Jews believed ʿUzayr (Ezra) to be the son of God:

> When the [Israelites] returned to Palestine, they did not have God's covenant with them, for the Torah was captured from them and burned and lost. And ʿUzayr was among the captives in Babylon and returned [with them] to the Land. He would cry over [the loss of] the Torah day and night, going off and wandering sorrowfully through the deserts and wadis. [Once] when he was sitting mourning and crying over the Torah a man approached him and said "O ʿUzayr, what has brought you to tears?"
>
> He answered: "I am crying for the Book of God and his covenant which was in our hands. Because of our sins and the Lord's anger against us, God has caused our enemy to rule over us, and they have killed our young men, destroyed our land, and burned our Book of God, and [that Book] alone can successfully guide us in this world and the next."
>
> Said [the man] "Would you like that [Book] to return to you?"
>
> Asked [Ezra], "Is there a way?"
>
> Answered [the man]: "Of course. Go back, fast, purify yourself and your clothing and [return] tomorrow to meet [me] in this place."
>
> ʿUzayr went back and fasted and purified himself and his clothing and returned to the place where they had met and sat there. Then the same man came to him with a vessel of water, and he was an angel God had sent to him, and he let him drink from the vessel. And the Torah returned [to his consciousness] and [ʿUzayr] returned to the children of Israel and he placed the Torah before them and they recognized it—what it allowed and what it forbade, its commandments and desirable acts and its punishments. And they loved him greatly, as they had never loved him before, and the Torah remained in their possession and they fared well with it. ʿUzayr, too, stayed with them, acting righteously until God took him to himself. . . .
>
> After that, events resumed, until they called ʿUzayr son of God, and God once again sent them a prophet, as was his way, in order to mend their ways and command them to observe the Torah and what was in it.[45]

The relation of this text to 4 Esdras is clear, and, as is explained in Appendix 2, several Arab translations of 4 Ezra had been made from a very early period.

One early commentator on these verses in the Koran is Ibn Ḥazm of Spain (Abu Muḥammad ʿAli b. Aḥmad b. Ḥazm, 994–1064). He was the author of two works, *Ṭawq al-ḥamāma* (*The Ring of the Dove*) and *Kitāb al-aklāq wa'l-siyar* (*The*

Book of Character and Conduct).[46] Each of these works contains a section on the Jews, whom the author divides into five sects. The majority group is the Rabbanites, who follow the teachings of the rabbis. The ʿAnānites (also called Karaites), in contrast, reject the teachings of the rabbis, whom they brand as liars; they adhere only to the books of the Torah and the Prophets.[47] A third group is the ʿIsāwiyya, who believe that Jesus was a prophet sent to the Israelites and that Mohammed was a prophet sent to the Arabs and to the children of Ishmael.[48] A fourth group is the Samaritans, who deny the mission of every prophet after Moses and Joshua. They do not believe in the resurrection and deny the existence of the *jinn*, or supernatural creatures.[49] According to Ibn Ḥazm, the fifth sect is that of the Ṣadūqiyya (Zaddokites?, Sadducees?) who follow a certain Ṣadoq. They lived in Yemen, and their most prominent characteristic was that they believed that Ezra was the son of God.[50] Ibn Ḥazm had never been to Yemen, however, and there is no evidence of Zadokites or Sadducees having been in Yemen.[51] According to Hirschberg, Yemenite Jews do not name their children Ezra, moreover, because of their tradition that Ezra had cursed them with poverty for not having moved to Israel.[52] This fifth group of Jews, according to Ibn Ḥazm, also believes that Melchizedek, Elijah, Pinhas, and others never died but are still alive.[53]

The accusation that the Jews call Ezra the son of God may go back to the following verses in 4 Ezra in which God speaks to Ezra: "And now I say to you: Lay up in your heart the signs that I have shown you, the dreams that you have seen, and the interpretations that you have heard; for you shall be taken up from among humankind, and henceforth you shall live with my Servant and with those who are like you, until the times are ended" (4 Ezra 14:7–9). The Latin and the later Christian translations of it read "Son" in 14:9, instead of "Servant." The Hebrew "Servant" can be translated into Greek by παῖς, which means both "servant" and "son." There is no intimation in the verse itself that Ezra is like the Servant or the Son; it suggests only that he and others who are like Ezra (not like the Son) would be "taken up" and would live with the Son, or Servant. The confusion is understandable, however.

Ezra Censured Because He Questioned Predestination and God's Ability to Revive the Dead

Besides censuring the Jews for revering Ezra as the son of God, Muslims also condemned Ezra himself for questioning predestination and God's ability to revive the dead (Sura 2:259).

We read in the Koran (2:259): "[Consider] the like of him [ʿUzayr] who passed by a town, and it had fallen down upon its roofs; he said: How will God give it life after its death?" Thus ʿUzayr doubts God's power to resurrect the dead, a central pillar of Islam.

> So God caused him to die for a hundred years, then raised him to life. He [God] said: How long have you slept [that is, how long were you dead]?
>
> [ʿUzayr] said: I have slept a day, or a part of a day.
>
> Said [God]: Nay! you have slept [been dead] a hundred years; yet look at your food and drink—years have not passed over it;[54] and look at your ass; and so that We may make you a sign to men, look at your bones, how We set them together, then clothed them with flesh.
>
> When it became clear to him, ʿUzayr said: I know that God has power over all things.

In discussing this verse, the mystic and philosopher Ibn ʿArabī (1165–1612) writes that ʿUzayr was censured not only for the hubris of questioning God's ability to raise the dead but also because ʿUzayr asked about the Decree (*qadr*) itself, that is, about the Day of Judgment of the dead. "When we saw that God censured ʿUzayr, peace be upon him, when he asked about the Decree [*qadr*], we knew that ʿUzayr was seeking this knowledge. Thus he was seeking to possess the power [*qudra*] which is connected to the decreed [*maqdur*]. This knowledge is only claimed by the One Who has absolute existence. Thus he sought the impossible."[55]

According to Ibn ʿArabī, not only was ʿUzayr (Ezra) doubting God's ability to raise the dead; he also wanted to know what God had decreed for those who had died and perhaps also for the power to determine the judgment itself. Both are accusations of hubris, and both may be based on 4 Ezra, in which Ezra does ask about all these things.

Ezra as the Falsifier of the Torah

In numerous places the Koran accuses the Jews of having deliberately misrepresented, even falsified, the word of God in their Torah. For example, we read:

> Do you [Muslims] then hope that they [the Jews] would believe in you, and a party from among them indeed used to hear the Word of God, then altered it after they had understood it, and they know [this]. (Sura 2:75)
>
> Most surely there is a party amongst those who distort the Book with their tongue that you may consider it to be [a part] of the Book, and they say, "It is from God," while it is not from God, and they tell a lie against God whilst they know. (Sura 3:78)
>
> Of those who are Jews (there are those who) alter words from their places [in the Book]. (Sura 4:46)
>
> But on account of their [the Jews'] breaking their covenant We [that is, God] cursed them and made their hearts hard; they altered the words from their places and they neglected a portion of what they were reminded of; and you [Muslims] shall always discover treachery in them excepting a few of them. (Sura 5:13)

> O followers of the Book [Jews and Christians]! indeed Our Apostle has come to you making clear to you much of what you concealed of the Book and passing over much; indeed, there has come to you light and a clear Book from God. (Sura 5:15)

The Koran states further: "Woe, then, to those who write the book with their hands and then say: This is from God, so that they may take for it a small price; therefore woe to them for what their hands have written and woe to them for what they earn" (Sura 2:79).

According to Al-Ṭabarī (d. 923), this verse (Sura 2:79) refers to the description of Mohammed that had been included in the original divine version of the Torah but that the Jews had removed from its place.[56] Al-Ṭabarī continues by quoting ʿUthman (579–656), the third Caliph (or Successor to Mohammed), who states that "the Jews added to the Torah what they liked and deleted from it what they hated, for example, Mohammed's name. Thus they brought God's anger upon themselves, and so God recalled or took back to heaven parts of the Torah."[57] To Al-Ṭabarī, the Torah currently in use among Jews is not even the actual Torah that Ezra wrote but a distorted second Torah that was written by some rabbis and presented as genuine.[58] Instead of charging Ezra with falsifying the Torah, he blames the rabbis.

According to al-Maqdisī (946–1000), however, it was Ezra's student who distorted the Torah:

> When Nebuchadnezzar destroyed Jerusalem, burned the Torah, and exiled the Israelites to the land of Babylon, the Torah disappeared from among the Jews until the time when Ezra renewed it for them, according to what they say. It has been learned from those knowledgeable about history and legends that Ezra dictated the Torah at the end of his life, and died soon after having completed his task.
>
> [Before his death, however, Ezra] had handed the book over to one of his disciples, and ordered him to read it before the people after his death. It is from this disciple that they [the Jews] have taken their Torah and subsequently copied it. They claim that it was this disciple who corrupted [the text], adding to it and distorting it. This is why distortions and corrupted passages occur in it and why certain words of the Torah have been replaced by others, because it is the work of a man living after Moses, for in it is related what happened to Moses, such as how he died, how he gave his last instructions to Joshua, son of Nun; how the Israelites grieved and wept over him, and other things of which it is obvious to anyone endowed with reason that they are not the word of God nor the word of Moses.[59]

Al-Maqdisī assumes that the Torah was distorted and falsified because of the fact that Moses's death is reported in it but also because Mohammed is not predicted in it and because of the discrepancies among the Hebrew Torah, the Christian and Greek Old Testament, and the Samaritan texts: "All this points to distortions and alterations effected by them, since it is inconceivable that [the Torah] should contain contradictions coming from God. I have explained all this to you, so that you will not be discouraged when they say that Muḥammad is not mentioned in the Torah."[60]

Most prominent in his castigation of the Jews for their falsification of scripture, however, is Ibn Ḥazm. His book contains a chapter of more than two hundred pages with the title "Chapter on the obvious contradictions and clear lies in the book which the Jews call 'Torah' and in others of their books, as well as in the four Gospels, which will demonstrate convincingly that they have been corrupted and are different from what God, praised be He, has revealed."[61] Among the corruptions are the chronological impossibilities of the antediluvian patriarchs surviving the flood, the geographic impossibility of the four rivers coming from Eden, the theological impossibility of man being in the image of God and of all the anthropomorphisms that describe God, and the attribution of lies and sins to the patriarchs, such as Lot sleeping with his daughters; Jacob cheating his brother; Abraham lying about Sarah, his wife, and marrying his sister; Judah sleeping with his daughter-in-law because he thought she was a harlot; David cheating with Bathsheba and killing Uriah, her husband; and Solomon being induced to idolatry because of his wives. To Ibn Ḥazm, these stories could have been written only by a heretic who mocks the sacred. He compares these stories to the unreliable and contradictory stories in the four Gospels.

According to Ibn Ḥazm, the one who deliberately falsified the text, the heretic who mocked religion, is none other than Ezra the Scribe.[62] It was Ezra himself who inserted the malicious lies about the patriarchs and the monarchs, who ridiculed faith, and who made a mockery of God and his prophets.[63] Indeed Ibn Ḥazm (994–1064) may have been the first among the Muslims to portray Ezra as the deliberate falsifier of the biblical text.[64] He writes in his book against Ibn al-Nagrīlah:

> They [the Jews] acknowledge that throughout the entire period of their rule, the Torah was in the sole possession of the priests. Thus, for a period of almost 1200 years, the Torah was handed down from one single person to another—a situation that [almost] guarantees alterations, substitutions, distortions, interpolations and omissions, all the more so since most of their kings and all of the masses throughout most of the period were idol-worshippers who had turned their backs on their faith and even killed their own prophets.[65] It must therefore be assumed that the true Torah was undoubtedly lost and changed under these conditions. . . . They admit even that Ezra, who wrote [the Torah]) for them from his memory after it was lost, was only a scribe and not a prophet.[66]

Ibn Ḥazm was followed by Samau'al al-Maghribi, a twelfth-century scholar and physician who lived in present-day Syria, Iraq, and Iran. Brought up a Jew, Samau'al converted to Islam and wrote a tract against the Jews and Judaism. According to Samau'al, too, it was Ezra who falsified and corrupted the Torah:

Ezra's tomb (east view over lower Tigris). Courtesy of the Art, Architecture and Engineering Library Lantern Slide Collection, University of Michigan Library.

> Moses gave the Torah to the sons of Aaron, depositing it among them and keeping it away from all others. These Aaronide priests, who knew the Torah and had memorized most of it, were slain by Nebuchadnezzar in a massacre at the conquest of Jerusalem. Memorizing the Torah was neither obligatory nor traditional, but each Aaronide used to memorize a section of it. When Ezra saw that the Temple of the people was destroyed by fire, that their state had disappeared, their masses dispersed and their book vanished, he collected some of his own remembrances and some still retained by the priests, and from these he concocted the Torah that the Jews now possess. That is why they hold Ezra in such high esteem and claim that a light appears over his tomb [discussed in the next section], situated near the marshes of Iraq, even unto the present day; for he has produced a book that preserves their religion. Now this Torah that they have is in truth a book by Ezra, and not a book of God. This shows that the person who collected the sections now in their possession was an empty man, ignorant of divine attributes. That is why he attributed anthropomorphism to God, [and why he attributed to him] regret over His past actions and the promise of abstention from similar acts in the future.[67]

Samau'al provided a motive though for Ezra's actions: "Ezra, being of a priestly family, sought to prevent the rule of the Davidic dynasty during the days of the Second Temple as it had in the times of the First. For that reason, Ezra invented tales of incest to sully David's origins; and in fact, he achieved his goal: During the Second Temple period the regime was in the hands of priests of the House of Aaron, not the Davidic dynasty."[68] The Torah in the possession of the Jews is thus *Kitāb ʿAzrā,* The Book of Ezra, and not *Kitāb Allāh,* the Book of God.

Ezra's Tomb

According to Islamic tradition, Ezra's tomb lies on the banks of the Tigris near Basra, Iraq. It is a pilgrimage site for the local Marsh Arabs and Jews. The Andalusian poet Judah al-Ḥarizi (1170–1235) reports that, while journeying to the Near East in the first quarter of the thirteenth century, he was told of lights ascending from the tomb of Ezra the priest in the Iraqi village of Basra.[69] Al-Ḥarizi states: "There goes up from his grave on certain nights an illumination that dispels the thick darkness. Because of this phenomenon the people believe that the Glory of the Lord shines upon him [כבוד יהוה זרח עליו], and many people make pilgrimage to him. Round about him are the graves of the seven upright saints. On certain nights lights [descend] upon them, sparkling from the highest heaven and their rays come down upon earth."[70] A twelfth-century Jewish traveler, Petaḥiyah of Regensburg, also asserts that "Ezra, the scribe, is buried on the boundary of the land of Babylon. When the pillar of fire is over his grave, the structure erected on it is not visible on account of the brightness over his grave."[71]

Ezra's tomb is noted elsewhere as well. In 1414 C.E., Rabbi Yiṣhaq Elfarra of Málaga was told while on pilgrimage to Jerusalem that a cloud ascends from the tomb of Ezra the scribe in the Aleppan village of Taduf.[72]

Ezra in Rabbinic Tradition

In contrast to Samaritan, Christian, and Islamic traditions of Ezra, rabbinic traditions about him are entirely positive. The rabbis saw themselves as scribes and as Torah scholars and so identified with him. Thus there are a good many rabbinic tales about Ezra the scribe.

Ezra as Prophet

According to the rabbis, Ezra had prophetic stature and was actually the prophet Malachi. One reason for latching on to Malachi, the last prophet in the "book of twelve," is that the Hebrew word "*mal'aki*" is open to interpretation. Rather than being a proper name, it may mean "my messenger" as in Malachi 3:1 (הִנְנִי שֹׁלֵחַ מַלְאָכִי [See, I am sending my messenger (or Malachi)]).

In fact, it is translated "messenger" in the Septuagint, except that the final letter "i" (*yud,* י) was mistaken for a *vov* (ו), a common confusion, and was thus translated "his messenger," rather than "my messenger." The Targum of Malachi, that is, the ancient Aramaic translation of the prophetic book (ca. 110 C.E.), actually reads "my messenger whose name is called Ezra the scribe"; thus the assimilation between the two is very old. The rabbis of the Talmud naturally debate the truth of this ascription:

> It has been taught: R. Joshua b. Korha said: Malachi is the same as Ezra. But the Sages say that Malachi was his proper name.
>
> R. Nahman said: There is good ground for accepting the view that Malachi was the same as Ezra. For it is written in the prophecy of Malachi, "Judah has dealt treacherously and an abomination is committed in Israel and in Jerusalem, for Judah has profaned the sanctuary of YHWH which he loves and has married the daughter of a foreign God." And who was it that put away the foreign women? Ezra, as it is written, "And Shechaniah the son of Jehiel, one of the sons of Elam answered and said unto Ezra: We have broken faith with our God and have married foreign women." (Megillah 15a)

The implication of Ezra being the last prophet, Malachi, that is, God's messenger, is that, with Ezra's death, prophecy ended, and for the rabbis that meant that a new era began with his death. "After the later prophets Haggai, Zechariah, and Malachi had died, the Holy Spirit [the spirit of prophecy] departed from Israel" (*Yoma* 9b). This was to be an era in which God communicated to his people Israel not through prophecy but through Torah and Torah scholars (i. e., through the rabbis themselves). "Moses received the Torah at Sinai and transmitted it to Joshua, Joshua to the elders, the elders to the prophets, and the prophets to the men of the Great Assembly" (*Aboth* 1.1).

The Torah referred to here is the oral Torah, understood to be the whole body of custom and interpretation that is finally crystallized in the Talmud. The imagined Great Assembly was an assembly of Torah scholars. According to its self-understanding, the Talmud is the codified, written deposit of tradition transmitted orally from Moses until it was finally written down. According to the sequence proposed in this passage, the transmission process altogether avoided the temple and its priesthood, the central institution of second-temple Judaism.[73] The Talmud does not state where Ezra fits into this line of tradition, but Maimonides (1135–1204 C.E.), the preeminent medieval Jewish philosopher and Torah scholar, extrapolates:

> The whole of the Law was written down by Moses our teacher before he died, in his own hand. He gave a scroll of the Law to each tribe; and he put another scroll by the Ark for a witness, as it is written "take this book of the Law, and put it by the side of the Ark of the Covenant of YHWH your God, that it may be there for a witness against you" (Deut. 31:26).
>
> But the Commandment, the interpretation of the Law—he did not write it down, but gave orders concerning it to the elders, to Joshua, and to all the rest of Israel, as it is written "all this word which I command you, that shall ye observe to do . . ." (Deut. 13:1). For this reason, it is called the Oral Law.

> Although the Oral Law was not written down, Moses our teacher taught all of it in his court to the seventy elders. . . . And to his student Joshua, Moses our teacher passed on the Oral Law and ordered him concerning it. And so Joshua throughout his life taught it orally.
>
> Many elders received it from Joshua, who passed it to . . . [list of prophets]. . . . Baruch son of Neriah received it from Jeremiah and his court, and Ezra and his court received it from Baruch and his court.
>
> Ezra's court is called the Men of the Great Assembly, and they were Haggai, Zechariah, and Malachi, and Daniel, Hananiah, Mishael, and Azariah, and Nehemiah son of Hachaliah, and Mordechai, and Zerubbabel; and many other sages were with them, numbering altogether one hundred twenty elders.
>
> The last of them was Simon the Just, who was included among the one hundred twenty, and received the Oral Law from all of them; and he was High Priest after Ezra.

Maimonides inserts Ezra between the prophets and Simon, using Baruch, Ezra's putative teacher (discussed later) as the lynchpin.[74] His method of reasoning is clear. If the prophets received it, then Jeremiah must have been among them; and if Jeremiah, then necessarily Baruch ben Neriah, his secretary; and if Baruch, then Ezra, who (according to the Talmud) was Baruch's student. Scholars debate the identity of Simon the Just in the Talmudic passage. He is either Simon I (high priest at the end of the fourth century BCE) or Simon II (high priest at the end of the third).[75] However, an Ezra who would know both Baruch ben Neriah (ca. 586 BCE) and Simon (even Simon I) would compress the nearly three-hundred-year time frame of the Babylonian and Persian periods to the span of a single person's adult lifetime.

Maimonides continues with a list of known rabbinic scholars, making the authors of the Talmud the direct heirs of Ezra and Moses and the Talmud itself Moses's Oral Law written down. As the deposit of the Oral Torah that Moses received at Sinai, the Talmud becomes God's communication with his people. The chain of transmission outlined in both the Talmud (*Aboth*) and Maimonides implies that the age of prophecy had ended and the age of the Torah scholar, that is, the rabbinic age, had begun with Ezra's death. This is the meaning of Ezra for the rabbis.

The rabbis give the three prophets of the return, Haggai, Zechariah, and Malachi (Ezra), an important role in rebuilding the temple. Ezra 3 states that the altar was built and sacrifices laid on it even before the temple's foundations were laid. According to the rabbis, this anomalous act could not have been done without prophetic permission, and they determined that Ezra/Malachi was the one who gave it:[76] "Rabbah b. Hanah said in R. Johanan's name: Three prophets went up with them from the Exile: one testified to them about [the dimensions of] the altar; another testified to them about the site of the altar; and the third testified to them that they could sacrifice even though there was no Temple (because the site was holy for all time)" (*Zevachim* 62a).

The rabbis asked first how it was possible to recognize the site of the destroyed altar after all those years. Some say it was because the prophets saw the angel Michael standing at the spot and offering sacrifices on it, whereas others point to a more terrestrial reason—they could still smell the sacrifices and the incense: "As for the Temple, it is well, for its outline was distinguishable [by the stones of the old foundation]; but how did they know [the site of] the altar [the sacrificial altar outside the temple]?—Said R. Eleazar: They saw [in a vision] the altar built, and Michael the great prince standing and offering upon it. While R. Isaac Nappaha said: They saw Isaac's ashes lying in that place.[77] R. Samuel b. Nahman said: From [the site of] the whole House they smelled the odor of incense, while from there [the site of the altar] they smelled the odor of limbs" (*Zevachim* 62a).

The Date of Ezra's Ascent to the Land of Israel

The problem with Ezra being the third prophet of the three who determined the location of the temple is that according to the biblical text, Ezra did not return until after the temple was already finished and dedicated (cf. Ezra 6; Ezra 7). The rabbis can only wonder why Ezra went up to Jerusalem so late. Why did he not come at the earliest opportunity under Cyrus? One view was that he would not leave his aged teacher, Baruch ben Neriah, Jeremiah's amanuensis (Jer. 36:4), alone in Babylon: "R. Samuel b. Martha—said: The study of the Torah is superior to the building of the Temple, for as long as Baruch b. Neriah was alive Ezra would not leave him to go up to the land of Israel" (*Megillah* 16b).

The study of Torah is superior to building the temple, because that is what the rabbis themselves did all day—study Torah! According to another rabbinic source (*Shir Hashirim Rabbah* 5:5), God commanded Ezra to stay in Babylon as long as Jeshua the son of Jehozadak was alive and was high priest in Jerusalem. This high priest was the scion of a family that had been high priests since the time of Solomon and Zadok. If Ezra had come to the Holy Land during the lifetime of Jeshua, he would have had a better claim on the office than did Jeshua because of his superior merit. Out of respect for Jeshua, he remained in Babylon until Jeshua's death.[78] The thought that Ezra as Torah scholar would have had a better claim on the office of high priest than the high priest himself fits with the general rabbinic attitude of superiority toward the priesthood. A third reason for Ezra's delay is also proposed—he was working on his family tree: "Ezra wrote the book that bears his name and the genealogies of the Book of Chronicles up to his own time. This confirms the opinion of Rab, since Rab Judah has said in the name of Rab: Ezra did not leave Babylon to go up to Eretz Yisrael until he had written his own genealogy. Who then finished it [the Book of Chronicles, Ezra, and Nehemiah]?—Nehemiah the son of Hachaliah" (*Baba Bathra* 15a).

A fourth reason for the delay is offered (*Qiddušin* 69a): "For R. Eleazar said: Ezra did not go up from Babylon until he made it (that is, Babylon) like pure sifted flour: then he went up." That is, he would not leave Babylon until he could bring out of Babylon all the Judeans of impure bloodline there so that all those remaining would be pure. (This quotation from the Babylonian Talmud was written by Judeans who were themselves descended from those who had not gone up to Israel but had remained in Babylon.)

The rabbis disputed whether the people who went up with Ezra to the land of Israel went up voluntarily or against their will:

> Abaye said: We learned: "they went up" [that is, voluntarily];
>
> Raba said: We learned: He [Ezra] brought them up [that is, against their will].
>
> And they differ over R. Eleazar ['s dictum,] viz.: "Ezra did not go up from Babylon until he made it like pure sifted flour: then he went up."
>
> Abaye rejects it, Raba accepts it [since such a purging could have been carried out only by compulsion]. Alternatively, all accept R. Eleazar's dictum, but they differ in this: One teacher [Abaye] holds that he [merely] separated them [those with pure bloodline from those without such], whereupon they [those without a pure bloodline] voluntarily ascended [to Palestine]: the other teacher holds that [even so] he led them up against their will.

Again, this discussion reflects the fact that the rabbis living in Babylon and writing this text did not themselves go up to Israel. A fifth (Midrashic) reason why Ezra did not go up at the first opportunity under Cyrus is also proposed: "God told Daniel to bring Zerubbabel and Ezra before Cyrus to inform him [Cyrus] that God has commanded him to rebuild the temple in Jerusalem. Ezra then traveled through the cities and announced to the Israelites that it was time to return to Jerusalem and rebuild it. However, the Israelites thought that Ezra was lying, and they sought to kill him. Ezra discovered the plot and prayed to God; thereupon, God hid Ezra from the mob. [Therefore,] Ezra did not return with Zerubbabel at this time because he was hiding from those seeking to kill him. It was their fault, not Ezra's, that he did not participate in rebuilding the temple."[79] The Midrashist attempts to exonerate Ezra for not going up to Israel when he definitely could have gone. All these responses assume that Ezra was alive in the time of Cyrus and that he certainly could have gone up had he wanted to.

Ezra as High Priest

The rabbis also assume that Ezra became high priest upon his entrance into Israel. They describe him as being one of only a few people who prepared the ashes of the red heifer (*Parah,* chapter 3; Mishnah 5; cf. Num. 19:2–7), an act devolving upon the high priest. The rabbis comment, "In Ezra 7:5, we read 'the son of Aaron, the High Priest,' and in the next verse (7:6) we read, 'this Ezra,' so by putting these together, we have 'Aaron the High Priest is this Ezra' [that is, Ezra is equal to Aaron]. Ezra would have been esteemed even over his illustrious ancestor Aaron, had the latter been alive then" (*Yalkut Shimoni* 114).[80]

Ezra as Second Moses

The rabbis saw Ezra as a second Moses. Like Moses, Ezra is said to have reached such a level of holiness that he was able to pronounce the divine name "as it is written."[81] His piety is especially extolled by the rabbis (Midrash Psalms on 105: 2):

> And Ezra blessed the Lord, the great God [Neh. 8:6]. What does "great" imply?
>
> —R. Joseph said in the name of Rab: "He magnified Him by [pronouncing] the Ineffable Name [the tetragrammaton]."
>
> R. Giddal said:
>
> [He recited], "Blessed be the Lord, the God of Israel, from everlasting even to everlasting."
>
> Said Abaye to R. Dimi: But perhaps it means that he magnified Him by [pronouncing] the Ineffable Name?
>
> He answered: One does not pronounce the Ineffable Name outside [the limits of the Temple].
>
> But may one not? Is it not written: "And Ezra the scribe stood upon a pulpit of wood, which they had made for the purpose. [. . . and Ezra praised the great God]."
>
> And R. Giddal [commenting thereupon] said: He magnified Him by [pronouncing] the Ineffable Name.—That was a decision in an emergency [that is, it is not to be taken as a precedent]. (*Yoma* 69b)

Ezra's merit before God carried over onto all his descendants, even to the tenth generation. The rabbis were attempting to appoint one among them to arbitrate a dispute between R. Joshua and R. Gamaliel. They ask:

> Whom shall we appoint [to arbitrate]? We can hardly appoint R. Joshua, because he is one of the parties involved!
>
> We can hardly appoint R. Akiba because perhaps Rabban Gamaliel will bring a curse on him because he has no ancestral merit.
>
> Let us then appoint R. Eleazar b. Azariah, who is wise and rich and the tenth in descent from Ezra. He is wise, so that if anyone puts a question to him he will be able to answer it. He is rich, so that if occasion arises for paying court to Caesar he will be able to do so. He is tenth in descent from Ezra, so that he has ancestral merit and he [Rabban Gamaliel] cannot bring a curse on him. They went and said to him: Will Your Honor consent to become head of the Academy? (*Berakoth* 27b)

According to the rabbis, Ezra's major goal was the spread of Torah so that it became the common property of the people at large.[82] Because of this it was said of him that if Moses had not already brought the Torah to the people Israel, then Ezra would have merited doing so, because he was a second Moses:

> It has been taught: R. Jose said: Had Moses not preceded him, Ezra would have been worthy of receiving the Torah for Israel. Of Moses it is written, "And Moses went up unto God" [Exod. 19:3] and of Ezra it is written, "He, Ezra, went up from Babylon" [Ezra 7:6]. As the going up of the former refers to [receiving the] law, so does the going up of the latter. Concerning Moses, it is stated: "And the Lord commanded me at that time to teach you statutes and judgments" (Deut. 4:14), and concerning Ezra, it is stated: "For Ezra had prepared his heart to expound the law of the Lord [his God] to do it and to teach Israel statutes and judgments" [Ezra 7:10]. (*Sanhedrin* 21b)

Since similar words are used to describe both Moses and Ezra, they must have performed a similar task and would have been similarly worthy of it. It was only an accident of history then that caused Moses to receive the Torah and not Ezra. Since it was only his desire to expound the law and to do it and to teach in Israel statutes and judgments that made him worthy, not his piety or his brilliance, anyone with that desire (i. e., the rabbis themselves) would be just as worthy.[83]

Tradition has it that to further his purpose still more, Ezra ordered that additional schools for children be established everywhere, though the old ones sufficed to satisfy the demand (*Baba Bathra* 21b). He thought that the rivalry between the old and the new institutions would redound to the benefit of the pupils. Ezra was also considered a second Moses because the rabbis assumed that the Torah had been forgotten, that it was absent from the land of Israel, and that Ezra had brought it into the land in the same way that Moses had. "For in ancient times when the Torah was forgotten from Israel, Ezra came up from Babylon and established it" (*Sukka* 20a). Even though the Torah was not given through him (originally), its writing was changed through him: "Originally the Torah was given to Israel in [paleo-]Hebrew characters and in the sacred [Hebrew] language; later, in the times of Ezra, the Torah was given in Assyrian script [the square script used in modern Hebrew] and Aramaic language. [Finally], they selected for Israel [or Israel selected] the Assyrian script and Hebrew language, leaving the [paleo-] Hebrew characters and Aramaic language for the Samaritans" (*Sanhedrin* 21b).

Here we see that the Samaritans merited the original script but not the original language. That was left for Israel. That the rabbis did not consider the Samaritans to be part of Israel is amply demonstrated here and in a late rabbinic tradition that recalls the total excommunication of the Samaritans, allegedly proclaimed by Ezra in the presence of three hundred priests, three hundred children, and three hundred scrolls of the Torah and with the accompaniment of three hundred trumpets (Tanhuma on Vayeshev 2 end, *Pirqe de-Rabbi Eliezer* 37 [38]).[84]

Ezra is said to have written all the genealogies in Chronicles up to his own time (*Baba Bathra* 15a) as well as a portion of the Psalms (*Song of Songs Rabbah* 4.19). Also ascribed to Ezra is the division of the Torah into readings for the Sabbath and holiday synagogue services, as well as the following so-called ten regulations of Ezra:

1) That [portions of] the Torah be read [publicly] in the Minhah [afternoon] service on Sabbath [the regulations also delineate the portions to be read];
2) that the Torah be read [publicly] on Mondays and Thursdays [these were market days when people would be out and in the town squares];
3) that Courts be held on Mondays and Thursdays [for the same reason, people would be in town];
4) that clothes be washed on Thursdays [and be fresh for the Sabbath];
5) that garlic be eaten on Fridays [garlic was believed to increase semen count, and Friday nights were to be devoted to conjugal delights];
6) that the housewife rise early to bake bread [so that it would be available to the poor, should they come begging];
7) that a woman must wear a *sinnar* [no one is sure what this is];
8) that a woman must comb her hair before performing immersion [so that her hair will not be tangled when she is in the ritual bath and the water can reach all parts of it];
9) that peddlers [selling spices and perfumes desirable to women] be allowed to travel about in the towns [and go door to door];
10) He also decreed immersion [in a ritual bath] to be required by those to whom [seminal] pollution had occurred. (*Baba Kama* 82a)

Ezra as a Second Joshua

Ezra is also perceived as a second Joshua because he led the Judeans into the land of Israel in his day just as Joshua had in his day, but if so, the rabbis ask, why were there no miracles in the time of Ezra as there were in the time of Joshua? They reply: "The intention was to perform a miracle for Israel in the days of Ezra, even as it was performed for them in the days of Joshua bin Nun, but sin caused [the miracle to be withheld]" (*Berakot* 4a).

Indeed, according to the rabbis, the area occupied by those returning from Babylon is the area of "true Israel" and is holy for all time. This is the area of Israel that is obligated by the Sabbatical and Jubilee laws (that is, the area of land that may not be cultivated during these periods). The rest of Israel—those areas conquered by Joshua and those areas beyond the Jordan that were conquered by David—decrease both in holiness and in the degree to which they belong to the land of Israel proper. The conquest of the Holy Land on the first occasion [by Joshua] consecrated it for the time being but not for the future, whereas those areas settled by the returnees from Babylon were consecrated for all time (*Ḥullin* 7a). Thus, we find that Palestine is divided into three areas of decreasing holiness with reference to the Sabbatical Law:

1. [The fruit of] that territory occupied by those who came up from Babylon, namely from Eretz Israel as far as Achzib, may not be eaten nor may its soil be cultivated.
2. [The fruit of] that territory occupied by those who came up from Egypt, namely from Achzib to the River [Orontes] and up to [Mount] Amanus may be eaten but not cultivated. (*Shevi'ith* 6.1)
3. In Syria [that is, "greater Palestine, conquered by David] one may perform work on such produce as had been detached from the soil [without being concerned about how it became detached], but not on such produce still attached. They may thresh, winnow, and tread [this detached grain], and even bind it into sheaves, but they may not reap the grain, cut the grapes, or harvest the olives. (*Shevi'ith* 6.2)

The rabbis also asked which people were holier, the people of the first temple or the people of the second. Some answer the first, since God did not dwell in the second temple.

> R. Johanan said: The fingernail of the earlier generations is better than the whole body of the later generations.
>
> Said Resh Lakish to him: On the contrary, the latter generations are better, although they were oppressed by [other] governments, they occupied themselves with the Torah.
>
> [R. Johanan] replied: The Sanctuary will prove [my point] for it came back to the former generations, but not to the latter ones.
>
> Even if they had all come up in the time of Ezra, the Divine Presence would not have rested over the second Sanctuary, for it is written: "God shall enlarge Japheth, and he shall dwell in the tents of Shem," [that means that] although God has enlarged Japheth [Persia], the Divine Presence rests only in the tents of Shem [Solomon]. (*Yoma* 9a–b)

That God did not dwell in the second temple refers to the rabbinic dictum that the first sanctuary differed from the second in that five things were missing from the second that were present in the first: the ark, the ark cover, and Kerubim; the fire; the Shechinah [the in-dwelling divine presence]; the Holy Spirit [of Prophecy]; and the *Urim*-and-*Thummim* (*Yoma* 21b).[85]

Reaction to the Fall of the Temple

The rabbis blamed the people's idolatry for the fall of the first temple, and they projected onto the returnees from Babylon a fear for the fall of the second temple.

They tell this colorful story, all of which is supposed to have taken place when Ezra read the Book of the Law in front of the water gate (Neh. 8):

> And [they] cried with a great [loud] voice unto the Lord, their God [Neh. 9:4].
>
> What did they cry?—Woe, woe, it is he [the Evil Inclination] who has destroyed the Sanctuary, burnt the Temple, killed all the righteous, driven all Israel into exile, and is still dancing around among us!
>
> Thou hast surely given him to us so that we may receive reward through him. (*Yoma* 69b)

That is, because if they would overcome the Evil Inclination, Israel would be rewarded. The people respond that they want neither the Evil Inclination nor a reward through it. "We want neither him, nor reward through him! Thereupon a tablet fell down from heaven for them, upon which the word 'truth' was inscribed." That is, God agrees that it is better not to have the Evil Inclination at all, even if it means giving up the reward for overcoming it—whereupon the Evil Inclination leaves them.

> R. Hanina said: One may learn from this that the seal of the Holy One, blessed be He, is truth.
>
> They ordered a fast of three days and three nights, whereupon he [the Evil Inclination] was surrendered to them.
>
> He came forth from the Holy of Holies like a young fiery lion. Thereupon the Prophet [evidently Zechariah] said to Israel:
>
> This is the evil desire of idolatry, as it is said:
>
> And he said: This is wickedness [Zech. 5:8].
>
> As they took hold of him [that is, of the Evil Inclination], a hair of his beard fell out, he raised his voice and it was audible for four hundred parasangs. Thereupon they said: "What shall we do? Perhaps, God forbid, they might have mercy upon him in heaven!"—[so therefore they should not kill him].
>
> The prophet [Zechariah] said unto them:
>
> "Cast him into a leaden pot, and close its opening with lead, because lead absorbs the voice," as it is said:
>
> "And he said: 'This is wickedness.' So he thrust him back into the pot, and pressed the leaden weight down on its mouth" (Zech. 5:8).
>
> They said: "Since this is a time of Grace, let us pray for mercy for the Tempter to evil."
>
> They prayed for mercy, and he was handed over to them.
>
> He [God] said to them:
>
> "Realize that if you kill him [that is, the Evil Inclination], the world perishes."
>
> They imprisoned him for three days, then looked in the whole land of Israel for a fresh egg and could not find it. (*Yoma* 69b)

That is, once the Evil Inclination is imprisoned, there is no lust anywhere in the world. "They put out his eyes, but they let him go" (*Yoma* 69b). The rabbis assert by this story that without the Evil Inclination nothing is produced (not even an egg), and it is better to have the world as we know it than the sterile world of Gan Eden. Without the Evil Inclination, the world perishes.

Conclusion

A comparison of these different traditions about Ezra reveals Ezra as a sort of Rorschach, a blank slate upon which the reader may project his own anxieties, fears, and self-perceptions. The writings of the Church Fathers, the Samaritans, and the Muslims reveal a certain anxiety about the authenticity of their own scripture and condemn Ezra for having falsified the Jewish texts. The rabbis, in contrast, project upon Ezra their own self-image. Ezra was another Moses who created Torah and brought it to Israel. This was how the rabbis saw themselves as well, as creators or promulgators of Torah (albeit the Oral Torah) and as the ones who bring it to the people Israel. These descriptions of Ezra tell us about the groups describing him but not about Ezra himself or about the Torah that he is reputed to have brought. This is also true of modern scholars who attempt to describe Ezra's activities, as we will now see.

9

Ezra in Modern Scholarship

Modern biblical scholars have tended to credit Ezra with the creation of Judaism, and some have even claimed that without Ezra's bringing the Torah to Jerusalem, Judaism could not have existed. This line of thought goes back to Eduard Meyer, a nineteenth-century historian, and before that to the seventeenth-century scholars who asserted not only that Ezra brought the Torah to Judah but that in fact he wrote it. The seventeenth century marked a sea change in biblical interpretation, for it was then that scholars began to consider the Bible as just another ancient text, a product of human hands, the result of human experiences and culture. According to this view, biblical literature could be studied in much the same way that any ancient literature was studied. Attribution of Mosaic authorship of the Pentateuch slowly fell by the wayside, and the ascription of its final composition to Ezra began to take its place.

Seventeenth Century—Moses No Longer

We may begin our survey of modern biblical scholarship with the Englishman Thomas Hobbes (1588–1679), who wrote in his *Leviathan* (published in 1651) that if the Apocrypha (4 Ezra) may be believed, then Ezra wrote the Pentateuch:

> Who the original writers of the several books of Holy Scripture were has not been made evident by any sufficient testimony of other history. . . . The light therefore that must guide us in this question must be that which is held out unto us from the books themselves: and this light, though it show us not the writer of every book, yet it is not unuseful to give us knowledge of the time wherein they were written.
>
> If the books of the Apocrypha (which are recommended to us by the Church, for not canonical but yet profitable books for our instruction) may in this point be credited, the scripture was set forth in the form we have it by Ezra, as may appear according to that which he himself has said, in 4 Ezra 14:21, 22 where, speaking to God, he says thus: "Your law is burnt up; therefore no man knows the things which you have done, or the works that are to begin. But if I have found grace before you, send the holy spirit into me, and I shall write all that has been done in the world, since the beginning, which were written in your law, that men may find your path, so that they who will live in the latter days, may live." And verse 45:

> "And it came to pass, when the forty days were fulfilled, that the Highest spoke, saying, The first that you have written, publish openly, that the worthy and unworthy may read it; but keep the seventy last, that thou may deliver them only to such as be wise among the people" (Hobbes, *Leviathan*, chapter 33).

Thus Hobbes assumes from 4 Ezra 14 that the biblical text was burnt up in the conflagration that destroyed the first temple and that Ezra re-created it (or perhaps wrote it anew). Hobbes continues that it was also Ezra, as high priest at the time of the return, who enforced the scriptures as laws for the Jews:

> Between the time when the law was lost (which is not mentioned in the Scripture, but may probably be thought to be the time of Rehoboam when Shishak, King of Egypt, took the spoil of the Temple [I Kings 14: 26]) and the time of Josiah, when it was found again (II Kings 22–23), they had no written word of God, but ruled according to their own discretion, or by the direction of such as each of them esteemed a prophet.
>
> From hence we may infer that the Scriptures of the Old Testament, which we have at this day, were not canonical, nor a law unto the Jews, till the renovation of their covenant with God at their return from the Captivity, and restoration of their Commonwealth under Ezra. But from that time forward they were accounted the law of the Jews, and for such translated into Greek by seventy elders of Judaea, and put into the library of Ptolemy at Alexandria, and approved for the word of God. Now seeing Ezra was the high priest, and the high priest was their civil sovereign, it is manifest that the Scriptures were never made laws, but by the sovereign civil power. (Hobbes, *Leviathan,* chapter 42)

Hobbes wants to see Ezra as the civil authority so that he can more readily understand how Torah law became law for the Jews and, not incidentally, so that he may assert the right of a civil authority over an ecclesiastical one. Hobbes does not mention King Artaxerxes's role in enforcing Torah law but ascribes this function entirely to Ezra.

The *Tractatus Theologico-Politicus* published anonymously in 1670 by Baruch Spinoza (1632–1677) of Amsterdam, may have been influenced by Hobbes as well as by the works of Ibn Ezra (Rabbi Abraham ben Meir Ibn Ezra [1089–1167]) of Spain, one of the earliest pioneers of biblical criticism. Beginning to doubt with Ibn Ezra the Mosaic authorship of the Pentateuch, Spinoza concluded with Hobbes that Ezra wrote all of the first nine books, Genesis through 2 Kings, the books now collectively known as the Primary History. Spinoza quotes and elaborates upon Ibn Ezra as follows:

> Wherefore, Ibn Ezra, a man of enlightened intelligence, and no small learning, who was the first, so far as I know, to treat of this opinion, dared not express his

> meaning openly, but confined himself to dark hints which I shall not scruple to elucidate, thus throwing full light on the subject. (Spinoza, *Tractatus Theologico-Politicus* 8:9)
>
> When we put together these three considerations, namely, the unity of the subject of all the books, the connections between them, and the fact that they are compilations made many generations after the events that they relate had taken place, we come to the conclusion, as I have just stated, that they are all the work of a single historian.
>
> Who this historian was, it is not so easy to show; but I suspect that he was Ezra, and there are several strong reasons for adopting this hypothesis. (Spinoza, *Tractatus Theologico-Politicus* 8:99–100)

> The historian whom we already know to be but one individual brings his history down to the liberation of Jehoiakim, and adds that he himself sat at the king's table all his life—that is, at the table either of Jehoiakim, or of the son of Nebuchadnezzar, for the sense of the passage is ambiguous: hence it follows that he did not live before the time of Ezra. But Scripture does not testify of any except of Ezra (Ezra 7:10), that he "prepared his heart to seek the law of the Lord, and to set it forth, and further that he was a ready scribe in the law of Moses." Therefore, I can not find anyone, save Ezra, to whom to attribute the sacred books. (Spinoza, *Tractatus Theologico-Politicus* 8:101–3)

Thus, once Spinoza had decided that all the books were written by one man and that he had to have lived long enough after the death of Jehoiakim to know that the latter was present at the king's table all his life, then there was no one to whom Spinoza felt he could ascribe the writing except Ezra.

To advocate for Mosaic authorship in the light of these works, Richard Simon (1638–1712) wrote in his 1678 volume *Critical History of the Old Testament* that Moses wrote the Pentateuch originally but that it had been revised and added to over the centuries until the time of Ezra, who put on the final touches. It was in fact Ezra's additions that were the source of the contradictions and repetitions in the biblical text.[1]

Eighteenth Century—The Documentary Hypothesis

Biblical criticism changed sharply in 1711, when Henning Bernard Witter published his discussion of the beginning chapters of Genesis.[2] He showed that separate and independent sources in Genesis could be isolated on the basis of certain easily recognized criteria. He noticed, for example, that the story of creation in Genesis 1:1–2:3 differed markedly from the story in Genesis 2:4–3:24. The names used for God differed—Elohim (God) in Genesis 1 and YHWH Elohim (LORD God) in Genesis 2–3; more important, the order of creation was completely different in the two versions.

In an attempt to defend Mosaic involvement, Jean Astruc (1684–1766) argued in 1753 that Moses used the sources identified by Witter to compile not only the first few chapters of Genesis but all of the Hexateuch, Genesis-Joshua.[3] Like Witter's, Astruc's division into sources was based on differences in the divine name but also on the doublets and triplets of narratives found in Genesis. Astruc identified three separate narrative sources or documents that constituted Genesis. The first, by the Yahwist or, in German, the Jahwist, J, or the J writer, that author who used either the divine name alone—YHWH (JHWH in German), translated in English as "The LORD," or YHWH Elohim, translated as "LORD God." The second was by the E writer, who did not use the divine name but simply used Elohim (God) to refer to the deity. The third source was one whose contribution he could not assign to either source J or E. He traced these documents all the way up into Joshua. Moses had combined (but had not written) these separate sources and in combining them created doublets and inconsistencies.

Following Astruc, Johan Gottfried Eichorn (1752–1825) in his *Introduction* (1780–83) agreed that the entire Pentateuch was composed of several complete, parallel, and independent documents.[4] Thus began the so-called Documentary Hypothesis, which is still with us today. Beyond J and E, a priestly source P, responsible for the law codes of Exodus, Leviticus, and Numbers, as well as some narratives, was added, and D, or Deuteronomy, was included as a separate document. It was recognized that P used Elohim prior to Exodus 6:6, when God introduces himself to Moses under his own personal name, YHWH, but then used YHWH afterwards. Both Astruc and Eichorn argued that it was Moses, not Ezra, who put the strands together, for, they argued, if Ezra had really written the Pentateuch, the Samaritans could not have accepted it.[5]

The system of dividing the Hexateuch into these four documentary sources (J, E, P, and D) plus an editor became the modus operandi of critical biblical research. What remained was to determine the order of the documents. Until the nineteenth century the priestly source, P, was viewed as the earliest, the basis upon which the others were grafted, while D, Deuteronomy, was viewed as written last; in between lay the J and E sources.

The Nineteenth Century—The Laws Are Jewish, Not Israelite

This order of the documents was turned on its head in 1805, when de Wette concluded that the reforms of Josiah to centralize the cult (2 Kings 23) were based on the laws proclaimed in Deuteronomy, especially Deuteronomy 12:5–6, which demands that God be worshipped in only one place.[6] He argued that the book found in the temple by Josiah (2 Kings 22) must therefore have been the book of Deuteronomy. He went further, however, to assert that it was not simply found there but actually had been written then in the reign of Josiah (622 B.C.E.) by Levitical priests. This provided the fulcrum upon which all the other documents could be dated. Deuteronomy 12 commands that God be worshipped in only one place, "the place that God will choose to put his name there." Thus, those texts that presupposed the centralization of the cult in Jerusalem were necessarily written after Josiah, and those that did not presuppose it were necessarily written before.

Graf, writing in 1866, expanded upon the work of de Wette. He realized that the pre-exilic prophets did not mention P's ritual laws and that therefore, he concluded, these laws, which are similar to those described by the post-exilic prophet Ezekiel, must be postexilic.[7] This theory assumes that Ezekiel was not describing a situation that he knew from his experiences as a priest in the Jerusalem temple, but was rather making these laws up anew in Babylon, apparently from a general guilt about the temple's destruction. The theory assumes further that the pre-exilic prophets would not have ignored the temple ritual laws had they been operative.

It was Julius Wellhausen who brought Graf's theory into prominence by the success of his *Prolegomena to the History of Israel* (1883). Wellhausen, like his contemporaries of the Romantic period, viewed history as a decline and degeneration from a pure spontaneous past:[8]

> [Romanticism] validated strong emotion as an authentic source of aesthetic experience, placing new emphasis on such emotions as trepidation, horror, and terror and awe—especially that which is experienced in confronting the sublimity of untamed nature and its picturesque qualities, both new aesthetic categories.
>
> Romanticism elevated folk art and ancient custom to something noble, made spontaneity a desirable characteristic (as in the musical impromptu), and argued for a 'natural' epistemology of human activities as conditioned by nature in the form of language and customary usage.[9]

In this Romantic view, the early past was by definition free, spontaneous, connected to nature, and untamed. Furthermore, only the "natural," the "free," the "spontaneous" was "authentic," and only it was to be admired. Civilization, in contrast, was rigid, conformist, rational, and controlled. Wellhausen and his contemporaries read their theory of history into the biblical texts and ordered the documents that they had isolated according to it. Wellhausen could not see the "rigid," "legalistic," "ritual-based" religion (which he believed resulted from the Deuteronomic reform and which was further constrained in the priestly sources) as part of the religion of the pre-exilic prophets whom he loved. He saw a decline into rigidity beginning with Josiah and his forced centralization and ritualization of worship. Adhering to the work of Graf, he maintained that all the laws and rituals of P were post-exilic and late and therefore had nothing to do with either the prophets or even the religious life portrayed in the books of Samuel.

Wellhausen's aim in his *Prolegomena,* therefore, was to prove that the main legal sections of the Pentateuch (Exod. 12; 25–31; 35–40; all of Leviticus; plus the legal material in Numbers that constitutes the priestly code [P]), were in fact a reflection of postexilic Judaism and must therefore be considered a deviation from the authentic, spontaneous Israelite religion of the pre-exilic prophets that preceded it. He was also concerned to show that free, spontaneous, natural religion characterized Israelite religion prior to the Deuteronomic reforms of Josiah. The Priestly Code, he maintained, was the "constitution" of Judaism, which arose as an entirely new (degenerate) and legalistic phenomenon after the return from the Exile.[10] The Day of Atonement described in Leviticus 16, for example, is not known in the J portions of the Pentateuch, in Deuteronomy, or in the historical or prophetic books. It begins to show itself in embryo only in the exile.[11] Zechariah (8:19) knows nothing of it, for to him the fast of the seventh month is the fast of Gedaliah, commemorating Gedaliah's assassination and the end of the Kingdom of Judah (2 Kings 25:22–26). Ezra reads the law in the beginning of the seventh month, and they proceed to the holiday of Succoth, on the fifteenth, without mentioning the Day of Atonement on the tenth. According to Wellhausen, it is only after the exile that the great fast of the tenth day of the seventh month becomes the holiest day of the year. Guilt over the destruction of the temple brought about the emphasis on the law and indeed led to the creation of an entirely new holiday, the holiday of Yom Kippur, the Day of Atonement. "It is as if the temper of the exile had carried itself into the time of liberation also, . . . it is as if men had felt themselves not as in an earlier age only momentarily and in special circumstances, but unceasingly, under the leaden pressure of sin and wrath."[12]

After the exile, Wellhausen argues, the priests took control and introduced a theocracy, so "natural" religion died and "legalism" took over. Indeed, to Wellhausen, the law first became "canonical only through the influence of Ezra and Nehemiah."[13] Canonical validity was given to the Torah "by a single public and formal act (described in Neh. 8–10), through which it was introduced as the Magna Carta of the Jewish communion."[14] The law marked the beginning of the stagnation that is Judaism and had nothing to do with the people Israel or the spontaneous, "authentic," Israelite religion of the pre-exilic prophets.

Following quickly on Wellhausen's heels was Eduard Meyer (1896), who argues in *Die Enstehung des Judentums* (*The Origin of Judaism*) that Judaism was a creation of the Persian Empire. Without the Persian Empire and Artaxerxes's mandate of Torah law, there would have been no Judaism. Ezra did not simply bring the Pentateuch to Jerusalem, nor did he simply edit it, as Wellhausen proposes; Meyer states that Ezra was the author of at least the priestly law code and that it was Ezra who made the entirety law for Jews in the satrapy Beyond-the-River (*Abar Nahara*). Meyer states:

> Ezra is commissioned by the king and his ministers with a mission to Judah and Jerusalem. He is to investigate the situation in the community living there and to organize it on the basis of the law book of the law of God *which he had written.*

> This law had binding power over the Jews in [the satrapy of] Beyond-the-River. Ezra is to install judges who are to judge according to this law, and if they don't know the law, to teach it to them.
>
> This determination is indispensable for the entire edict. The law book of Ezra is by this introduced as a binding law for the Jewish community. Whoever will not join will be out of the community, their belongings confiscated. This law is not a private agreement among members of a religious gathering, but a legally binding basic law of the state for a recognized community. The introduction of this type of law book for a certain circle of subjects is only possible if it is sanctioned by the state.
>
> This is expressly stated in v. 26. Although it is said to apply to all the people in *Abar Nahara*, it really only applies to the Israelite people.[15]

Simply put, by mandating Torah law in Judah, the Persians created Judaism.

The Fallacy behind the Theories of Wellhausen and Meyer

This theory of the Documentary Hypothesis was foundational for the practice of biblical criticism. Four sources had been identified: J (the Yahwist or Jahwist), who wrote in the south during the tenth or ninth centuries B.C.E.; E (the Elohist), who wrote in the eighth century B.C.E. in the north in the days of the northern prophets; D (the Deuteronomist), who wrote in the time of King Josiah and mandated centralization of worship in Jerusalem; and P (the priestly writer), who wrote the law codes of the Torah during the exile or shortly thereafter. These four strands were then assembled and redacted as part of Ezra's reforms (Neh. 8). There is a fallacy in the ordering of these sources, however.[16]

The Place of Worship

Wellhausen begins his arguments with the place of worship.[17] He finds in the biblical portrayal of the earliest history of Israel not a hint of a fixed sanctuary.[18] He sees described in Genesis, as well as in the books of Judges and Samuel, a multiplicity of altars. Abram builds an altar and sacrifices on it spontaneously wherever YHWH appears to him. He builds one at the oak of Moreh, near Shechem (Gen. 12:7), another between Bethel and Ai (Gen. 12:8), one at Hebron (Gen. 13:18), another at Mount Moriah (22:9, 13). Isaac builds an altar and sacrifices on it at Beer Sheba (Gen. 26:25). Jacob builds one near Shechem (Gen. 33:20) and another at Beth-el (Gen. 35:7). Moses builds an altar at Riphidim after the victorious battle against Amelek (Exod. 17:15). In Judges and Samuel we read that Gideon builds an altar and sacrifices on it at Ophrah (Judges 6:24), Manoa builds an altar and sacrifices on it in the area of Dan (Judges 13:19–20), the people build an altar at Bethel and sacrifice on it (Judges 21:4), Samuel builds an altar at Ramah (1 Sam. 7:17), Saul builds an altar in the midst of his battle against the Philistines (1 Sam.

14:35), and David builds an altar at the threshing floor of Araunah and sacrifices on it (2 Sam. 24:25).

To Wellhausen and his followers, this is an accurate portrayal of Israel's earliest history and describes an authentic, natural, and spontaneous Israelite religion. The difficulty, and what Wellhausen couldn't have known, is that this description of the patriarchs going about building altars and sacrificing on them wherever they experienced an epiphany is in reality a description of classic Greek religion and has nothing to do with the religions of the ancient Near East (Mesopotamia, Egypt, and of the Fertile Crescent), the context in which historical Israel was actually located.

The Role of Temples and Altars in the Ancient Near East

In contrast to Greek religion, in the ancient Near East and Egypt the temples were always the fixed homes of the gods, where the gods lived and where the daily life of the gods was carried out. There they were washed, clothed, and fed their two meals daily (morning and evening) by the priests who composed their household staff.[19] It is exactly this view of the temple and of the god that is reflected in the priestly portions of the biblical text. Like their counterparts throughout the ancient Near East, the priestly writers saw YHWH as inhabiting the tabernacle: "Moses was not able to enter the tent of meeting because the cloud settled upon it, and YHWH's glory filled the tabernacle" (Exod. 40:35), as well as the temple: "And when the priests came out of the holy place, a cloud filled the house of YHWH, so that the priests could not stand to minister because of the cloud; for YHWH's glory filled YHWH's house" (1 Kings 8:10–11). The cloud was the physical manifestation of YHWH's presence.

As was routine in the ancient Near East, the sacrifices were the god's daily meals. So also in the priestly portions of the biblical text, we read that the morning and evening temple sacrifices constituted YHWH's daily food ration.[20] As everywhere in the ancient Near East, the gods in ancient Israel are depicted receiving their meals (the sacrifices) in their homes (the temples) at fixed times, twice a day, a morning and evening meal, as was customary in antiquity. This was also the case in Judah. "Command the Israelites, and say to them: My offering, my food, for my fire, my offerings of pleasing odor, you shall take care to offer to me at its appointed time . . . two male lambs a year old without blemish, daily, as a regular offering. One lamb you shall offer in the morning, and the other lamb you shall offer at twilight" (Num. 28:2–4).

Because the temples were the homes of the gods, ancient Near Eastern temples went through a regular annual purgation ritual, usually as part of the preparation for the New Year's celebration. This is similar to the purgation ritual described in Leviticus 16. Contrary to Wellhausen, Leviticus 16 does not prescribe a day of atonement for sin. Yom Kippur should not be translated "Day of Atonement."

Rather, it is simply a day of purgation, of cleansing the sanctuary, and it occurred once a year, during the regular fall New Year's activities.[21] Such annual purgation rites were typical of ancient Near Eastern temples. The word *kuppuru* is Akkadian and means "to purge," to "wipe off," "to cleanse [magically]," and commonly refers to temple purification rites.[22] We read, for example, the following purgation ritual for the temple of Marduk in Babylon.[23]

> On the fifth day of the month of Nisannu [the first month of the Babylonian year], the *šešgallu* priest shall arise and wash . . . he shall put on a linen robe in front of the god Bel [that is, Marduk] and the goddess Beltiya.
>
> He shall enter the temple Ezida, into the cella of the god Nabu [Marduk's son] with censer, torch, and *egubbū*-vessel to purify the temple. He shall sprinkle on the sanctuary water from the cisterns of the Tigris and Euphrates. He shall smear all the doors of the sanctuary with cedar oil. In the court of the cella, he shall place a silver censer, upon which he shall scatter aromatic ingredients and cypress. He shall call a slaughterer to decapitate a ram, the body of which the *mašmašu*-priest shall use in performing the *kuppuru* ritual for the temple. He shall recite the incantations for exorcising the temple. He shall purify the whole cella, including its environs, and shall remove the censer. The *mašmašu*-priest shall lift up the body of the aforementioned ram and proceed to the river. Facing west he shall throw the body of the ram into the river. He shall then go out into the open country. The slaughterer shall do the same with the ram's head. The *mašmašu*-priest and the slaughterer shall go out into the open country. As long as the god Nabu is in Babylon, they shall not enter Babylon, but stay in the open country from the fifth to the twelfth day (of Nissanu).

As in Judah, the *kuppuru* or temple purification rites in Babylon were simply part of the annual ritual for the New Year's Day, indicating Judah and Israel's participation in the global culture of the ancient Near East. The New Year's *kuppuru* rite thus has nothing to do with either exile or any perceived "leaden weight of sin and wrath" on Judean shoulders. That neither Zechariah nor Nehemiah saw the tenth day of the seventh month as a fast day demonstrates that the command to "afflict" or "humble yourself" (Lev. 16:29) did not include a day-long fast; if it did, it did not include one for the general population but for the priests only.

A similar purgation ritual can be seen in Hittite texts:

> [The priestess] wraps up a small piece of tin in the bowstring and attaches it to the sacrificers' right hands and feet. She takes it off them again and attaches it to a mouse [with the words]: "I have taken the evil off of you and transferred it to this mouse. Let this mouse carry it on a long journey to the high mountains, hills and dales.

> She turns the mouse loose [saying]: "Alauwaimis! This one pursue! [If you do] I shall give you a goat to eat.
>
> She sets up an altar of wood and breaks one long sacrificial loaf for the Alauwaimis gods, she breaks one sacrificial loaf for Alauwaimis, she breaks one sacrificial loaf for Mammas and she puts them on the altars.
>
> She then consecrates a goat for Alauwaimis [saying]: "Eat!"
>
> In front of the loaves she cuts up [the goat] and takes off its right shoulder. She cooks it on a fire and puts it in a place apart from the loaves. The liver she offers in the same manner [for the Alauwaimis gods and for Mammas].[24]

These sorts of purification rituals were common throughout the ancient Near East, and the rite described in Leviticus 16 must be understood in this way. The Israelite temple priests belonged to the same global culture as did the priests of Marduk and the Hittite priestess, and the rites prescribed cannot be considered to be the result of any specific historical event.

The Role of Temples in Ancient Greece

The Greek view of temples stands in stark contrast to the view prevalent throughout the ancient Near East, Canaan, and Egypt. Ancient Greeks, like other ancient peoples, prayed and made offerings to their gods in each god's sanctuary. Unlike sanctuaries in the ancient Near East, however, the sanctuary most common throughout the ancient Greek world consisted simply of an altar with a surrounding fence delineating the *temenos,* the sacred district, with no temple present at all.[25] There were sanctuaries that did include both temples and a statue of the god, of course, but there were only about twenty of these, whereas there were thousands of the simpler kind consisting of an altar only. In fact, the altar was the only essential ingredient in the Greek cult and sacrifice the only essential form of worship. The gods did not require a house to live in; rather, most lived in the sky or on Mount Olympus.[26] On the occasion of a sacrifice, the worshipper would begin with a prayer inviting the god to enter the sacred area and receive the offering. If a temple was built later, it would have been built primarily to shelter the many votive offerings dedicated to the god, one such offering being perhaps a statue of the god himself, but the temple was not built to house the statue. The statues, moreover, were the work of famous artists, known by name, and were simply gifts in which the god delighted. The god was not considered present in his statue; the statue was simply another, albeit more grandiose, offering to him. There was no rite like the "opening of the mouth ceremony" that existed in Mesopotamia to give life to the cult image, and because the god was not present in his statue there was no ceremony to induct it into the temple, as was required in the ancient Near East.[27] Nor were sacrifices conducted twice daily in the sanctuary to provide him with food but only occasionally, as at his festival days or at special times of the worshipper's personal need or thanksgiving.

The great temple of Asclepius at Epidaurus is typical, and the presence there of a large number of inscriptions that record the course of temple building enables us to understand the temple-building process in the Greek world.[28] The sanctuary of Asclepius was established toward the end of the sixth century at a site three and one-half miles west of the city of Epidaurus. The first step in establishing a cult in the Greek world, and the first step at Epidaurus, was to set up an altar to the god and to begin conducting sacrifices on it.[29] The altar dedicated to Asclepius dates to the end of the sixth century B.C.E.[30] A plague broke out in Athens in 430 and again in 427 B.C.E., and this was likely when a roofed building was built east of the altar. It was closed on three sides but open on the west facing the altar. It is thought that it contained an upper story on the three closed sides with galleries where the sick could sleep. It was not until around 375 B.C.E., however, that a decision was made to build a temple to Asclepius and not until 370 that the foundations for it were laid.[31] Thus, the altar was erected two and one-half centuries before there was any thought of building a temple.

The descriptions of the patriarchs, of Saul and even David, setting up isolated altars and sacrificing on them, a description that Wellhausen found so spontaneous, primitive, natural, and authentic, is a description of religion throughout the Greek world, not a description of religion in the ancient Near East. These texts, which have been assigned to the J writer and which Wellhausen and later biblical scholars see as the earliest of the biblical writings, were most likely the latest. This writer certainly wrote after Greek influence became paramount throughout the ancient Mesopotamian world. It is rather the priestly writer's description of the cult and its rituals that reflects the deepest antiquity of the ancient Near East, not J's.

Rules of Sacrifice

Wellhausen next investigates the way in which sacrifices were performed. He sees described in the priestly texts the minutia of the sacrificial rituals, whereas the sacrifices described in Genesis, Judges, and Samuel, purportedly describing Israel's earliest history, are done spontaneously, with little concern for ritual. Wellhausen complains that in the priestly texts disproportionate attention is given to the *when,* the *where,* the *by whom,* and the *how* of the sacrifices and that it is apparently from these that the sacrifice obtains its value, not from the god to whom it is given.[32] Again, this emphasis on procedure is the difference between the Greek and the ancient Near Eastern views of cult. As an example, we read the ritual for the daily sacrifices to the gods of Uruk in ancient Babylon:[33]

> Every day in the year, for the main meal of the morning, you shall prepare—in addition to the *sappu*-vessels of the *maqqānē*—eighteen gold *sappu*-vessels on the

> tray of the god Anu. Of these [eighteen vessels], you shall prepare before the god Anu seven *sappu*-vessels on the right—three for barley-beer and four for mixed beer, one for *zarbabu*-beer, and one alabaster *sappu*-vessel for milk—and four gold *sappu*-vessels for "pressed" wine. Similar [preparations shall be made] for the second [meal] of the morning as well as for the main and second [meals] of the evening. Among the gold *sappu*-vessels for the tray, there are five gold *sappu*-vessels which are bound with [strings of] inexpensive stones.

The text continues for another fifty lines on the obverse. The reverse begins: "[Below are enumerated] the bulls and rams for the regular offerings [to be made] every day of the year to the deities Anu, Antu, Ishtar, Nana, and the [other] gods dwelling in the Resh Temple, the Irigal Temple, and the Esharra Temple, [which is] the topmost level of the temple-tower of the god Anu. From the first day of the month Nisannu (that is, the first day of the year) through the thirtieth day of the month Adaru (the last day of the year) [they shall be offered] for the main meal of the evening." This also continues for another fifty lines. This is what it means for the sacrifices to be considered the daily meals of the gods. Not only are the ingredients of each meal specified, but also the times, the exact sets of dishes to be used, the precise placement of the dishes on the trays, the specification of which item is to be served in which dish, and, equally important, who is to do the serving. All this sort of ritual that Wellhausen objects to is reflected in Leviticus and Numbers. The prescriptions we read there for the daily and festival meals are similar to ritual texts everywhere in the ancient Near East. They were manuals for the temple priesthood that served as the god's household staff. Such texts were not needed in ancient Greece, since sacrifices there were primarily conducted by lay people on special occasions of celebration or lamentation to which the god was invited to participate.

The Judeans living in the Nile island of Elephantine in the Persian period shared the same world view: their temple was the home of their god, YHW, and could be destroyed only if the god who had been living in it had abandoned it.[34] The temple of YHW at Elephantine had been destroyed, so therefore YHW must have abandoned it. The Judeans at Elephantine complain:

> They came to the fortress of Elephantine with their weapons, broke into that temple, demolished it to the ground . . . and since this has been done [to us], we with our wives and children have been wearing sackcloth and fasting and praying to YHW Lord of Heaven . . . from the month of Tammuz, year 14 of King Darius [when the temple was destroyed] and until this day [the twentieth of Marḥešvan, year 17 of King Darius] we have been wearing sackcloth and fasting; our wives are made as widow[s]; (we) do not anoint [ourselves] with oil and do not drink wine. Moreover, from that [time] and until this day they did not make meal-offering or incense nor whole burnt offering in that Temple.[35]

There was no point in performing sacrifices on the altar at the site where the temple had once stood since the god who had been living in it was no longer in residence to consume them. For at least three years, the temple of YHW in Elephantine lay in ruins. During that time the Judeans of Elephantine were in mourning, sitting in sackcloth and ashes. They were in mourning for their god in the same way that the Israelites mourned after YHWH when the ark was kept at Kiriath-jearim: "From the day that the ark was lodged at Kiriath-jearim, a long time passed, some twenty years, and all the house of Israel mourned after YHWH" (1 Sam. 7:2).

This view of a god who partakes of the sacrifices as his daily meals is evident even in Persian period biblical texts. We read in Malachi (1:6–8) that YHWH complains that the people are offering him polluted food:

> A son honors his father, and servants their master. If then I am a father, where is the honor due me? And if I am a master, where is the respect due me? says YHWH of hosts to you, O priests, who despise my name. You say, "How have we despised your name?"
>
> By offering polluted food on my altar. And you say, "How have we polluted it?"
>
> "By thinking that YHWH's table may be despised.
>
> "When you offer blind animals in sacrifice, is that not wrong? And when you offer those that are lame or sick, is that not wrong? Try presenting that to your governor; will he be pleased with you or show you favor?" says YHWH of hosts.

YHWH compares himself to the Persian governor. As you would not offer polluted food to your governor, how can you offer it to your god? The parallel is informative. Food for the governor is equated with food for the god. This worldview, which we see expressed in the ritual and legal texts of the Hebrew Bible, is very ancient, but it also continued into the Persian period. Its continuation into the Persian period is a sign of the deep conservatism of the priests and of the priestly writers, not of angst over the destruction of the temple. New rituals could not be substituted for the ancient practices that had been part of the pre-exilic temple.

Wellhausen compares the stories of the patriarchs in Genesis, Judges, and Samuel to the laws described in the priestly writings and to descriptions there of the organization of the priesthood. In each case he misconstrues "simple" as "early" and "complex" as "late," when in reality the complex reflects the great temples of Babylon, Assyria, Egypt, and even the Bronze Age temples of Canaan with their huge staffs of priests, scribes, and accountants. It certainly reflects temple practices observed in the pre-exilic temple as well. In contrast, the simple practices revealed in the stories of the J writer actually reflect the Greek way of interacting with their gods in simple sanctuaries that had no temples and no priesthoods associated with them. The J writer was a product of the Hellenistic Age, when Greek thought and Greek ways of doing things pervaded the Mesopotamian world. The P texts reflect the situation in the ancient world well before these Hellenistic influences were felt.

The Role of Ezra in Wellhausen's Thought

Wellhausen saw the story of Josiah's finding the law book in the temple (2 Kings 23) as a true story except he believed that the law book was actually written then, not simply found then.[36] According to Wellhausen, the reforms of Josiah proclaimed Deuteronomy as a law code, and with it all the old freedoms that are described in the J and E texts were ended. In addition, the enforcement of Deuteronomy 18 brought with it the death of prophecy.[37] Whereas D was written in the time of Josiah, the priestly code was written for the first time only in Babylon as priests who had gathered around Ezekiel put to writing a system that Wellhausen refers to as "an artificial systematizing of given materials."[38] Wellhausen asserts that the priestly code, inserted into the Pentateuch only in Babylon under Ezekiel, was not introduced as law until 444 B.C.E. and that by Ezra, a century and a half after the exile.[39] Deuteronomy alone had been known in the interval between the return and Ezra's appearance. To quote Wellhausen: "The man who made the Pentateuch the constitution of Judaism was the Babylonian priest and scribe, Ezra."[40] He had come from Babylon in 458 at the head of a company of "zealous" Jews and was "provided with a mandate from the Persian king empowering him to reform, according to the law, the congregation of the temple.[41] Even if the letter from Artaxerxes in Ezra 7 is spurious, Wellhausen suggests it must still reflect the views of his contemporaries. Wellhausen states further that "the expression taken from Ezra's own memoirs (7:27) leaves no doubt that he was assisted by Artaxerxes in the objects he had in view," namely to install the priestly code as law in Judah.[42] He waited thirteen years to actually promote it because he needed the backing of the Persian governor, and this he did not have until the arrival of Nehemiah the Jew, cupbearer to the king.[43]

Wellhausen argues further that "as we are accustomed to infer the date of the composition of Deuteronomy from its publication and introduction by Josiah, so we must infer the date of the composition of the Priestly Code from its publication and introduction by Ezra and Nehemiah," so that the codification of temple ritual took place only in the postexilic period.[44] Wellhausen denies that Ezra was the author of P and asserts only that Ezra was the real and principal editor of the entire Hexateuch (Genesis–Joshua).[45]

Wellhausen asserts, moreover, that "Ezra and Nehemiah, and the eighty-five men of the Great Assembly (Neh. 8–10) who are named as signatories of the covenant [Neh. 10], are regarded by later tradition as the founders of the covenant."[46] By "later tradition" he means rabbinic tradition, but, as we have seen (chapter 8), according to rabbinic tradition, Ezra and his colleagues are regarded not as the founders but simply as having received the tradition from their predecessors and passed it on. To Wellhausen, it was Ezra's introduction and promulgation of the Pentateuch in his covenant renewal ceremony (Neh. 8–10) that caused the Jewish people to become "the people of the book." The Israelite religion that had once been free and spontaneous was now Jewish, rigidly prescribed and ossified. We have seen in chapters 2 and 3, however, that the ceremony portrayed in Nehemiah 8–10 that Wellhausen relies on so heavily is not historical.

Wellhausen admits that the elaborate and expensive worship system that is described in the priestly portions of the Pentateuch could not have survived without a state apparatus to collect the taxes and provide for the clergy.[47] He suggests that this apparatus was provided by the Jerusalem monarchy, as Wellhausen admits: "Under the shelter of the monarchy the priests of Jerusalem had grown great and had . . . attained . . . a position of legitimacy."[48] To Wellhausen this began only with Josiah, and did not date from the time of the temple's inception under Solomon. According to Wellhausen, however, after the fall of the monarchy and the subsequent return from captivity, the priests were the only ones who had the power and felt the obligation to place themselves at the head of the new state arising at the time of the return, so they created a theocracy.[49] In point of fact, as has been shown on numerous occasions, Yehud under the Persians was not a theocracy and was not ruled by its priesthood.[50] As in every province in the Persian Empire, all political power was in the hands of Persian garrison commanders, governors, and satraps. The role of the high priest was to serve the god, though he also tried to represent the Judeans to the Persian officials as best as he could and to represent as best as he could the will of the Persian officials to the people.[51] The priesthood held political power for only a very short while under the Maccabees, but this may have created in Josephus's mind the model of what Judean society was supposed to be (*Against Apion* 2:165).

The Twentieth Century and Ezra's Law Book

Wellhausen's conclusions were taken for granted in the early and mid-twentieth century by all but a few.[52] Discussions in the early and mid- twentieth century regarding Ezra concentrated on the identity of the law book that he is shown reading in Nehemiah 8 and on the date of his arrival in Jerusalem. Did he arrive in Jerusalem before or after Nehemiah? Was the law book the entire Pentateuch, or was it just P?[53] Most mid-twentieth-century commentaries on Ezra assumed that laws from the entire Pentateuch were in mind, although perhaps not in the form we now have them.[54]

A sea change occurred, however, in the understanding of the composition of the biblical text toward the end of the century. Scholars recognized that the E writer was a willow-o'-the-wisp. E was considered a northern writer, connected somehow to Elijah and Hosea, but certain texts that appeared to stem from a northern locale did not use Elohim, and some even used YHWH, so many began to question E's existence.[55] Moreover, other vignettes from the Abraham and Isaac narratives that were assigned to E had a decided southern cast, set as they were in the region of Beer Sheba and the Negev.

Just as E began to disappear from scholarly discourse, the J writer (who had been seen as the great historian and theologian of Solomon's court)[56] began to be viewed as postexilic, his writings a response to the exile, and the patriarchs as postexilic fictions.[57] Moreover, the existence of even three (let alone four) separate independent narratives combined by a postexilic editor was beginning to be doubted. By the end of the century it was held that the Pentateuch was composed of small independent literary units, combined by a postexilic Deuteronomic editor.[58] This mimics the theory proposed for the composition of the Gilgamesh epic in which isolated independent legends about the various characters were later combined by an epic writer or two.[59] There were thus no separate independent documents covering the whole history of Israel, just small chunks combined later into epic narratives. The documentary hypothesis as Wellhausen knew it was dead or dying. Reference to the example of the Gilgamesh epic strengthened the proposal that Babylonian literary traditions influenced the creation of the biblical story and that these were felt most keenly during the exile and after.

The Role of Ezra in Late-Twentieth- and Early Twenty-First-Century Scholarship

Blum took the role of Ezra seriously. He proposed that the Pentateuch was a combination of two independent epic works (each composed of smaller units), a priestly (PK or Priestly Komposition) and a Deuteronomic (DK or Deuteronomic Komposition).[60] These were combined only under Persian influence because, according to Blum, when the Persian government decided to grant political autonomy to Judah it needed to establish a single "constitution" by which to govern it. Under Ezra and the Persians, the Pentateuch became the official law code for Jews, especially Jews in Judah. This assumption is based on a literal reading of the Artaxerxes letter in Ezra 7.

Blenkinsopp too asserts that it was Persian imperial policy to insist on "local self-definition inscribed primarily in a codified and standardized corpus of traditional law backed by the central [Persian] government and its regional representatives."[61] Thus it was Persian insistence, with Ezra as Persia's representative in Judah, that led to the creation and the canonization of the Pentateuch as law and so to the creation of Judaism.

Both Blum and Blenkinsopp rely heavily on Frei's theory of Persian imperial authorization of local laws (discussed further later).[62] According to this theory, Ezra came to Judah with a mandate from the Persian king to set up a system whereby nonobservance of Torah law would be penalized with the backing of the Persian king. Having pushed the composition of the Pentateuch to the Persian period, scholars now seem willing to accept Persian period biblical texts verbatim and provide them with a credulity that previous readers lent to Moses and Abraham.

Imperial Authorization of Local Law and the Creation of Judaism

Biblical scholars today tend to regard the transformation of Torah law into a legally binding law code for Jews and, indeed, the creation of Judaism itself as a function of Persian imperial power with Ezra as its representative. This is largely because of their acceptance of Frei's theory of Persian imperial authorization of local norms.[63] Frei began by asking to what degree local communities within the Persian Empire had the authority to regulate their own interests. He assumed that since the Persian imperial ruling classes could not quickly build an efficient administration that could be managed by its own members, they needed to concede administrative responsibilities to the conquered.[64] After a survey of several Persian period inscriptions, Frei concludes that the Achaemenid Empire created a process by which local norms were not only approved by the imperial authority but adopted as its own.[65] That is, according to Frei, laws freely proposed by members of the local population were legitimated and enforced by the central government. In this bottom-up theory, imperial authorization was neither essential nor obligatory but was desired by local communities, since through it "the legal norms of a local body with subordinate status were elevated to the status of imperial legislation."[66] The most that the central authority did was to order local communities to codify their laws and norms and so make them known for authorization and enforcement. In this way, locally determined laws and customs became imperialized.

Frei bases his theory on Darius's so-called codification of local Egyptian laws;[67] on the trilingual inscription from Xanthus;[68] and on the so-called Elephantine Passover Letter.[69] Each of these is examined in this chapter.[70] Frei also bases his theory on Artaxerxes's letter in Ezra 7.[71] In fact, Ezra 7 is a major pillar of his theory that the Achaemenid Empire mandated the Pentateuch as the law code for all Judeans living in the satrapy of Beyond-the-River (Ezra 7:14, 25, 26).[72] As is obvious, the theory is not new. Frei's treatment of Ezra 7 rephrases Wellhausen's and Meyers's old argument that it was the Persian Empire that authorized, publicized, and mandated Torah law in Judah and that without it Judaism would not have been created.

In its form revived by Frei, the theory has received a great deal of support among biblical scholars. Blenkinsopp maintains that "the combination of the P history with Deuteronomy, resulting in a narrative from creation to the death of Moses, and the concentration of all the legal material within this narrative framework, cannot be explained exclusively in terms of circumstances, exigencies, and events intrinsic to the Jewish community."[73] The combination of P and D required an outside force—the Persian Empire. Blenkinsopp claims that "one aspect of this imperial policy [by which local norms were authorized] was the insistence on local self-definition inscribed primarily in a codified and standardized corpus of traditional law backed by the [Persian] central government and its regional representatives."[74] Blenkinsopp sees Ezra's mission and the letter of Artaxerxes as historical and as authorizing Ezra to establish the "laws of your god and the laws of the king" in Judah and to set up judicial proceedings to enforce compliance. Thus, again, Judaism is defined by its law codes. The impetus for its creation was external and came from the Persian king with Ezra crucial to its implementation.

Crüsemann also claims that even if we regard Artaxerxes's letter as pure invention, we "must acknowledge that it asserts a kernel of historical reality."[75] He continues: "While skeptical about the Artaxerxes decree, we must accept the important statement in Ezra 7:25, which equates the [Torah] laws of God and of the Persian king as both legally applicable and juridically binding."[76] This was the creation of Judaism. Both Crüsemann and Blenkinsopp base these conclusions on Frei's theory of imperial authorization of local norms. Albertz argues similarly: "Even if the so-called Ezra decree is hardly authentic in the form which has been handed down to us, it nevertheless reflects a Persian legal practice which can also be demonstrated from other sources and which Frei calls 'imperial authorization.'"[77] Albertz opines that "the imperial authorization offered the Jewish people a unique chance of claiming the support of the Persian imperial organization in securing its cultural and religious identity. But it could only seize this chance if it finally formulated a text which was binding on all its members, and which it could present to the Persian authorities for approval and authorization."[78] Thus, again, without the Persian Empire the various documents that make up the Torah would not have been combined. Moreover, it would not have become authoritative for Judeans, it would not have become the source for Jewish law, and Judaism would not exist. Konrad Schmid has defended the theory against some recent detractors.[79] Schmid calls for the separation of two distinct issues: (1) whether there was such an institution in the Achaemenid Empire as "imperial authorization of local norms," and (2) whether the completion of the Torah was connected to it. Schmid does not discuss the first question but assumes it has already been proved by Frei: "There is no reason to deny that at least some local laws indeed were authorized by higher authorities such as the satraps. This is the unavoidable minimal interpretation of the trilingual inscription of Xanthus, which prompted Frei to develop his theory."[80] Schmid asks further "how can we best describe processes whereby Persian authorities created local autonomy—processes that can only be expected and that can be substantiated beyond any doubt?"[81]

Based on the Xanthus inscription (to be discussed), Schmid concludes that "we must assume processes whereby local norms were authorized by the Persian Empire."[82] Schmid asserts further that Ezra 7 shows that the formation of the

Torah must have had something to do with this process. "This basic assumption [of imperial authorization of local norms] is made clear," he says, "by the Artaxerxes decree in Ezra 7, completely independent of whether the text is authentic or not or whether it is Persian or Hellenistic. Ezra 7 shows us that the author of this text was familiar with processes of authorizing local norms and that he described Ezra's presentation of the Torah to his readers in this context." Thus Schmid argues that Ezra 7 can be used to prove the theory, even if it is late and even if it is entirely fictitious.

David Carr also credits the Persians with creating the circumstances whereby the Torah became legally sanctioned public law.[83] He suggests that it was "recognition probably by local Persian authorities (albeit in the name of the king) of locally produced texts as valid Persian law" that impelled the various strands of the Torah known from scribal education to gain the force of law.[84] According to Carr, without external imperial support the Torah would never have been moved from its place in the temple as part of scribal education to its public role as local law. Of course, his evidence for this claim that Torah law had actually become law in Judah is the book of Ezra itself, and if the text is fictive, which most admit, then in what way does it serve as evidence?

Anselm Hagedom also agrees that Ezra 7 is fictive but that "this author uses formulations and information known in the Persian period, so a certain knowledge of Persian imperial structures can be assumed."[85] According to Hagedom, "this knowledge is independent of any actual date of the Ezra narrative . . . even if one favors a Hellenistic composition of the Ezra narrative . . . the context provided by the biblical documents themselves still remains Persian."[86] Thus, even though the text is fictional and Hellenistic, the fact that the story is *set* in the Persian period means that it accurately describes Persian behavior. This is strange reasoning. The stories of Abraham are placed in a Bronze Age nomadic setting, but few scholars today would argue that the author had accurate knowledge of what Bronze Age nomadic life was like. How can it be assumed that an author writing in the Hellenistic period would accurately describe Persian-period administrative procedures? The arguments are circular: because Ezra 7 is assumed to describe Persian administrative practices, the author must have known how the Persians administered their empire. Thus, it is claimed, the text can be used to understand Persian administrative practices.

The Fallacy behind Frei's Theory of Imperial Authorization

Frei's theory of imperial authorization of local norms encountered criticism in the articles of *Persia and Torah: The Theory of Imperial Authorization of the Pentateuch*, edited by James W. Watts,[87] in Jean Louis Ska's *Introduction to Reading the Pentateuch*,[88] and in my *The Priest and the Great King: Temple-Palace Relations in the Persian Empire.*[89] In fact, there was no concept of a law code in the Achaemenid

Empire and no local autonomy anywhere in it. None of Frei's arguments adduced to support it can stand.[90]

The So-Called Demotic Chronicle

The first pillar of Frei's theory is Column C of the so-called Demotic Chronicle.[91] Column C of the Chronicle includes a report of Darius's so-called codification of Egyptian *hpw*, usually translated as "laws." As Redford points out, however, these *hpw* are not laws but customs and traditions. There were no laws in Egypt for Darius to codify.[92] What Darius most likely did was to codify and put into Aramaic a copy of cadastral land surveys to indicate the borders of the great landed estates of the various institutions for purposes of taxation.[93] Thus the so-called Demotic Chronicle actually refers to the codification of the procedures, mechanisms, and titles of personnel involved in running those Egyptian institutions, such as the temples, that were productive of wealth.[94] These enabled the Persian satrap and the provincial governors to know, for example, who among the temple personnel were responsible for the management of the finances and who would be responsible for the temple's payment of taxes. Darius's collection and codification of this type of data are also revealed in the Murašu archives of Babylonia.[95]

The Xanthus Inscription

The second pillar of Frei's theory is the Xanthus inscription.[96] The Xanthus stele relates the supposed free desire of Lycians to install a cult to a foreign Carian god in the middle of the Lycian sanctuary to their own gods, a decision that was then "ratified" and authorized by their newly appointed Carian satrap, Pixodarus. This inscription thus deals not with local laws at all but merely with Lycian acquiescence in setting up a shrine to a foreign Carian god within their own sanctuary. Schmid declares that the Carian satrap of Lycia is said to publish the decision of the people of Xanthus *as his own decree*.[97] To Frei, Schmid, and others, this implies "evidence of the elevation of local legislation to [the level of] imperial legislation."[98] Debord asks, however, how great the margin of maneuverability would have been for a people under a Carian satrap, a Carian *archon* (governor), and a Carian *epimeltes* (garrison commander) with his certainly Carian garrison to refuse to establish a Carian god in their sanctuary.[99] It is not likely that the Lycians could have refused to accept the Carian god. Rather than implying satrapal ratification of a local decision, it implies satrapal and indeed military coercion. The establishment of a cult to the Carian god was not for the benefit of the local Lycians. It was for the benefit of the Carian soldiers who made up the garrison installed there. The decision reflects and indeed symbolizes Carian power over Lycia. The fact that the Xanthus stele phrases the establishment of this foreign cult as the idea of the Lycians is typical of inscriptions of conquered Greek cities pretending to be free and independent.[100]

The So-Called Passover Letter

Frei also uses the so-called Passover Letter, dated to the fifth year of Darius II, 419–418 B.C.E., to support his theory of imperial authorization of local norms.[101] Instead, the letter should be understood in the same vein as the Xanthus stele. The Passover Letter is an Aramaic letter to the priesthood of a foreign god on the Nile island of Elephantine. Again, the temple to the foreign god was erected solely for the benefit of the members of the Persian garrison installed there, not for the benefit of the local population. Instead of Carians, this garrison was composed of Judeans, however, and the temple was dedicated to the foreign Judean god YHW. Unlike the Xanthus stele, which authorizes the installation of that garrison's foreign god, the Passover Letter authorizes the members of the garrison to follow the precepts of their god's foreign rituals. Because of the fragmentary nature of the letter, it cannot be determined whether it included instructions for the traditional Passover sacrifice, the sacrifice of the Pascal lamb, coincidentally the icon of the local god Khnum, but we do know that nine years later the garrison commander agreed to the demands of Khnum to destroy this foreign and intruding Judean temple.[102]

Authorization of the customs of Persian garrisons that were billeted throughout the empire cannot be construed as authorization of local norms. These customs authorized by the empire on behalf of their own garrisons may indeed have actually contradicted the local norms of the subject populations.

Artaxerxes's Letter to Ezra

As noted, a major pillar of Frei's theory is Ezra 7 of the biblical text.[103] Frei writes: "Ezra was sent by the Persian ruler to Judah. His mission included among other things [to promote] a religiously founded law book. The introduction of this law book by an empowered commissioner was not possible without the license of its contents by the central administration."[104] Even though Frei admits later that this text may be fictional, he asserts that "real institutions can be introduced in fictive documents."[105]

Frei argues that the law book that Ezra brought was the Torah and that the Persians authorized it as the operative body of law, the constitution, for Judeans living in the satrapy of Beyond-the-River. Frei assumes this to be the case, even though he allows the possibility that the entire text of Ezra is fictional! As Ska points out, however, the Pentateuch could not possibly have been the basis of a legal code, nor would it have been authorized by the Persian imperial administration. The Pentateuch is not a legal document; rather, its laws are embedded in a narrative. Further, the laws disagree.[106] Exodus 21, for example, refers to male and female Hebrew slaves. The male is to be released after six years but not the female. According to Deuteronomy 15:12, however, the female slave must also go out in the seventh year, whereas according to Leviticus 25:39–40 you shall not enslave your fellow Hebrew at all, but they shall serve you only as hired laborers. The laws thus conflict and cannot form the basis of a law code. Perhaps more serious, the narrative includes a promise to the descendants of Abraham of a grant of land extending from the River of Egypt to the Euphrates River (Gen. 15:18). Why would the Persian authorities validate that? The Pentateuch is actually a subversive document that claims that the land is YHWH's and does not belong to any earthly king (Lev. 25:33).

Indeed, it is possible for a fictional document to reflect real institutions, but the fictional element cannot be used without external proof of the reality behind it. Unfortunately, none of the proofs that Frei and others have brought to support this reality withstand historical scrutiny. (See chapter 2 for a discussion of the historical Ezra.)

Q: Then How and When Did Torah Law Become Legally Binding on Jews? A: It Never Did.

If the Persians did not mandate Torah law, how and when did it become legally binding on Jews? The answer is that it never did. The entire question rests on a profound confusion between taboos and venerable ancestral customs on the one hand and laws on the other. Customs are socially—not legally—enforced. The ancient Israelite avoidance of pork, for example, is "widely known and well-established" as an "important cultural and even ethnic trait in Iron Age Israel."[107] This pork taboo did not require a written law code with judges to enforce it. Judeans from Lachish are shown in reliefs being escorted from their homes by Assyrian soldiers and wearing long garments with fringes on the hem (cf. Num. 15:38).[108] This style of dress similarly required no written law code. Faust exploits biblical and sociological evidence to suggest that the Israelites began to circumcise themselves in the Iron I period as an ethnic marker to distinguish themselves from the "uncircumcised" Philistines.[109] Other ethnic markers also appear in the archaeology of Israel—for example, the ubiquitous four-room house and unpainted pottery. None of these customs would have needed to be legally enforced.

Custom and taboo, not judges and magistrates, controlled Jewish life even in the Persian period.[110] As noted in chapter 3, if we search for the word *tôrâ* in what are considered the authentic portions of Nehemiah's memoir (the first-person accounts: Nehemiah 1:1–3, 11c; 2:1–7:4; 11:1–2; 12:27–43; 13:4–31) dated to the mid-fifth century and the reign of Artaxerxes I, we see that the word never appears.[111] Nehemiah did not need a written law code to tell him what right and wrong were; he simply took it upon himself to enforce long-held Judean customs and taboos.

In order for laws to be *legally* binding, judges need to enforce them and sanctions need to be applied—hence the reliance on Ezra 7:25–26 to support Frei's theory. In fact, as discussed in chapter 2, royal and provincial judges throughout the Persian Empire were ethnically Persian, either brought in from Persia themselves or the sons of Persian judges who inherited their father's positions. They would not have known Judean customs, let alone have cared to enforce them. Indeed, the laws of neither Torah nor Talmud were observed by the vast majority of the Jewish population.[112] One striking proof of this lies in the injunction in the Torah against making pictures of anything that exists in the heaven above or on the earth below (Exod. 20:4). Jews in antiquity nevertheless did make such pictures and incorporated them as meaningful symbols everywhere, even in their synagogues and on their gravestones.[113] There was no authority that was able to prevent it or interested in doing so. Jewish courts evidently existed (2 Cor. 11:24), but they were voluntary.[114] They had the status of an arbitration. It was not until 398 C.E. that the Roman emperor ruled that Roman provincial courts should enforce decisions made by arbiters.[115] Even then, Torah laws had no imperial status. Observance was always voluntary.

If the biblical story of Persian authorization of Ezra's law code in Ezra 7 is not historical, if it is not consistent with Persian norms and behavior, why was it written? The story of Ezra was created by biblical writers in the Hellenistic period. Written under the Ptolemies or the Seleucids, the story of a Jewish scribe having a Persian mandate to enforce Judean customs was created in the face of Ptolemaic or Seleucid religious persecutions. It was likely written in an attempt to provide its readers with the proof that the very norms for which they were being persecuted had received the imprimatur and authorization of the Persian Empire and so were legitimate, valid, and vital.

Postscript

REFLECTIONS ON EZRA AND THE LAW

To the writers of both Ezra-Nehemiah and 1 Esdras, it was the failure to observe Torah law that caused the destruction of the temple and the Babylonian exile. Now their temple and their cities were rebuilt, the purified population had heard the law, and the law was installed as an icon of the deity in their newly dedicated temple. Adhering to Torah law, it was hoped, would preserve them from impurity and maintain them on their land. The writer of 4 Ezra, writing after the destruction of the second temple, saw that this was not to be. The people of Judah had kept Torah law to the best of their ability, but doing so had not protected them. God had allowed their temple and their cities to be destroyed anyway. The only conclusion possible was that their observance must have been inadequate. God gave them the law, but he did not give them the ability to keep it. Because they did not keep it sufficiently, God delivered his city and his temple into the hands of their enemy, a people who did not know him. The author of 4 Ezra responds that he would test God! If God wanted Torah observance, then he would give God Torah observance. He would teach the people the Torah (4 Ezra 14).

This defiant response of the author of 4 Ezra to the disaster of the temple's destruction was also Emil Fackenheim's response to the Holocaust. Like the fall of the temple, the Holocaust symbolized to the modern Jew the failure of the covenant on whose terms Jews have traditionally based their faith and lived their lives.[1] Fackenheim's response to the Holocaust was his famous 11th (or actually 614th) commandment—not to give Hitler a posthumous victory but to defy God and Man and to live one's life as a Jew. This was the response of the author of 4 Ezra.

Fourth Ezra was absorbed into Christian communities around the world, as is witnessed by the Christian introduction (5 Ezra), its triumphal conclusion (6 Ezra), the number of its Christian translations, and the many medieval Christian apocalypses that have spun off from it. The complaint that God had created the evil heart and had hemmed in mankind with laws but had not given him the ability to follow them that characterizes 4 Ezra is answered in these Christian translations. God did not create evil. God gave us the ability to follow his law, and he gave us free will. Evil results because God permits man to do evil. The iron that God created is neutral, but we may use it to kill or to till the ground.

Does it matter which we choose, to kill or to plow? Does God reward the righteous? Does he punish the wicked? These questions are at the heart of the Christian apocalypses. Foundational for their authors is that what we do does matter and that there is a God to whom it matters. There are rewards and punishments depending on one's response to God's laws—if not in this life, then in the next. The solution offered in these medieval apocalypses is that to believe this is enough, or not even to believe but to act as though one did believe, to act as though God's laws matter, that is enough. Perfection itself is not required. This is also Fackenheim's response: act as though your behavior matters.

Only among the nineteenth- and twentieth-century scholars, most notably Wellhausen and Meyer, did we see a change in the attitude toward God's laws. To them, rather than bringing life, the law brings death. Perhaps this is a reflex of Paul (Rom. 7:5; 8:2; 2 Cor. 3:7) and of Luther (1483–1546). To them, reliance on the law creates an ossified religion. Laws written on paper stultify. In true religion, law is what is in your heart (Rom. 2:29).

These scholars did not know what the authors of the apocalypses already realized, that what is written in one's heart cannot be trusted. You may look in your heart, but you will not find God's laws written there. Even describing mankind after the destruction of the flood, the biblical writer knew that man's heart is evil from his youth, יֵצֶר לֵב הָאָדָם רַע מִנְּעֻרָיו (Gen. 8:21). The continuing interest in Ezra affirms the ongoing debate regarding the efficacy of God's laws as antidote to the evil inclinations of the heart.

Appendix I

CHRONOLOGY

Kings of Ancient Mesopotamia

The Neo-Babylonian Dynasty

1. Nabopolassar	625–605[1]
2. Nebuchadnezzar II	604–562
3. Evil-Merodach	561–560
4. Neriglissar	559–556
5. Labaši-Marduk	556 (three months)
6. Nabonidus	555–539

The Achaemenid Rulers

1. Cyrus II	559–530
2. Cambyses II	529–522
3. Bardija	522 (six months)
4. Nebuchadnezzar III	522 (two months)
5. Nebuchadnezzar IV	521 (three months)
6. Darius I	522–486
7. Xerxes I	486–465
8. Artaxerxes I	465–424
9. Darius II	424–405
10. Artaxerxes II	405–359
11. Artaxerxes III	358–338
12. Artaxerxes IV	338–336
13. Darius III	336–331

The Macedonian Dynasty

Alexander III	330–323

Egyptian Pharaohs

Dynasty XXVI

1. Necho II	610–595[2]
2. Psammetichus II	595–589

3. Apries (Hofra)	589–570
4. Amasis	570–526
5. Psammetichus III	526–525

Dynasty XXVII

1. Cambyses II	525–522
2. Darius I	522–486
3. Xerxes I	486–465
4. Artaxerxes I	465–424
5. Darius II	424–405
6. Artaxerxes II	405–359

Dynasty XXVIII

1. Amyrtaeus	404–399

Dynasty XXIX

1. Nepherites I	399–393
2. Psammuthis	393
3. Achoris	393–380
4. Nepherites II	380

Dynasty XXX

1. Nectanebo I	380–362
2. Tachos	362–360
3. Nectanebo II	360–343

Dynasty XXXI—Second Persian Period

1. Artaxerxes III	343–338
2. Artaxerxes IV	338–336
3. Darius III	336–332
4. Khababash	333 (last known indigenous Egyptian ruler)

The Macedonian Dynasty

Alexander III	332–323
Ptolemy I Soter	323–282
Ptolemy II Philadelphos	282–246
Ptolemy III Euergetes	246–222

Appendix 2

VERSIONS AND TRANSLATIONS OF 4 EZRA

Among all the Pseudepigraphal books, 4 Ezra has enjoyed a privileged position, as is suggested by the large number of languages and editions into which it has been translated and reworked. From the original Hebrew, it was translated into Greek and from the Greek into Latin, Syriac, Armenian, Ethiopian, Georgian, Coptic (of which we possess only a fragment), and two different Arabic translations. A third Arabic text is a translation from the Syriac.[1] Neither the Hebrew nor the Greek texts have survived, and evidence suggests that all these various versions are actually translations of two different Greek text families.[2] The Latin, Syriac, Ethiopic, Georgian, Syro-Arabic, and Coptic seem to go back to one Greek text family, whereas the Armenian and the two other Arabic translations seem to be based on a completely different Greek text family. The first text family can be divided further, with the Latin and Syriac on the one hand and the Ethiopic and Georgian on the other. The major witnesses to these two text families are discussed later. All of the translations include the section in 4 Ezra on the impermissibility of interceding for the dead, the section that had been removed from a prominent Latin manuscript in the Vatican (4 Ezra 7:36–105). Further, none of these translations includes the Christian additions to the Latin version of 4 Ezra (5 and 6 Ezra, discussed in chapter 6), so all these translations are translations of the earlier Greek text. They are all Christian.

Fourth Ezra in the Armenian Tradition

The Armenian translation of 4 Ezra[3] is a faithful rendering of an original Greek text that Stone suggests was already reworked in the Greek before the translation was made.[4] Agathangelos, who lived at the latest in the mid-fifth century, cites from the Armenian translation, so it must have been completed by that date.[5] The Greek version from which this was made, like the ones from which all these translations were made, was the work of a Christian who may also have had other Jewish sources available to him.[6] It did not include 5 or 6 Ezra.

This translation may be construed as a debate with the original 4 Ezra, many of whose ideas are grappled with and altered. The Latin text of 3:4 reads, for example: "Did you not speak at the beginning when you planted the earth—and that without help—and commanded the dust and it gave you Adam, a lifeless body? Yet he was the creation of your hands, and you breathed into him the breath of life, and he was made alive in your presence" (Lat. 4 Ezra 3:4–5), whereas the Armenian reads: "Did you not make the heavens and the earth and everything which is in them? And after that you created a man with your incorruptible hands and you breathed into him the breath of life."

Besides the fact that the Armenian reads "man," not "Adam," as does the Hebrew Bible, a remarkable difference exists in the Latin's stress on God's acting through speech and not manually. According to the Latin, God commanded the dust, and the dust gave forth Adam, even though the Latin admits that he was the creation of God's hands. The Armenian reads simply that God made a man with his incorruptible hands. This difference also exists between the first two Arabic translations (discussed later). *Ar1* stresses that "God spoke and it happened," whereas *Ar2* reads: "You said at the beginning that you made Adam with your holy hands."[7] Stone suggests that *Ar1* and the Latin go back to a common *Vorlage* not shared with the Armenian or *Ar2*.[8] The latter texts reflect the original Hebrew, in which God made a man with his own hands. Uniquely, the Armenian version gives a reason for the man receiving his single commandment: "that he might know the Lord."[9]

Human Free Will as Justification for Evil

A major feature of the Armenian is the avoidance of a role for God in creating evil. The Latin of 3:8 refers to the peoples who came forth from Adam "who walked after their own will; they did ungodly things in your sight and rejected your commands, and you did not hinder them." This accusation against God, present in all the versions, is omitted in the Armenian, which reads: "who transgressed the laws of your holy commandments."

Similarly, in the Latin of 4 Ezra 3:19–20, we read: "You gave the law to the descendants of Jacob, and your commandments to the posterity of Israel. Yet you did not take away their evil heart from them, so that your law might produce fruit in them" (Lat. 4 Ezra 3:19–20). In contrast, the Armenian version has simply "You gave them the law, but they did not observe it" (3:19). It does not accuse God of failing to take away their evil heart or of not preventing their evil acts.

Further, whereas in the Latin we read: "for a grain of evil seed was sown in Adam's heart from the beginning" (Lat. 4 Ezra 4:30), in the Armenian it is changed to "the little transgression of Adam perpetrated that much evil." In the Armenian translation Adam is not a passive recipient of an evil heart that was sown in him at the beginning, rather he is an actor with free will.

Armenian Ezra does come close to accusing God of making Adam vulnerable to sin but does not go all the way. In an addition to 6:54 when the acts of creation on the first six days are described, Armenian Ezra says: "But you did not make him [the man] needful of any earthly instrument," perhaps implying that God did not make man receptive to instruction or to change (Arm. 6:54D). This is still far different from alluding to an "evil seed" that God put in Adam's heart from the beginning.

Instead of blaming God for creating man with an evil heart, which led to the world of toil and hardship that mankind has inherited, as in the Latin (7:11–14), the Armenian version states that God gave men the law, but, though he made them capable of observing it, they chose not to but abandoned it, and so the Most High abandoned them: "He said to me, 'Similarly, a portion of inheritance will be given to Israel. For God made this world for the sake of men, and he filled it with every produce and he gave them the law by which they might be educated and rule a good and modest and blameless kingdom; but they did not observe (it), but abandoned it, and the Most High decided to abandon those who had revolted against him'" (Arm. 4 Ezra 7:10–11).

In the Armenian, God is the knowable God of Deuteronomy, the God of the quid pro quo. Man abandons God, so God abandons man. As in Ezra-Nehemiah and 1 Esdras, God's abandonment is proof that man has not kept the law. Stone sees this verse as an anti-Judaic polemic, which is certainly possible. Yet, it might also be seen as a universalization of the promise to Israel. God made the world not just for the sake of Israel but for all mankind, and then he gave the law to "them," that is, to all mankind. It was, then, all mankind that rejected the law, not just Israel, and all mankind that in turn is rejected by God. The Latin reads simply: "He said to me, 'So also is Israel's portion. For I made the world for their sake, and when Adam transgressed my statutes, what had been made was judged'" (Lat. 4 Ezra 7:10–11).

The Latin blames Israel's failure to keep the law on Adam and on the fact that God did not give Adam and his descendants the possibility of keeping it. This accusation toward God is avoided in the Armenian. Adam sinned, but Israel and all mankind separately sinned. Each person has been given the law, and each has rejected it. The sin is not Adam's alone but belongs to each of us. Therefore, when the following verse (7:12) reads in both the Armenian and the Latin (as well as the other versions) that "because of that, the entrances of this world are narrow, difficult, hard and full of suffering," the implication in the Latin and in the other versions is that this is due to Adam's sin. In the Armenian, however, it is due to each person's sin, each person's rejection of the law. This view is also expressed in another change that the Armenian makes. Where the Latin and other versions read: "O Adam, what have you done? For though it was you who sinned, the fall was not yours alone, but ours also who are your descendants" (Lat. 4 Ezra 7:118), implying that all mankind participated in Adam's fall from grace, the Armenian reads: "Oh, Adam, what have you done? You alone sinned, but the affliction was not yours alone, but common to all who were descended from you." In the Armenian version, it was not in Adam's sin that mankind participated but in his affliction, that is, in his continuing decision to reject the law.

In addition to omitting any reference to the "evil heart" or "evil seed" that was placed in Adam in the beginning, the Armenian denies that there is a fixed amount of evil in the world that must be harvested before the good can appear. In contrast to the Latin, which reads: "For the evil about which you ask me has been sown, but the harvest of it has not yet come. If therefore that which has been sown is not reaped, and if the place where the evil has been sown does not pass away, the field where the good has been sown will not come" (Lat. 4 Ezra 4:28–29), the Armenian has instead: "Since it is not able to bear the evil of its time because the men of this world are full of every wickedness, therefore, too, the threshing will pass over them [that is, over the evil men]; for if the harvest will not first come upon them, neither will that which is the fruit of goodness reach the righteous." In the Armenian it is the evil men who are harvested, not a fixed amount of evil that was sown in the beginning. Of that, there is no mention.

Why God Made Evil

Only in the Armenian is it directly asked why God made evil: "Is that why he created so many souls, so that he might destroy them? God forfend! Is he not full of knowledge? Would he not know what man would do, before his birth, and is he not familiar with everything before it happens" (Arm. 4 Ezra 7:140)? And only in the Armenian is a direct answer given: "He [Uriel] answered and said to me, 'Speak not that which is above you and do not dissemble before God; consider that which is permitted you. He made this world for the sake of many but that one, for the sake of few. For, although his prescience is abundant, still he granted men free-will, the knowledge of their actions, so that they might know what to do so that they will not be punished and what to do that they will be punished'" (Arm. 4 Ezra 8:1).

Not only does man have free will, but it is a free will with foresight. Man knows what good and bad are, which actions will net reward in the world to come, and which will lead to punishments. This emphasis on man's free will is an explicit theme throughout the Armenian translation. As in the Latin, the other versions blame God for creating man with an evil inclination and for not preventing his evil acts. The Armenian is alone, however, in asking God why he made evil in the first place, since by it man is induced to do what God hates. Ezra asks: "Why indeed did you create evil at all, that we should have it and through it we might sin" (Arm. 4 Ezra 8:62G)? God answers that he did not create evil: "That which was created well, he [man] did not use well and he sinned. Not that I created anything evil, but everything which I created was very good: each thing which existed, existed for its own purpose, just as iron existed, not that it might kill, but that it might work the ground and fulfill the needs of all men. But men did not remain in that same state in which they were created, but they undertook that which was not done for good. Thus, also other things that came into the world for good, they changed to evil. The cause was then not he who creates things well, but he who did not use them well, by which he offended their Creator" (Arm. 4 Ezra 8:62L–N).

Only in the Armenian is it thus emphasized that everything that God created was for good. Mankind, however, by his free will perverts the good things that were made and uses them for evil. God, however, allows the evil act to stand.[10] The solution in all the versions is the same: God gave man the law and the commandments to protect him against his evil inclination so that he might live by them and not die. The Armenian is alone among all the versions in stressing that God gave man the ability to keep the law. "The Lord answered me and said, 'I commanded nothing above man nor anything impossible; but . . . just as you wish to be honored by your servant, you too do the same to the living God'" (9:16C). God did not instill in Adam a wicked heart that his descendants inherited. Each man sins only as a result of his own decisions and with complete knowledge of the effects of his sin on his reward in the world to come. In the Armenian version there is no condemnation of God for making mankind as he is, since he has given him the choice.

God Is Merciful

Besides the emphasis on man's free will and on God's creating only good and not evil, the God in the Armenian version is portrayed entirely differently from the way in which he is depicted in the other versions. In the Latin and elsewhere, we read that God concerns himself not with sinners but only with the righteous (8:38–40): "For indeed I will not concern myself with the fashioning of those who have sinned, or about their death, their judgment, or their destruction; but I will rejoice over the creation of the righteous, over their pilgrimage also, and their salvation, and their receiving their reward. As I have spoken, therefore, so it shall be" (Lat. 4 Ezra 8:38–40). In the Armenian, in complete opposition to the other versions, we read: "If the sinners will indeed return to me with all their hearts, I will not think to requite them according to their former sins, but as I shall find and judge them at the end of their giving up the ghost; and I shall be as happy over those who return to good deeds as I shall be happy over my righteous ones" (Arm. 4 Ezra 8:37–39).

This insistence on God's clemency during a man's life is repeated: "The Most High will be longsuffering towards them for, if they who act wickedly will repent instead of that and will do good things, they will live, but if not, they will be punished" (Arm. 4 Ezra 8:41B). This Jewish view that the gates of repentance are always open during a man's life is emphasized in this Christian text, in strong contrast to the probable Hebrew original, in which God is described as not merciful, not patient, not long-suffering, and not forgiving toward those who have sinned.

In the Latin and in the other versions, there are only two types of people, the sinner and the righteous, with the vast majority falling into the first group. Only in the Armenian version is there the possibility that a man may cross over from the group of sinners to the group of the righteous, with his previous sins forgiven him.[11]

More Than One Creator?

A jarring verse in the Aramean version, however, is 5:23, which seems to imply the existence of more than one creator God. After he finishes his fast, Ezra says "before the Most High": "O Lord, you are he, who by the will of the Most High, made and prepared everything and by your wisdom you conduct everything and you requite each according to his ways" (Arm. 4 Ezra 5:23). Whom is Ezra talking to who created everything "by the will of the Most High"? If he is talking to Uriel, then is Uriel an angelic demiurge who created the world according to God's orders?[12] This conflicts with Ezra's statement at the beginning whereby he affirms that God made the world alone and everything in it (Arm. 4 Ezra 3:4). The passage is reminiscent of the prologue to the Gospel of John, however, so, rather than talking to an angelic demiurge, Ezra most likely is addressing Jesus, Lord and Judge of this world. The Armenian continues with the text as it is in other versions: "You Lord, out of all the woods of trees you chose for yourself one vine, . . . and out of all the people, you chose for yourself the seed of Abraham. The Law, which you chose above everything, you bestowed upon your beloved people." Then Ezra asks why he turned over the people he loved to the heathens (Arm. 4 Ezra 5:24–28). It is hard to imagine that these words would be addressed to an impersonal demiurge, but they could be addressed to Jesus.

Chapter 6 of this version begins with a long insertion in response to the following verse: "I said, 'I implore you, O Lord, if I have found favor in your sight, show your servant through whom you will visit your creation'" (Arm. 4 Ezra 5:56). To the writer, the answer could only be through Jesus:[13]

> And I said to him, "How will the Most High come, or when will his coming be?"
>
> And he [Uriel] said, "First of all, he will come after a little time in the form of a Son of Man, and he will teach hidden things: and they will dishonor him and they will be rejected and do themselves evil. And after that, acts of wickedness will increase; the spirit of error will lead them astray, to flatten the mountains with anger and to work signs so as to lead astray certain of the holy ones. After that, the Most High shall come again in a vision of great glory and he shall put an end to the sprit of error and he shall rule, and he shall requite the holiness of the holy ones and the wickedness of the impious" (Arm. 6:1f–1h).

In this long addition to 6:1, the Armenian text describes God's interjection into the world in the form of a mortal man. It describes a first coming and then a second, indicating that Jesus is referred to here, not the two messianic figures described later in 4 Ezra. Armenian 4 Ezra then continues as in the other versions. In the other versions, God is simply stating that he planned the world from the beginning, but in the Armenian it is clear from this preamble to chapter 6 that it was God's coming in the form of a mortal man, his rejection, and his second coming that had all been planned from the beginning.

Strikingly different from the other versions is also the Armenian description of the Messiah. Gone are the verses in the Latin that state that the Messiah shall live only four hundred years and that he and all who are with him shall then die (Lat. 4 Ezra 7:28, 29). By skipping immediately from the appearance of the Messiah to the description of the resurrection of the dead and the universal day of judgment, the Armenian text asserts that resurrection and judgment follow immediately upon the Messiah's second coming, with no intervening "Messianic Age." Moreover, neither in its description of the anointed one as the lion who rebukes the eagle nor its presentation of the man who ascends from the sea is there an intimation that this messianic figure existed from the beginning and had been kept in reserve. In both cases, the Armenian version reads that the Most High will send him "at the time of the end" or "after many times" (12:32; 13:26). In the case of the lion, it is the Anointed One who will be sent. In the case of the man rising out of the sea, however, it the Most High himself, who appears in power (13:32). The Anointed One, the Son or the Servant, who appears in the other versions is in the Armenian no separate being but God himself. In 14:9, where the Latin reads: "For you shall be taken up from among men, and henceforth you shall live with my Son [or Servant] and with those who are like you, until the times are ended" (4 Ezra 14:9), the Armenian reads: "For you will be raised up from among men and henceforth you and whoever is like you will be with me until the end of times"—"with me," not "with my Servant." The Anointed in the mind of this translator is no doubt Jesus, God Most High.

Fourth Ezra According to the Syriac Translation

The Syriac is extant in a single manuscript, the great Ambrosian Bible Codex in Milan, which is dated to the sixth or seventh century.[14] It was translated into English by G. H. Box, in 1917. It is nearly identical to the Latin of 4 Ezra, so both are evidently literal translations of the same Greek text. One striking difference in the Syriac is the change in the length of the Messiah's life to thirty years from four hundred, perhaps to correspond to the presumed length of Jesus's life (4 Ezra 7:28).

Fourth Ezra in the Ethiopic Tradition

The first edition of the Ethiopic version to be published in a European language was prepared by Ricardo Laurence, who translated the Ethiopic version into English in 1820.[15] August Dillman, in 1894, created an eclectic version based on the ten manuscripts available to him, and this version forms the third column of Bruno Violet's synoptic text.

There are various differences between the Latin and the Ethiopic, and it is interesting to contemplate whether one or the other reflects the original Hebrew more faithfully. In 3:5, for example, the Latin includes the name of the man, Adam, whereas the Ethiopic (1:5) omits the name and reads simply "a man." The Ethiopic translation reflects the Greek and Latin translations of Genesis which also read only "a man," and that is certainly what is intended in the Hebrew (where adam is the normal word for "human being"). The Ethiopic reflects the original here.[16]

No Predestination

A more profound difference between the Latin and the Ethiopic resides in the attitude toward predestination. In 3:14, the Latin reads: "you loved him [Abraham], and to him alone you revealed the end of the times," whereas the Ethiopic speaks of (3:16) "the end of the time," in the singular, referring (according to Laurence) only to the time of Abraham's life, not to the time of the end of the world.[17] If so, the Ethiopic avoids the intimation present in the Latin that the whole future course of history is already known to God and is thus predetermined. This is also illustrated by comparing the response of the angel Jeremiel in the two versions. In the Latin, God has measured and numbered the ages and the times: "And the archangel Jeremiel answered and said, 'When the number of those like yourselves is completed; for he has weighed the age in the balance, and measured the times by measure, and numbered the times by number; and he will not move or arouse them until that measure is fulfilled'" (Lat. 4 Ezra 4:36–37). In the Ethiopic, in contrast, God has measured only the world and the sea as it existed at the time: "For in a balance has the world been weighed, and with a measure has he measured the sea; neither will he command silence, nor utter a voice, until the allotted measure shall be fulfilled" (Ethiop. 4 Ezra 4:46).

This attitude toward predestination is also revealed in Ezra's second conversation with the angel Uriel. According to the Latin, Ezra asks: "I implore you, O Lord, if I have found favor in your sight, show your servant through whom you will punish[18] your creation" (Lat. 4 Ezra 5:56). In the Latin, God answers that there is no other power but himself: "I planned these things, and they were made through me alone and not through another; just as the end shall come through me alone and not through another" (4 Ezra 6:6).[19] The answer in the Ethiopic, however, reads: "First by means of the son of man, and then by myself" (Ethiop. 6:1).

Although the phrase "son of man" is a term for the Messiah in the New Testament, it is likely that the Ethiopic simply means "mortal man." The Ethiopic elsewhere denies the eternal preexistence of a Son of Man, for it records God as saying "at that time [before the creation of the world] I considered that I myself existed, but no other" (Ethiop. 6:13). The Ethiopic points here to Adam and Eve as the source of sin, through whom punishment came into the world.

No Antipathy against Rome

Another difference between the texts is that the Ethiopic does not exhibit the antipathy toward Rome that is present in the Latin. The Ethiopic omits the statement that to Abraham were given Isaac, Jacob, and Esau and that God rejected Esau but Jacob became a multitude, which is in the Latin (3:15, 16). Esau had come to stand for Rome,[20] and it may be that these verses were added in the Latin and were not present in the Greek from which the Ethiopic translation was made. (The rejection of Esau is also absent in the Armenian version, but it is present in the two Arabic translations of the Greek text, *Ar1* and *Ar2*). In this regard, where the Latin predicts the ruin and destruction of Rome (5:3), the Ethiopic turns it around and predicts the rule of a country that is now in ruins and desolate. The Latin reads: "And the land that you now see ruling shall be a trackless waste, and people shall see it desolate" (Lat. 4 Ezra 5:3), whereas the Ethiopic reads: "A country, which you now behold waste and destroyed, shall rule, and the earth shall be desolated" (Ethiop. 4 Ezra 5:4). Either translation could result from a misunderstanding of the Greek. The Ethiopic, however, is more consistent with the verses predicting the arrival of the Messiah that immediately follow and that are present in both versions. It is not the rulers who will be devastated; rather, it is the devastated who will rule by the hand of the Messiah.

Some Omissions of the People Israel

While for most of the text the Ethiopic seems to be a literal translation of the presumed Greek, some references to the people Israel are omitted. One such omission occurs in chapter 8. The Latin refers explicitly to the people Israel, but this reference is missing from all the Ethiopic manuscripts.[21] The Latin reads: "[I ask] about your inheritance, for whom I lament, and about Israel, for whom I am sad, and about the seed of Jacob, for whom I am troubled" (Lat. 4 Ezra 8:16). In the Ethiopic, we read: "Yet for your people, and for your inheritance I experience anxiety. This it is, on account of which I lament, this it is, on account of which I have begun to supplicate you for myself and for them" (Ethiop. 4 Ezra 8:20–21).

It may have been obvious to the translator and to the readers of his translation to whom "your people" and "your inheritance" refers, but evidently the composer of the Latin version felt it necessary to explicate the reference. Rather than an addition in the Latin, however, it is more likely a deliberate omission in the Ethiopic. A similar minus in the Ethiopic is the reference in the vision of the mourning woman to Jerusalem as "our mother." In the Latin we read: "You most foolish of women, do you not see our mourning, and what has happened to us?

For Zion, the mother of us all, is in deep grief and great distress. It is most appropriate to mourn now, because we are all mourning, and to be sorrowful, because we are all sorrowing; you are sorrowing for one son, but we, the whole world, for our mother" (Lat. 4 Ezra 10: 6–7). The Ethiopic, however, reads: "Do you not perceive the grief in which we are involved on account of Zion, how that we are all plunged into the bitterest affliction? And now truly do you mourn and grieve? All of us indeed mourn and grieve; but you are troubled for the loss of a single son" (Ethiop. 4 Ezra 10:9–10). The reference to Zion as "mother" is missing in all the Ethiopic manuscripts but is present in the Latin and the Syriac, as well as in the Arabic and the Armenian.[22] This could simply be a scribal error, as Violet suggests, but, when taken together with the previous omission of references to "Israel" and the "seed of Jacob," it is possible to perceive a pattern of purposeful alteration of the Judean background to the text.

This type of difference between the Ethiopic and the Latin is visible elsewhere. In the Latin we read: "But in mercy he will set free the rest of my people, those who have been saved throughout my borders" (Lat. 4 Ezra 12:34), whereas in the Ethiopic we read: "As to the rest of the people, them will I redeem in mercy, those who have been saved in my judgment" (Ethiop. 4 Ezra 12:40). The notion of God having a people is absent. Moreover, in the Ethiopic the salvation is not within physical borders, as in the Latin; rather, the saved are saved in judgment, at the last day.

Again we read in the Latin: "Therefore write all these things that you have seen in a book, put it in a hidden place; and you shall teach them to the wise among your people, whose hearts you know are able to comprehend and keep these secrets" (Lat. 4 Ezra 12:37–38), whereas in the Ethiopic we read: "But write in a book all the things which you have seen, and conceal them; teaching them to the wise among the people, who you are assured will keep them secret in their hearts" (Ethiop. 4 Ezra 12:43). One speaks of "the people," the other of "your people." Similarly, we read in the Latin that when Ezra's friends prevail upon him to join them, he replies: "As for me, I have neither forsaken you nor withdrawn from you; but I have come to this place to pray on account of the desolation of Zion, and to seek mercy on account of the humiliation of your sanctuary" (Lat. 4 Ezra 12:48). In the Ethiopic we read, strangely: "But I came into this place to pray on account of the desolation of Zion, and that I might seek mercy on account of the severe humiliation of our joys" (Ethiop. 4 Ezra 12:55). It is true that Zion is mentioned here, as it is in other places. Nevertheless, while the reader might suppose that the temple is set above our chief joy (Psalm 137:4) and that the temple is referred to here, it is not stated.

Similarly, in the vision of the man who comes out of the sea (chapter 13) the Latin reads (vs. 48): "those who are left of your people, who are found within my holy borders, [shall be saved]," whereas the Ethiopic reads: "And therefore was it, that you saw a multitude of people proceeding to, and attaining, my blessed borders. When too he shall have destroyed the numerous crowd who shall have been collected against him, then shall the people who remain be strengthened" (Ethiop. 4 Ezra 13:50–51). Although God's borders are mentioned, there is no intimation here that these are the people Israel. Similarly, where the Latin has God tell Ezra to retain the seventy books for the wise among "your" people (Lat. 4 Ezra 14:46), the Ethiopic reads simply "the wise among the people" (Ethiop. 4 Ezra 14:51).

Colophon

The Latin ends with "and I did so," whereas the Ethiopic agrees with the Syriac, *Ar1,* and the Armenian by having a more detailed ending:

> Thus I did in the fourth of the sabbatical years, in the five thousandth and ninety-second year after the creation of the world, on the tenth night of the third month.
> Then Ezra was taken up into the region of those who resembled him.
> All these things he wrote.
> And he was called the scribe of the wisdom of the Most High, to whom be glory for ever and ever.
> The end of Ezra I.

The Ethiopic version that Laurence used also has a colophon: "Upon him who caused this book to be written, the Abbuna, servant of Christ, upon him who wrote it, upon him who read it, and upon him who accurately heard the voice of the reader, upon all of us together, may God, who is full of glory, have mercy! Amen, Amen, Amen."

4 Ezra in the Arabic Versions

There are three Arabic versions of 4 Ezra. The first (*Ar1*), a somewhat free translation from the Greek, is known in only one manuscript, belonging to the Bodleian Library at Oxford University (Ms. 251).[23] It was translated by a Coptic Christian in 1354 C.E. and published by H. Ewald.[24] It is column four in Violet. A second, literal, but greatly abbreviated Arabic translation (*Ar2*), published by J. Gildemeister, may have been made from the same Greek text, since these two versions have a lacuna in the same spot (8:50–63).[25] It is column five in Violet. A third Arabic version of 4 Ezra (*Ar3*), unknown to Violet, was found in a codex from Mount Sinai (#589) and identified by P. Sj. van Koningsveld[26] and M. E. Stone.[27] It appears to be a translation of the sole surviving intact Syriac manuscript of the Ambrosian Codex, although fragments in Arabic have been found elsewhere.[28] This translation of the Syriac is not identical to any other Arabic version of 4 Ezra, as these others have all been translated from the Greek. Since the Syriac is extant in only one manuscript and since the Arabic is extant in only the one manuscript, these versions are each used to fill in lacunae in the other.

Arabic Translation 1 (*Ar1*)

This is a free translation[29] that attempts to further the ideology of the Christian milieu in which it was created.[30] It was evidently based directly on a Greek text, not on the Latin.[31] Both this translation and the following Arabic translation (*Ar2*) have a large gap in Vision 3, namely chapter 8:50–9:1, suggesting that the same Greek text was used as their *Vorlagen*.[32] The text begins with the superscription: "To the name of the Holy Trinity, the first volume of the book of ʿAzrah, scribe of the law." Instead of being narrated by "Shaltiel, who is also called Ezra," this text is told by " ʿEzra who is called Shealtiel," that is, he is so called because he is the one who questions God. Unlike the other versions, this one also names the destroyed city, Jerusalem.

Denial of Predestination and Emphasis on Free Will

Like the Armenian, this work stresses man's free will and denies predestination. For example, the Latin text (3:8–9) reads: "And every nation walked after its own will; they did ungodly things in your sight and rejected your commands, and you did not hinder them. But again, *in its time* you brought the flood upon the inhabitants of the world and destroyed them." The phrase "in its time" may imply that the flood (and the sinning) was planned even before the creation of the world. In contrast, *Ar1* reads: "They transgressed before you and committed crimes by their own will, and you did not prevent it: then you formed the flood *at this time, for the people of this period.*" This translation asserts that the flood was a reaction to sin, and not planned from the start.[33] *Ar2* also avoids the implication that the times were planned in advance. It reads simply: "And after a time, you sent over them the flood and destroyed them altogether." The Armenian reads likewise: "you brought the flood upon them and destroyed them," with no hint that all this was planned from the start.

A more telling example occurs in 3:14, when, according to the Latin, God reveals to Abraham the end of times: "you loved him, and to him alone you revealed the end of the times, secretly by night" (4 Ezra 3:14). *Ar1* reads instead that God made known to Abraham "a time of repose," referring perhaps to Genesis 15:12, when God causes a heavy sleep to fall upon him.[34] As in the Ethiopic, God could not have made known to Abraham the end of times, since it was not determined in advance. *Ar2* is similar, reading only "You loved him," and omits the rest of the verse entirely. Another example also shows that the possibility of knowing the future is denied in this Arabic translation. The Latin of 4:26 reads: "If you are alive, you will see, and if you live long, you will often marvel, because the age is hurrying swiftly to its end." In contrast, *Ar1* reads: "If you interrogate me, you will see, and if you ask with perseverance and constancy, you will know promptly, for this age about which you ask me is rapidly declining." *Ar2* agrees with *Ar1* here against the Latin, stating that "the world is hurrying swiftly by," and not that it is "hurrying swiftly to its end." There is no predetermined end in these texts.

The next verse is similar. According to the Latin, the righteous will not receive their rewards planned for them: "It will not be able to bring the things that have been promised to the righteous in their appointed times, because this age is full of sadness and infirmities" (Lat. 4 Ezra 4:27). *Ar1* reads: "The promise of the just will not come to this age, because it is full of infirmities and sadness of heart" (*Ar1* 4 Ezra 4:27). In this translation, there are no "appointed times," no planned end of the age. The promised reward to the righteous will not come in this age only because of its infirmities and sadness. *Ar2* reads similarly: "the promises of God to the faithful may not continue because the world is full of sorrow and misery." There is no hint in these two Arabic texts of events fixed from the beginning.

Similarly, where the Latin reads: "And the archangel Jeremiel answered and said, 'When the number of those like yourselves is completed; for he has weighed the age in the balance, and measured the times by measure, and numbered the times by number; and he will not move or arouse them until that measure is fulfilled'" (Lat. 4 Ezra 4:36–37), *Ar1* omits the entire passage, thereby denying that the times can be measured and numbered. The avoidance of predestination is also evident in *Ar1's* version of 4 Ezra 9:4–5, where the Latin again implies that the end is known in the beginning: "For just as with everything that has occurred in the world, the beginning is evident, and the end manifest; so also are the times of the Most High: the beginnings are manifest in wonders and mighty works, and the end in penalties and in signs" (Lat. 4 Ezra 9:5–6). *Ar1* reads: "For what was not known at the beginning, the end will appear through power and wonders and acts and works and signs. The end will not be known until it is the time of the end, it is not known and was not determined in advance." Another difference from the Latin is that in *Ar1* the Messiah does not die. The phrase in 7:29 that predicts the death of the Messiah is simply omitted. After the Messianic period, the seven days that are quiet like the first begin immediately, with no intervening death of the Messiah.

God Is Merciful, Evil Is from the Enemy

The major difference between this version and all the others, however, is its understanding of the origin of evil. This translation asks: "what is God's justice considering the existence of evil in the world?" It answers the question by acknowledging man's free will, as does the Armenian, but in contrast to the Armenian and to every other text it attributes the origin of evil not to God but to the Enemy.[35] According to the Latin (7:48), "an evil heart has grown up in us which has alienated us," whereas in *Ar1* we read: "Evil has [put] in our heart every bad thing, by which it has misled and seduced us." In the other translations, it is our own evil heart that has alienated us from God, whereas in *Ar1* evil is portrayed as an active external force.[36] This is made explicit in *Ar1* 7:75 (= L 7:92): those who see the Most High will have seen degrees of consolation (L= seven types of joy); the first, according to the Latin, is: "Because they have striven with great effort to overcome the evil thought that formed within them, so that it might not lead them astray from life into death." In *Ar1,* however, we read: "The first is because they have struggled in order to defeat him who was created with them, namely the Enemy, and all his evil deeds and sordid thoughts." In *Ar1,* Evil is the Enemy, a separate created being created when Adam was created.

A final surprising difference between this version and the others is the emphasis on God's mercy, rather than on his justice. Whereas the Latin reads (4 Ezra 7:33–34): "The Most High shall be revealed on the seat of judgment, and compassion shall pass away, and patience shall be withdrawn. Only judgment shall remain, truth shall stand, and faithfulness shall grow strong," *Ar1* reads: "The Most High will appear on his seat of judgment; at that moment mercy shall *come,* clemency shall *approach, goodness* and *patience* are reunited." This is in direct contradiction to the presumed original Jewish text (represented by the Latin), in which at the time of the resurrection of the dead mercy and compassion will cease. In *Ar1,* it is then that God's mercy arrives. God's mercy can be stressed in this Arabic text, because the source of evil belongs to another. The notion of a separate source of evil and the emphasis on God's mercy is the ultimate exoneration of God. The text does not ask, however, why the merciful God allows the Enemy to exist.

Arabic Translation 2 (*Ar2*)

As both Violet and Gunkel point out, *Ar2* is a greatly shortened but generally literal translation of a Greek translation of the original Hebrew, the same Greek text, they suggest, from which *Ar1* was made.[37] Because it is often so abbreviated, it cannot always be determined if this is so and whether or not it agrees with *Ar1* in its interpretation of the text. *Ar2* begins with this prescript: "In the name of the living holy God, I begin with a compendium of the book of Ezra the Prophet. Thus spoke Ezra." In the rest of the translation, however, the speaker names himself not Ezra, as in the prescript, but El-Useir, Ezra's name as it appears in the Koran (see chapter 8), and as the son of Shealtiel, not Shealtiel himself.

There are differences between *Ar2* and *Ar1. Ar2* is far less pessimistic and dark than the other versions. It omits, for example, the verse in 4:12 in which Ezra declares to Uriel: "It would have been better for us not to be here than to come here and live in ungodliness, and to suffer and not understand why" (4 Ezra 4:12), a verse present in *Ar1* and in all the other versions. *Ar2* also omits the following verse, which is present in all the other translations: "For not of your own will did you come into the world, and against your will you depart, for you have been given only a short time to live" (Lat. 4 Ezra 8:5). It reads instead: "For they are few who escape death," thus providing a far less dour view of life.

Even so, *Ar2*'s text is often dramatic. As elsewhere, the turning point of 4 Ezra occurs in Ezra's conversation with the woman in the field. It appears even more stark in *Ar2,* however, for *Ar2* alone adds Ezra's statement to the woman to the effect that if she does not admit that the grief of the earth is greater than her own grief, then she opposes the Lord (*Ar2* 10:15).

In Vision V, the vision with the eagle, the lion who speaks to him is interpreted as the "King" in *Ar2,* instead of the Messiah, as in the Latin. Nor does he save "my people," as in the Latin; instead, he saves "the people who have known my miracles" (12:34). Those saved will have quiet until the end of time. Later in this text the Messianic figure is labeled "my Servant" (13:32). It is Jesus who is in mind here—instead of "he shall stand on top of Mount Zion (13:35)," we read "and a man will ascend onto Mount Golgotha in Zion."

Arabic Translation 3 (*Ar3*)

This final Arabic manuscript[38] is a fairly faithful translation not of the Greek but of a Syriac text closely related to the Syriac of the Ambrosian Codex, discussed earlier.[39] On the basis of the paleography, scholars believe it was likely made in the late ninth or early tenth century.[40] It is not identical to the other Arabic translations, which were translated from the Greek, even if we exclude the many Christian insertions in the form of chapter headings and marginal comments. These insertions are helpfully written in red ink, by the same hand as wrote the manuscript. They indicate how the copyist interpreted his text.

The text begins with an introduction that is not present in the Syriac or Latin versions. This introduction, which follows the heading, must have been in the *Vorlage,* since it is in black ink. It reads:

> In the name of God, the Merciful, the Compassionate. We begin, with God's help, The Book of the Writings of Ezra, the Teacher, the Scribe, the Pen of the Lord, which God threw into his heart and which Ezra dictated to the five persons whom God ordered him to take with him to the plain, that they should write that with which God inspired him and which he recited to them. So they wrote, in a script with which they were not previously acquainted, ninety-four books. Of these, God ordered him to make public twenty-four books, to be read in public, and to hide the remaining seventy, which they did.
>
> These are the names of the five persons: Sarâyâ, Darâyâ, Shalamyâ, Halqanâ, and Ashâyil.

The heading, in red, reads: "*The Book of the Writings of Ezra, the Teacher, the Scribe, the Pen of the Lord.*" There are interesting emendations from the Syriac. This translation also names the city in where the destruction occurred, Jerusalem, as in *Ar1.* It differs from the Latin of 3:9 and from the Syriac in that, instead of using the phrase "in its time you brought the flood," as does the Latin, or "in the appointed time," as does the Syriac, it reads: "at one time, you brought the flood." This does not indicate a lack of belief in predestination, however, since we read in 4:36–37 the same as in the Latin and the Syriac: "for he has weighed the age in the balance, and measured the times by measure, and numbered the times by number; and he will not move or arouse them until that measure is fulfilled.'"

This Arabic version does differ from the Latin or its Syriac *Vorlage* in several ways, however. Instead of reading in 3:20 that "you did not remove their evil heart from them [the people Israel], we read in *Ar3* that "the evil heart was not removed from them." The change to the passive voice removes the onus from God. Further, instead of "the first Adam, burdened with an evil heart, transgressed," *Ar3* reads: "the first Adam *put on* an evil heart" (3:21), also removing the onus from God.

In addition to such minor differences, there are insertions and marginal comments in red. The Arabic of 5:3–4 reads the same as the Latin, but before and after it we read marginal comments in red:

> *Prophecy of Ezra about the crucifixion of the Messiah and about his disciple.*
>
> And the land that you now see ruling shall be a trackless waste, and people shall see it desolate. But if the Most High grants that you live, you shall see it thrown into confusion after the third period; and the sun shall suddenly begin to shine at night, and the moon during the day [Lat. 4 Ezra 5:3–4].
>
> *Prophecy about the crucifixion of the Messiah.*

The copyist interprets the verse as a prediction not about the fall of Rome but about the signs that will appear at the Messiah's (Jesus's) crucifixion.

Another inserted heading occurs before 5:20: "*This is the prayer of Ezra and his request to his Lord. Meaning of Uriel, the angel: Uriel is the light of God—powerful and exalted is he who is the revealer.*" Uriel is thus interpreted as God himself or his emanation. There is also a marginal note beside 5:50. Verse 5:50 in *Ar3* reads as follows: "Then I inquired and said, 'Since you have now given me the opportunity, let me speak before you. Zion, our mother, of whom you have told me, is she still young? Or is she now approaching old age?'" It differs from the Latin in that the Latin inquires about the earth or the ages, not Zion. The marginal comment next to it reads: "*About the incarnation of our Lord the Messiah.*" Thus, in this interpretation, the question refers to the time of the second coming of Christ.

Further, where the Latin and Syriac read: "show your servant through whom you will visit [or punish] your creation" (5:56), *Ar3* reads: "show your servant through whom you will redeem your creation." Drint suggests that since the two Syriac words look very similar, it is likely just a misreading.[41] However, misreadings are shaped by ideology; the copyist has the coming of the Messiah in mind. Next to the Arabic text, there is another marginal comment in red: *"Prophecy about the sins of the people of the Messiah."* The people have sinned, but the Messiah will redeem them.

The Latin states that God alone will punish mankind: "At the beginning of the circle of the earth, before the portals of the world were in place, and before the assembled winds blew, . . . I planned these things. They were made through me alone and not through another" (Lat. 4 Ezra 6:1, 6). These verses are omitted in the Syriac and also from *Ar3.* Box suggests that they were omitted for dogmatic Christian reasons.[42] It was not through God alone but through Jesus as well that the world was made.

Next to 6:19 is another marginal comment: "*Prophecy about the baptized and the descending of the Spirit into them.*" The Latin reads: "The days are coming when I draw near to visit the inhabitants of the earth, and when I require from the doers of iniquity the penalty of their iniquity, and when the humiliation of Zion is complete" (6:18–19). God visiting (or punishing) the inhabitants of the earth is interpreted here to refer to the descending of the spirit into the baptized and the rejection (apparently) of those who are not. There is another marginal comment next to 7:26. Verse 7:26 reads in the Latin: "For indeed the time will come, when the signs that I have foretold to you will come to pass, that the city that now is not seen shall appear, and the land that now is hidden shall be disclosed" (Lat. 4 Ezra 7:26). The Syriac reads "that the bride will be revealed appearing as a city" (cf. Rev. 21:2). *Ar3* reads, however, "bridegroom" instead of bride. The marginal note reads: *"About the prophecy of the Messiah and his apostles."* The substitution of bridegroom for bride is intended to denote the coming of the Messiah.[43]

As in the Syriac, this text changes the length of time that the Messiah shall live from the four hundred years that is in the Latin and doubtless in the Hebrew to thirty years to conform to the life of Christ. The Latin reads: "Everyone who has been delivered from the evils that I have foretold shall see my wonders. For my Servant [or Son] the Messiah shall be revealed with those who are with him, and those who remain shall rejoice four hundred years. After those years my son the Messiah shall die, and all who draw human breath" (Lat. 4 Ezra 7:27–29). The Syriac and *Ar3* read "thirty years" instead of "four hundred": "Whoever is delivered from these evils which have been predicted, he shall see my wonders. For my son the Messiah shall be revealed together with those who are with him, and shall rejoice those that remain thirty years. And it shall be after these years, my son the Messiah shall die, and all those in whom is human breath." It seems, then, that by the time of the Syriac text, it was well understood that the one held in reserve until the end of time was the same one who had lived for thirty years on earth, that is, Jesus, known as the Christ.

NOTES

Chapter 1: Introduction to the Continuing Story of Ezra, Scribe and Priest

1. For a recent discussion of the devastation and the causes of the catastrophic drop in the population from the Babylonian conquest, see now Faust, "Deportation and Demography," and references cited there.

2. For the crucial role of the king in temple building, see my "The Land Lay Desolate."

3. Most notably Edelman, *Origins of the 'Second' Temple.*

4. Klein, "Were Joshua, Zerubbabel, and Nehemiah Contemporaries?," 697–701.

5. I have attempted to explain this in my "Ezra's Use of Documents in the Context of Hellenistic Rules of Rhetoric," 11–26.

6. For example, Williamson, *Ezra, Nehemiah,* xlvi–vii; Blenkinsopp, *Ezra-Nehemiah,* 44–45; and most recently Pakkala, *Ezra the Scribe,* 167–70.

7. Williamson, "1 Esdras as Rewritten Bible?," 237–49.

8. For discussions of the relationship between 1 Esdras and Ezra-Nehemiah, see the articles in Fried, *Was 1 Esdras First?*

Chapter 2: The Historical Ezra

1. Wills, *The Jewish Novel.*

2. Torrey, *Ezra Studies,* 240.

3. Kapelrud, *The Question of Authorship,* 95.

4. Mowinckel, *Die Ezrageschichte,* 11; so also Noth, *The Chronicler's History,* 187ff. For a literary discussion of the effect of person in the narrative of Ezra-Nehemiah, see Eskenazi, *In an Age of Prose,* 129–35.

5. Mowinckel, *Die Ezrageschichte,* 13.

6. Dor, *Did They Really Divorce the Foreign Women*?, 13–98.

7. Ibid., 18.

8. Campbell, "The Narrator as 'He,' 'Me,' and 'We'," 385–407.

9. Ibid., 402.

10. VanderKam, *From Joshua to Caiaphas,* 43–111; Fried, "A Silver Coin of Yohanan Hakkôhen," 65–85, Pls. II–V. For the idea that Ezra-Nehemiah is indeed one book and that the information in Nehemiah 12:22 applies to both books, Ezra and Nehemiah, see Japhet, "The Supposed Common Authorship of Chronicles and Ezra-Nehemiah Investigated Anew," 330–71; Japhet, "The Relationship between Chronicles and Ezra-Nehemiah," 298–313; and my "Who Wrote Ezra-Nehemiah?," 75–97. For the varying views on whether Ezra and Nehemiah form one book or two, see the discussions in Boda and Redditt, *Unity and Disunity.*

11. E. Stern, *Material Culture;* Ambar-Armon and Kloner, "Archaeological Evidence," 1–22; Eshel, "Hellenism in the Land of Israel," 116–24; as well as references cited in these works.

12. Hölbl, *A History of the Ptolemaic Empire,* 25. Although this is described for Egypt, the same is true for the rest of the empire.

13. Pakkala, *Ezra the Scribe;* Wright, *Rebuilding Identity.*

14. As asserted by Lebram, "Die Traditionsgeschichte der Esragestalt," 103–38.

15. Grabbe, "'Persian Documents,'" 531–70; Williamson, "The Aramaic Documents in Ezra Revisited," 41–62; Schwiderski, *Handbuch,* 343–82.

16. Porten and Yardeni, *Textbook of Aramaic Documents from Ancient Egypt,* A6.9.

17. Wellhausen, *Prolegomena,* 405–6.

18. Briant, *From Cyrus to Alexander,* 130–37.

19. Steiner, "The *mbqr* at Qumran, the Episkopos in the Athenian Empire," 623–46.

20. Liddell and Scott, *A Greek-English Lexicon,* ἐπίσκοπος (Definition 5).

21. Gehman, "'Επισκέπομαι, ἐπίσκεψις, ἐπίκοπος, and ἐπισκοπή," 197–207; Thiering, "*Mebaqqer* and *Episkopos,*" 59–74.

22. Balcer, "The Athenian Episkopos," 252–63.

23. Liddell and Scott, *A Greek-English Lexicon;* Balcer, "The Athenian Episkopos," 252–63; Steiner, "The *mbqr* at Qumran," 623–46.

24. Balcer, "The Athenian Episkopos."

25. Ibid., 255–56.

26. Porten and Yardeni, *Textbook of Aramaic Documents from Ancient Egypt,* A4.5:9, 10.

27. Ibid.

28. Porten, *Elephantine Papyri in English,* 136, fn. 10; Porten, *Archives from Elephantine,* 50, fn. 83.

29. Olmstead, *History of the Persian Empire,* 59.

30. Balcer, "The Athenian Episkopos," 262.

31. Stolper, "The Neo-Babylonian Text from Persepolis," 299–310.

32. Porten and Yardeni, *Textbook of Aramaic Documents from Ancient Egypt,* A6.2.

33. Stolper, "Registration and Taxation of Slave Sales in Achaemenid Babylonia," 80–101; Heltzer, "A Recently Published Babylonian Tablet," 57–61.

34. Translation is that of Kent, Old Persian: Grammar, Texts, Lexicon, 119.

35. Ibid., 138.

36. Ibid., 142.

37. *Dinātu,* plural, does not refer to "Law" in the general sense (*pace* Malbran-Labat, *La Version Akkadienne,* 134). The Laws listed in Hammurabi's law codes are not laws in our sense but simply scribal opinion of what justice looks like. See my "'You Shall Appoint Judges,'" 63–89, and references cited there.

38. Kent, *Old Persian: Grammar, Texts, Lexicon,* 152.

39. Dandamayev and Lukonin, *Cultures and Social Institutions,* 116–17.

40. Briant, "Polythéismes et empire unitaire," 425–29; Wiesehöfer, "Reichsgesetz' oder 'Einzelfallgerechtigkeit?,'" 36–46.

41. It also appears on one tablet from the time of Cyrus and in four texts from the Seleucid period (Démare-Lafont, "*Dātū Ša Šarri,*" note 8), but these will not be discussed here.

42. *Assyrian Dictionary of the Oriental Institute of the University of Chicago* 3:123

43. *Assyrian Dictionary of the Oriental Institute of the University of Chicago* 3:123

44. Jursa, "Nochmals Akkad," 101–4.

45. Ibid., 104; Stolper, *Late Achaemenid Texts,* 61.

46. Jursa et al., "Three Court Cases," 255–59.

47. Jursa et al. originally suggested that it refers to a "royal rule book" for regulating general disputes over the status of slaves. Jursa recently recanted this view in a lecture before the College de France (Jursa, "Achaemenid Babylonia: Political History and Administration," *Histoire et civilisation du monde achéménide et de l'empire d'Alexandre, Collège de France,* January 10, 2012, http://www.college-de-france.fr/site/pierre-briant/Conference_du_10_janvier_2012_.htm).

48. Kratz, *Translatio imperii,* 226; Démare-Lafont, "*Datu Ša Šarri,*" 544.

49. Dupont-Sommer, "La stèle trilingue du Letoon," 129–78; Fried, *The Priest and the Great King,* 140–54.

50. Dandamayev and Lukonin, *The Culture and Social Institutions,* 116–17.

51. Grätz, "Gottesgesetz und Königsgesetz," 3. Of course he considers the whole letter to be a fiction from the Hellenistic period: Grätz, *Das Edikt des Artaxerxes.*

52. *Assyrian Dictionary of the Oriental Institute of the University of Chicago* D153, Q180

53. Porten and Yardeni, *Textbook of Aramaic Documents from Ancient Egypt,* A4.7, 8.

54. YHW is the spelling used by the Elephantine Judeans for the Judean god Yahweh. In the Hebrew Bible it is spelled YHWH, but the pronunciation of the name and the identity of the god indicated are the same.

55. Porten and Yardeni, *Textbook of Aramaic Documents from Ancient Egypt,* A9.

56. Röllig, "Baal-Shamem," 149–51.

57. Ibid.

58. Schmid, "Persian Imperial Authorization," 37, fn. 50.

59. Hallock, *Persepolis Fortification Tablets,* 353–54.

60. The Hebrew reads "your god," but the possessive adjective "your" appears in none of the ancient versions, so it was likely added by a late copyist. All the versions read "the wisdom of God." It is even missing in the New Revised Standard Version English translation. However, the versions do include the possessive adjective "your" after God in the second part of the verse (not quoted here).

61 This phrase, "which is in your hand," is missing in 1 Esdras, and Talshir (*1 Esdras: A Text Critical Commentary,* 408) suggests it was not in the translator's *Vorlage,* that is, not in the Hebrew, but was added later.

62. The Hebrew reads "judges and judges," with the first word being the Hebrew word for "judge" and the second being the Aramaic. The first was probably added as a gloss by the biblical writer. Greek Ezra translates the first word as γραμματεῖς (scribes, perhaps, lawyers, experts in the law, that is, the very title this version applies to Ezra). First Esdras translates the first word as "judges" but the second as "jurors," those who sit in judgment in Athenian court cases.

63. I have discussed the Persian ethnicity of royal judges in numerous locations: Fried, "What the Aramaic Documents Tell Us about the Achaemenid Administration of Empire"; "Artaxerxes' Letter and the Mission of Ezra—noch einmal"; "Implications of 5th and 4th

Century Documents for Understanding the Role of the Governor in Persian Imperial Administration"; The Priest and the Great King, 90–92; "'You Shall Appoint Judges,'" 63–89.

64. Dandamayev, and Lukonin, *The Culture and Social Institutions,* 122.

65. Ibid., 118, n.12, 122.

66. Ibid.,123.

67. The Aramaic is in the plural here; only 1 Esdras puts it into the singular. I supply "judges" as the probable subject of the verb.

68. Grabbe, "Persian Documents."

69. *Pace* Pakkala (*Ezra the Scribe,* 37), who argues that these three verses (14, 25–26) were added later because they conflict with the basis text as he understands it.

70. Van Hoonacker, "Néhémie et Esdras," 151–84, 317–51, 389–400.

71. I discuss the authenticity of Darius's letter to Gadatas in Fried, *The Priest and the Great King,* 110–16.

72. Although the priest was exempted, the taxes were paid, picked up by the citizens of Xanthus.

73. *The Assyrian Dictionary of the Oriental Institute of the University of Chicago,* M. Part 1, 13–16, esp. 15.

74. *The Assyrian Dictionary of the Oriental Institute of the University of Chicago,* I-J, 73–81, esp. 80.

75. Grabbe, "Persian Documents."

76. Daniel E. Fleming and H. G. M. Williamson, personal communications.

77. *Hebrew and Aramaic Lexicon of the Old Testament,* 1:741. For Nehemiah's method of self-presentation, see Clines, "The Nehemiah Memoir: The Perils of Autobiography," 124–64.

78. Fried, "A Silver Coin of Yohanan Hakkôhen."

79. Levine, *Numbers 21–36,* 96

80. Porten, *Archives from Elephantine,* 28–35.

81. Tuplin, "Xenophon and the Garrisons," 167–245; Briant, "Contrainte militaire," 48–98; Briant, From Cyrus to Alexander; Fried, The Priest and the Great King; Fried, "The Political Struggle of Fifth Century Judah," 9–21; Fried, "What the Aramaic Documents Tell Us about the Achaemenid Administration of Empire."

82. Shaked, *Le satrape de Bactriane.*

83. This section is taken from Fried, "The Concept of 'Impure Birth,'" 121–42; it had its impetus in Eskenazi, "The Missions of Ezra and Nehemiah."

84. Osborne, "Law, the Democratic Citizen, and the Representation of Women," 3–33.

85. Jacoby, "Philochoros," 328F 119; Davies, "Athenian Citizenship," 105–21.

86. Manville, *The Origins of Citizenship in Ancient Athens,* 184.

87. Davies, "Athenian Citizenship."

88. Although quoted in a mid-fourth-century document, it has not been possible to date the laws themselves. Patterson, *Pericles' Citizenship Law,* 95.

89. Osborne, "Law and the Representation of Women," 3–33.

90. Ibid., 6–7.

91. Ibid., 9.

92. Humphreys, "The *Nothoi* of Kynosarges," 88–95, esp. 93–94; Samons, "Introduction: Athenian History and Society," 14.

93. Briant, *From Cyrus to Alexander,* 83, 501.

94. Brosius, *Women in Ancient Persia,* 47. Cambyses II is reputed to have married the daughter of Pharaoh, for example (ibid., 45).

95. Ibid., 47–64.

96. Ibid., 37–39.

97. For further discussion of the relations between local elites and the Persian Empire see Briant, *From Cyrus to Alexander;* Fried, "The Political Struggle of Fifth Century Judah," 9–21; Fried, *The Priest and the Great King;* Tuplin, "The Administration of the Achaemenid Empire"; Tuplin, "Xenophon and the Garrisons of the Achaemenid Empire."

98. *Pace* Eskenazi, "The Missions of Ezra and Nehemiah," who sees the entire episode of the mass divorce as driven by opposition to the priestly elites and does not admit to Persian motivation behind this opposition. For further discussion of possible imperial motivations, see Hoglund, *Achaemenid Imperial Administration,* 226–40.

99. Duverger, "Le Concept d'Empire," 12.

100. Shallit, "The Reforms of Gabinius," 41.

101. Lewis, *Life in Egypt,* 32–33. The code of regulations of the Privy Purse is BGU 1210 at the Berlin Egyptian Museum. Cf. R. Bagnall and B. Frier, *The Demography of Roman Egypt,* 28–29.

Chapter 3: Ezra in the Hebrew Bible

1. By canonical, we refer to the books in the Hebrew Bible. By Apocryphal, we refer to those books that were added in the Greek translation (1 Esdras) or to those added in the Latin Vulgate (4, 5, and 6 Esdras). For discussions of the relative dating of canonical Ezra and 1 Esdras, see now the several articles in Fried, *Was 1 Esdras First?*

2. Harvey Jr., "Darius' Court and the Guardsmen's Debate," 179–90.

3. Japhet, *I & II Chronicles,* 151.

4. *Pace* Rudolph, *Esra und Nehemia,* 66; and *pace* in der Smitten, *Esra,* 8.

5. So also Kapelrud, *The Question of Authorship,* 20. See Johnson, *The Purpose of the Biblical Genealogies.*

6. Pakkala, *Ezra the Scribe,* 42–43.

7. Williamson, "The Composition of Ezra i–vi," 1–30, Williamson, *Ezra, Nehemiah,* xxxiii–xxxv.

8. So also Gunneweg, *Esra,* 121.

9. Parker and Dubberstein, *Babylonian Chronology.*

10. Porten and Yardeni, *Textbook of Aramaic Documents from Ancient Egypt,* B.4. For a discussion of scribal activity at Elephantine, see Botta, *Aramaic and Egyptian Legal Traditions at Elephantine.*

11. Porten and Yardeni, *Textbook of Aramaic Documents from Ancient Egypt,* B.4.

12. See the articles in Gammie and Perdue, *The Sage,* and in Perdue, *Scribes, Sages, and Seers,* as well as Kratz, *Das Judentum,* 111–18.

13. Stolper, "Registration and Taxation of Slave Sales in Achaemenid Babylonia," 80–101; Heltzer, "A Recently Published Babylonian Tablet," 57–61.

14. See Lichtheim, "The Satire of the Trades," 184–92, a text from Egypt's Middle Kingdom. It is a humorous instruction from a father to his son, which belittles the trades in

order to encourage his son to apply himself to his scribal studies. See also Rollston, "Ben Sira 38:24–39:11 and the 'Egyptian Satire of the Trades.'"

15. Lindenberger, The Aramaic Proverbs of Ahiqar; Kottsieper, "The Aramaic Tradition."

16. Kottsieper, "The Aramaic Tradition," 109–24.

17. Gunneweg, *Esra,* 127.

18. Fishbane, *Biblical Interpretation,* 245.

19. In der Smitten, *Esra,* 10; van der Toorn, "The Iconic Book," 229–48.

20. I thank Erica Arnold, one of my students, for this phrase.

21. Lim, "Defilement of the Hands," 501–15.

22. Quoted from Goodman, "Sacred Scripture," 102.

23. Barton, *The Spirit and the Letter,* 108–21; Goodman, "Sacred Scripture," 99–107; Lim, "Defilement of the Hands."

24. Niditch, *Oral World and Written Word,* 106.

25. This has also been the view of many modern scholars; see chapter 9.

26. For example, Rudolph, *Esra und Nehemia,* 74.

27. Hartman and Di Lella, *Daniel,* 13.

28. Duggan, *Covenant Renewal,* 1.

29. See, for example, Torrey, *Ezra Studies,* 252–84, and any of the commentaries on Ezra-Nehemiah.

30. Cazelles, "La mission d'Esdras," 113–40.

31. Ibid.

32. The idea that Nehemiah 8 was dislocated from an original position in Ezra was perhaps initiated by Torrey, *The Composition and Historical Value of Ezra-Nehemiah,* 14–34, and has been followed by nearly every other commentator since.

33. This is so, whatever the date of the historical Ezra.

34. Wright, *Rebuilding Identity,* 327.

35. This verse seems to be a late addition by a second author anyway (ibid., fn. 37).

36. So also Rendtorff, "Esra und das 'Gesetz,'" 165–84; Rendtorff, "Noch einmal," 89–91; VanderKam, "Ezra-Nehemiah or Ezra and Nehemiah?" 55–75.

37. The following sections are based on my article "A Greek Religious Association in Second Temple Judah?," 75–93.

38. Most English versions have inserted "and Ezra said" at the beginning of Nehemiah 9:6, but it is not in the Hebrew.

39. Baltzer, *The Covenant Formulary,* 43–8; Duggan, *Covenant Renewal,* 5–7.

40. Welch, "The Source of Nehemiah IX," 175–87; Japhet, "Sheshbazzar and Zerubbabel," 66–98; Williamson, *Ezra, Nehemiah,* 309; Boda, *Praying the Tradition,* 32–41; Duggan, *Covenant Renewal,* 9. See Baltzer, *The Covenant Formulary,* 43, for the opposing view.

41. Boda, *Praying the Tradition,* 32–41.

42. Williamson, *Ezra, Nehemiah,* 330; Blenkinsopp, *Ezra-Nehemiah,* 312–14, sees it as a free composition of the Chronicler.

43. Duggan, *Covenant Renewal,* 120.

44. Ibid., 121.

45. Baltzer, *The Covenant Formulary,* 43–48; Duggan, *Covenant Renewal;* Freedman and Miano, "People of the New Covenant," 7–26.

46. See McCarthy, *Treaty and Covenant;* Weinfeld, "The Covenant of Grant," 184–203.

47. Baltzer, *The Covenant Formulary,* 43–48.

48. Ibid., 45.

49. McCarthy, "Covenant and Law in Chronicles-Nehemiah," 25–44.

50. McCarthy, in ibid., did note a similarity, but the idea is absent from Duggan's recent study, *Covenant Renewal,* fn.1.

51. Quoted in and translated by Jones, *The Associations of Classical Athens,* 34, from Gaius's Digest 47.22.4.

52. Weisberg, *Guild Structure.*

53. De Cenival, *Les associations religieuses en Égypte;* de Cenival, "Comptes d'une association religieuse," 13–29 (the index number of the papyrus is stated incorrectly in the article's title; it is E 7841); Hughes and Junker, *The Sixth Day of the Lunar Month.* For a recent review and bibliography of associations in Ptolemaic Egypt see Muhs, "Membership in Private Associations," 1–21.

54. Jones, *The Associations of Classical Athens.*

55. Fried, "A Greek Religious Association in Second Temple Judah?," 75–93.

56. The following is derived from my article "Who Wrote Ezra-Nehemiah," 75–97.

57. Polak, "The Covenant at Mount Sinai," 119–34.

58. Polak, in ibid., points out the importance of this location in the Sinaitic covenant.

59. In the story of the Exodus there are no foreigners; anyone who is there receives the Torah. The three days of abstinence prior to the law reading are enough to purify the people. Aaron Demsky, "Who Came First, Ezra or Nehemiah?," 1–19, points out that the Temple Scroll (45: 7–12) also requires three days of abstinence as a purification rite. The three days of abstinence are separated in Ezra-Nehemiah into a three-day delay and then a mass divorce. In First Esdras too the law reading is placed at the end of the book (9:37–54) so that it occurs after the people have been purified by divorcing their foreign wives (9:5–36).

60. In the story of 1 Esdras, the Apocryphal story of Ezra, the story of the law reading is told after the mass divorce, at the end of Chapter 10. For studies of the relationship between the Canonical Ezra and 1 Esdras, see chapter 4 as well as the articles in Fried, *Was 1 Esdras First?*

61. Polak, "The Covenant at Mount Sinai."

62. That is, the rest of Nehemiah 8 and all of Nehemiah 9–12:30 were added secondarily by later authors. See my discussion in "Did the Authors of Ezra-Nehemiah Think That YHWH Dwelt in the Second Temple?" and also the analysis of the growth of the text of Nehemiah in Wright, Rebuilding Identity.

63. Eskenazi, *In an Age of Prose,* 120.

64. Langdon, *Die neubabylonischen Königsinschriften,* 258; *apud* Hurowitz, *I Have Built You an Exalted House,* 278.

65. Josephus reports that Torah scrolls were laid up in the temple (Ant. 3:38; 5:61).

66. Polak, "The Covenant at Mount Sinai."

67. See now the articles in Frevel, *Mixed Marriages.*

68. As Japhet ("Theodicy in Ezra-Nehemiah," 430) emphasizes, "In these rhetorical pieces, past and present are viewed as connected by a relationship of cause and effect, the past being the root of the present, the origin and cause of its circumstances in all their aspects."

69. Ibid., 432.

70. See in particular James L. Crenshaw's chapter, "Punishment for Sin," in Crenshaw, *Defending God*, 117–31.

71. *Pace* Rabbi Kushner, *When Bad Things Happen to Good People.*

72. The various biblical responses to calamity are always intended to justify God's innocence in the face of evil. See the essays in Crenshaw, *Defending God.*

73. See the various commentaries on Ezra.

74. Weinfeld, *Deuteronomy 1–11*, 362–64. Except for the Canaanites, the peoples listed here are from Anatolia (Asia Minor) and had fled to Canaan when the Sea Peoples invaded at the end of the Bronze Age. According to Weinfeld, the order reflects the usage of the Geographical-gentilic terms in neo-Assyrian inscriptions of the seventh century B.C.E.

75. Van Seters, "'Amorite' and 'Hittite,'" 64–81.

76. Japhet, "Theodicy in Ezra-Nehemiah," 442.

Chapter 4: First, or Greek, Esdras—The Law Triumphant

1. See Honigman, *The Septuagint and Homeric Scholarship.*

2. For discussions of the relationship between 1 Esdras and Ezra-Nehemiah, see the articles in Fried, *Was 1 Esdras First?*

3. Williamson, "1 Esdras as Rewritten Bible?," 237–49.

4. This section is based on my article "Another Look at 1 Esdras."

5. This question is indeed the focus of the articles in Fried, *Was 1 Esdras First?*

6. Pohlmann, *Studien zum dritten Esra.* For a history of research see De Troyer, "Zerubbabel and Ezra," 30–60.

7. For example, Torrey, *Ezra Studies*, 11–36; Pohlmann, *Studien zum dritten Esra;* Schenker, "La Relation d'Esdras A' au Texte Massorétique," 218–48; Schenker, "The Relationship between Ezra-Nehemiah and 1 Esdras," 45–58; Böhler, *Die heilige Stadt in Esdras α und Esra-Nehemia;* Böhler, "On the Relationship between Textual and Literary Criticism," 35–50. See also Fulton and Knoppers, "Lower Criticism and Higher Criticism," 11–29; Grabbe, "Chicken or Egg?," 31–43.

8. For example, Talshir, *1 Esdras: From Origin to Translation*; Talshir, "Ancient Composition Patterns," 109–29; Becking, "The Story of the Three Youths," 83–71; De Troyer, "The Second Year of Darius," 73–81; Fried, "Why the Story of the Three Youths in 1 Esdras?," 83–92; Pakkala, "Why 1 Esdras Is Probably Not an Early Version," 93–107; VanderKam, "Literary Questions," 131–43; Wright, "Remember Nehemiah," 145–63.

9. This is the conclusion of a majority of scholars writing in Fried, *Was 1 Esdras First?*

10. Harvey Jr., "Darius' Court and the Guardsmen's Debate," 179–90. See this work also for a discussion of the antiquity of the genre as well as related bibliography.

11. For example, Fried, "Why the Story of the Three Youths in 1 Esdras?," 83–92; Japhet, "1 Esdras: Genre, Literary Form, and Goals," 209–23; Williamson, "1 Esdras as Rewritten Bible?," 237–49; Wright, "Remember Nehemiah," 145–63.

12. For a discussion of the use of these letters in Ezra 1–6, see now my "Ezra's Use of Documents in the Context of Hellenistic Rules of Rhetoric," 11–26. For the historical background of the letters and why they were actually directed toward stopping the city wall from being built, see my "The Artaxerxes Correspondence of Ezra 4, Nehemiah's Wall, and Persian Provincial Administration," 35–58.

13. Wright, "Remember Nehemiah," 145–63.

14. Klein, "The Rendering of 2 Chronicles 35–36 in 1 Esdras," 225–35.

15. See Honigman, "Cyclical Time and Catalogues," 191–208, for a discussion of 1 Esdras's cyclical construction.

16. Or because they "thoroughly understood the words": Talshir, *1 Esdras: A Text Critical Commentary,* 495.

17. Honigman, "Cyclical Time and Catalogues," 191–208. See also Eskenazi, "The Chronicler and the Composition of 1 Esdras," 39–61; Van der Kooij, "On the Ending of the Book of 1 Esdras," 37–49; Williamson, "1 Esdras," 851–58.

18. *Pace* Wright, "Remember Nehemiah," 145–63.

19. Feldman, "Josephus," 981–98.

20. Ibid., 987.

21. Ibid., 194.

22. See the examples in MacMullen, *Enemies of the Roman Order,* particularly the chapter on urban unrest, 163–91.

23. Feldman, "Josephus' Portrait of Ezra," 190–214.

24. A Greek or Attic talent was 26 kilograms (57 lbs.), a Roman talent was 32.3 kilograms (71 lbs.), an Egyptian talent was 27 kilograms (60 lbs.), and a Babylonian talent was 30.3 kilograms (67 lbs.). Ancient Israel and other Levantine countries adopted the Babylonian talent but later revised the mass. The heavy common talent, used in New Testament times, was 58.9 kilograms (130 lbs.). Powell, "Weights and Measures."

25. Feldman, "Josephus' Portrait of Ezra," 190–214.

26. Ibid., 191.

Chapter 5: Fourth Ezra—The Ezra Apocalypse

1. Bogaert, "Versions [of the Bible]," 799–803.

2. Stone, *Fourth Ezra,* 10–11.

3. Collins, "Introduction: Towards the Morphology of a Genre," 1–20; Yarbro Collins, "The Early Christian Apocalypses," 61–121; Himmelfarb, *Ascent to Heaven,* 95–114; Himmelfarb, *Tours of Hell. Pace* Stone, "Apocalyptic, Vision, or Hallucination?" 47–56, in which the opposite view is maintained; it is reiterated later in his commentary on 4 Ezra (Stone, *Fourth Ezra*) and again in a recent article (Stone, "A Reconsideration of Apocalyptic Visions," 167–80).

4. Collins, "Introduction: Towards the Morphology of a Genre," 9.

5. All translations of 4 Ezra are from the New Revised Standard Version (1989) unless otherwise noted.

6. For example, Box, *The Ezra-Apocalypse,* 516; and Denis, *Introduction à la littérature religieuse Judéo-Hellénistique,* 818–19.

7. Stone, *Fourth Ezra,* 11–23.

8. Collins, "Introduction: Towards the Morphology of a Genre," 9.

9. Crenshaw, "Introduction: The Shift from Theodicy," 148, speaking not of Ezra directly but of all those theodicies which put their hope in another world, another time.

10. Mark 2:19 is printed in pink by the members of the Jesus Seminar (meaning that between 50 percent and 75 percent assign it to Jesus himself, whereas Mark 2:20 is printed in black, as being later or not Jesus (Funk, Hoover, and The Jesus Seminar, *Five Gospels,* 47).

Verse 20 is derived from and implied by verse 19. There were certainly annual fasts for the destruction of the first temple (Zech. 7:5, 8:19).

11. Pious Jews have been fasting and mourning on the ninth day of the Hebrew month of Av for almost two thousand years for the fallen first and second temples.

12. This image of the heavenly Jerusalem on earth is reminiscent of that in Revelation 21:1–5.

13. Stone, *Fourth Ezra,* 365; thus the same time as Josephus.

14. For a discussion of Cyrus as Messiah, see my "Cyrus the Messiah?," 373–93.

15. Or Son. The word for "servant" and "son" is the same in Greek, from which this Latin translation was made.

16. Stone, *Fourth Ezra,* 441.

17. Ibid., 97.

18. Bauckham, *The Fate of the Dead,* 34

19. Stone, "The Concept of the Messiah in 4 Ezra," 295.

20. Stone, *Fourth Ezra,* 348.

21. Stone, "The Concept of the Messiah in 4 Ezra," 295–312, addresses this anomaly.

22. Reading with the Greek.

23. Stone, *Fourth Ezra,* 222.

24. Metzger, "The Lost Section," 153–56; Robert Bensly undertook a search for the missing section and finally found a complete Latin manuscript in a library in Amiens. He published it with a commentary in 1875 (Bensly, *The Missing Fragment of the Latin Translation of the Fourth Book of Ezra*). The introduction details the story of the find.

25. Stone, *Fourth Ezra,* 334–35; Stone, "The City in 4 Ezra," 402–7.

26. On evil as punishment for sin and man's power over God, see Crenshaw, "Punishment for Sin," in Crenshaw, *Defending God,* 117–31.

27. For a discussion of the many biblical texts in which God is shown punishing his own people without cause, see Whybray, "Shall Not the Judge of All the Earth Do What Is Just?," 1–19.

28. For the appeal to the mysteriousness of God and the ignorance of man in the face of innocent suffering see the many commentaries on Job as well as Crenshaw, "Mystery: Appealing to Human Ignorance," 165–75.

29. Note the title of G. B. Sayler's book on 2 Baruch: *Have the Promises Failed?*

30. For recourse to another time and another place in a discussion of God's justice, see Crenshaw, "Justice Deferred."

31. Whybray ("Shall Not the Judge of All the Earth Do What Is Just?," 9) characterizes the Deuteronomistic History as a work "whose aim is to justify God's punitive behavior toward his people."

32. For a discussion of this approach to justifying God, see Crenshaw, "Justice Deferred."

33. Longenecker, *2 Esdras,* 92.

Chapter 6: The Christian Additions to the Ezra Apocalypse

1. *Pace* Yarbro Collins, "The Early Christian Apocalypses," 79.

2. Kraft, "Towards Assessing the Latin Text," 158–69.

3. Ibid., 165.

4. Bergren, *Fifth Ezra,* 318–20.

5. Ibid.

6. Dunn, *The Partings of the Ways,* 248

7. Ibid.

8. Bergren, *Sixth Ezra,* 15–16, 103–15.

9. Fox, *Pagans and Christians,* 450. Jews were exempt from this requirement, having been grandfathered in.

10. Ibid., 455.

11. Southern, *The Roman Empire,* 74–75.

12. Fox, *Pagans and Christians,* 455.

13. Bergren, *Sixth Ezra,* 16–17, 116–32.

14. Gutschmid, "Die Apokalypse des Esra," 1–81; see also Bergren, *Sixth Ezra,* 116–32.

15. For Procopius, see Stoneman, *Palmyra and Its Empire,* 78; for Malalas, see Millar, *The Roman Near East,* 160.

16. Wiesehöfer, "Ardašir I," 371–76; Stoneman, *Palmyra and Its Empire,* 90–91.

17. Stoneman, *Palmyra and Its Empire,* 77; Teixidor, "Palmyra in the Third Century," 181.

18. Stoneman, *Palmyra and Its Empire,* 92.

19. Barraclough, *HarperCollins Atlas,* 79; Bosworth, "ARAB: i. Arabs and Iran in the Pre-Islamic Period," 201–3.

20. Frye, "Appendix 5: The Inscription of Shapur I at Naqsh-e-Rustam," 371–74.

21. Stoneman, *Palmyra and Its Empire,* 107.

Chapter 7: Ezra Ascends to Heaven and Goes to Hell

1. The text used here is based on Stone, "Greek Apocalypse of Ezra," 561–79.

2. Stone, "The Metamorphosis of Ezra," 5.

3. Himmelfarb, *The Apocalypse,* 18. Earlier she argues for an early third-century date for Ap. Paul (Himmelfarb, *Tours of Hell,* 18). Stone, "Greek Apocalypse of Ezra," 563. For discussion of this tradition in general see Alexander, *The Byzantine Apocalyptic Tradition.*

4. Evans, *Age of Justinian,* 163.

5. Himmelfarb, *The Apocalypse,* 127.

6. Tartarus is mentioned in Hesiod as a dark abyss, as deep below Hades as earth is below heaven, the prison of the Titans, and so on. Liddell and Scott, *A Greek-English Lexicon.* The term appears in the Septuagint of Proverbs 30:16; in Job 40:20; 41:24; and in 2 Peter 2:4.

7. Bauckham, *The Fate of the Dead,* 34. J. Crenshaw (personal communication) reminds me, however, that the story of Lazarus in Abraham's bosom (Luke 16:19–31) belies the notion of a linear development in the concept of the time of the judgment after death.

8. Denis, *Introduction à la littérature religieuse Judéo-Hellénistique,* 861.

9. Mueller and Robbins, "Vision of Ezra," 581–90; Himmelfarb, *Tours of Hell;* Himmelfarb, *The Apocalypse.*

10. Kraft, "The Multiform Jewish Heritage," 180.

11. The text used here is based on the translation of Mueller and Robbins, "Vision of Ezra," 582.

12. Yarbro Collins, "The Early Christian Apocalypses," 87.

13. These are interpolated into a second, longer version of the text in which both signal the coming of the last days. See Denis, *Introduction à la littérature religieuse Judéo-Hellénistique,* 865–66. In the longer text there is also Ezra's fear of dying and a plea for clemency for those who read this book.

14. Mueller and Robbins, "Vision of Ezra," 584.

15. The translation used is that of Stone, "Questions of Ezra," 591–99.

16. Ibid., 591.

17. Ibid., 597, fn h.

18. Ibid., 593.

19. The translation used is that of Agourides, "Apocalypse of Sedrach," 606. It is extant in a single fifteenth-century Greek manuscript, located in the Bodleian Library.

20. Ibid.

21. Ibid.

22. This label is proposed by Stone, "The Metamorphosis of Ezra," 4.

23. This discussion is based on the translation into French by J. B. Chabot ("L'Apocalypse d'Esdras des Arabes," 242–43, 333–46).

24. Ibid., 242.

25. Ibid., 344.

26. Based on the French translation and commentary of Halévy, *Te'ezaza Sanbat.*

27. Ibid., iii–xxxii.

28. Ibid., xxxii.

29. Ibid., xxxiii.

30. Ibid., xxxiv–xxxv.

31. Ibid., xix; cf. Isaac, "The Ethiopic Apocalypse of Enoch," 5–89.

32. The translation is that of Fiensy, "Revelation of Ezra," 601–4.

33. Charlesworth, "Jewish Astrology in the Talmud," 190 and fn. 22.

Chapter 8: Ezra among Christians, Samaritans, Muslims, and Jews of Late Antiquity'

1. Quoted in Kraft, "'Ezra ' Materials," 125.

2. Ibid.

3. Ibid.

4. Ibid., quoted from Hippolytus Commentary on Daniel 4:30–31.

5. Kuhn, "A Coptic Jeremiah Apocryphon," 95.

6. Ibid., 96, 102.

7. Ibid., 103.

8. Ibid., 309–10.

9. Ibid., 315.

10. Adler, "The Jews as Falsifiers," 3.

11. Gilliard, "Paul and the Killing of the Prophets," 259–70; Halpern-Amaru, "The Killing of the Prophets," 153–80.

12. Quoted in Stern, *From Tacitus to Simplicius,* 480, emphasis mine.

13. Rufinus, *Apology against Jerome* 2.36, quoted in Adler, "The Jews as Falsifiers," 9.

14. Jeffery, "Ghevond's Text," 277.

15. Ibid., 289–90.

16. Ibid., 288.

17. Translation from Anderson and Giles, *Tradition Kept,* 101, with my slight emendation.

18. Stern and Magen, "The First Level of the Samaritan Temple," 119–24; Stern and Magen, "Archaeological Evidence," 49–57; Magen, "The Dating of the First Phase of the Samaritan Temple," 157–211.

19. Adang, *Muslim Writers on Judaism,* 232.

20. Hjelm, *The Samaritans,* 101; Anderson and Giles, *Tradition Kept,* 143.

21. Stenhouse (*The Kitab al-Tarikh of Abu 'l-Fath,* xxi, fn. 306) states that the king is usually associated with Darius, since the name is that of Darius spelled backwards in the consonantal text (דריוש vs. שורדי, and the number of years proposed for his reign is the same, thirty-six years (*The Chronicle of Abu 'l-Fatḥ* 80).

22. That is the whole Hebrew Bible, including the history of the Davidic kings, not included in the Samaritan Bible, which includes only the Pentateuch.

23. Stenhouse, *Kitab al-Tarikh of Abu 'l-Fath,* 92–93.

24. Ibid., 96.

25. I have suggested that the story of Samaritan opposition told in Ezra 4 and the one in Nehemiah are actually the same story told twice. See my "The Artaxerxes Correspondence," 35–58.

26. Hjelm, *The Samaritans,* 100; Stenhouse, "Samaritan Chronicles," 540.

27. Meshorer and Qedar, *The Coinage of Samaria.*

28. That is, they added the five final consonantal forms that are not in paleo-Hebrew.

29. Stenhouse, *Kitab al-Tarikh of Abu 'l-Fath,* 97–98.

30. Anderson and Giles, *Tradition Kept,* 36. The Samaritan Pentateuch can add this as a tenth commandment, since it views the statement "I am YHWH your god who brought you out of the land of Egypt out of the house of bondage" as simply a preamble, rather than as the first of the commandments, as the Jews consider it.

31. Ayoub, "'Uzayr," 6.

32. Lazarus-Yafeh, *Intertwined Worlds,* 52.

33. Ayoub, "'Uzayr," 9; Comerro, "Esdras est-il le fils de Dieu?," 165.

34. Comerro, "Esdras est-il le fils de Dieu?," 165.

35. Ayoub, "'Uzayr," 9.

36. Ibid., 11.

37. Ibid.

38. Ibid., 6.

39. Adang, *Muslim Writers on Judaism,* 11.

40. Ibid., 116.

41. Quoted in Ayoub, "'Uzayr," 12.

42. Ibid.

43. Ibid.

44. The following quotations are cited in Ayoub, "'Uzayr," 14–15.

45. Quoted in Lazarus-Yafeh, *Intertwined Worlds,* 54–55.

46. Adang, *Muslim Writers,* 59–60.

47. Ibid., 95.

48. Ibid., 96.

49. Ibid., 97.

50. Ibid., 98.

51. Hirschberg, "Ezra [in Islam]," 653.

52. Ibid.

53. Adang, *Muslim Writers,* 98.

54. J. Crenshaw (personal communication) points out that bread is also used to mark the days that Gilgamesh sleeps (XI:5), but there the bread marks time by becoming moldy, whereas here it is preserved fresh by God, proving God's ability to preserve life and resurrect the dead.

55. Ibn 'Arabī, "The Seal of the Wisdom of the Decree," 62–66.

56. Lazarus-Yafeh, *Intertwined Worlds,* 20.

57. Quoted from ibid., 20–21.

58. Adang, *Muslim Writers,* 231.

59. Quoted from ibid., 233–34.

60. Quoted from ibid., 234.

61. Lazarus-Yafeh, *Intertwined Worlds,* 27 and n. 25.

62. Adang, *Muslim Writers,* 246.

63. Lazarus-Yafeh, *Intertwined Worlds,* 67 and n. 50.

64. Ibid., 66.

65. This is based on Christian polemic; see Gilliard, "Paul and the Killing of the Prophets," 259–70; Halpern-Amaru, "The Killing of the Prophets," 153–80.

66. Quoted in Lazarus-Yafeh, *Intertwined Worlds,* 67–68.

67. He refers here to God's regret over the flood and his promise not to destroy the world by flood again.

68. Quoted from Lazarus-Yafeh, *Intertwined Worlds,* 69.

69. Meri, *The Cult of Saints,* 21.

70. Quoted from ibid.

71. Ibid., 22.

72. Ibid., 24. The rabbi repeats this in a letter to his son, dated 1435 (ibid., 237).

73. Boccaccini, *Roots of Rabbinic Judaism,* 4.

74. See Wright, *Baruch Ben Neriah,* for a study of Baruch in history and tradition, including rabbinic tradition.

75. For the dates of these and other high priests of the second temple, see VanderKam, *From Joshua to Caiaphas.*

76. Building an altar and sacrificing on it without a temple (Ezra 3) was quite anomalous in the Mediterranean world but customary among the Greeks. See chapter 9. I also discuss this issue and its relevance for the composition of the biblical book of Ezra in Fried, "Did the Authors of Ezra-Nehemiah Think That YHWH Dwelt in the Second Temple?"

77. This refers to rabbinic midrash in Genesis 22, where it is held that Isaac was bound at the spot where the temple was to be built and a ram sacrificed in his stead. The ram's ashes are counted as Isaac's ashes.

78. Ginzberg and Stern, *Legends of the Jews,* 1123, fn. 35.

79. Quoted by Porton, "Ezra in Rabbinic Literature," 315, fn. 37.

80. Quoted in Rabinowitz, *The Book of Ezra,* 153–54.

81. Feldman, "Josephus' Portrait of Ezra," 192.

82. Ginzberg and Stern, *Legends of the Jews,* 1122.

83. Porton, "Ezra in Rabbinic Literature," 319.

84. Cited from Feldman, "Josephus' Portrait of Ezra," 191. This is doubtless based on the events described in 4 Ezra, although Ezra himself is not described as participating in them.

85. I have argued that both the divine presence and the *urim* and *thummim* were believed present in the second temple: Fried, "Did Second Temple High Priests Possess the *Urim* and *Thummim*?"; and Fried, "Did the Authors of Ezra-Nehemiah Think That YHWH Dwelt in the Second Temple?"

Chapter 9: Ezra in Modern Scholarship

1. Simon, *A Critical History of the Old Testament,* 5.

2. Witter, *Jura Israelitarum in Palaestinam.*

3. Astruc, *Conjectures sur les mémoires originaux.*

4. Eichhorn, *Einleitung in das Alte Testament.*

5. Houtman, "Ezra and the Law," 97–98.

6. De Wette, *Dissertatio critico-exegetica qua Deuteronomium;* Ska, *Introduction to Reading the Pentateuch,*106.

7. Graf, *Die geschichtlichen Bücher des Alten Testaments.*

8. Ska, *Introduction to Reading the Pentateuch,* 110.

9. *Encyclopædia Britannica Online,* "Romanticism."

10. Weinfeld, *Place of the Law,* xi.

11. Wellhausen, *Prolegomena,* 110.

12. Ibid., 112.

13. Ibid., 2.

14. Ibid.

15. Meyer, *Die Entstehung des Judentums,* 66. Emphasis mine.

16. This has also been proposed by Kaufmann, *The Religion of Israel,* and his numerous followers, but not for the reasons suggested here. They count P as the earliest of the sources and date it to the pre-exilic period. I agree that the ritual texts associated with the priestly writers undoubtedly reflect practices of the pre-exilic temple, but the date of P must rely on assessment of when the narratives assigned to P were written, not on the date of the laws and rituals.

17. Parts of the following sections are taken from my article "Did the Authors of Ezra-Nehemiah Think That YHWH Dwelt in the Second Temple?"

18. Wellhausen, *Prolegomena,* 17.

19. Oppenheim, *Ancient Mesopotamia,* 188; Anderson, *Sacrifices and Offerings in Ancient Israel,* 15; Margueron, "Mesopotamian Temples," 165.

20. Anderson, *Sacrifices and Offerings in Ancient Israel,* 15.

21. Milgrom, *Leviticus 1–16,* 1009–84, esp. 1079–84.

22. *The Assyrian Dictionary of the Oriental Institute of the University of Chicago,* K. 178–79.

23. *Ancient Near Eastern Texts Relating to the Old Testament,* 3rd ed., 331–34; Milgrom, *Leviticus 1–16,* 1067–68.

24. *Ancient Near Eastern Texts Relating to the Old Testament,* 3rd ed., 348.

25. Mikalson, *Ancient Greek Religion*; Zaidman and Pantel, *Religion in the Ancient Greek City,* 55.

26. Burkert, *Greek Religion,* 92. Levine ("*Lpny YHWH,*" 259–69) discusses the Edomite open-air altar of Hurvat Qitmit and compares it to the *bāmāh* of 1 Samuel 9. As Levine recognizes, both of these have buildings associated with them, which may be assumed to house the god. Levine bases his discussion primarily on the open-air sanctuaries described in Genesis. At the time of his writing (1993), these texts were associated with the J and E writers and dated to the monarchic period. Such an early dating is no longer maintained by scholars (see, for example, the essays in Dozeman and Schmid, *A Farewill to the Yahwist?*).

27. Burkert, *Greek Religion,* 91.

28. Burford, *The Greek Temple Builders at Epidauros.* I thank Professor B. A. Levine for calling this work to my attention.

29. Ibid., 47.

30. Ibid., 48–49.

31. Ibid., 54.

32. Wellhausen, *Prolegomena,* 52–53.

33. *Ancient Near Eastern Texts Relating to the Old Testament,* 3rd ed., 343–44.

34. For a discussion of divine abandonment, see Fried, "The Land Lay Desolate," 21–54, and references cited there.

35. Porten and Yardeni, *Textbook of Aramaic Documents from Ancient Egypt,* A4.7.

36. Wellhausen, *Prolegomena,* 402. I and others have tried to show that there is no archaeological evidence for a Josianic reform. See my "The High Places (Bamôt) and the Reforms of Hezekiah and Josiah" and references cited there.

37. Wellhausen, *Prolegomena,* 403.

38. Ibid., 405.

39. Ibid.

40. Ibid.

41. Ibid.

42. Ibid., 406, fn. 1.

43. Ibid., 407.

44. Ibid., 408.

45. Ibid., 409, fn. 1.

46. Ibid.

47. Ibid., 412.

48. Ibid., 420.

49. Ibid., 419.

50. Cataldo, *A Theocratic Yehud?;* see also Fried, *The Priest and the Great King;* Fried, "What the Aramaic Documents Tell Us about the Achaemenid Administration of Empire"; Fried, "Artaxerxes' Letter and the Mission of Ezra—noch einmal"; and Fried, "Implications of 5th and 4th Century Documents."

51. The role of the high priest in Judah can be seen in the documents describing the role of the priest Jedenaiah of the Elephantine community: Porten and Yardeni, *Textbook of Aramaic Documents from Ancient Egypt.*

52. Primarily Y. Kaufmann and his students; see n. 21.

53. See the commentaries for the different opinions and Kellermann, "Erwägungen zum Esragesetz," 373–85. Kellermann himself proposes that it was the legal portions of D.

54. For example, Blenkinsopp, *Ezra-Nehemiah,* 152–57; Williamson, *Ezra, Nehemiah,* xxxvii–xxxi. Mowinckel (*Die Ezrageschichte,* 124–41) concludes that it cannot be known, since the description of the law all comes from the biblical writer and not from Ezra himself; Grabbe, *Ezra-Nehemiah,* 147, agrees and concludes that the biblical writer understands the entire Pentateuch by it. Houtman, "Ezra and the Law," 91–115, considers that various forms of the Pentateuch existed during the period of the restoration.

55. Ska, *Introduction to Reading the Pentateuch,* 132–33.

56. See for example, von Rad, *Genesis,* 24–26.

57. Van Seters, *Abraham in History and Tradition;* Thompson, *Historicity of the Patriarchal Narratives.* Neither of these employs the reasons that I have suggested.

58. For a review of the literature, see Blenkinsopp, *Pentateuch,* 24.

59. Tigay, "The Evolution of the Pentateuchal Narratives," 21–52; Fleming and Milstein, *The Buried Foundation of the Gilgamesh Epic;* Carr, *Writing on the Tablet of the Heart.*

60. Blum, *Die Komposition der Vätergeschichte;* Blum, "Die Komposition der jüdischen Tora," 333–60; Blum, "Esra, die Mosetora und die Persische Politik," 231–77.

61. Blenkinsopp, *Pentateuch,* 239.

62. Blum, "Die Komposition der jüdischen Tora," 333–60; Blum, "Esra, die Mosetora und die Persische Politik," 231–77; Blenkinsopp, *Pentateuch,* 239–42; Frei and Koch, *Reichsidee und Reichsorganisation,* second edition.

63. Frei, "Zentralgewalt und Localautonomie," 8–131; Frei, "Persian Imperial Authorization: A Summary," 5–40.

64. Ibid., 6.

65. Ibid., 7.

66. Ibid., 38.

67. Frei, "Zentralgewalt und Localautonomie," 16–18, 47; Spiegelberg, *Die sogenannte demotische Chronik;* Olmstead, "Darius as Lawgiver," 247–49. Redford, "The So-Called 'Codification' of Egyptian Law;" see also my chapter on Egypt and on the impact of Darius in Fried, *The Priest and the Great King,* 75–86.

68. Frei, "Zentralgewalt und Localautonomie," 12–16, 39–47; Metzger, Demargne, et al., *Fouilles de Xanthos VI.* See also Fried, *The Priest and the Great King,* 140–54.

69. Frei, "Zentralgewalt und Localautonomie," 18–20, 48–49; Porten and Yardeni, *Textbook of Aramaic Documents from Ancient Egypt,* A4.1; Porten, *Elephantine Papyri in English,* B13; Fried, *The Priest and the Great King,* 88–89.

70. Frei also bases his theory on an inscription recording Droaphernes's donation of a statue to a temple of Zeus in Sardis and on a record of a border dispute between Miletus and Myus (Frei, "Zentralgewalt und Localautonomie," 96–97). I discuss each of these in my book *The Priest and the Great King,* and there is no need to discuss them further here.

71. Frei, "Zentralgewalt und Localautonomie," 20–22, 49–61.

72. Blenkinsopp reiterated this theory recently in *Judaism: The First Phase.*

73. Blenkinsopp, *Pentateuch,* 239.

74. Ibid.

75. Crüsemann, *The Torah,* 336.

76. Ibid.

77. Albertz, *Israelite Religion,* 2:467.

78. Ibid.

79. Schmid, "Persian Imperial Authorization as a Historical Problem," 23–38.

80. Ibid., 27.

81. Ibid.

82. Ibid., 33.

83. Carr, "The Rise of Torah."

84. Ibid., 54.

85. Hagedom, "Local Law in an Imperial Context," 71.

86. Ibid.

87. Watts, *Persia and Torah.*

88. Ska, *Introduction to Reading the Pentateuch,* 218–25.

89. Fried, *The Priest and the Great King.*

90. I have repeatedly tried to show this: Fried, "'You Shall Appoint Judges.'" 63–89; Fried, *The Priest and the Great King;* Fried, "What the Aramaic Documents Tell Us about the Achaemenid Administration of Empire"; Fried, "Artaxerxes' Letter and the Mission of Ezra—*noch einmal*"; and Fried, "Implications of 5th and 4th Century Documents for Understanding the Role of the Governor in Persian Imperial Administration."

91. Frei, ""Zentralgewalt und Localautonomie," 16–18, 47; Spiegelberg, *Die sogenannte demotische Chronik,* 11.

92. Redford, "The So-Called 'Codification' of Egyptian Law," 135–59. See also Wiesehöfer, "Reichsgesetz' oder 'Einzelfallgerechtigkeit?,'" 36–46. For the correct definition of *hpw,* see Bontty, *Conflict Management in Ancient Egypt,* 62–73; Nims, "The Term *hp,*" 243–60.

93. Redford, "The So-Called 'Codification' of Egyptian Law," 135–59

94. Cruz-Uribe, "The Invasion of Egypt by Cambyses," 47–50. See also my "What the Aramaic Documents Tell Us about the Achaemenid Administration of Empire."

95. Kuhrt, "Babylonia from Cyrus to Xerxes," 112–38; Kuhrt and Sherwin-White, "Xerxes' Destruction of Babylonian Temples," 69–78; Stolper, *Entrepreneurs and Empire;* Joannès, "Pouvoirs locaux," 173–89.

96. Frei, "Zentralgewalt und Localautonomie," 12–16, 39–47. Dupont-Sommer, "La stèle trilingue du Letoon," 129–78; Metzger, *La stèle trilingue du Létoôn.*

97. Schmid, "Persian Imperial Authorization as a Historical Problem," 27.

98. Ibid.

99. Debord, *L'Asie Mineure,* 67.

100. Jones, *The Greek City,* 95–112.

101. Frei, "Zentralgewalt und Localautonomie," 18–20, 48–49; Porten and Yardeni, *Textbook of Aramaic Documents from Ancient Egypt,* A4.1; Porten, *Elephantine Papyri in English,* B13.

102. Porten and Yardeni, *Textbook of Aramaic Documents from Ancient Egypt*, A4.7, 8.

103. Frei, "Zentralgewalt und Localautonomie," 20–22, 49–61.

104. Ibid., 20.

105. Ibid., 52.

106. Ska, *Introduction to Reading the Pentateuch*, 222.

107. Rather, the presence of pork faunal remains indicates the site is not Israelite. Faust, *Israel's Ethnogenesis*, 35, and references cited there.

108. Ussishkin, *Conquest of Lachish*. The fringes are not shown in the drawings but do appear in the actual reliefs.

109. Faust, *Israel's Ethnogenesis*, 85–91.

110. Grabbe, "Elephantine and the Torah." Grabbe points out that the Judean community at Elephantine kept the temple sacrifices, the Passover holiday, and the Sabbath without needing a written law code to do it. Other Judean customs were also likely kept; there is no mention of pork among the foods to be eaten.

111. Cazelles, "La mission d'Esdras," 113–40.

112. In his introduction (xiv) to Goodenough's *Jewish Symbols*, Neusner sums up the author's work as confirming in synagogue after synagogue and in Jewish cemetery after Jewish cemetery, from "Tunisia to Dura, from Rome to the Galilee," that "the legacy of most Jews is not recorded in the Talmud."

113. Goodenough, *Jewish Symbols in the Greco-Roman Period*.

114. Harries, *Law and Empire in Late Antiquity*, 201–2. Paul would have submitted to the Jewish court voluntarily.

115. Ibid., 201.

Postscript: Reflections on Ezra and the Law

1. Rubinoff, "In Search of a Meaningful Response to the Holocaust," 253.

Appendix 1: Chronology

1. After Oppenheim, *Ancient Mesopotamia*, 340.
2. After Grimal, *A History of Ancient Egypt*, 394–95.

Appendix 2: Versions and Translations of 4 Ezra

1. See Stone, *Fourth Ezra*, 1–9, for a discussion of the versions, with references.
2. Klijn, *Die Esra-Apokalypse*, xiv.
3. This is based on the work of Stone, *Textual Commentary on the Armenian Version*, and on Stone, *The Armenian Version of IV Ezra*, from which the translations are taken.
4. Stone, *Textual Commentary on the Armenian Version*, ix–xiii.
5. Ibid; Stone, *The Armenian Version of IV Ezra*, 35.
6. Stone, *The Armenian Version of IV Ezra*, ix.
7. Violet, *Die Esra-Apokalypse*, 5.
8. Stone, *Textual Commentary on the Armenian Version*, 6.
9. Ibid., 9.
10. In spite of all the commentary on the Cain and Abel story, I have not seen discussion of the fact that although he accepts Abel's offering, God still does not protect him from

Cain. One response is the Kabbalistic notion of *tsimtsum,* in which God withdraws himself to make room for human action. For a discussion of God withdrawing his power to allow mankind free will, see Crenshaw, "Limited Power and Knowledge."

11. We read the same theology in Ezekiel 18:23: "Have I any pleasure in the death of the wicked, says the Lord YHWH, and not rather that they should turn from their ways and live?"

12. So Stone, *Textual Commentary on the Armenian Version,* 95.

13. Ibid., 122.

14. Box, *The Apocalypse of Ezra,* ix–x; Stone, *Fourth Ezra,* 6.

15. This section is based on the translations of Laurence, *Primi Ezræ Libri,* and of Violet, *Die Esra-Apokalypse.*

16. Klijn, *Die Esra-Apokalypse,* xv.

17. Laurence, *Primi Ezræ Libri,* 200.

18. This translation of *visitare* is suggested by Stone, *Fourth Ezra,* 155. It is supported in the Ethiopic (see Violet, *Die Esra-Apokalypse,* 88).

19. Stone, *Fourth Ezra,* 142, suggests that 6:1 in the Latin has fallen out and that it originally agreed with the Ethiopic. It seems to me that the Latin answers the question in 6:6.

20. Stone, *Fourth Ezra,* 72.

21. So Violet, *Die Esra-Apokalypse,* 226–27.

22. Ibid., 286–87.

23. Comerro, *Le Quatrième Livre d'Esdras,* 24.

24. Ewald, *Das vierte Ezrabuch,* 133–230.

25. Gildemeister, *Esdrae Liber Quartus;* Stone disagrees, *Textual Commentary on the Armenian Version,* 6.

26. Van Koningsveld, "An Arabic Manuscript of the Apocalypse of Baruch," 207.

27. Stone, "A New Manuscript of the Syro-Arabic Version of the Fourth Book of Ezra," 183–84.

28. Drint, *Mount Sinai Arabic Version of IV Ezra,* ii.

29. This translation from the Arabic is provided by Comerro, *Le Quatrième Livre d'Esdras.* See also Violet, *Die Esra-Apokalypse,* where it is labeled Arab Ew [ald] after Ewald, *Das vierte Ezrabuch,* its first publisher.

30. Comerro, *Le Quatrième Livre d'Esdras,* 54.

31. Violet, *Die Esra-Apokalypse,* xxxvii.

32. Ibid., xxxviii. However, Stone, *Textual Commentary on the Armenian Version,* 6, seems to disagree.

33. Ibid., 103.

34. Ibid., 105.

35. Comerro, *Le Quatrième Livre d'Esdras,* 54.

36. Ibid., 219.

37. This translation is based on the German of Violet, *Die Esra-Apokalypse,* xxxviii. It was originally published by Gildemeister, *Esdrae Liber Quartus.*

38. This discussion is based on the translation of Drint, *Mount Sinai Arabic Version of IV Ezra.*

39. Ibid., i–vi.
40. Ibid.
41. Ibid., 23, fn.119.
42. Box, *The Syriac Apocalypse of Ezra*, 39, fn. 11.
43. Drint, *Mount Sinai Arabic Version of IV Ezra*, 38, fn. 57.

BIBLIOGRAPHY

Adang, Camilla. *Muslim Writers on Judaism and the Hebrew Bible: From Ibn Rabban to Ibn Hazm.* Islamic Philosophy, Theology and Science: Texts and Studies, vol. 22. Leiden: Brill, 1996.

Adler, William. "The Jews as Falsifiers: Charges of Tendentious Emendation in Anti-Jewish Christian Polemic." In *Translation of Scripture: Proceedings of a Conference at the Annenberg Research Institute, May 15–16, 1989,* edited by David M. Goldenberg, 1–27. Jewish Quarterly Review Supplement. Philadelphia: Annenberg Research Institute, 1990.

Agourides, Savas. "Apocalypse of Sedrach." In *The Old Testament Pseudepigrapha,* edited by J. H. Charlesworth, 1:605–13. Garden City, N.Y.: Doubleday, 1983.

Albertz, Rainer. *From the Exile to the Maccabees.* Vol. 2 of *A History of Israelite Religion in the Old Testament Period.* Translated by John Bowden. Old Testament Library. Louisville, Ky.: Westminster John Knox, 1994.

Alexander, Paul J. *The Byzantine Apocalyptic Tradition.* Edited by Dorothy de F. Abrahamse. Berkeley: University of California Press, 1985.

Ambar-Armon, Einat, and Amos Kloner. "Archaeological Evidence of Links between the Aegean World and the Land of Israel in the Persian Period." In *A Time of Change: Judah and Its Neighbours in the Persian and Early Hellenistic Periods,* edited by Y. Levin, 1–22. London: T&T Clark, 2007.

Anderson, Gary A. *Sacrifices and Offerings in Ancient Israel: Studies in their Social and Political Importance.* Harvard Semitic Museum Monographs, vol. 41. Atlanta, Ga.: Scholars Press, 1987.

Anderson, Robert T., and Terry Giles. *Tradition Kept: The Literature of the Samaritans.* Peabody, Mass.: Hendrickson, 2005.

Astruc, Jean. *Conjectures sur les mémoires originaux dont il paraît que Moyse s'est servi pour composer le livre de la Genèse.* 1753. Reprint with introduction and notes by P. Gilbert Paris 1999. Brussels: E. H. Fricx, 1999.

Ayoub, Mahmoud. "'Uzayr in the Qur'an and Muslim Tradition." In *Studies in Islamic and Judaic Traditions: Papers Presented at the Institute for Islamic-Judaic Studies,* edited by William M. Brinner and Stephen D. Ricks, 3–18. Studies in Islamic and Judaic Traditions, vol. 110. Atlanta: Scholars Press, 1986.

Bagnall, Roger S., and Bruce W. Frier. *The Demography of Roman Egypt.* Cambridge: Cambridge University Press, 1994.

Balcer, Jack Martin. "The Athenian Episkopos and the Achaemenid 'King's Eye'." *American Journal of Philology* 98, no. 3 (1977): 252–63.

Baltzer, Klaus. *The Covenant Formulary in Old Testament, Jewish, and Early Christian Writings.* Translated by D. Green. Philadelphia: Fortress Press, 1971.

Barraclough, Geoffrey. *HarperCollins Atlas of World History.* Ann Arbor, Mich.: Borders Press, 1989.

Barton, John. *The Spirit and the Letter: Studies in the Biblical Canon.* London: Society for Promoting Christian Knowledge, 1997.

Bauckham, Richard. *The Fate of the Dead: Studies on the Jewish and Christian Apocalypses.* Supplements to Novum Testamentum, vol. 93. Leiden: Brill, 1998.

Becking, Bob. "The Story of the Three Youths and the Composition of 1 Esdras." In *Was 1 Esdras First? An Investigation Into the Nature and Priority of First Esdras,* edited by Lisbeth S. Fried, 83–71. Ancient Israel and Its Literature, vol. 7. Atlanta: Society of Biblical Literature, 2011.

Bensly, Robert L. *The Missing Fragment of the Latin Translation of the Fourth Book of Ezra.* Cambridge: Cambridge University Press, 1875.

Bergren, Theodore A. "Ezra and Nehemiah Square Off in the Apocrypha and Pseudepigrapha." In *Biblical Figures Outside the Bible,* edited by M. E. Stone and T. A. Bergren, 340–65. Harrisburg, Pa.: Trinity Press International, 1998.

——. *Fifth Ezra: The Text, Origin, and Early History.* Society of Biblical Literature Septuagint and Cognate Studies, vol. 25. Atlanta: Scholars Press, 1990.

——. *Sixth Ezra: The Text and Origin.* Oxford: Oxford University Press, 1998.

Blenkinsopp, Joseph. *Ezra-Nehemiah, a Commentary.* Old Testament Library. Philadelphia: Westminster Press, 1988.

——. *Judaism: The First Phase. The Place of Ezra and Nehemiah in the Origins of Judaism.* Grand Rapids, Mich.: Eerdmans, 2009.

——. *The Pentateuch: An Introduction to the First Five Books of the Bible.* Anchor Bible Reference Library. New York: Doubleday, 1992.

Blum, Erhard. "Esra, die Mosetora und die Persische Politik." In *Religion und Religionskontakte im Zeitalter der Achämeniden,* edited by Erhard Blum, 231–77. Gütersloh: Gütersloher Verlagshaus, 2002.

——. "Die Komposition der Jüdischen Tora und die Persische Politik." In *Studien zur Komposition des Pentateuch,* edited by Reinhard G. Kratz, 333–60. Beihefte zur Zeitschrift für die alttestamentliche, vol. 189. Berlin: De Gruyter, 1990.

——. *Die Komposition der Vätergeschichte.* Wissenschaftliche Monographien Zum Alten und Neuen Testament, vol. 57. Düsseldorf: Neukirchener Verlag, 1984.

Boccaccini, Gabriele. *Roots of Rabbinic Judaism: An Intellectual History, from Ezekiel to Daniel.* Grand Rapid, Mich.: Eerdmans, 2002.

Boda, Mark J. *Praying the Tradition: The Origin and Use of Tradition in Nehemiah 9.* Beihefte zur Zeitschrift für die alttestamentliche, vol. 277. Berlin: De Gruyter, 1999.

Boda, Mark J., and Paul L. Redditt. *Unity and Disunity in Ezra-Nehemiah: Redaction, Rhetoric, and Reader.* Hebrew Bible Monographs, vol. 17. Sheffield: Sheffield Phoenix Press, 2008.

Bogaert, Pierre-Maurice. "Versions [of the Bible], Ancient (Latin)." In *Anchor Bible Dictionary,* 6:799–803. New York: Doubleday, 1992.

Böhler, Dieter. *Die Heilige Stadt in Esdras a und Esra-Nehemia: Zwei Konzeptionen der Wiederherstellung Israel.* Orbis Biblicus et Orientalis, vol. 158. Göttingen: Vandenhoeck & Ruprecht, 1997.

——. "On the Relationship between Textual and Literary Criticism: The Two Recensions of the Book of Ezra: Ezra-Neh (Masoretic Text) and 1 Esdras (Septuagint)." In *The Earliest Text of the Hebrew Bible: The Relationship between the Masoretic Text and the Hebrew Base of the Septuagint Reconsidered,* edited by A. Schenker, 35–50. Septuagint and Cognate Studies, vol. 52. Atlanta: Society of Biblical Literature, 2003.

Bontty, Monica M. "Conflict Management in Ancient Egypt: Law as a Social Phenomenon." Ph. D. diss., University of California at Los Angeles, 1997.

Bosworth, Clifford Edmund. "ARAB: i. Arabs and Iran in the Pre-Islamic Period." In *Encyclopaedia Iranica.* New York: Columbia University Press, 1987: 201–203.

Botta, Alejandro F. *The Aramaic and Egyptian Legal Traditions at Elephantine: An Egyptological Approach.* Library of Second Temple Studies, vol. 64. London: T&T Clark Ltd, 2009.

Box, George Herbert. *The Apocalypse of Ezra (II Esdras III–XIV) Translated from the Syriac Text, with Brief Annotations.* Translations of Early Documents: Palestinian Jewish Texts (Pre-Rabbinic), Series 1. London: Society for Promoting Christian Knowledge, 1917.

——. *The Ezra-Apocalypse.* London: Pittman, 1912.

Briant, Pierre. "Contrainte militaire, dépendance rurale et exploitation des territoires en Asie Achéménide." *Index* 8 (1978–79): 48–98.

——. *From Cyrus to Alexander: A History of the Persian Empire.* 1996. Translated by Peter T. Daniels. Winona Lake, Ind: Eisenbrauns, 2002.

——. "Polythéismes et empire unitaire (remarques sur la politique religieuse des Achéménides." In *Les grandes figures religieuses fonctionnement pratique et symbolique dans l'antiquité,* 68:425–43. Paris: Centre de recherches d'histoire ancienne, 1986.

Brosius, Maria. *Women in Ancient Persia (559–331 B.C.).* Oxford Classical Monographs. Oxford: Clarendon Press, 1996.

Burford, Alison. *The Greek Temple Builders at Epidauros: A Social and Economic Study of Building in the Asklepian Sanctuary during the Fourth and Early Third Centuries B.C.* Liverpool Monographs in Archaeology and Oriental Studies. Liverpool: Liverpool University Press, 1969.

Burkert, Walter. *Greek Religion.* Translated by John Raffan. Cambridge, Mass.: Harvard University Press, 1985.

Campbell, William Sanger. "The Narrator as 'He,' 'Me,' and 'We': Grammatical Person in Ancient Histories and in the Acts of the Apostles." *Journal of Biblical Literature* 129, no. 2 (2010): 385–407.

Carr, David M. "The Rise of Torah." In *The Pentateuch as Torah: New Models for Understanding Its Promulgation and Acceptance,* edited by Gary N. Knoppers and Bernard M. Levinson, 39–56. Winona Lake, Ind.: Eisenbrauns, 2007.

——. *Writing on the Tablet of the Heart: Origins of Scripture and Literature.* Oxford: Oxford University Press, 2005.

Cataldo, Jeremiah W. *A Theocratic Yehud? Issues of Government in a Persian Province.* Library of Hebrew Bible/Old Testament Studies, vol. 498. London: T&T Clark, 2009.

Cazelles, Henri. "La mission d'Esdras." *Vetus Testamentum* 4 (1954): 113–40.

Chabot, Jean-Baptiste. "L'Apocalypse d'Esdras touchant le royaume des Arabes." *Revue Semitique d'Épigraphie et d'Histoire Ancienne* 2 (1894): 242–43, 333–46.

Charlesworth, James. "Jewish Astrology in the Talmud, Pseudepigrapha, the Dead Sea Scrolls, and Early Palestinian Synagogues." *Harvard Theological Revue* 70, no. 3/4 (1977): 183–200.

Clines, David J. A. "The Nehemiah Memoir: The Perils of Autobiography." In *What Does Eve Do to Help?: And Other Readerly Questions to the Old Testament,* edited by David J. A. Clines,124–64. Sheffield: Journal for the Study of the Old Testament Press, 1990.

Collins, John J. "Introduction: Towards the Morphology of a Genre." In *Apocalypse: The Morphology of a Genre,* edited by John J. Collins, 1–20. Semeia, vol. 14. Missoula, Mont.: Scholars Press, 1979.

——. "The Jewish Apocalypses." In *Apocalypse: The Morphology of a Genre,* edited by John J. Collins, 21–59. Semeia, vol. 14. Missoula, Mont.: Scholars Press, 1979.

Comerro, Viviane. "Esdras est-il le fils de Dieu?" *Arabica* 52, no. 2 (2005): 165–81.

——. "Le quatrième livre d'Esdras dans la littérature arabe: La transmission d'un texte juif 'perdu' en milieu chrétien et musulman." Ph.D. diss., U. F. R. des science historiques: Institut des sciences de l'antiquité, Université Marc Bloch de Strasbourg, 2002.

Crenshaw, James L. *Defending God: Biblical Responses to the Problem of Evil.* Oxford: Oxford University Press, 2005.

——. "Justice Deferred: Banking on Life beyond the Grave." In *Defending God: Biblical Responses to the Problem of Evil,* edited by James L. Crenshaw, 149–63. Oxford: Oxford University Press, 2005.

——. "Limited Power and Knowledge: Accentuating Human Freedom." In *Defending God: Biblical Responses to the Problem of Evil,* edited by James L. Crenshaw, 75–86. Oxford: Oxford University Press, 2005.

——. "Introduction: The Shift from Theodicy to Anthropodicy." In *Urgent Advice and Probing Questions: Collected Writings on Old Testament Wisdom,* edited by James L. Crenshaw, 141–54. Macon, Ga.: Mercer University Press, 1995.

——. "Mystery: Appealing to Human Ignorance." In *Defending God: Biblical Responses to the Problem of Evil,* edited by James L. Crenshaw, 165–75. Oxford: Oxford University Press, 2005.

Crüsemann, Frank. *The Torah: Theology and Social History of Old Testament Law.* Translated by Allan W. Mahnke. Minneapolis, Minn.: Fortress, 1996.

Cruz-Uribe, Eugene. "The Invasion of Egypt by Cambyses." *Transeuphratène* 25 (2003): 9–60.

Dandamayev, Muhammad A., and Vladimir G. Lukonin. *The Culture and Social Institutions of Ancient Iran.* Cambridge: Cambridge University Press, 1989.

Davies, John K. "Athenian Citizenship: The Descent Group and the Alternatives." *Classical Journal* 73 (1977–78): 105–21.

——. "Comptes d'une association religieuse rhébaine datant des années 29 à 33 du roi Amasis." *Revue d'Égyptologie* 37 (1986): 13–29.

Debord, Pierre. *L'Asie Mineure au IVe siècle (412–323 a. C.): Pouvoirs et jeux politiques.* Bordeaux: Ausonius, 1999.

De Cenival, Francoise. *Les associations religieuses en Égypte d'après les documents démotiques.* Cairo: Imprimerie de l'Institut français d'archéologie orientale, 1972.

Démare-Lafont, Sophie. "*Datu Ša Šarri.* La « loi du roi » dans la Babylonie Achéménide et Séleucide = *Datu Ša Šarri.* The 'Law of the King' in Achaemenid and Seleucid Babylonia." *Droit et Cultures [en ligne]* 52 (2006). http://droitcultures.revues.org/544.

Demsky, Aaron "Who Came First, Ezra or Nehemiah?" *Hebrew Union College Annual* 65, no. 1 (1994): 1–19.

Denis, Albert-Marie. *Introduction à la littérature religieuse judéo-hellénistique.* Turnhout, Belgium: Brepols, 2000.

De Troyer, Kristin. "The Second Year of Darius." In *Was 1 Esdras First? An Investigation into the Nature and Priority of First Esdras,* edited by Lisbeth S. Fried, 73–81. Ancient Israel and Its Literature, vol. 7. Atlanta: Society of Biblical Literature, 2011.

———. "Zerubbabel and Ezra: A Revived and Revised Solomon and Josiah? A Survey of Current 1 Esdras Research." *Currents in Research: Biblical Studies* 1:3–4 (October 2002): 30–60.

De Wette, Wilhelm Martin Leberecht. "Dissertatio Critico-Exegetica Qua Deuteronomium a Prioribus Pentateuchi Libris Diversum." Ph.D. diss., Literis Etzdorfii, 1805.

Dor, Yonina. *Did They Really Divorce the Foreign Women? The Question of the Separation in the Days of the Second Temple* (Hebrew). Jerusalem: Magnes Press, 2006.

Dozeman, Thomas B., and Konrad Schmid, Eds. *A Farewell to the Yahwist? The Composition of the Pentateuch in Recent European Interpretation.* Society of Biblical Literature Symposium Series, vol. 34. Atlanta: Society of Biblical Literature, 2006.

Drint, Adriana. *The Mount Sinai Arabic Version of IV Ezra.* Corpus Scriptorum Christianorum Orientalium, vol. 564, no. Scriptores Arabici 49. Lovanii: Peeters, 1997.

Duggan, Michael W. *The Covenant Renewal in Ezra-Nehemiah (Neh 7:72b-10:40): An Exegetical, Literary, and Theological Study.* Society of Biblical Literature Dissertation Series, vol. 164. Atlanta: Society of Biblical Literature, 2001.

Dunn, James D. G. *The Partings of the Ways between Christianity and Judaism and Their Significance for the Character of Christianity.* London: SCM Press, 1991.

Dupont-Sommer, A. "La stèle trilingue du Letoon: L'inscription araméenne." In *La stèle trilingue du Létoôn.* Vol. 6 of *Fouilles de Xanthos,* edited by H. Metzger, 129–78. Paris: Klincksieck, 1979.

Duverger, Maurice. "Le Concept d'Empire," in *Le Concept d'Empire.* Paris: Presses universitaires de France, 1980.

Ebbinghaus, Hermann. *On Memory: A Contribution to Experimental Psychology.* New York: Teachers College. 1913.

Edelman, Diana. *The Origins of the "Second" Temple: Persian Imperial Policy and the Rebuilding of Jerusalem.* London: Equinox, 2005.

Eichhorn, Johann Gottfried. *Einleitung in das Alte Testament.* 3 vols. Leipzig: Weidmann, 1803.

Encyclopædia Britannica Online. "Romanticism." http://www.britannica.com/EBchecked/topic/508675/Romanticism. Accessed January 11, 2012.

Eshel, Hanan. "Hellenism in the Land of Israel from the Fifth to the Second Centuries B.C.E. in Light of Semitic Epigraphy." In *A Time of Change: Judah and Its Neighbours in the Persian and Early Hellenistic Period,* edited by Yigal Levin, 116–24. London: T&T Clark, 2007.

Eskenazi, Tamara Cohn. "The Chronicler and the Composition of 1 Esdras." *Catholic Biblical Quarterly* 48 (1986): 39–61.

——. *In an Age of Prose: A Literary Approach to Ezra-Nehemiah.* Atlanta: Scholars Press, 1988.

——. "The Missions of Ezra and Nehemiah." In *Judah and the Judeans in the Persian Period,* edited by O. Lipschits and M. Oeming, 509–29; Winona Lake, Ind.: Eisenbrauns, 2006.

Evans, J. A. S. *Age of Justinian: The Circumstances of Imperial Power.* London: Routledge, 2000.

Ewald, H. *Das Vierte Ezrabuch Nach Seinem Zeitalter, Seinen Arabischen Übersetzungen, und einer Neuen Wiederherstellung.* Abhandlungen der Historisch-Philogischen Klasse 11 (1862/1863): 133–230.

Faust, Avraham. "Deportation and Demography in Sixth Century B.C.E. Judah." In *Interpreting Exile: Interdisciplinary Studies of Displacement and Deportation in Biblical and Modern Contexts,* edited by B. E. Kelle et al., 91–103. Atlanta: Society of Biblical Literature, 2011.

——. *Israel's Ethnogenesis: Settlement, Interaction, Expansion, and Resistance.* London: Equinox, 2006.

Feldman, Louis H. "Josephus." In *Anchor Bible Dictionary,* 3:981–98. New York: Doubleday, 1992.

——. "Josephus' Portrait of Ezra." *Vetus Testamentum* 43, no. 2 (1993): 190–214.

Fiensy, David A. "Revelation of Ezra." In *The Old Testament Pseudepigrapha,* edited by J. H. Charlesworth, 1:601–4. Garden City, N.Y.: Doubleday, 1983.

Fishbane, Michael. *Biblical Interpretation in Ancient Israel.* Oxford: Clarendon Press, 1985.

Fleming, Daniel E., and Sara J. Milstein. *The Buried Foundation of the Gilgamesh Epic.* Cuneiform Monographs. Leiden and Boston: Brill, 2010.

Fox, Robin Lane. *Pagans and Christians: Religion and the Religious Life from the Second Century A.D., When the Gods of Olympus Lost Their Dominion and Christianity with the Conversion of Constantine Triumphed in the Mediterranean World.* New York: Knopf, 1989.

Freedman, David Noel, and David Miano. "People of the New Covenant." In *The Concept of the Covenant in the Second Temple Period,* edited by Stanley E. Porter and Jacqueline C. R. de Roo, 7–26. Leiden: Brill, 2003.

Frei, Peter. "Persian Imperial Authorization: A Summary." In *Persia and Torah: The Theory of Imperial Authorization of the Pentateuch,* edited by James W. Watts, 5–40. Society of Biblical Literature Symposium Series, vol. 17. Atlanta: Society of Biblical Literature, 2001.

——. "Zentralgewalt und Localautonomie im Achämenidenreich." In *Reichsidee und Reichsorganisation im Perserreich,* edited by P. and K. Koch Frei, 8–131. Fribourg: Universitätsverlag, 1996.

Frei, Peter, and Klaus Koch. *Reichsidee und Reichsorganisation im Perserreich.* 2nd ed. Göttingen: Vandenhoeck & Ruprecht, 1996.

Frevel, Christian ed., *Mixed Marriages: Intermarriage and Group Identity in the Second Temple Period.* Library of Hebrew Bible/Old Testament Studies, vol. 547. London: T&T Clark, 2011).

Fried, Lisbeth S. "Another Look at 1 Esdras: The Law Triumphant." In *Making a Difference: Essays on the Bible and Judaism in Honor of Tamara C. Eskenazi,* edited by David J.A. Clines, Kent Harold Richards, and Jacob L. Wright. Hebrew Bible Monographs 49: Sheffield-Phoenix Press, 2012:132–38.

——. "The Artaxerxes Correspondence of Ezra 4, Nehemiah's Wall, and Persian Provincial Administration." In *'Go Out and Study the Land' (Judges 18:2): Archaeological, Historical and Textual Studies in Honor of Hanan Eshel,* edited by A. M. Maeir, J. Magness, and L. H. Schiffman, 35–58. Supplement to the Journal for the Study of Judaism. Leiden: Brill, 2011.

——. "Artaxerxes' Letter and the Mission of Ezra-*Noch Einmal.*" In *Festschrift for Charles Krahmolkov,* edited by Philip Schmitz, David Howard, and Robert Miller II. Alter Orient und Altes Testament. Münster: Ugarit-Verlag, in press.

——. "The Concept of 'Impure Birth' in Fifth Century Athens and Judea." In *In the Wake of Tikva Frymer-Kensky: Tikva Frymer-Kensky Memorial Volume,* edited by S. Holloway, R. H. Beal, and J. Scurlock, 121–42. Piscataway, N.J.: Gorgias Press, 2009.

——. "Cyrus the Messiah? The Historical Background of Isaiah 45:1." *Harvard Theological Revue* 95 (2002b): 373–93.

——. "Did Second Temple High Priests Possess the Urim and Thummim?" *Journal of Hebrew Scriptures* 7 (2007): Article 3.

——. "Did the Authors of Ezra-Nehemiah Think That YHWH Dwelt in the Second Temple?" In *Reflecting upon Divine Presence and Absence in the Exile and Persian Period,* edited by N. MacDonald and Izaak de Hulster. Tübingen: Forschungen zum Alten Testament; Mohr Siebeck, in press.

——. "Ezra's Use of Documents in the Context of Hellenistic Rules of Rhetoric." In *New Perspectives on Ezra-Nehemiah: History and Historiography, Text, Literature and Interpretation,* edited by Isaac Kalimi, 11–26. Winona Lake, Ind.: Eisenbrauns, 2012.

——. "A Greek Religious Association in Second Temple Judah? A Comment on Nehemiah 10." *Transeuphratène* 30 (2005): 75–93.

——. "The High Places (Bamôt) and the Reforms of Hezekiah and Josiah: An Archaeological Investigation." *Journal of the American Oriental Society* 122 (2002a): 437–65.

——. "Implications of 5th and 4th Century Documents for Understanding the Role of the Governor in Persian Imperial Administration." In *In the Shadow of Bezalel. Aramaic, Biblical, and Ancient Near Eastern Studies in Honor of Bezalel Porten,* edited by A. F. Botta. 319–31, Culture and History of the Ancient Near East. Leiden: Brill, 2003.

——. "The Land Lay Desolate: Conquest and Restoration in the Ancient Near East." In *Judah and the Judeans in the Neo-Babylonian Period,* edited by Oded Lipschits and Joseph Blenkinsopp, 21–54. Winona Lake, Ind.: Eisenbrauns, 2003.

——. "The Political Struggle of Fifth Century Judah." *Transeuphratène* 24 (2002): 9–21.

——. *The Priest and the Great King: Temple-Palace Relations in the Persian Empire.* Biblical and Judaic Studies from the University of California, San Diego, vol. 10. Winona Lake, Ind.: Eisenbrauns, 2004.

——. "A Silver Coin of Yohanan Hakkôhen." *Transeuphratène* 26 (2003): 65–85, Pls. II–V.

——. "What the Aramaic Documents Tell Us about the Achaemenid Administration of Empire." In *Arshama's Peoples,* edited by John Ma and Christopher Tuplin. Oxford: Centre for the Study of Ancient Documents, Oxford University Press, in press.

——. "Who Wrote Ezra-Nehemiah—and Why Did They?" In *Unity and Disunity in Ezra-Nehemiah: Redaction, Rhetoric, and Reader,* edited by M. J. Boda and P. L. Redditt, 75–97. Hebrew Bible Monographs, vol. 17. Sheffield: Sheffield Phoenix Press, 2008.

——. "Why the Story of the Three Youths in 1 Esdras?" In *Was 1 Esdras First? An Investigation into the Nature and Priority of First Esdras,* edited by Lisbeth S. Fried, 83–92. Atlanta: Society of Biblical Literature, 2011.

——. "'You Shall Appoint Judges': Ezra's Mission and the Rescript of Artaxerxes." In *Persia and Torah: The Theory of Imperial Authorization of the Pentateuch,* edited by James W. Watts, 63–89. Society of Biblical Literature Symposium Series, vol. 17. Atlanta: Society of Biblical Literature, 2001.

Fried, Lisbeth S., ed. *Was 1 Esdras First? An Investigation into the Priority and Nature of 1 Esdras.* Ancient Israel and Its Literature, vol. 7. Atlanta: Scholars Press, 2011.

Frye, Richard N. "Appendix 5: The Inscription of Shapur I at Naqsh-e-Rustam." In *History of Ancient Iran,* 371–74. Handbuch der Altertumswissenschaft, Part 3, vol. 7. Munich: Beck, 1984.

Fulton, Deirdre N. "Jeshua's 'High Priestly' Lineage? A Reassessment of Nehemiah 12.10–11." In *Exile and Restoration Revisited: Essays on the Babylonian and Persian Periods in Memory of Peter R. Ackroyd,* edited by Gary N. Knoppers and Lester L. Grabbe with Deirdre Fulton, 94–115. London: T&T Clark, 2009.

Fulton, Deirdre N., and Gary N. Knoppers. "Lower Criticism and Higher Criticism: The Case of 1 Esdras." In *Was 1 Esdras First? An Investigation into the Nature and Priority of First Esdras,* edited by Lisbeth S. Fried, 11–29. Ancient Israel and Its Literature, vol. 7. Atlanta: Society of Biblical Literature, 2011.

Funk, Robert W., Roy W. Hoover, and The Jesus Seminar. *The Five Gospels: The Search for the Authentic Words of Jesus.* New York: Macmillan, 1993.

Gammie, John G., and Leo G. Perdue, eds. *The Sage in Israel and the Ancient Near East.* Winona Lake, Ind.: Eisenbrauns, 1990.

Gehman, Henry Snyder. "'Επισκέπομαι, ἐπίσκεψις, ἐπίκοπος, and ἐπισκοπή in the Septuagint in Relation to פקד and Other Hebrew Roots: A Case of Semantic Development Similar to That of Hebrew." *Vetus Testamentum* 22, no. 2 (1972): 197–207.

Gildemeister, Johannes. *Esdrae Liber Quartus Arabice E. Codice Vaticano Nunc Primum Editus.* Bonn, Germany: 1877.

Gilliard, Frank D. "Paul and the Killing of the Prophets in 1 Thess. 2:15." *Novum Testamentum* 36 (1994): 259–70.

Ginzberg, Louis, and David Stern. *Legends of the Jews, Vols. 1 and 2.* 2nd ed. Philadelphia: Jewish Publication Society, 2003.

Goodenough, Erwin R. *Jewish Symbols in the Greco-Roman Period.* Edited and abridged by Jacob Neusner. Princeton: Princeton University Press, 1988.

Goodman, Martin. "Sacred Scripture and 'Defiling the Hands'." *Journal of Theological Studies* ns 41 (1990): 99–107.

Grabbe, Lester L. "Chicken or Egg? Which Came First, 1 Esdras or Ezra-Nehemiah?" In *Was 1 Esdras First? An Investigation into the Nature and Priority of First Esdras,* edited by Lisbeth S. Fried, 31–43. Ancient Israel and Its Literature, vol. 7. Atlanta: Society of Biblical Literature, 2011.

——. "Elephantine and the Torah." In *In the Shadow of Bezalel. Aramaic, Biblical, and Ancient Near Eastern Studies in Honor of Bezalel Porten,* edited by A. F. Botta, 125–35. Culture and History of the Ancient Near East. Leiden: Brill, 2013.

——. *Ezra-Nehemiah.* Old Testament Readings. London: Routledge, 1998.

——. *Leading Captivity Captive.* Journal for the Study of the Old Testament Supplement Series, vol. 278. Sheffield: Sheffield Academic Press, 1998.

——. "The 'Persian Documents' in the Book of Ezra: Are They Authentic?" In *Judah and the Judeans in the Persian Period,* edited by O. Lipschits and M. Oeming, 531–70. Winona Lake, Ind.: Eisenbrauns, 2006.

Graf, Karl Heinrich. *Die Geschichtlichen Bücher des Alten Testaments: Zwei Historisch-Kritische Untersuchungen.* Leipzig: T. O. Weigel, 1866.

Grätz, Sebastian. *Das Edikt des Artaxerxes: Eine Untersuchung zum Religionspolitischen und historischen Umfeld von Esra 7, 12–26.* Beihefte zur Zeitschrift für die alttestamentliche, vol. 337. Berlin: De Gruyter, 2004.

——. "Gottesgesetz und Königsgesetz: Esr 7 und die Autorisierung der Tora." *Zeitschrift für Theologie und Kirche* 106 (2009): 1–19.

Grimal, Nicolas. *A History of Ancient Egypt.* Oxford: Blackwell, 1993.

Gunneweg, Antonius H. J. *Esra.* Kommentar zum Alten Testament. Gütersloh: Gütersloher Verlagshaus Mohn, 1985.

Gutschmid, Alfred von. "Die Apokalypse des Esra und ihre spätern Bearbeitungen." *Zeitschrift für wissenschaftliche Theologie* 36 (1860): 1–81.

Hagedom, Anselm C. "Local Law in an Imperial Context: The Role of Torah in the (Imagined) Persian Period." In *The Pentateuch as Torah: New Models for Understanding Its Promulgation and Acceptance,* edited by Gary N. Knoppers and Bernard M. Levinson, 57–76. Winona Lake, Ind.: Eisenbrauns, 2007.

Halévy, Joseph. *Te'ezaza Sanbat (Commandements du Sabbat).* Bibliothèque de l'École des hautes études, vol. 137. Paris: Ministère de l'instruction publique, 1902.

Hallock, R. T. *Persepolis Fortification Tablets.* University of Chicago Oriental Institute Publications, vol. 92. Chicago: University of Chicago Press, 1969.

Halpern-Amaru, Betsy. "The Killing of the Prophets: Unraveling a Midrash." *Hebrew Union College Annual* 54 (1983): 153–80.

Harries, Jill. *Law and Empire in Late Antiquity.* Cambridge: Cambridge University Press, 1999.

Hartman, Louis F., and Alexander A. Di Lella. *The Book of Daniel: A New Translation with Introduction and Commentary.* Anchor Bible, vol. 23. New York: Doubleday, 1978.

Harvey Jr., Paul B. "Darius' Court and the Guardsmen's Debate: Hellenistic Greek Elements in 1 Esdras." In *Was 1 Esdras First? An Investigation into the Nature and Priority of First Esdras,* edited by Lisbeth S. Fried, 179–90. Ancient Israel and Its Literature, vol. 7. Atlanta: Society of Biblical Literature, 2011.

Heltzer, Michael. "A Recently Published Babylonian Tablet and the Province of Judah after 516 B.C.E." *Transeuphratène* 5 (1992): 57–61.

Himmelfarb, Martha. *The Apocalypse: A Brief History.* Wiley Online Library, 2010. http://onlinelibrary.wiley.com/book/10.1002/9781444318210.

——. *Ascent to Heaven in Jewish and Christian Apocalypses.* Oxford: Oxford University Press, 1993.

——. *Tours of Hell: An Apocalyptic Form in Jewish and Christian Literature.* Philadelphia: Fortress Press, 1983.

Hirschberg, Haïm Z'ev. "Ezra [in Islam]." In *Encyclopaedia Judaica,* 2nd ed., edited by Michael Berenbaum and Fred Skolnik, 68:653. Detroit: Macmillan Reference USA, 2007.

Hjelm, Ingrid. *The Samaritans and Early Judaism: A Literary Analysis.* Journal for the Study of the Old Testament Supplement Series, vol. 303. Sheffield: Sheffield Academic Press, 2000.

Hobbes, Thomas. *Leviathan, or the Matter, Forme, & Power of a Common-Wealth Ecclesiasticall and Civill.* Oxford: Clarendon Press, 1909.

Hoglund, Keneth G. *Achaemenid Imperial Administration in Syria-Palestine and the Missions of Ezra and Nehemiah.* Society of Biblical Literature Dissertation Series, vol. 125. Atlanta: Scholars Press, 1992.

Hölbl, Günther, 2000. *A History of the Ptolemaic Empire.* Translated by Tina Saavedra. London: Routledge, 2001.

Honigman, Sylvie. "Cyclical Time and Catalogues: The Construction of Meaning in 1 Esdras." In *Was 1 Esdras First? An Investigation into the Nature and Priority of First Esdras,* edited by Lisbeth S. Fried, 191–208. Ancient Israel and Its Literature, vol. 7. Atlanta: Society of Biblical Literature, 2011.

——. *The Septuagint and Homeric Scholarship in Alexandria: A Study in the Narrative of the Letter of Aristeas.* London: Routledge, 2003.

Hoonacker, Albin van. "Néhémie et Esdras, une nouvelle hypothèse sur la chronologie de l'époque de la restauration." *Le Muséon* 9 (1890): 151–84, 317–51, 389–400.

Houtman, Cornelis. "Ezra and the Law: Observations on the Supposed Relation between Ezra and the Pentateuch." In *Remembering All the Way—A Collection of Old Testament Studies Published on the Occasion of the Fortieth Anniversary of the Oudtestamentisch Werkge,* edited by Bertil Albrektson, 91–115. Oudtestamentische Studiën, vol. 21. Leiden: Brill, 1981.

Hughes, George R., and Herman Junker. *The Sixth Day of the Lunar Month and the Demotic Word for "Cult Guild."* Wiesbaden: Otto Harrassowitz, 1958.

Humphreys, Sarah C. "The Nothoi of Kynosarges." *Journal of Hellenic Studies* 94 (1974): 88–95.

Hurowitz, Victor (Avigdor). *I Have Built You an Exalted House: Temple Building in the Bible in Light of Mesopotamian and Northwest Semitic Writings.* Journal for the Study of the Old Testament Supplement Series, vol. 115. Sheffield: Sheffield Academic Press, 1992.

Ibn Arabī, Muhi-e-Din. "The Seal of the Wisdom of the Decree (Qadar) in the Word of 'Uzayr (Ezra)." In *Fusus al-Hikam (The Seals of Wisdom),* edited by A. D. Crown and Raymond Apple. Studies in Judaica, vol. 1. Sydney: Sydney University Press, 1985. http://www.sufi.ir/books/download/english/ibn-arabi-en/fusus-al-hikam-en.pdf.

In der Smitten, Wilhelm Th. *Esra: Quellen, Überlieferung und Geschichte.* Assen: Van Gorcum, 1973.

Isaac, Ephraim. "The Ethiopic Apocalypse of Enoch, or 1 Enoch." In *The Old Testament Pseudepigrapha,* edited by James H. Charlesworth, 1:5–89. Garden City, N.Y.: Doubleday, 1983.

Jacoby, Felix. "Philochoros." In *Die Fragmente der griechischen Historiker.* Berlin: Weidmann, 1923: 328F, 119.

Japhet, Sara. "1 Esdras: Its Genre, Literary Form, and Goals." In *Was 1 Esdras First? An Investigation into the Nature and Priority of First Esdras,* edited by Lisbeth S. Fried, 209–23. Ancient Israel and Its Literature, vol. 7. Atlanta: Society of Biblical Literature, 2011.

——. *I & II Chronicles*. Louisville, Ky.: Westminster/John Knox Press, 1993.

——. "The Relationship between Chronicles and Ezra-Nehemiah." In *Congress Volume: Leuven 1989*, edited by J. A. Emerton, 298–313. Leiden: Brill, 1991.

——. "Sheshbazzar and Zerubbabel—Against the Background of the Historical and Religious Tendencies of Ezra-Nehemiah." *Zeitschrift für die alttestamentliche Wissenschaft* 94 (1982): 66–98.

——. "The Supposed Common Authorship of Chronicles and Ezra-Nehemiah Investigated Anew." *Vetus Testamentum* 18 (1968): 330–71.

——. "Theodicy in Ezra-Nehemiah and Chronicles." In *Theodicy in the World of the Bible*, edited by Antti Laato, and Johannes C. De Moor, 429–69. Leiden: Brill, 2003.

Jeffery, Arthur. "Ghevond's Text of the Correspondence between 'Umar II and Leo III." *Harvard Theological Revue* 37, no. 4 (1944): 269–332.

Jellicoe, Sidney. *The Septuagint and Modern Study*. Cambridge: Cambridge University Press, 1968.

Joannès, Francis. "Pouvoirs locaux et organisations du territoire en Babylonie Achéménide." *Transeuphratène* 3 (1990): 173–89.

Johnson, Marshall D. *The Purpose of the Biblical Genealogies*. 1969 Cambridge University Press Monograph Series, 2nd ed. Eugune, Ore.: Wipf and Stock, 2002.

Jones, Arnold Hugh Martin. *The Greek City from Alexander to Justinian*. 2nd ed. Oxford: Clarendon Press, 1998.

Jones, Nicholas F. *The Associations of Classical Athens: The Response to Democracy*. New York: Oxford University Press, 1999.

Jursa, Michael. "Achaemenid Babylonia: Political History and Administration." Lecture presented at the conference "Histoire et civilisation du monde Achéménide et de l'empire d'Alexandre," Collège de France, January 10, 2012. http://www.college-de-france.fr/site/pierre-briant/Conference_du_10_janvier_2012_.htm

——. "Nochmals Akkad." *Wiener Zeitschrift für die Kunde des Morgenlandes* 87 (1997): 101–10.

Jursa, Michael, Joanna Paszkowiak, and Caroline Waerzeggers. "Three Court Cases." *Archiv für Oreintforschung* 50 (2003/2004): 255–68.

Kapelrud, Arvid S. *The Question of Authorship in the Ezra-Narrative: A Lexical Investigation*. Oslo: I Kommisjon Hos Jacob Dybwad, 1944.

Kaufmann, Yehezkel. *The Religion of Israel: From Its Beginnings to the Babylonian Exile*. Translated by Moshe Greenberg. Chicago: University of Chicago Press, 1960.

Kellermann, Ulrich. "Erwägungen zum Esragesetz." *Zeitschrift für die alttestamentliche Wissenschaft* 80, no. 3 (1968): 373–85.

Kent, Roland G. *Old Persian: Grammar, Texts, Lexicon*. New Haven: American Oriental Society, 1953.

Klein, Ralph W. "The Rendering of 2 Chronicles 35–36 in 1 Esdras." In *Was 1 Esdras First? An Investigation into the Nature and Priority of First Esdras*, edited by Lisbeth S. Fried, 225–35. Ancient Israel and Its Literature, vol. 7. Atlanta: Society of Biblical Literature, 2011.

——. "Were Joshua, Zerubbabel, and Nehemiah Contemporaries? A Response to Diana Edelman's Proposed Late Date for the Second Temple." *Journal of Biblical Literature* 127, no. 4 (2008): 697–701.

Klijn, A. Frederik J. *Die Esra-Apokalypse (IV Esra): Nach dem lateinischen Text unter Benutzung der anderen Versionen Übersetzt und Herausgegeben.* Die Griechischen Christlichen Schriftsteller der ersten Jahrhunderte. Berlin: Akademie-Verlag, 1992.

Koningsveld, Pieter Sjoerd van. "An Arabic Manuscript of the Apocalypse of Baruch." *Journal for the Study of Judaism* 6 (1974/75): 207.

Kooij, Arie van der. "On the Ending of the Book of 1 Esdras." *Seventh Congress of the International Organization for Septuagint and Cognate Studies.* Atlanta: Scholars Press, 1991.

Kottsieper, Ingo. "The Aramaic Tradition: Aḥikar." In *Scribes, Sages, and Seers: The Sage in the Eastern Mediterranean World,* edited by L. G. Perdue, 109–24. Forschungen zur Religion und Literatur des Alten und Neuen Testaments, vol. 219. Göttingen: Vandenhoeck & Ruprecht, 2008.

Kraft, Robert A. "'Ezra' Materials in Judaism and Christianity." *Aufstieg und Niedergang der Römischen Welt* 2 (1979): 119–36.

——. "The Multiform Jewish Heritage of Early Christianity." In *Christianity, Judaism, and Other Greco-Roman Cults: Studies for Morton Smith at Sixty,* edited by Jacob Neusner, 174–99. Leiden: Brill, 1975.

——. "Towards Assessing the Latin Text of '5 Ezra': The 'Christian' Connection." *Harvard Theological Revue* 79, no. 1 (1986): 158–69.

Kratz, Reinhard G. *Das Judentum im Zeitalter des zweiten Tempels.* Forschungen zum Alten Testament, vol. 42. Tübingen: Mohr Siebeck, 2004.

——. *Translatio Imperii: Untersuchungen zu den Aramäischen Danielerzählungen und ihrem theologiegeschchtlichen Umfeld.* Wissenschaftliche Monographien zum Alten und Neuen Testament, vol. 63. Neukirchen-Vluyn: Neukirchener Verlag, 1991.

Kuhn, Karl Heinz. "A Coptic Jeremiah Apocryphon." *Le Muséon* 83 (1970): 95–135, 291–350.

Kuhrt, Amélie. "Babylonia from Cyrus to Xerxes." In *Persia, Greece and the Western Mediterranean c.525–479,* 112–38. Cambridge Ancient History, vol. 4. Cambridge: Cambridge University Press, 1988.

Kuhrt, Amélie, and Susan Sherwin-White. "Xerxes' Destruction of Babylonian Temples." In *The Greek Sources,* edited by Heleen Sancisi-Weerdenburg and Amélie Kuhrt, 69–78. Achaemenid History, vol. 2. Leiden: Nederlands Instituut voor het Nabije Oosten, 1987.

Kushner, Harold S. *When Bad Things Happen to Good People.* New York: Schocken Books, 1981.

Langdon, Stephen. *Die Neubabylonischen Königsinschriften.* Translated by R. Zehnpfund. Vorderasiatische Bibliothek, vol. 4. Leipzig: Hinrichs, 1912.

Laurence, Ricardo. *Primi Ezræ Libri, Qui Apud Vulgatam Appellatur Quartus, Versio Æthiopica; Nunc Primo in Medium Pro'ata, et Latine Angliceque Reddita.* Oxford: Oxford University Press, 1820.

Lazarus-Yafeh, H. *Intertwined Worlds: Medieval Islam and Bible Criticism.* Princeton: Princeton University Press, 1992.

Lebram, Jürgen C. H. "Die Traditionsgeschichte der Esragestalt und die Frage nach dem Historischen Esra." In *Achaemenid History I: Sources, Structures and Synthesis,* edited by H. Sancisi-Weerdenburg, 103–38. Leiden: Nederlands Instituut voor het Nabije Oosten, 1987.

Levine, Baruch A. "*Lpny YHWH*–Phenomenology of the Open-Air Altar in Biblical Israel." In *In Pursuit of Meaning: Collected Studies of Baruch A. Levine*, edited by Andrew D. Gross, 1:259–69. Winona Lake, Ind.: Eisenbrauns, 2011.

——. *Numbers 21–36.* Anchor Bible, vol. 4A. New York: Doubleday, 2000.

Lewis, Naphtali. *Life in Egypt Under Roman Rule.* Oxford: Clarendon Press, 1983.

Lichtheim, Miriam. "The Satire of the Trades." In *The Old and Middle Kingdom*, vol. 2 of *Ancient Egyptian Literature*, edited by Miriam Lichtheim, 184–92. Berkeley: University of California Press, 1975.

Liddell, H. G. and R. Scott. *Greek-English Lexicon with a Revised Supplement.* Oxford: Clarendon Press, 1996.

Lim, Timothy H. "The Defilement of the Hands as a Principle Determining the Holiness of Scriptures." *Journal of Theological Studies* ns 61 (2010): 501–15.

Lindenberger, James M. *The Aramaic Proverbs of Ahiqar.* Baltimore: Johns Hopkins University Press, 1983.

Longenecker, Bruce W. *2 Esdras.* Sheffield: Sheffield Academic Press, 1995.

MacMullen, Ramsay. *Enemies of the Roman Order: Treason, Unrest, and Alienation in the Empire.* New York: Routledge, 1992.

Magen, Yitzhak. "The Dating of the First Phase of the Samaritan Temple on Mount Gerizim in Light of the Archaeological Evidence." In *Judah and the Judeans in the Fourth Century* B.C.E., edited by G. N. Knoppers, O. Lipschits, and R. Albertz, 157–211. Winona Lake, Ind.: Eisenbrauns, 2007.

Malbran-Labat, Florence. *La version akkadienne de l'Inscription trilingue de Darius à Behistun.* Documenta Asiana, vol. 1. Rome: Gruppo Editoriale Internazonale, 1994.

Manville, Philip B. *The Origins of Citizenship in Ancient Athens.* Princeton: Princeton University Press, 1997.

Margueron, Jean-Claude. "Mesopotamian Temples." In *The Oxford Encyclopedia of Archaeology in the Near East,* edited by Eric M. Meyers, 5:165–69. Oxford: Oxford University Press, 1997.

McCarthy, Dennis J. "Covenant and Law in Chronicles-Nehemiah." *Catholic Biblical Quarterly* 44 (1982): 25–44.

——. *Treaty and Covenant.* Analecta Biblical, vol. 21. Rome: Pontifical Biblical Institute, 1963.

Meri, Josef W. *The Cult of Saints among Muslims and Jews in Medieval Syria.* Oxford Oriental Monographs. Oxford: Oxford University Press, 2002.

Meshorer, Ya'akov, and Shraga Qedar. *The Coinage of Samaria in the Fourth Century* B.C.E. Jerusalem: Numismatic Fine Arts, 1991.

Metzger, Bruce M. "The Lost Section of II Esdras (= IV Esdras)," *Journal of Biblical Literature* 76 (1957): 153–65.

Metzger, Henri, Pierre Demargne, et al. *Fouilles de Xanthos VI: La stèle trilingue du Létôon.* Paris: Klincksieck, 1979.

Meyer, Eduard. *Die Entstehung des Judentums.* 1896. Hildesheims: Olms, 1965.

Mikalson, Jon D. *Ancient Greek Religion.* Blackwell Ancient Religions, no. 2nd. West Sussex, UK: Wiley-Blackwell, 2010.

Milgrom, Jacob. *Leviticus 1–16.* Anchor Bible Commentary, vol. 3A. New York: Doubleday, 1991.

Millar, Fergus. *The Roman Near East 31 B.C.–A.D. 337.* Cambridge, Mass.: Harvard University Press, 1993.

Mowinckel, Sigmund. *Die Ezrageschichte und das Gesetz Moses.* Studien zu dem Buche Ezra-Nehemiah, vol. 3. Oslo: Universitetsforlaget, 1965.

Mueller, James R., and Gregory A. Robbins. "Vision of Ezra." In *Apocalyptic Literature and Testaments.* In *The Old Testament Pseudepigrapha,* edited by J. H. Charlesworth, 1:581–90. Garden City, N.Y.: Doubleday, 1983.

Muhs, Brian. "Membership in Private Associations in Ptolemaic Tebtunis." *Journal of the Economic and Social History of the Orient* 44, no. 1 (2001): 1–19.

Niditch, Susan. *Oral World and Written Word.* Ancient Israelite Literature. Louisville, Ky.: Westminster John Knox Press, 1996.

Nims, Charles. "The Term *Hp,* 'Law,' 'Right,' in Demotic." *Journal of Near Eastern Studies* 7 (1948): 243–60.

Noth, Martin. *The Chronicler's History.* Translated by H. G. M. Williamson. Sheffield: Sheffield Academic Press, 1987.

Olmstead, Albert Ten Eyck. "Darius as Lawgiver." *American Journal of Semitic Languages and Literatures* 51, no. 4 (1935): 247–49.

——. *History of the Persian Empire.* Chicago: University of Chicago Press, 1948.

Oppenheim, A. Leo. *Ancient Mesopotamia: Portrait of a Dead Civilization.* 2nd ed. Edited by Erica Reiner. Chicago: University of Chicago Press, 1977.

Osborne, Robin. "Law, the Democratic Citizen and the Representation of Women in Classical Athens." *Past and Present* 155 (1997): 3–33.

Pakkala, Juha. *Ezra the Scribe: The Development of Ezra 7–10 and Nehemiah 8.* Beihefte zur Zeitschrift für die alttestamentliche Wissenschaft, vol. 347. Berlin: De Gruyter, 2004.

——. "Why 1 Esdras Is Probably Not an Early Version of the Ezra-Nehemiah Tradition." In *Was 1 Esdras First? An Investigation into the Nature and Priority of First Esdras,* edited by Lisbeth S. Fried, 93–107. Ancient Israel and Its Literature, vol. 7. Atlanta: Society of Biblical Literature, 2011.

Parker, Richard A., and Waldo H. Duberstein. *Babylonian Chronology 626 B.C.–A.D. 75.* Brown University Studies, vol. 19. Providence: Brown University Press, 1956.

Patterson, Cynthia B. *Pericles' Citizenship Law of 451/50 B.C.* New York: Arno Press, 1981.

Perdue, Leo G., ed. *Scribes, Sages, and Seers: The Sage in the Eastern Mediterranean World.* Göttingen: Vandenhoeck & Ruprecht, 2008.

Pohlmann, Karl-Friedrich. *Studien zum Dritten Esra: Ein Beitrag zur Frage nach dem Urspruünglichen Schluss des Chronistischen Geschichtswerkes.* Forschungen zur Religion und Literatur des Alten und Neuen Testaments 104. Göttingen: Vandenhoeck & Ruprecht, 1970.

Polak, Frank H. "The Covenant at Mount Sinai in the Light of Texts from Mari." In *Sefer Moshe: The Moshe Weinfeld Jubilee Volume,* edited by C. Cohen, A. Hurvitz, and S. Paul, 119–34. Winona Lake, Ind.: Eisenbrauns, 2004.

Porten, Bezalel. *Archives from Elephantine: The Life of an Ancient Jewish Military Colony.* Berkeley: University of California Press, 1968.

———. *The Elephantine Papyri in English: Three Millennia of Cross-Cultural Continuity and Hange.* 2nd ed. Leiden: Brill, 2011.

Porten, Bezalel, and Ada Yardeni. *Textbook of Aramaic Documents from Ancient Egypt: Volumes I–IV Newly Copied, Edited and Translated into Hebrew and English.* Winona Lake, Ind.: Eisenbrauns, 1986–1999.

Porton, Gary G. "Ezra in Rabbinic Literature." In *Restoration: Old Testament, Jewish, and Christian Perspectives,* edited by James M. Scott, 305–34. Supplements to the Journal for the Study of Judaism, vol. 72. Leiden: Brill, 2001.

Powell, Marvin A. "Weights and Measures." *Anchor Bible Dictionary,* Vol. 6. Edited by David Noel Freedman. New York: Doubleday, 1992: 897–908.

Rabinowitz, Yosef. *The Book of Ezra.* ArtScroll Tanach Series. Brooklyn, N.Y.: Mesorah Publications, 1984.

Rad, Gerhard von. *Genesis: A Commentary.* Translated by John H. Marks. Old Testament Library. Philadelphia: SCM Press, 1972.

Redford, Donald B. "The So-Called 'Codification' of Egyptian Law under Darius I." In *Persia and Torah: The Theory of Imperial Authorization of the Pentateuch,* edited by James W. Watts, 135–59. Atlanta: Society of Biblical Literature, 2001.

Rendtorff, Rolf. "Esra und das 'Gesetz.'" *Zeitschrift für die alttestamentliche Wissenschaft* 96, no. 2 (1984): 165–84.

———. "Noch Einmal: Esra und das 'Gesetz.'" *Zeitschrift für die alttestamentliche Wissenschaft* 111 (1999): 89–91.

Röllig, Wolfgang. "Baal-Shamem." In *Dictionary of Deities and Demons in the Bible,* 2nd ed., edited by B. Becking, K. van der Toorn, and P. van der Horst, 149–51. Grand Rapids, Mich.: Eerdmans, 1999.

Rollston, Chris A. "Ben Sira 38:24–39:11 and the 'Egyptian Satire of the Trades': A Reconsideration." *Journal of Biblical Literature* 120 (2001): 131–39.

Roth, Martha T, ed. *The Assyrian Dictionary.* Chicago: The Oriental Institute, 1964–2010.

Rubinoff, Lionel. "In Search of a Meaningful Response to the Holocaust: Reflections on Fackenheim's 614th Commandment." In *Emil L. Fackenheim: Philosopher, Theologian, Jew,* edited by M. Yaffe, Sharon Portnoff and J. Diamond. Brill, 2008, 251–94. Brill E-Books. Accessed June 7, 2012, http://dx.doi.org/10.1163/ej.9789004157675.i-342.

Rudolph, Wilhelm. *Esra und Nehemia Samt. 3 Esra.* Tübingen: Mohr, 1949.

Samons II, Loren J. "Introduction: Athenian History and Society in the Age of Pericles." In *The Cambridge Companion to the Age of Pericles,* edited by Loren J. Samons II, 1–24. Cambridge: Cambridge University Press, 2007.

Sayler, Gwendolyn B. *Have the Promises Failed? A Literary Analysis of 2 Baruch.* Society of Biblical Literature Dissertation Series, vol. 72. Chico, Calif.: Scholars Press, 1984.

Schenker, O.P., Adrian. "La relation d'Esdras A au texte massorétique d'Esdras-Néhémie." In *Tradition of the Text: Studies Offered to Dominique Barthélemy in Celebration of His 70th Birthday,* edited by G. J. Norton and S. Pisano, 218–48. *Orbis Biblicus et Orientalis,* vol. 109. Freiburg: Universitätsverlag, and Göttingen: Vandenhoeck & Ruprecht, 1991.

———. "The Relationship between Ezra-Nehemiah and 1 Esdras." In *Was 1 Esdras First? An Investigation into the Nature and Priority of First Esdras,* edited by Lisbeth S. Fried. Ancient Israel and Its Literature, vol. 7. Atlanta: Society of Biblical Literature, 2011: 45–58.

Schmid, Konrad. "The Persian Imperial Authorization as a Historical Problem and as a Biblical Construct: A Plea for Distinctions in the Current Debate." In *The Pentateuch as Torah: New Models for Understanding Its Promulgation and Acceptance,* edited by Gary N. Knoppers and Bernard M. Levinson, 23–38. Winona Lake, Ind.: Eisenbrauns, 2007.

Schwiderski, Dirk. *Handbuch des nordwestsemitischen Briefformulars: Ein Beitrag zur Echtheitsfrage der aramäischen Briefe des Esrabuches.* Beihefte zur Zeitschrift für die alttestamentlich Wissenschaft 10. Berlin: de Gruyter, 2000.

Seters, John van. *Abraham in History and Tradition.* New Haven: Yale University Press, 1975.

——. "The Terms 'Amorite' and 'Hittite' in the Old Testament." *Vetus Testamentum* 22, no. 1 (1972): 64–81.

Shaked, Shaul. *Le satrape de Bactriane et son gouverneur: Documents araméens du IVe s. avant notre ère provenant de Bactriane.* Paris: De Boccard, 2004.

Shallit, A. "The Reforms of Gabinius," *World History of the Jewish People,* Ser. 1, Vol. 7. New Brunswick: Rutgers University Press, 1975.

Simon, Richard. *A Critical History of the Old Testament. Written Originally in French by Father Simon and since Translated into English by a Person of Quality.* Translated by Richard Hampden and Henry Dickinson. London: Walter Davis in Amen-Corner, 1682.

Ska, Jean-Louis. *Introduction to Reading the Pentateuch.* Translated by Sr. Pascale Dominique. Winona Lake, Ind.: Eisenbrauns, 2006.

Southern, Pat. *The Roman Empire from Severus to Constantine.* London: Routledge, 2001.

Spiegelberg, W. *Die sogenannte demotische Chronik des Pap. 215 der Bibliothéque Nationale de Paris.* Leipzig: Hinrichs, 1914.

Spinoza, Baruch de., *The Chief Works of Benedict de Spinoza,* rev. ed. Translated by R. H. M. Elwes. London: G. Bell and Sons, 1909.

Steiner, Richard C. "The *mbqr* at Qumran, the *episkopos* in the Athenian Empire, and the Meaning of *lbqr'* in Ezra 7:14: On the Relation of Ezra's Mission to the Persian Legal Project." *Journal of Biblical Literature* 120 (2001): 623–46.

Stenhouse, Paul. *The Kitab al-Tarikh of Abu 'l-Fatḥ.* Studies in Judaica, vol. 1. Sydney: Sydney University Press, 1985.

——. "Samaritan Chronicles." (Hebrew) In *The Samaritans* (Hebrew), edited by Ephraim Stern and Hanan Eshel, 539–61. Jerusalem: Yad Izhak Ben-Zvi, 2002.

Stern, Ephraim. *Material Culture of the Land of the Bible in the Persian Period, 538–332 B.C.* Warminster, Wiltshire, England, and Jerusalem, Israel: Aris & Phillips Israel Exploration Society, 1982.

Stern, Ephraim, and Yitzhak Magen. "Archaeological Evidence for the First Stage of the Samaritan Temple on Mount Gerizim." *Israel Exploration Journal* 52 (2002): 49–57.

——. "The First Level of the Samaritan Temple on Mt. Gerizim: New Archaeological Evidence." (Hebrew) *Qadmoniot* 33 (2000): 119–24.

Stern, Menahem. *From Tacitus to Simplicius.* Greek and Latin Authors on Jews and Judaism: Edited with Introductions, Translations, and Commentary, vol. 2. Jerusalem: Israel Academy of Sciences and Humanities, 1980.

Stolper, Matthew W. *Entrepreneurs and Empire: The Murašû Archive, the Murašû Firm, and Persian Rule in Babylonia.* Leiden: Nederlands Instituut voor het Nabije Oosten, 1985.

——. *Late Achaemenid, Early Macedonian, and Early Seleucid Records of Deposit and Related Texts.* Annali, vol. 53, Supplement n. 77. Naples: Instituto Universitario Orientale, 1993.

——. "The Neo-Babylonian Text from the Persepolis Fortification." *Journal of Near Eastern Studies* 43 (1984): 299–310.

——. "Registration and Taxation of Slave Sales in Achaemenid Babylonia." *Zeitschrift für Assyriologie* 79 (1989): 80–101.

Stone, Michael E. "Apocalyptic, Vision, or Hallucination?" *Milla Wa Milla* 148 (1974): 47–56.

——. *The Armenian Version of IV Ezra.* University of Pennsylvania Armenian Texts and Studies 1. Missoula, Mont.: Scholars, 1979.

——. "The City in 4 Ezra." *Journal of Biblical Literature* 126, no. 2 (2007): 402–7.

——. "The Concept of the Messiah in 4 Ezra." In *Religions in Antiquity: Essays in Memory of Erwin Ramsdell Goodenough,* edited by Jacob Neusner, 295–312. Leiden: Brill, 1968.

——. *Fourth Ezra.* Hermeneia. Minneapolis, Minn.: Fortress Press, 1990.

——. "Greek Apocalypse of Ezra." In *Apocalyptic Literature and Testaments.* In *The Old Testament Pseudepigrapha,* edited by J. H. Charlesworth, 1:561–79. Garden City, N.Y.: Doubleday, 1983.

——. "The Metamorphosis of Ezra: Jewish Apocalypse and Medieval Vision." *Journal of Theological Studies ns* 33 (1982): 1–18.

——. "A New Manuscript of the Syro-Arabic Version of the Fourth Book of Ezra." *Journal for the Study of Judaism* 8 (1976/7): 183–84.

——. "Questions of Ezra." In *Apocalyptic Literature and Testaments.* In *The Old Testament Pseudepigrapha,* edited by J. H. Charlesworth, 1:591–99. Garden City, N.Y.: Doubleday, 1983.

——. "A Reconsideration of Apocalyptic Visions." *Harvard Theological Revue* 96, no. 2 (2003): 167–80.

——. *A Textual Commentary on the Armenian Version of IV Ezra.* Septuagint and Cognate Studies Series, vol. 34. Atlanta: Society of Biblical Literature, 1990.

Stoneman, Richard. *Palmyra and Its Empire: Zenobia's Revolt against Rome.* Ann Arbor: University of Michigan Press, 1992.

Talshir, Zipora. *1 Esdras: A Text Critical Commentary.* Atlanta: Society of Biblical Literature, 2001.

——. *1 Esdras: From Origin to Translation.* Atlanta: Society of Biblical Literature, 1999.

——. "Ancient Composition Patterns Mirrored in 1 Esdras and the Priority of the Canonical Composition Type." In *Was 1 Esdras First? An Investigation into the Nature and Priority of First Esdras,* edited by Lisbeth S. Fried, 109–29. Ancient Israel and Its Literature, vol. 7. Atlanta: Society of Biblical Literature, 2011.

Teixidor, Javier. "Palmyra in the Third Century." In *Journey to Palmyra: Collected Essays to Remember Delbert R. Hillers,* edited by Eleonora Cussini. Leiden: Brill, 2005: 181–225.

Thiering, Barbara E. "*Mebaqqer* and *Episkopos* in the Light of the Temple Scroll." *Journal of Biblical Literature* 100, no. 1 (1981): 59–74.

Thompson, Thomas L. *The Historicity of the Patriarchal Narratives.* Berlin: De Gruyter, 1974.

Tigay, Jeffrey H. "The Evolution of the Pentateuchal Narratives in the Light of the Evolution of the Gilgamesh Epic." In *Empirical Models for Biblical Criticism,* edited by Jeffery H. Tigay, 21–52. Philadelphia: University of Pennsylvania Press, 1985.

Toorn, Karel van der. "The Iconic Book Analogies between the Babylonian Cult of Images and the Veneration of the Torah." In *The Image and the Book: Iconic Cults, Aniconism, and the Rise of Book Religion in Israel and the Ancient Near East,* edited by Karel van der Toorn, 229–48. Leuven: Peeters, 1997.

Torrey, Charles C. *The Composition and Historical Value of Ezra-Nehemiah.* Beihefte zur Zeitschrift für die alttestamentliche Wissenschaft, vol. 2. Giessen: J. Ricker, 1896.

——. *Ezra Studies.* New York: Ktav, 1970.

Tuplin, Christopher. "The Administration of the Achaemenid Empire." In *Coinage and Administration in the Athenian and Persian Empires,* edited by I. Carradice, 109–66. British Archaeological Reports International Series, vol. 343. Oxford: British Archaeological Reports, 1987.

——. "Xenophon and the Garrisons of the Achaemenid Empire." *Archäologische Mitteilungen Aus Iran* 20 (1987): 167–245.

Ussishkin, David. *The Conquest of Lachish by Sennacherib.* Tel Aviv: Tel Aviv University, 1982.

VanderKam, James C. "Ezra-Nehemiah or Ezra and Nehemiah?" In *Priests, Prophets and Scribes: Essays on the Formation and Heritage of Second Temple Judaism in Honour of Joseph Blenkinsopp,* edited by J. W. Wright, E. Ulrich, and R. P. Carroll, 55–75. Journal for the Study of the Old Testament Supplement, no. 149. Sheffield: Sheffield Academic Press, 1992.

——. *From Joshua to Caiaphas: High Priests after the Exile.* Minneapolis, Minn.: Fortress Press, 2004.

——. "Jewish High Priests of the Persian Period: Is the List Complete?" In *Priesthood and Cult in Ancient Israel,* edited by G. A. Anderson and S. M. Olyan, 67–91. Journal for the Study of the Old Testament Supplement, vol. 125. Sheffield: Sheffield Academic Press, 1991.

——. "Literary Questions between Ezra, Nehemiah, and 1 Esdras." In *Was 1 Esdras First? An Investigation into the Nature and Priority of First Esdras,* edited by Lisbeth S. Fried, 131–43. Ancient Israel and Its Literature, vol. 7. Atlanta: Society of Biblical Literature, 2011.

Violet, Bruno. *Die Esra-Apokalypse (IV. Esra).* Leipzig: J. C. Hinrichsche Buchhandlung, 1910.

Watts, James W., ed. *Persia and Torah: The Theory of Imperial Authorization of the Pentateuch.* Atlanta: Society of Biblical Literature, 2001.

Weinfeld, Moshe. "The Covenant of Grant in the Old Testament and in the Ancient Near East." *Journal of the American Oriental Society* 90, no. 2 (April–June 1970): 184–203.

——. *Deuteronomy 1–11.* Anchor Bible, vol. 5. New York: Doubleday, 1991.

——. *Place of the Law in the Religion of Ancient Israel.* Leiden: Brill, 2004.

Weisberg, David. *Guild Structure and Political Allegiance in Early Achaemenid Mesopotamia.* New Haven: Yale University Press, 1967.

Welch, Adam C. "The Source of Nehemiah IX." *Zeitschrift für die Alttestamentliche Wissenschaft* 47, no. 1st (1929): 130–37.

Wellhausen, Julius. *Prolegomena to the History of Ancient Israel.* 1878. New York: Meridian Books, 1957.

Whybray, R. N. "'Shall Not the Judge of All the Earth Do What Is Just?' God's Oppression of the Innocent in the Old Testament." In *Shall Not the Judge of All the Earth Do What*

Is Right? Studies on the Nature of God in Tribute to James L. Crenshaw, edited by David Penchansky and Paul L. Redditt, 1–19. Winona Lake, Ind.: Eisenbrauns, 2000.

Wiesehöfer, Josef. "'Reichsgesetz' oder 'Einzelfallgerechtigkeit'? Bemerkungen zu P. Freis These von der achämenidischen 'Reichsautorisation.'" *Zeitschrift für altorientalische und biblische Rechtsgeschichte* 1 (1995): 36–46.

——. "Ardašir I." In *Encyclopaedia Iranica.* New York: Center for Iranian Studies Columbia University, 1987.

Williamson, H. G. M. "1 Esdras." In *Eerdmans Commentary on the Bible,* edited by James D. Dunn and John W. Rogerson, 851–58. Grand Rapids, Mich.: Eerdmans, 2003.

——. "1 Esdras as Rewritten Bible?" In *Was 1 Esdras First? An Investigation into the Nature and Priority of First Esdras,* edited by Lisbeth S. Fried, 237–49. Atlanta: Society of Biblical Literature, 2011.

——. "The Aramaic Documents in Ezra Revisited." *Journal of Theological Studies* 59, no. 1 (2008): 41–62.

——. "The Composition of Ezra i–vi." *Journal of Theological Studies Ns* 34 (1983): 1–30.

——. *Ezra, Nehemiah.* Word Biblical Commentary, vol. 16. Waco, Tex.: Word Books, 1985.

Wills, Lawrence M. *The Jewish Novel in the Ancient World.* Ithaca: Cornell University Press, 1995.

Witter, Henning Bernard. *Jura Israelitarum in Palaestinam Commentatione in Genesin Perpetua.* Hildesiæ: Sumtibus Ludolphi Schröderi, 1711.

Wright, Jacob L. *Rebuilding Identity: The Nehemiah-Memoir and Its Earliest Readers.* Beihefte zur Zeitschrift für die alttestamentliche Wissenschaft, vol. 348. Berlin: De Gruyter, 2004.

——. "Remember Nehemiah: 1 Esdras and the *Damnatio Memoriae Nehemiae.*" In *Was 1 Esdras First? An Investigation into the Nature and Priority of First Esdras,* edited by Lisbeth S. Fried, 145–63. Ancient Israel and Its Literature, vol. 7. Atlanta: Society of Biblical Literature, 2011.

Wright, J. Edward. *Baruch ben Neriah: From Biblical Scribe to Apocalyptic Seer.* Studies on Personalities in the Old Testament. Columbia: University of South Carolina Press, 2003.

Yarbro Collins, Adela. "The Early Christian Apocalypses." *Semeia* 14 (1979): 61–121.

Zaidman, Louise Bruit and Pauline Schmitt Pantel. *Religion in the Ancient Greek City* Cambridge: Cambridge University Press, 1992.

INDEX OF ANCIENT SOURCES

INDEX OF MODERN AUTHORS

SUBJECT INDEX

ABOUT THE AUTHOR

LISBETH S. FRIED is a visiting scholar in the Department of Near Eastern Studies at the University of Michigan, an emeritus program lecturer at Washtenaw Community College, and an associate editor for ancient Near Eastern religions for the forthcoming *Routledge Dictionary of Ancient Mediterranean Religions.* Fried is the author of *The Priest and the Great King: Temple-Palace Relations in the Persian Empire* and editor of *Was 1 Esdras First? An Investigation into the Priority and Nature of 1 Esdras.*